ONE SIGNAL
PUBLISHERS
ATRIA

ALSO BY CHARLES PILLER

Gene Wars: Military Control Over the New Genetic Technologies
(with Keith R. Yamamoto)

*The Fail-Safe Society: Community Defiance and the
End of American Technological Optimism*

DOCTORED

Fraud, Arrogance, and Tragedy
in the Quest to Cure Alzheimer's

CHARLES PILLER

ONE SIGNAL
PUBLISHERS

ATRIA

New York   Amsterdam/Antwerp   London   Toronto   Sydney   New Delhi

ONE SIGNAL
PUBLISHERS

ATRIA

An Imprint of Simon & Schuster, LLC
1230 Avenue of the Americas
New York, NY 10020

First One Signal Publishers/Atria Books hardcover edition February 2025

ONE SIGNAL PUBLISHERS / ATRIA BOOKS and colophon are trademarks
of Simon & Schuster, LLC

For information about special discounts for bulk purchases, please contact Simon &
Schuster Special Sales at 1-866-506-1949 or business@simonandschuster.com.

The Simon & Schuster Speakers Bureau can bring authors to your live event. For more
information or to book an event, contact the Simon & Schuster Speakers Bureau at
1-866-248-3049 or visit our website at www.simonspeakers.com.

Interior design by Jill Putorti

Manufactured in the United States of America

1 3 5 7 9 10 8 6 4 2

Library of Congress Cataloging-in-Publication Data has been applied for.

ISBN 978-1-6680-3124-7
ISBN 978-1-6680-3126-1 (ebook)

For Surry, Nate, Sandra, and Maya

Contents

Prologue

2021–2022

In December 2021, I fell into one of the biggest and most disturbing stories of my career. A credible whistleblower with strong credentials in dementia research tipped me to a major case of apparent misconduct in his field. He produced convincing evidence that lab studies at the heart of the dominant hypothesis for the cause of Alzheimer's disease might have been based on bogus data. My investigative story for *Science* magazine in July 2022 exposed those findings and their far-reaching significance, drawing global media attention. But I didn't suspect it would begin a yearslong, high-stakes journey into hidden, sordid corners of science and medicine.

Just a couple months later, two giant drug companies announced what many described as one of the most dramatic developments in the history of Alzheimer's. For decades scientists had struggled fruitlessly to offer hope to millions of patients who suffer the gradual, debilitating decline in their ability to think and remember loved ones, or enjoy self-aware lives. Finally, a major test seemed to prove that a new medication could alter the course of the disease.

That drug, Leqembi, strips away from brain tissues the sticky plaques and other toxic compounds that comprise a substance called "amyloid-beta." In so doing—said its makers, experts in their pay, and cheerleading journalists—Leqembi definitively validated the "amyloid hypothesis," the long-debated notion that Alzheimer's is caused by the buildup accumulation of amyloid in the brain. If true, its removal would lead to a cure.

Understandable excitement—hope against hope—greeted Leqembi. Alzheimer's afflicts nearly seven million Americans, about one in every nine over the age of sixty-five, making it the fifth leading cause of death among the elderly. Up to 360,000 adults in the prime of life—including people as young as thirty—suffer from early onset Alzheimer's. Comparable figures in the United Kingdom, Europe, and the rest of the world have made the leading cause of dementia a global scourge. And dementia totals will more than double by 2050.

In the United States alone, more than eleven million family members care for fathers and mothers and grandparents who have fallen prey to the cruel disease that begins by gradually stealing a person's mastery of everyday life, then cherished memories, and finally the sense of self that makes each of us human. Alzheimer's families face incalculable emotional costs—including lost dreams of retirement and pleasures with loving partners. For many, the disease also means financial impoverishment. Family caregivers in the United States provided a staggering $350 billion in care to Alzheimer's patients in 2023—nearly matching the amount paid for dementia care by all other sources, including Medicare.

Unfortunately, the Leqembi "breakthrough" amounted to just this: Alzheimer's patients lost their ability to remember, think clearly, and live normal lives only slightly less rapidly than others taking a bogus treatment. The drug offers so modest a benefit that doctors and patients might not perceive any effect whatsoever.

It was the latest example of the exaggeration, hype, and sheer fakery and fraud that has characterized Alzheimer's research for decades. By then I realized that I could tell the full story of how the hunt to cure the insidious and chilling illness went awry. I had to show why billions of dollars in spending by governments, pharma companies, and philanthropies had done little for desperate patients.

For decades, proponents of the dominant amyloid hypothesis have sidelined, starved for resources, and even bullied rebels behind other promising notions of how to treat Alzheimer's. If Leqembi and look-alikes with similarly lackluster results hold sway in drug development and dominate mindshare among patients and doctors, a genuine Alzheimer's cure might become even more remote.

Many patients take a leap of faith in such drugs as a hedge against creeping fear. Big pharma companies, among others, bet their bottom lines on that basic instinct. Alzheimer's research has offered endless opportunities for advancement and riches to corporate shysters and ruthlessly ambitious scientists who cut corners or engage in brazen deception.

I set out to unmask decades of arrogance, greed, fabulism, and error that have emptied research coffers and littered the drug development landscape with failure after failure.

My reporting followed the path of a junior professor who faced great personal risks to challenge his field's institutional powers. He uncovered hidden and fabricated data instrumental to keeping the amyloid hypothesis supreme at the expense of other possible solutions. As I dug deeper, a scientific underworld of deceit and lies rose into view. I gradually saw an opportunity to help reshape how scientists, doctors, and patients understand one of the most terrible human afflictions—and add realistic hope in the process.

The story begins where it must, with a deeply determined patient struggling with dementia. He dared to hope that he could be one of the first people living with Alzheimer's to find a transformative treatment.

Chapter 1

A Vanishing Mind

Tabernacle Township, New Jersey
2020–2022

"I have to handle things differently."

—STEPHEN PRICE,
RETIRED CONSTRUCTION CONTRACTOR
WHO LIVES WITH ALZHEIMER'S

Stephen Price and his son, Matt, had driven for an hour from the family home in Tabernacle Township, New Jersey, to a medical strip mall in Toms River, on the Jersey Shore, to begin the experimental drug simufilam. It was May 3, 2021. Cassava Sciences, a Texas biopharma company, developed simufilam to treat or cure Alzheimer's disease, the debilitating, ultimately deadly illness that afflicts tens of millions of people worldwide. Stephen was enrolling in a clinical trial—a human experiment to examine the drug's safety and effectiveness.

For experimental drugs that show promise in lab studies, the Food and Drug Administration (FDA) requires such trials to enforce rigorous standards for administering drugs and measuring their effects, and close monitoring to ensure that patients get help and treatment if they show unforeseen or worrisome side effects. Stephen had enrolled in a "phase 2" trial—a test of safety and possible benefits. It had followed a small, phase 1 safety trial meant to ensure that simufilam was not obviously toxic. Later, large phase 3 trials would test whether simufilam helped volunteers regain some of their memories and ability to cope with daily life—or at least slowed their gradual decline. If the results looked strong, the FDA might permit doctors to prescribe simufilam. Drug regulators in the European Union, the United Kingdom, and many other nations follow a similar, time-honored, apparently careful approach.

Matt was Stephen's "study partner"—necessary to help his dad, already impaired from the disease, negotiate the somewhat-complex process. Stephen, then seventy-three, had been diagnosed more than six years earlier. Simufilam, they hoped, would stop his memory, ability to concentrate, and mastery of daily life from continuing to ebb away.

In December 2022, trim-framed with neatly cropped gray hair, the seventy-four-year-old Stephen cut a handsome pose. He towered over Toni, his wife and high school sweetheart. They looked the picture of a quiet, middle-class retirement. Stephen had owned and operated a tiny construction firm for thirty years, mostly digging foundations for new homes and businesses. Toni had taught English to teens with behavioral challenges, then grew lavender on their land in the rural exurbs east of Philadelphia—sixty-seven acres of woods and fields. Their comfortable, two-story home rests at the end of a half-mile gravel drive. For most of his life, Stephen was a man who kept his own counsel. On that day, he spoke openly about his experience with Alzheimer's.

Gazing steadily from blue eyes behind heavy, black-framed glasses, Stephen spoke with a direct friendliness, albeit a bit guarded at times. He sometimes became confused about small matters or lost his train of thought. To hold up his end of a conversation, he favored short replies. He paused to find an elusive word or anecdote, smiling apologetically to fill the gaps.

Asked when he and Toni first met, Stephen looked upward for a few moments, pondering. "Before we entered high school," he said.

"No, no . . ." she interjected, gently.

"When you were doing the baton thing in the parades," Stephen replied, turning to his wife.

She replied softly, "Okay"—acquiescing to his version with a hint of polite frustration. Caring for someone with Alzheimer's calls for infinite patience.

"I have to handle things differently," Stephen said. "And it took a long time for my wife and Matt to catch up or get at the same speed I am on. I have to do things one thing at a time. And if I get interrupted—when, like, I'm putting my meds together, something like that—I have to go back to the beginning again and start all over. It's hard for other people to understand that. You know, it's, it's a very different world," he said, smiling again, this time sheepishly. Toni looked stressed.

Stephen wore a plaid flannel shirt over a white T-shirt. He looked ready to head out to dig a new foundation, as he chatted about career and business. "It was a smaller company where everybody knew everybody," Stephen said, gesturing with his arm, as if encircling his crew, who he said enjoyed each other's companionship in hard but satisfying work. "It was just a nice way to have a, have a business," he added.

Nowadays, despite his decline, Stephen regularly and fondly checks his remaining equipment that hasn't yet been sold off. An old front-end loader dominates a barn-sized warehouse down the drive from their home. He meanders around, scanning and moving small tools—more comforting ritual than inventory check. Matt and Toni installed video security inside. Not to safeguard the property. They don't want to worry about Stephen's well-being in case he becomes confused during a nostalgic visit.

Stephen has participated in various drug trials in his journey as a patient and research volunteer in the search for an Alzheimer's cure. He wants to feel like part of the solution to the great and terrible Alzheimer's mystery—to help scientists explore new treatments for patients who will follow. Two of those might be his own children. That's because Stephen carries two copies of a gene known as *APOE4*—a risk factor for coming down with Alzheimer's and passing it to the next generation. Matt remembers his dad saying "What can I do for society? What can I do for my family? And what can I do for myself?"

Matt likes to say that he knows "just enough about clinical trials to be dangerous." That's unduly modest. His sophistication about what to look for in a trial would put many physicians to shame. A Harvard-trained epidemiologist and global-health specialist, he knows how to assess a trial's structure and approach. I asked his father whether Matt showed this taste for studious diligence as a kid, foreshadowing his luminous scholarly achievements.

"He was very self-motivated," Stephen replied, with a self-effacing grin. "I don't know where it came from," he added, showing that he could still crack a small family joke.

Near the beginning of the simufilam trial Stephen was battling what he described as "some issues." He suffered from an often overlooked but common Alzheimer's symptom: depression. It traces back to the cruelty of the illness. As dementia first encroaches, many people sharply—painfully—witness their own gradual decline with conscious alarm. In the early stages, they can see their sense of self and intimacy with loved ones slowly wane. Medications usually provide meager benefits at best. And Stephen knew that Alzheimer's might kill him.

Antidepressants didn't help much. So, in 2020 Matt helped him join a clinical trial to see whether the mind-altering drug psilocybin could do better. Stephen and Toni had never used drugs recreationally. Consuming the mushroom-derived chemical—safely within the comfortable, closely supervised confines of Johns Hopkins University—was a novel experience.

The effects proved profound. "It kind of got my head on straight. I wish I could go back there again," Stephen said. (He thought the trial lasted two or three years—perhaps a reflection of how favorably he remembered it. Including therapy and follow-up, it ran less than a year.)

"At the time, Dad reported that it was among the most meaningful experiences he's had in his life. During the session it was traumatic, but he came to view it as a positive experience," Matt recalled. The psilocybin alleviated some distressing feelings from his childhood, and helped Stephen express his deep compassion for Toni—who had faced her own health problems at the time. Matt described his views of Stephen's experience:

"Eye-opening. I was surprised by how much it seemed to help him accept his illness for a period of at least a few months."

In that "open-label" trial, investigators and participants knew that all volunteers received psilocybin, rather than some getting a placebo—a dummy treatment, like the classic sugar pill. Such small, early experiments aim to gather initial readings on side effects or benefits. They rarely convince the FDA to approve a drug for marketing. For that, the agency normally requires randomized, controlled, and double-blinded trials, in which volunteers are divided into groups that get either the drug or a placebo. (Treatments for late-stage cancers, for example, in which it would be unethical to give a dying person a placebo, can be an exception.) Expectations by investigators or participants can change outcomes, sometimes profoundly, independent of getting the study drug or a placebo. So neither volunteers nor investigators know who gets the real treatment. Double-blinding reduces the risk of bias, intentional or not. Guarding against that thumb on the scale can be essential to finding out if a treatment really works.

LIMITED OPTIONS

Then thirty-seven, Matt had been trying to get his father into a trial for a drug that, unlike psilocybin, was designed to be "disease modifying." Rather than calming symptoms, the goal would be to slow, stop, or reverse cognitive decline—or for people who have no symptoms, prevent them—by attacking Alzheimer's biochemical cause. When he first heard about simufilam, it sounded exciting. In principle, the drug repairs a brain protein, filamin A—one of the many proteins that accelerate chemical reactions and form key structures in cells. Filamin A, according to Cassava, can block sticky brain deposits, or "plaques" of another protein—amyloid-beta, widely seen as a hallmark of the disease. The amyloid hypothesis holds that two types of amyloid proteins—plaques that form between nerve cells, and toxic forms of amyloid that can dissolve into the cerebrospinal fluid that surrounds brain tissues—spark a biochemical chain of events that ends with Alzheimer's devastating impairment. According to Cassava, simufilam also affects the brain in other ways that might cure the disease, such as reducing amyloid's toxic downstream effects.

If simufilam could improve cognition, Stephen might regain the capacity to navigate everyday activities and enjoy life more. Perhaps he could recapture the person he and his family saw slipping away, Stephen, Toni, and Matt thought. If the company was right, simufilam might be their best hope.

Matt read Cassava's scientific explanations and research underpinning the trial and talked them over with a friend—a physician and PhD scientist trained at Harvard and the Massachusetts Institute of Technology. Doubts immediately emerged. The logic of Cassava's approach—far from the mainstream and not robustly validated by independent researchers—"seemed weird and bit thin," Matt said.

Matt had looked for other trials of potential disease-modifying drugs. Those only accepted volunteers who suffered from mild cognitive impairment, an early stage of Alzheimer's. Investigators for such trials by major pharmaceutical companies rejected Stephen. In cognitive tests, his Alzheimer's seemed too advanced—in the "moderate" range of impairment.

So they circled back to simufilam. Despite Matt's misgivings, the trial offered appealing qualities: Many experimental treatments require uncomfortable and potentially dangerous intravenous infusions in a clinic. Simufilam is a pill Stephen could take at home. Most important, Cassava didn't share the qualms of other companies about accepting people with moderate impairment.

Matt worried about the rigor of the trial. Some experts saw Cassava's screening criteria to qualify patients for the trial as suspect. For example, it relied on a test called the Mini-Mental State Examination (MMSE), widely considered imprecise and easily susceptible to coaching. "It seems unthinkable that the diagnosis of a devastating illness such as Alzheimer's disease would hinge on the results of a rough-and-ready 5 minute test," as two neurologists wrote in a 2016 analysis, calling for the test's retirement.

Individuals who scored in the MMSE's "normal" range—no apparent dementia—could still be included in the simufilam trial if a scan showed shrinkage in the hippocampus, the part of the brain responsible for emotion and memory. Alzheimer's notoriously causes brain atrophy, but so do other conditions that cause dementia.

The broad range of likely patients in the trial—people with mild or moderate Alzheimer's, and others with no symptoms of dementia—could make the results of the experiment impossible to accurately compare to conventional studies.

Still, the relatively lax criteria offered a distinct advantage: Stephen got in. Matt recalled driving home from Toms River that day in 2021 after his dad took that first dose. "We were encouraging each other. We were saying, 'We're not sure if this is going to work out. But even if it doesn't we're doing the best that we can to fight.'" Matt paused, gathering his thoughts. "We were kind of rehearsing that narrative. Dad was optimistic."

The trial used a hybrid format—open-label for the first twelve months, double-blinded for the next six, then another six months of open-label. So for at least eighteen months of the twenty-four-month trial, participants would know they were getting the study drug, rather than possibly a placebo. Such an approach makes it much easier to recruit people who see themselves living on borrowed time, but harder to interpret the results.

By December 2022, Stephen had lost track of those details, though he remained hopeful. "I think I'm on the drug now, but I don't know that I have the full effect of the drug. Because I'd like to be a little bit more 'with it' than I am presently," he said.

Tests of drugs to treat conditions like cancer use objective biomedical measures—for example, a tumor shrinks or grows—that can show definitively if a drug is helping or failing. Fading memory or a waning ability to manage routine tasks can't be measured biologically. That requires nuanced, often-subjective tools. Scientists use memory tests, along with questionnaires about the experience of home life, to probe trial participants and gather the assessments of loved ones and clinicians. They try to map the contours of thought to find some ground truth about whether a drug might be working.

Cassava hired private contract-research sites—typical in large trials recruiting volunteers across the nation, or even internationally—to test participants on tasks including memory quizzes, copying shapes like diamonds and boxes, and completing simple tasks. For example, they told Stephen to place a pencil on a card, then move it to a different location on the desk. They used the Alzheimer's Disease Assessment Scale-Cognitive Subscale (ADAS-Cog). Although widely accepted, bias can still infect the scoring, results, and interpretation of the test. Scientists who study Alzheimer's regard it as a poor substitute for other assessments. Statistician Suzanne Hendrix of Pentara Corp., an expert in such testing and a reviewer for Cassava's findings, had coauthored an article that described the unreliability of ADAS-Cog. She debunked the idea that it is an accurate test for patients with mild Alzheimer's. It was more accurate for those who suffer from a moderate case of the disease, Hendrix wrote. In other words, if ADAS-Cog was useful, it might work better for patients like Stephen Price.

To people living with Alzheimer's and their loved ones, efforts to find a cure can seem like an impenetrable black box of scientific complexity. But Matt had the expertise to crack the box open. As the trial progressed, he began to study simufilam and its maker. What he learned renewed his earlier doubts, then left him frankly concerned. Over the next two years, Matt began to see his father's experience as a sign of how clinical research might succumb to expediency—and why big ideas to cure a disease are not always what they seem.

When he compared his dad's experience, and his own as a study partner, against the disclosure documents, Matt came to view certain aspects of the trial as ethically problematic. For example, at the outset, a clinician sampled Stephen's cerebrospinal fluid, which bathes the brain and spinal cord. Cassava needed it to look for signs of Alzheimer's biomarkers. If Stephen did not show certain biomarker levels, he would not qualify for the trial. Investigators used a standard lumbar puncture or "spinal tap." They inserted a needle between two vertebrae, into Stephen's spinal column, to collect the precious fluid. The procedure is routine, but hardly risk free. In rare cases it causes paralysis or even death. Yet Cassava listed none of the serious side effects on the consent forms Stephen signed.

The forms also said any trial participant could obtain their own spinal-tap results. Matt and Stephen wanted to see the levels of amyloids and other proteins in that fluid—in part to get a reading on the possible trajectory of Stephen's symptoms. But several requests went nowhere, as Matt began to wonder if the samples were ever actually tested.

Cassava might have been leery about handing over the data because their testing program had apparently violated a New York State lab licensing and inspection requirement meant to safeguard clinical trial participants. Spinal fluid and other samples for Stephen's trial would have been tested by Cassava's close collaborator Hoau-Yan Wang, a City University of New York (CUNY) neuropharmacologist. The state requires all labs that test such samples to be certified and inspected, but no lab at CUNY was on the certified list. That might have been why Cassava abruptly changed the trial protocol in June 2021: It would test spinal fluid for twenty-five patients only. Most likely, Stephen's fluid wasn't tested. Cassava said it could not reply about a contractor's licensure, and Wang did not respond to questions about lab certification.

It seemed a foreboding misstep, given the experience of another ambitious medical company, Theranos. Infamously, that Silicon Valley start-up claimed to build a device that could conduct a multitude of tests on a single drop of blood—an advance that could revolutionize laboratory efficiency and render the discomfort of blood draws from a vein nearly obsolete. But a key step in the firm's ultimate exposure as an elaborate deception came when one of its employees contacted the same New York regulators who apparently called Cassava's bluff and they learned that Theranos's testing evidently violated the same state rules.

Matt also questioned how the final data would be interpreted. The six-month, double-blinded interlude, sandwiched between two open-label periods, allowed Cassava to say it used the gold-standard approach, in part. But the blinded interval in this multipart trial was regarded by many scientists as too short to demonstrate a clear effect or provide statistical reliability.

Matt again reached out to his friend, an expert in a nerve-cell receptor called TLR4. Such receptors can perceive the presence of toxins and affect inflammation that can harm brain cells. Cassava says TLR4 plays a central role in how simufilam works. Matt's friend reviewed some test-tube and mouse experiments that the company said supported the idea that the drug was promising, partly due to its impact on TLR4. The papers were key to Cassava's justification that simufilam was ready to test in people. The linkages looked "very tenuous," the friend concluded.

But Matt didn't want his skepticism, however justified, to wipe out his family's hopes. From his own work in global health, Matt knew that aggressive trials with drugs that posed a relatively low risk for even a small chance of a stunning reward could be worth trying. Although the ledger didn't favor simufilam, he thought it might still be worth the benefit of the doubt.

"WHAT'S POSSIBLE IS SHRINKING"

Before the trial, Stephen could remember words and places and times, draw shapes, and follow simple instructions with ease. By December 2022, about eighteen months into the trial, he had trouble remembering words like "apple" and "chair" moments after being asked to read them aloud. He couldn't fold a letter and place it into an envelope or recall the word "harmonica" when shown the instrument. He couldn't name Toms River, where his trial clinic was located, or remember the year or day of the week. Asked for the current month, he answered correctly—only to forget that fact seconds later.

In a March 2023 examination, Stephen was shown an example of a circle and asked to draw his own version. He produced a crude facsimile, like the artwork of a toddler. For a diamond, he drew an indecipherable squiggle.

"On the ride back, he just mentioned offhand that he is acutely aware of his own deficits, like when he's asked to draw shapes," Matt said. "Most of his days he kind of stays within the universe of things he feels he can do most of the time. Being subjected to a series of tests, I think it's a real downer for him—not like the beginning of the study. He does have insight that he's not getting better."

Still, certain hints of normalcy give Matt and Toni hope. Tai Chi, the slow, controlled martial art, has become a calming routine. Sometimes he reads news articles. "With some difficulty and hesitation, he comments on them in ways that reflect some retention," Matt said. Although Stephen hasn't driven on the road in many years and needs help putting on a seat belt, he sometimes drives his old pickup truck to collect leaves around their property.

"Yet afterwards, he will not know how to take off his own boots," Matt added, pausing to gather his thoughts. "At dinner, he sometimes looks at the fork, thinking about which end to hold. We're trying to support his independence as much as possible, while coming to the broader realization that what's possible for him is shrinking."

For Stephen, Alzheimer's was winning. Simufilam was failing.

As the family's struggle unfolded, an obscure researcher hundreds of miles away was preparing to send shudders through the Alzheimer's research world and well beyond.

Chapter 2

"Magic Hands"

Big Timber, Montana;
Cambridge, Massachusetts; Atlanta; Austin; New York City
1965–2021

"I mean, this is wild. It's zombie science!"

—ROGER NICOLL, NEUROLOGIST,
UNIVERSITY OF CALIFORNIA SAN FRANCISCO

One word captures Lindsay Burns: exceptional. From her beginnings in the remote western ranchlands of tiny Big Timber, Montana—midway between Yellowstone National Park and the Crazy Mountains—to the heights of academia and Olympic stardom, she worked phenomenally hard and aimed high. In everything she touched, the muscular, poised, sandy-haired athlete and scholar with a brilliant, toothy smile seemed destined for greatness.

She would lead research behind simufilam, an effort to turn the experimental Alzheimer's drug from Cassava Sciences into the most important medicine in the history of dementia.

Born in 1965, Burns spent her formative years on the family spread, with its one thousand head of cattle. The founding patriarch of the western branch of the Burns family was Lindsay's great-grandfather, Horatio Hutchinson Burns. He migrated out west and by 1884, at twenty-four, owned a cattle and sheep ranching operation in Northern Wyoming.

Horatio's son, Robert Horatio Burns, became a cow puncher at thirteen, among his proudest achievements. It was a generational signal that the family—which prospered on the vast Wyoming range—fully embraced the cowboy culture. But Horatio still dispatched Robert, fresh off his coming-of-age adventures, to a polar-opposite world: New Hampshire's elite Phillips Exeter Academy, a preeminent college-prep boarding school. Robert went on to Harvard, where he earned a degree in economics in 1927. So began the family heritage of merging east coast erudition with love for the vast, open west.

After college, Robert returned to work with his father amid Wyoming's windswept expanses. Then in 1951 the family moved operations two hundred miles northwest to the spectacular vistas of Big Timber, buying a ranch on rugged acres near meandering Swamp Creek, north of the tiny town center. Nestled in the foothills, four thousand feet up, with views of the snow-peaked "Crazies," even Hollywood found irresistible romance in that scenic land. Robert Redford shot his acclaimed dramas *The Horse Whisperer* and *A River Runs Through It* in and around Big Timber. Robert Burns built deep civic connections to his chosen community—joining the Masons, Shriners, Elks, the local Farm Bureau, and the Montana Wool Growers.

But in that isolated land—peopled by individualists and sometimes-restive skeptics of authority—he took an ominous political turn, according to a declassified Federal Bureau of Investigation report from 1964. It described Robert as affiliated with the Minutemen, a right-wing extremist group. They stockpiled weapons to fight an anticipated communist takeover of the United States.

"BURNS SHOULD BE CONSIDERED ARMED AND POSSIBLY DANGEROUS," the memo blared in scare-caps. "Burns is obtaining an old model Lewis machine gun." The World War I–era weapon could fire five hundred to six hundred rounds per minute. It added: "Also he desires to obtain some cheap shotguns that could have the barrels sawed off to twenty inches for use by their group."

The FBI believed Burns was distributing "None Dare Call It Treason," an anti-Soviet screed that sold millions of copies. The book praised staunch anticommunist Barry Goldwater and red-baited moderate candidates. It was credited as a key factor in Goldwater's 1964 Republican nomination for president. "None Dare" promoted the conspiracy theory that the US State Department was riddled with communists, and blamed Soviet and homegrown communist infiltration for tearing apart bonds between churches, civic groups, schools, and their communities. Sweet Grass County—home to Big Timber—voted solidly for Goldwater in the general election, giving him the second-highest margin of any Montana county.

Despite Robert Burns's alleged radicalism, he was never arrested and lived out his life peacefully as a successful rancher. His son, Lindsay's father Horatio "Rasch" Winspear Burns, was born in 1931 in Sheridan, Wyoming, a relative metropolis with its population of about nine thousand. On Rasch's fourth birthday, his mother died, a tragedy that seemed to cement his inheritance of Robert's steadfast self-reliance.

In 1945, at age fourteen, Rasch followed his father's example, stepping onto a transcontinental train to attend a different boarding school—Milton Academy in Massachusetts, also among the nation's most prestigious. After surviving "a severe case of culture shock," he continued on to Harvard to take a degree in economics as his father had done. He added a passion that would prove central to his daughter Lindsay's future—rowing crew.

After his Ivy League education, Rasch rejected graduate school and turned down job offers from Ford Motor Company and NASA. Again, the allure of the distant Burns ranch and the life of an outdoorsman proved impossible to resist. In early 1953 he rejoined his father, who by then was in Big Timber. Like Robert, Rasch built deep connections to the local community, becoming senior deacon of the Masonic lodge, a representative on various ranching organizations, and vice president of the local rifle club.

An avid hunter, he traveled to Point Hope, Alaska, just across the Bering Strait from Siberia, to shoot a polar bear. It was among several bear-hunting trips, including two to Russia. In 30 degrees below zero weather, he traveled via ski-plane searching for polar bears, peering down from one hundred feet above the icy terrain. After a heart-stopping landing,

Rasch shot a nearly ten foot tall, "cunning and crafty" bear from about 185 yards, scoring three direct hits. The hunter and his guide skinned the animal, giving what they considered the "questionably edible" meat to the native Alaskans. The pelt was tanned for the Burns home in Big Timber.

ATHLETIC STRATOSPHERE

Rasch and Sheila Ellen Shepherd married in 1961 and raised their own family of high achievers. Lindsay and her brother, Cameron, emerged from a rich stew of civic engagement, love of the land, guns and hunting, and plenty of athletic competitions. From the start, the siblings showed keen competitive drives, particularly Lindsay. Among the first of dozens of mentions about her exploits in the local paper, the *Big Timber Pioneer*, was a victory at age seven in the local sack races.

Lindsay's young life was filled with joyful, rural Americana, including membership in the local 4-H club. At age ten, she and her family made and sold candy suckers at the local Christmas bazaar; their effort earned a charming feature photo in the *Pioneer*.

In a first hint of her research ambitions, during grammar school Lindsay and a friend surveyed the number of trees in town—a formidable project. "There's a lot of 'timber' in Big Timber," an article in the *Pioneer* duly noted. "And if you don't believe it, just ask Christy Drivdahl and Lindsay Burns." The girls counted a sampling of trees and houses, then extrapolated their findings to come up with 10,560 trees—about seven times as many trees as people—"not counting bushes." The precocious grasp of something approximating scientific methodology hinted at her future professional endeavors.

The fourth-generation rancher often herded cattle on horseback and traversed family fields cutting hay on a giant mower. But when she reached age fourteen, following the family tradition, Rasch dispatched his daughter to boarding school. She followed in his footsteps to Milton, whose alumni include Ted Kennedy, Robert F. Kennedy Sr., T. S. Eliot, the legendary World War II general Douglas MacArthur, and Illinois governor and billionaire JB Pritzker.

The school's rarefied environment set the academically minded young woman on a glide path to Harvard in 1983, where she excelled in psychobiology, and—again, like her father—rowing, a sport in which she would soon eclipse him. Weighing no more than 130 pounds, Burns rowed primarily as a lightweight. The term thoroughly mischaracterized her in every other way, especially her unbridled determination and sheer competitive drive.

As a freshman, she cracked a rib, a painful stress fracture common to rowers, but tried to ignore it. "I rowed on it until it was ugly," she said. The same year, she flipped her boat in the "icy March waters" of the Charles River in Boston. Burns called it "a lesson on hypothermia, not to mention some details about boats and gravity." She loved the sport so much that she insisted on practicing on weekends. Harvard's stately Weld Boathouse was closed, so Lindsay scaled its brickwork like Spider-Woman to enter through a second floor window to get to her boat. (Administrators later nailed the window shut.)

The hard work paid off. Rising steadily through the ranks, Burns traveled to Copenhagen in 1987 for the world championships. She outfitted her team of four with lucky rattlesnake earrings—easy to find in southern Montana. They edged out competitors from West Germany and China. It would be the first major triumph of an illustrious career that took her to Tasmania, Vienna, Prague, and Tampere, Finland.

Burns continued rowing as a PhD student in neuropsychology at the University of Cambridge in England—another of the world's greatest and most selective institutions of higher learning. Afterward, she returned to Boston to train as a postdoctoral fellow at the Harvard-affiliated McLean psychiatric hospital. Her work involved the successful transplantation of fetal pig cells to rats in an effort to replenish cells killed by neurological disorders. It signified her growing fascination with dementia research.

Burns extended her rowing career to a thirteenth year to compete in the 1996 Atlanta Olympics—which added a lightweight division—in the double sculls, where one rower sits behind another. Before a wildly cheering American crowd, she and Teresa Zarzeczny were narrowly edged out by the German team. The silver medal still provided a glittering capstone to an illustrious athletic career. The exhilarating global recognition paled beside the party in her honor where it mattered most. Big Timber's "Lindsay Burns Day" that August featured speeches by local dignitaries and a potluck feed for all of Sweet Grass County. "Don't miss out on this chance of a lifetime! Come celebrate with Lindsay Burns!" the announcement in the local paper trumpeted.

SCIENTIFIC AMBITIONS

Grounded in rough-hewn Western self-confidence, imbued with Ivy League privilege, and armed with the success of world-class accomplishment at a young age, Burns seemed equal to any new challenge. Her next was drug development.

After bouncing around a couple of biotechs, in 2002 she joined the tiny pharma company Pain Therapeutics. Its big idea, amid the raging opioid-addiction epidemic, was an "abuse-deterrent, extended-release gel formulation of oxycodone." The encapsulated, sticky goo was meant to address a daunting problem: Addicts crushed and snorted or smoked oxy, or dissolved it and shot it up, turning a painkiller designed to work over several hours into an instant, fleeting high. The company named its drug "Remoxy"—described as a narcissistic mash-up of CEO Remi Barbier's first name and oxycodone. Remoxy "can serve a meaningful social purpose and, potentially, may save lives during the worst drug crisis in American history," the company boasted in a press release.

Barbier, a finance guy who had spent his career in the drug development business, previously had worked for Exelixis and ArQule, cancer medicine companies. The dark-haired, well-groomed CEO often showed a touch of informality reflected in his open-collar, jeans-clad pose in occasional features about his company in business magazines. Barbier subsidized work on Remoxy with investments from potential partners and investors, supplemented by federal grants. Pain Therapeutics amassed a sizeable research and development war chest.

Burns had trained under illustrious neuroscientist Trevor Robbins at the University of Cambridge, but her work was not notable among his protégés. According to Neurotree, a website that chronicles the influence of leading scholars, forty-three of Robbins's students went on to esteemed positions in the field. Burns didn't make the cut. Yet she joined Pain Therapeutics as vice president for neuroscience. Burns and Barbier began a romance. They wed in June 2005 and lived in the Bay Area, where the company was headquartered. Later they bought a luxury home in Austin, Texas, where Pain Therapeutics relocated executive offices in 2011.

Burns formed half of the brain trust behind Remoxy's development. The other half was Hoau-Yan Wang, a graying but boyish-looking professor at the City University of New York (CUNY) who favors large rectangular glasses. Wang, now in his midsixties, had long conducted basic research on the brain's dopamine receptors, which play a key role in memory, learning, emotions, and the neural reward system. He was particularly interested in how the habitual use of recreational drugs or painkillers—including cocaine and opioids—promoted deeper addiction by flattening the response of dopamine receptors and sparking demands for more drugs to get the same high. Pain Therapeutics had no labs. Wang conducted much of its bench science at CUNY.

Wang has his own equally driven but less brand-name success story. He emigrated from his native Taiwan in the early 1980s to complete a master's degree at St. John's University, then earned his PhD degree in pharmacology at the Medical College of Pennsylvania, which later became part of Drexel University. His collaboration with Burns began in the mid-2000s, when he endured a grueling daily commute between his home in Philadelphia and his new job teaching and running a small lab at CUNY. The cost of the commute weighed on his finances. "New York real estate is very expensive, and my wife and kids are happy in Philadelphia," he said at the time. When Amtrak raised the price of its monthly pass to more than one thousand dollars, Wang took a slower transit route to save money, he said. "Otherwise, we might as well send my paycheck straight to Amtrak by direct deposit."

Pain Therapeutics apparently noticed Wang because his basic research examined drug development targets for pain relief, which fit the company's opioid focus. When he became its research collaborator and scientific advisor, Wang's long-standing interest in filamin A—the brain protein that he later concluded holds the key to Alzheimer's disease—also became Burns's central focus. Filamin A provides cellular scaffolding that affects the brain's opioid receptors. In one of their earliest joint scholarly papers, published in 2008, Wang and Burns said their data established filamin A as a key target to both improve opioid pain relief, yet "prevent opioid tolerance and dependence." The company viewed the protein as vital to lift its prospects in a crowded marketplace.

It was the start of a rich research collaboration by Burns and Wang, who ultimately shared inventor credit on fourteen patents related to filamin A. In each case, they assigned Pain Therapeutics the rights to use the intellectual property.

The company worked for more than fifteen years to move Remoxy through the drug approval pipeline. The Food and Drug Administration (FDA) rejected its application for marketing over and over. Shareholders accused Pain Therapeutics of failing to report the agency's concerns about the drug—including its chemistry and manufacturing—leading to an abrupt drop in the company's share price. Without admitting wrongdoing, Barbier and his company settled the case for up to $8.5 million. It would not be the last time they faced a shareholder revolt.

Remoxy didn't work as described, the FDA concluded. Barbier called the move a "horrible travesty," and blamed a convoluted and sometimes-confusing regulatory maze for the failure. With alliterative flourish, the company cited "math errors, material mistakes, or misrepresentations" in the FDA's review. Its "lack of transparency, clarity, or helpfulness" stifled innovation, sending more than $100 million down the drain, company officials said in February 2019. "We can't work with shambolic regulations," they added. The bitter turn of phrase would later be deployed against his company to caustic effect.

THE NEW BIG IDEA

Barbier had always been one of Pain Therapeutics's largest individual shareholders, and Burns also received blocks of stock and options—the right to buy shares later at a preset price. Over the years their ownership had been reduced by stock sales that earned the pair many millions of dollars; they still held about 5 percent of the company. But Pain Therapeutics never won federal approval for its drug. With Remoxy moribund, the company looked to be circling the drain. On paper, Pain Therapeutics was worth just $19 million, compared to $470 million a decade earlier. The Barbier-Burns family stake shrank in value to less than a paltry $1 million.

Barbier needed a new big idea fast. Wang and Burns supplied it. Filamin A might not lead to a tamperproof opioid, but it offered a tantalizing prospect for something that could be even more important, and breathtakingly lucrative: a remedy for Alzheimer's disease.

The duo had been erecting the scientific scaffolding for the company's new organizing principle just as another bold scientific venture was beginning to unravel under intense scrutiny. In 2015, then-billionaire Elizabeth Holmes, CEO of the once-revolutionary lab-test company Theranos, made a comment that seemed apt for Pain Therapeutics, "When you have that passion, you will get back up when you get knocked down. And you will get knocked down over and over and over again, and you win by getting back up . . . that's what winning is about." A few years later, she was infamously exposed as a fraud. As Burns commented about Holmes on LinkedIn at the time: "She has a lot more explaining to do." Those words would later haunt Burns herself.

Many experts believe that Alzheimer's dementia can be traced to harm caused by certain hallmark proteins: One of those, "tau," resides inside neurons, the brain cells central to cognition. Tau deposits are called "tangles"—after their convoluted shape, like a mass of knotted string. The second protein, amyloid-beta, creates sticky "plaques," amorphous deposits that occupy spaces between the cells, as well as a soluble, toxic form that can kill neurons, according to many scientists.

Wang and Burns offered a novel hypothesis: Alzheimer's occurs due to a misfolded form of filamin A, twisted into an abnormal shape. Instead of performing its normal scaffolding role, misfolded filamin A causes inflammation and promotes the formation of tau and amyloid-beta proteins, according to the two scientists. Burns and Wang developed an experimental drug—code-named PTI-125—that they said returns filamin A to a benign shape and reverses those terrible effects—the promotion of tau and amyloid-beta proteins—produced by its misfolded evil twin. They said the drug, which could be developed in pill form to treat Alzheimer's, also lessens resistance to insulin, which regulates blood sugar and has been tied to the formation of amyloid plaques by some scientists. In short, unlike most other Alzheimer's drugs, PTI-125 purportedly offers a grab bag of "mechanisms of action"—the scientific term for how the drug affects the body biochemically. It adopted several ideas advocated as central to Alzheimer's by factions in the competitive world of drug discovery. For Wang, it must have been an enormous source of pride. His grandmother and both of his parents-in-law were living with Alzheimer's.

Pain Therapeutics pivoted hard and fast. Barbier transformed the company's core mission and changed its name to the stylishly enigmatic Cassava Sciences, "to better reflect a new strategic focus on drug development for neurodegenerative diseases, such as Alzheimer's." The name was pulled from the street in the tony Austin neighborhood where Barbier and Burns made their home, according to some observers. It seemed an odd choice. Cassava root is widely touted in online forums and nutritional-supplement ads as a brain-health remedy, including claims that it counters Alzheimer's symptoms—without a shred of credible evidence. Ironically, some varieties of cassava naturally contain the poison cyanide. If improperly prepared, ingesting the root causes cognitive decline. Nor did it boost the company's credibility when, a few months later in a corporate presentation, it represented the chemical structure of the hallucinogen LSD as that of PTI-125. For good measure, the LSD diagram apparently came from Wikipedia.

Soon after, Cassava developed a pill form of PTI-125 and adopted the chemical name *sumifilam* in August 2020. "A very famous author once asked, what's in a name?" said Barbier, riffing on Shakespeare's *Romeo and Juliet*. "With apologies to that author, that which we call sumifilam by any other name would still elicit palpable excitement for an absolutely new type of drug therapy for Alzheimer's disease." His comments resembled self-parody three months later, when it came out that sumifilam was already in use for another drug. Barbier transposed two vowels to rename his drug *simufilam*.

ZOMBIE SCIENCE

Despite the embarrassing snafus, if Burns and Wang were correct, associating the new Alzheimer's remedy with historically great literature might seem warranted. It could rank as a premier discovery in medical history.

The scientists had established simufilam's plausibility for tests in people based partly on research on human brain samples conducted in Wang's CUNY lab. His techniques evoked a different literary masterpiece: Mary Shelley's *Frankenstein*.

Wang claimed to have effectively revivified long-dead brain tissue. The samples had been frozen at super-cold temperatures, in some cases ostensibly for years. He partly thawed, then chopped the donated tissue, and said it could transmit chemical signals between nerve cells. Wang dosed the still-subzero tissue with simufilam to test the experimental chemical's possibly beneficial effects. The technique, he and Burns wrote in scholarly papers, lent support to the overall idea that simufilam can counter the causes of Alzheimer's. The work's frigid novelty generated substantial interest in the idea that insulin resistance—akin to diabetes of the brain—plays a leading role. (Insulin, a hormone, regulates how the body processes sugar. People become diabetic when the body makes too little insulin or cells stop responding to it correctly.) A paper to that effect by Wang, Burns, and colleagues, published in the respected *Journal of Clinical Investigation*, has been cited by other scholars more than 1,800 times. After it appeared, NIH funding for insulin-related Alzheimer's work rose sharply.

The findings also raised eyebrows. How did an obscure lab at a university not known for cutting-edge neuroscience research make so momentous a discovery involving novel biochemical findings from postmortem brains, when no one had previously done so?

"It's hard for me to imagine how you could get any life from that tissue," said brain-slice expert Roger Nicoll of the University of California San Francisco. "I mean, this is wild. It's zombie science!"

Wang, with or without Burns, cited precedents for the extraordinary work—a standard element of any scientific paper, particularly one meant to establish credibility for an unusual technique. But the footnotes were self-referential, tracing back to earlier work by Wang himself.

The CUNY researcher seemed to have "magic hands"—a term scientists sometimes use to describe a preternatural talent to achieve hoped-for, problem-free results, time after time, experiment after experiment. A laboratory savant, Wang succeeded in work considered outlandish if not impossible by other experimentalists. Such a maven can become a fixer of sorts for other researchers, including top-tier professors who lack the patience for tedious, protracted lab work. Yet when ambitious collaborators get what they want, skepticism can be the first casualty. They'd rather conclude that the lab expert knows what he's doing.

Wang attracted elite coauthors from leading universities. They included Julie Schneider and David Bennett of Rush University—overseer of a major bank of donated brain samples—and Steven Arnold of Harvard. He even signed on the late John Trojanowski, a University of Pennsylvania scientist who was one of the most prolific and influential Alzheimer's scholars.

Such coauthors on the "zombie" papers conferred substantial credibility. Arnold, along with Burns's mentor Robbins and Robbins's neuroscientist spouse, Barbara Sahakian, and Jeffrey Cummings from the

University of Nevada—another prominent Alzheimer's researcher—joined Cassava's paid scientific advisory board. Such boards effectively vouch for a company's work. Given that Cassava had no record of commercial success after two decades of operations, it reassured funders, regulators, and investors. The famous names helped Cassava gain $20 million in grants for simufilam and other work by Wang or Burns from the premier federal funder, the National Institutes of Health (NIH). Their simufilam collaborators (including Arnold) gained tens of millions more for related studies. NIH would ultimately underwrite clinical trials necessary to gain eventual FDA approval. Cassava was suddenly on its way to testing simufilam not in frozen tissue, but where it really counts: in the brains of living Alzheimer's patients.

MISTAKES WERE MADE

The new strategy slowly lifted the company's battered share price—until it reported results from an early clinical trial of simufilam involving sixty-four participants. It was a bust. In May 2020, Cassava announced that the drug failed to reduce levels of tau or other targeted biomarkers associated with Alzheimer's. "Today's top-line results disappoint and are not consistent with previous clinical experience for reasons that are unclear," said Barbier. The company's stock lost three-quarters of its value overnight.

But a few months later, after a fresh analysis, Barbier had better news. Tau and other Alzheimer's biomarkers actually had improved sharply, he reported. Barbier blamed the earlier disappointing results on unspecified "mistakes" by a lab contractor. "It's hard for anyone to fess up to exactly what happened and when and who did what," Barbier said in a call with investors. "We did our forensic inquiries, we clearly see mistakes . . . we really rely exclusively on the second bioanalysis from this study."

Then he announced a more stunning development: Patients taking simufilam showed memory improvements after just a month—extraordinary for any Alzheimer's trial. "Filamin-binding molecules are new to Alzheimer's research and may represent an important advance if these data can be replicated in larger studies," crowed Cummings, the Cassava advisor, in a press release. He was identified by his academic credentials, with no mention of his role as paid consultant. "I am pleased to see early evidence of disease-modifying effects in patients," Cummings said. "The data appear to represent a step forward toward urgently needed treatments for Alzheimer's disease."

Cassava's share price rebounded instantly and sharply. And the good times kept rolling. In early February 2021, the company made public triumphant results for the same fifty patients after they had taken simufilam for six months. Their performance on cognitive tests showed that Alzheimer's-related measures—including memory, anxiety, and delusions—improved even more, this time by 10 percent.

For Wang, Barbier, and Burns, it wasn't just frozen brain tissue coming back to life. It looked like the kind of scientific resurrection that leads to Nobel Prizes, as some company boosters began suggesting on social media soon after. Less than two weeks later, Cassava announced that it had raised $200 million from investors in a public stock offering at a whopping $49 a share—several times the trading price only weeks earlier. "With solid science, the right people in place, cash in the bank and a clinical roadmap that makes sense, I think Cassava Sciences is positioned to becoming a premier organization to serve patients with Alzheimer's disease," Barbier said proudly, when announcing Cassava's stellar financial condition in March 2021.

The company unveiled more impressive data, described as unprecedented, in July. Simufilam improved cognitive test scores in two out of every three patients after nine months, and most others suffered only modest declines in cognition. "Cassava Sciences believes today's data is the first report of significant cognitive improvements at nine months that also track with robust improvements in biomarkers in patients with Alzheimer's," the company's press release noted.

Some leading scientists openly scoffed at the Cassava announcement. "Uninterpretable," said Lon Schneider, a physician and neuroscientist at the University of Southern California Alzheimer's research center. "Overblown, inappropriate, and naïve," said Rob Howard, an Alzheimer's researcher at University College London. "It's the sort of presentation that one might expect an undergraduate to make."

Those scientists and others cited basic concerns that would apply to any clinical trial for a new drug. The Cassava experiment's sample size at nine months was just fifty participants. So tiny a group offers exceedingly weak statistical power—a measure of how confident scientists can be that the findings were not due to chance alone. And the experiment used an open-label design; both experimenters and patients knew that they were getting simufilam pills, rather than a placebo. This made it vulnerable to bias compared to a double-blind, controlled design—particularly with results based on cognitive tests that rely on the subjective impressions of patients and their ever-hopeful caregivers and clinicians.

In an interview in 2021, Barbier was asked if later trials would include a placebo group. He provided a revealing and chilling reply: "It's an evil necessity."

Online boosters led a buying frenzy among small-time investors in the volatile stock. Cassava's market valuation rocketed into the stratosphere, topping $5.4 billion—280 times its value less than two years earlier. On paper, the Barbier and Burns family was suddenly worth $147 million.

They had reinvented the company and rescued it from failure and obscurity. "These clinical data . . . suggest highly encouraging and durable treatment effects for people living with Alzheimer's disease," Barbier said. To Cassava's true believers, simufilam was the long-awaited, ever-elusive pill to effectively treat or even cure one of the most terrifying diseases.

The jubilation didn't last long. On August 18, 2021, weeks after the company's stock reached an all-time high, two neuroscientists—Geoffrey Pitt of Weill Cornell Medical College and David Bredt, a former executive at drugmakers Eli Lilly and Johnson & Johnson—submitted a lengthy "citizen petition," in which individuals or a consumer group can ask the FDA to address concerns about an experimental drug—for simufilam. Their attorney provided evidence that dozens of scientific studies underlying simufilam's development contained manipulated scientific images. In short, they asserted, the work looked like it had been doctored.

The allegations called into question fundamental claims about simufilam and how it might affect Alzheimer's, if at all. Some of the research by Wang, Burns, and key collaborators, according to the petition, appeared to be "fraudulent."

The public announcements hit Wang hard. He "collapsed from stress and exhaustion, and due to the significant emotional trauma, he voluntarily admitted himself to Bryn Mawr Hospital for treatment," his wife later said in an affidavit.

Burns normally let Barbier announce good news and blast critics. This time Burns couldn't resist lashing out in her LinkedIn feed: "Cassava Sciences hit by false allegations," she said after the FDA filing, adding a thinly veiled legal threat. "Hit job by a law firm that admits it represents short sellers, makes its case in the Court of Public Opinion (as opposed to a Court of Law). Unreal." She had a point. Pitt and Bredt were also "shorting" the company's stock and would profit if Cassava shares fell. But documents provided by the neuroscientists—whatever their motives— were compelling and generated enormous uncertainty about simufilam.

The petition validated and extended growing doubts Matt Price had about the drug that his family was hoping against hope would help his dad, Stephen, gain a few better years. But like so many family members who lacked good options to help a loved one, he couldn't give up. Matt advised Stephen to stay in the trial. He continued taking simufilam twice daily. "I remembered a meme from the '90s TV show The X Files of this poster that says, 'I want to believe' beneath a little alien saucer," Matt said. "I wanted to believe that simufilam wasn't all a fraud."

The FDA petition's key findings were not only by Pitt and Bredt. Their lawyer hired a physician and neuroscientist who had the specialized knowledge and skill for the job.

Like Burns, the scientist emerged out of the remote rural west— a Washington State farming town with fewer than two thousand residents—about the size of Big Timber, Montana, five hundred miles east on Interstate 90. Like Burns, he was brilliant and ambitious. But he followed a more humble path into neuroscience—homeschooling, followed by undergraduate training in a less-august university by relatively obscure professors. He became an expert in the dominant amyloid hypothesis of Alzheimer's, which for decades has marked amyloid-beta proteins as the chief culprit.

During the course of his young career—he was thirty-six when the FDA petition was filed—the scientist had completed thousands of scientific images displaying proteins. In the process, he developed a seasoned eye for detecting digital manipulation with common software programs. Such images can easily be changed to better reflect researchers' hypotheses—sometimes leading to grants, influence, patents, and even riches. But doctored images, he knew, could also poison the scientific record—sending scientists down costly dead ends. They could even risk patients' lives.

The simufilam matter and the FDA petition formed the genesis of what would become an epic scientific journey. The young scientist would uncover a scandal that soon eclipsed the Cassava intrigues. His anonymous sleuthing would cast unprecedented doubt on the amyloid hypothesis. His work would lead to the discrediting of leading figures in Alzheimer's research. It would raise grave concerns about the trustworthiness of the scholarly press he found has been routinely publishing suspect or faked papers. And in the process, the researcher would mount a formidable challenge to billions of dollars in spending by the federal government and giant pharma companies.

The softspoken, nonchalantly rumpled junior professor at Vanderbilt University would become the most important whistleblower in the history of Alzheimer's.

The public announcements hit Wang hard. He "collapsed from stress and exhaustion, and due to the significant emotional trauma, he voluntarily admitted himself to Bryn Mawr Hospital for treatment," his wife later said in an affidavit.

Chapter 3

"Everything Is Figureoutable"

Davenport, Washington;

Grand Forks, North Dakota; Loma Linda, California; Nashville

1996–2022

"It's usually a very polite field.
People really don't want to have these arguments about fraud and data."

—MATTHEW SCHRAG

In his cramped, modest office at Vanderbilt University in Nashville, steps away from a buzzing refrigerator, neurologist and neuroscientist Matthew Schrag—a young-looking, sturdily built forty-year-old with a receding hairline and an easy smile—maintains a shelf-sized medical museum. Ten reflex hammers go back a century or more, as do ancient medical manuals. One for smallpox inoculations dates to 1752. An antique microscope pays homage to predecessors who applied painstaking bench science to medicine's endless enigmas.

A small sign on his desk reads, "Everything Is Figureoutable."

So far, Alzheimer's has proved a glaring exception to Schrag's inspirational maxim. But his background has left him comfortable with seemingly intractable contradictions, and the sacrifices required to unwind them.

Schrag's father, Paul Schrag, hails from a family of Mennonites, known for their philosophy of peacemaking. His ancestors migrated from Russia in the 1870s, after the czar revoked their right to refuse military service. Like thousands of their coreligionists, the Schrags ended up in the Midwest. They endured bitter times as Midwest farmers. "There were a number of hard winters where they lost a bunch of children to the cold and blizzards," Matthew said. So the family decamped to rural eastern Washington State, where Paul grew up.

Turning away from his pacifist ancestry, Paul joined the US Air Force, and worked in ROTC at the University of Massachusetts in Lowell, north of Boston. Matthew's mother, Nanette, grew up in small-town western Massachusetts and was an undergrad at Lowell, where the two met.

Later, Paul managed ground-launched cruise missile systems. "A substantial portion of what he did was classified, so we sort of have a vague concept of that to this day," Matthew said. An Air Force brat born in 1984, his peripatetic early years began in Tucson. When he was three they moved to Germany, then to Ely, England—a small town eighty miles north of London that dates to the seventh century and is known for its ancient cathedral. They lived in the local communities rather than on military bases. Matthew developed such a thick British accent that later, back in the States, he was cast as the lead in a production of the musical *Oliver*—based on Charles Dickens's *Oliver Twist*. (Not a trace of the accent remains.)

When Paul was ready to end his military career, he asked the Air Force for a last assignment in one of their home states—Georgia, where Nanette's family had moved, or Washington. Matthew was in middle school when they landed in Davenport, Washington—a flatter version of Lindsay Burns's Big Timber, Montana. (Paul retired from the military as a major during the Bill Clinton presidency.) Davenport, with its farmers and cattle ranchers, rests in the valley of Cottonwood Creek, where Schrag learned to fish. Its waters flow into Hawk Creek and finally empty into mighty Lake Roosevelt to the north. Davenport's a tiny cow town, where locals like to joke that their cows are as big as anyone's.

"It's in east Washington out in the middle of the wheatfields—a cute little town. A really nice place to grow up. People say it was stuck in the fifties. And it looked that way when you drove through," Matthew said. Today, the two-square-mile seat of Lincoln County calls itself the "Gateway to the Lake Roosevelt Recreation Area," created within the Columbia River by the Grand Coulee Dam. Davenport has a couple of motels, a block-long park, ten churches, and two pizza joints.

Overseas, Nanette homeschooled Matthew and his two brothers. The instruction was inspired by conservative, traditional values, and the pedagogy reflected rigor and discipline of the highest order. "Mom was tenacious and brilliant," Schrag recalled. "She gave us quite a gift. All that bouncing around could have been very hard. She created continuity in our education."

The curriculum featured lifelong evangelical religious training. "We were taught that the Bible was the physical word of God, and that we should live our lives by traditional Christian moral views," he said. "Bible study was the first class of the day.

"When you're a Christian, there's a code that you have to live by," Schrag said of his faith. "In its truest form, it's for imperfect people who know that they need forgiveness and are trying to live up to the standards that Christ set for us."

His family belonged to a church within the Countess of Huntingdon's Connexion—an obscure Calvinist Methodist offshoot formed in the eighteenth century, emphasizing God's sovereignty and the primacy of the Bible. Over the years, the family gradually began to identify as devout but nondenominational. Faith in God and the scientific method formed twin poles of Schrag's identity—nourishing his spirit and intellect absent any sense of conflict.

The Davenport area had an accelerated program for academically oriented kids, and Matthew took advanced classes for precocious high schoolers at the local community college, where he'd meet his teenage sweetheart and future wife, Sarah.

Matthew first encountered the toll of dementia through Paul, who attended nursing school on the GI Bill and worked in a local nursing home. "I remembered being mystified by a lot of the strange behaviors," Matthew said of his volunteer service there, calling it a formative experience "to see people struggling with such unfair symptoms." And he was impressed by the care Paul provided. It was a key influence from his dad for Matthew's future calling.

It wasn't the only way the father's choices swayed the son's thinking. Paul told Matthew that he left the military, in part, because he was too candid to expect promotion. Speaking one's mind was no way to appeal to the higher-ups.

COMMITTING TO SCIENCE

Schrag chose his father's scientifically unheralded alma mater, the University of North Dakota (UND), for his undergraduate degree. "Dad went there for his MBA, and he was stationed there with the intercontinental ballistic missile systems much earlier. He loved it," Matthew said.

UND offered a humble launchpad for a scientific career, and in its own way put Schrag ahead of Burns, whose father's footsteps led to Harvard, first in the biological sciences among US universities: UND ranks 186th. The year Schrag graduated, Harvard's vast, ultramodern labs garnered about $350 million in National Institutes of Health grants, compared to UND's $9 million.

"Not what I envisioned as an undergrad," Schrag said, of attending UND. "I had outstanding scores. But I think being homeschooled was not as well regarded then as it is now. A professor at the community college said that 'What matters is what you do. Getting into these Ivy League programs can seem like the be-all and end-all, but it's really about getting the right tools.' He said, 'Stop feeling sorry for yourself and go do something.' It was very good advice."

Schrag kept medical school in mind for the longer term, and soon learned that he'd need to do some research to get in. "I had this professor I liked—a botanist. I was like, 'They said I have to do some research. Can I come work in your lab?' He was like, 'They didn't mean botany.' Instead, he was steered to a young researcher named Othman Ghribi, a PhD in neuropharmacology, who was studying Alzheimer's disease at the time.

It proved a revelatory placement. Ghribi introduced Schrag to the seductive lure of scientific discovery. "The personal attention that I got from Othman and other people more than made up for the lack of pedigree at the University of North Dakota," Schrag said. Ghribi became a trusted mentor and close friend. Schrag spent long hours in his lab, absorbing the patient rhythms of science. He repeated experiments over and over, refining new skills.

That included the western blot. The test measures the amounts of specific proteins within a tissue sample. A blot device drives electricity through protein-rich samples—such as ground-up brain tissue—and then moves them through a gel that acts like a sieve to separate the proteins by size, based on their molecular structure. Heavier, larger protein molecules get stuck at the top of a roughly six-inch square plastic frame. Lighter ones migrate to the bottom—"exactly the opposite of panning for gold," Schrag said. The types and approximate quantities of brain-tissue proteins in a given sample can offer hints about why an experimental mouse—or a deceased person who had Alzheimer's—might have shown certain symptoms, compared to another who died free from cognitive distress. The blot provides a visual key. Distinct proteins of interest are fluorescently stained in the lab and individually illuminated on a digital display, where they often appear in a ladder-like pattern of stacked bands; the thicker the bands, the more of that particular protein is present in the sample.

Schrag couldn't have imagined then that his nascent skills in blot analysis would, years later, place him at the heart of a research drama of global proportions.

That destiny was equally determined by another major influence— Schrag's mom. Nan went back to finish college—long delayed by home-schooling and military-family duties—after her kids started college. She became a CPA who sniffed out fraud for the IRS, then a finance company. Nan developed into a scourge for scofflaws, aided by her type-A personality.

"I tend to be somewhat more laid back," Schrag said. His computer screen is dotted with dozens of files, although he always seems to locate the one he wants with ease. ("I appreciate a high level of organization," he said, admiring the pristine workstation of his lab manager, Alena Ko-zunda, who laughed knowingly. "But I haven't been able to impose it on myself!")

Nan's sense of moral duty, if not her organizational prowess, rubbed off. Schrag said he keeps his eyes open for anomalies in the research, in service of a higher purpose: "To me, it's about being stuck on solving this puzzle that we're trying to solve." The puzzle of Alzheimer's.

With his strong test scores and research history, Schrag was waitlisted for Dartmouth's prestigious medical school, but got tired of waiting and accepted an offer at the still-selective Loma Linda University—a Seventh-Day Adventist institution in Southern California.

For Schrag, whose faith always coexisted gently alongside his science, it was a match. "I think that an honest and humble view of our science and an honest and humble view of our theology would lead us to believe that they're both quite imperfect," Schrag said. "I would hope that if we had a perfect understanding of them both, there would be no conflicts. But I don't think it's necessary or even helpful to try to force them into an unnecessary harmony."

At Loma Linda, Schrag joined the lab of the late Wolff Kirsch, a noted neurosurgeon who had a large Alzheimer's grant. "Three years in, I was spending more time in the lab than I was studying for med school classes. They graciously, retroactively, put me in the MD-PhD program."

His first lesson in scientific sleuthing came during that PhD train-ing. A research group at another university found a link between amyloid plaques and iron metabolism in people—a novel discovery. Schrag had studied that topic in rabbits for his first-ever scientific paper, published in 2006 under Ghribi's watchful eye. Their paper examined how feeding rab-bits a high-cholesterol diet seemed to increase amyloid plaques and iron deposits in one part of their brains. Schrag and Ghribi had wondered: Could excess iron contribute to Alzheimer's dementia?

Encouraged by the other researchers' findings, Schrag poured his energy into trying to confirm their findings—and failed. There might have been some unknown factor that made their study accurate in a very specific sample of brain tissue. But Schrag identified what he considered flaws in the methodology, so simple human error might also explain the data. Or the results might have had a darker origin.

"It was my first brush with how to deal with a problem like that. You've got a group that's clearly an outlier. I suspected at the time that the work was fraudulent, although we didn't prove it," he said. Kirsch told him to calm down. "I remember him saying, 'It's much less important whose fault it is than it is to get back on track—to draw the right conclusions from the data.' I think that was very good advice at that time. And we could fairly conclusively determine what the right answer was.

"The way you handle this is you talk to the group that produced the data, you show them your data, you just put a spotlight on it," Schrag said Kirsch advised. The subsequent conversation proved awkward but civil. Schrag and his colleagues wrote a paper showing the other group's work as an unexplainable outlier.

"It's usually a very polite field. People really don't want to have these arguments about fraud and data. When you go to the top-tier research programs, they often know what's not reproducible, what's not trust-worthy," Schrag said, based on their intimate knowledge of every element of such experiments, every test for chemical and biological properties.

The experience introduced him to a disquieting element of Alzhei-mer's research. With this enigmatic, complex disease, even careful experi-ments done in good faith can fail to replicate, leading to dead ends and unexpected setbacks. It helped shape his scientific world view: Beware of dogma. Drill down to primary data behind big findings; they might prove troublingly thin. Treat everything with a degree of skepticism—especially one's own assumptions.

"I've got to believe most of the time, when things don't replicate, it's because of subtle details of the experimental approach. We don't ex-pect something nefarious around every corner," he hastened to add. But sometimes—too often, Schrag would learn—failure to replicate is a red flag. It may even suggest fraud, although Schrag avoids that word.

Soon after the iron episode, he moved on as a freshly minted physician and neuroscientist. The rabbit-brain paper—his proud, first scientific accomplishment as a callow undergrad—had faded into the mists of his early career. Years later, it would startlingly come back to life like Cassava Sciences' zombie brains.

GREAT BEAUTY WITHIN DISEASE AND DEATH

After moving over to Yale for his medical residency and a research fellowship, he and Sarah longed to settle down in someplace more spread-out and family friendly. In 2015 Schrag was offered a vascular neurology fellowship at Vanderbilt, which promised a faculty slot and lab the following year. They quickly moved to Nashville, where Schrag's independent-minded attitude found a good home, and Sarah's two pet horses from childhood could finally come along as they planned to expand their family. When he took me with him to his tiny "ranch" in the city's rural ex-urbs, classic sixties and seventies rock playing on the radio as we rode, Schrag's affection for Red Robin—a Tennessee Walker that Sarah calls her *alebrije*, or spirit animal—and Velvet, a striking palomino, was evident.

Schrag landed at Vanderbilt already an expert in cerebral amyloid angiopathy (CAA). In CAA, amyloid plaques attack and replace the smooth muscle fibers that support the blood vessels nourishing the brain. The condition turns flexible, life-sustaining plumbing into brittle, fragile pipes. Most Alzheimer's patients suffer from CAA. Half suffer moderate-to-severe cases that make them vulnerable to dangerous, sometimes fatal brain bleeds. The condition offers insights into the murky ambiguities of Alzheimer's, making Schrag's Vanderbilt clinic to treat CAA and other vascular diseases an unsurprising source of skepticism around potentially flawed thinking about how the conditions interact.

"There's absolutely no specific treatment for cerebral amyloid angiopathy," Schrag said in 2023. "My goal from the outset has been to get to that first treatment . . . Hopefully, it will work on Alzheimer's disease too. The best way to do that at the moment is to build a laboratory, then try to understand the disease mechanisms that may be treatable. The next stage will be to start a drug development program—pick a couple of those targets and develop therapeutics around them."

Schrag has spent thousands of hours creating and examining tens of thousands of western blots, microscopic images of brain tissue known as micrographs, and other scientific figures throughout his career. He hosts a tiny gallery in his lab's entryway. The striking display shows blood-vessel muscle fibers replaced by amyloids as shocks of fluorescent red, surviving vessel walls in brilliant green. The arresting images eerily depict great beauty within disease and death.

"We've invested very intentionally in technologies and tools to be able to say, 'How do we measure the relationships between things in these microscopy images?' That was the genesis of my ability to analyze images. Expertise comes from just from having done it. I've done it, and done it, and done it." With that exquisite intimacy, Schrag has learned to answer a key scientific question:

What should it look like?

NEGATIVE RESULTS

Eminent professors, scholarly journals, government officials, and university deans speak of the unique quality of the science to "self-correct." It amounts to this: When missteps, misconduct, or fraud steer science in wrong directions, research eventually returns to the right path. That truism usually holds over the long run. But outlandish or revolutionary—and false—scientific findings can stand for many years without public efforts to replicate or repudiate them, sometimes leading to catastrophic wastes of time, resources, and even lives.

That's partly because disproving someone else's experiment can be a death wish in science. "Negative results" can be impossible to publish—not a goal for a young scientist struggling to succeed in the ultracompetitive hothouse of scientific funding and fame. It's part of why many researchers agree that the scientific enterprise faces a "replication crisis."

Biological psychologist Marcus Munafo at the University of Bristol has worked for years to mitigate the replication problem. He said discoveries that break new ground are sometimes by nature based on soft evidence. "We want to be discovering new things but not generating too many false leads," Munafo said in a 2022 podcast.

But the incentive structures of academia and pharmacology remain. As Schrag put it, "The field is absolutely calibrated to the newest, most interesting, most cutting-edge discovery. It disincentivizes replication at every turn . . . It's not fun. It's not interesting." That's despite the fact that many researchers have attempted to replicate the experiments of others without success. Efforts leading to claims of apparent misconduct are rarer still.

When Schrag was approached in 2021 by the lawyer drafting the FDA citizen petition about the research behind Cassava Sciences' simufilam, he immediately saw many suspect images. But he worried about consequences to his career if his role became publicly known. The impending regulatory and scientific controversy seemed likely to become a bitter conflict and potential quagmire involving a billion-dollar company. The $18,000 Schrag earned for the work seemed a pittance considering the time he'd invest and the personal risk. So why do it?

"Any human discipline has an error rate, whether the error is intentional or unintentional, whether it's from instruments or from people," Schrag said. "Part of our job is trying to get that error rate as low as possible. We want to be working with ground truth as much as possible." In the case of Cassava, he decided that he couldn't stand back quietly. A drug seemingly based on misconduct was being taken by hundreds of unsuspecting Alzheimer's patients.

Chapter 4

The French Connection

Luc-sur-Mer and Caen, France

1974–2023

*"We are never safe from a student who would like to deceive us,
and we must remain vigilant."*

—DENIS VIVIEN, NEUROSCIENTIST, UNIVERSITY OF CAEN

Profanity rarely passes Matthew Schrag's lips, but his ferocity is evident in the light shadows forming under his eyes. That "Everything Is Figureoutable" ideal, his determination, and his indefatigable belief in the advancement of knowledge, seemed to mirror another noteworthy Alzheimer's scientist who was raised and trained a continent away.

Sylvain Lesné was born in 1974 in a remote, tiny, rural village, in a way suspended in time like the one where Schrag got his start—Luc-sur-Mer, France. He grew up amid seaside pleasures, quaint old buildings, and historic trauma and honor. Luc-sur-Mer ("Luke on the sea") nestles against "Sword Beach," the eastern attack point for the June 6, 1944, D-Day invasion that helped save France and the world from the Nazis.

As I walked along the town's shoreline on a drizzly, early summer day in 2023, the sun suddenly broke through clouds to illuminate the vast Normandy beaches, stretching for miles in both directions. The tank traps were gone, but otherwise it looked much as it did on that fated day in 1944. Still a moving scene.

While storming the beach and surging into town, British forces—with 177 French commandos, the only ones in the initial invasion force—took heavy losses. Lesné grew up with a keen sense of gratitude and pride of place. From his parents and neighbors, he learned about sacrifice and courage in the service of great goals. "As I grew up on Normandy beaches, each year I was reminded [of] the heroic actions and deep sacrifice of US and allied troops on D-Day," he wrote in 2019. "Today I am grateful once more [on] D-Day75thAnniversary."

Fields of wheat and rapeseed surround Luc-sur-Mer, which had scarcely more than two thousand residents when Lesné grew up. Similar small towns dot the landscape, competing for revenue from tourists and local beachcombers. Luc-sur-Mer flaunts reminders of its historic role. Banners profiling heroic British soldiers who gave their lives wave on lampposts, commemorative monuments face the beach with displays showing how the famous events unfolded. D-Day tourism has become central to the town's economy.

For nearly a century longer, Luc-sur-Mer has depended on its coastal allure, and on gambling. An iconic casino, a handsome, gabled behemoth built in 1883, stood guard over the surf as destroyed military vehicles and equipment began to litter Sword Beach. The bombardment ultimately destroyed the proud structure. Its boxy successor surrounded by parking lots, built during the no-frills 1950s recovery, dominates the scenic overlook and beachfront esplanade.

The town owns the casino, a key civic revenue source. In his way, Lesné adopted that heritage. He would gamble, over and over, that from modest beginnings he could innovate both experimental methods and the display of technical images about Alzheimer's disease in ways that would further his career and advance the science.

Lesné's parents—Bertrand, who worked for the French national railways, and Marie Carmen—apparently saw great possibilities for their bright son and sent him 115 miles east at age twelve to Collège Saint-Exupéry, a school in Forges-les-Eaux, small town known for its museum of resistance to the Nazis. He then attended a boarding high school in

Flers, about sixty miles south of Luc-sur-Mer. Lycée Jean Guéhenno honors as its namesake a leftist cultural critic who penned a famous testimony about life under Nazi occupation.

Neither school was exceptional compared to celebrated options in Paris, but they instilled in Lesné academic aspirations that would launch him into a life of discovery. For collegiate and advanced training, he stayed closer to home. In 1992, Lesné enrolled at the University of Caen, located in a small city of the same name just ten miles due south of Luc-sur-Mer.

Founded in 1432, one of Europe's oldest universities, Caen enjoys a proud history. Its alumni include pioneering chemists and mathematicians: In the seventeenth century, Nicolas Lémery became among the first to explain acid-base chemistry, and in the eighteenth century, Guillaume-François Rouelle expanded on Lémery's work. In the nineteenth century, Urbain Jean Joseph Le Verrier predicted the discovery and position of the planet Neptune using only mathematics. In the twentieth century, Gérard Férey innovated crystal chemistry.

After taking Sword Beach on June 7, British troops moved inland to capture Caen, a communication and transport hub. That objective required weeks of intensive fighting. Some 1,700 residents died when Allied bombers systematically destroyed nearly three-quarters of the city, including most of the university. After the war, the University of Caen was reborn as a complex of massive, brutalist buildings that belie the institution's late-medieval origins. Today, with a student body of more than thirty thousand, Caen ranks as the nation's thirty-eighth best university.

AUSPICIOUS SCHOLARLY BEGINNING

Handsome (a journalist would later compare his hair to George Clooney's), tall, athletic, energetic, Lesné flashes a high-wattage smile. Speaking English fluently with a lilting accent, his renown would grow as he became a gifted and popular ambassador for Alzheimer's research while seeing his work as a graduate student cited by other scholars more than a thousand times—extraordinary early career influence.

Three respected French neuroscience researchers served as his mentors. A PhD advisor, neuroscientist Denis Vivien, now leads a team of more than 140 at Cyceron, a secured, government-funded university research unit where Lesné trained. Vivien studies neurovascular disorders, including stroke, and aspects of Alzheimer's. Lesné's primary PhD advisor, Alain Buisson, examines the molecular mechanisms behind Alzheimer's at the University of Grenoble in southern France, where he moved from Caen some years ago.

Working under Vivien, Fabian Docagne led a team at Cyceron that explored the role of brain inflammation in neurological diseases such as multiple sclerosis. In 2022, he took a post in Paris with Inserm, the French health research agency. Docagne recently said his work is "dedicated to the relationship between science and society," focused on research involving "'experiential knowledge,' what people can know from their experiences, either as patients or as professionals." Asked by an interviewer for advice to students to fulfill their scientific ambitions, Docagne said, "Make choices that are sometimes radical."

All three wrote papers with Lesné during his time in Caen and in a few cases afterward. Lesné's own scientific work would later eclipse that triad, the wellspring of his pedigree. But the research ecosystem they helped create, combined with the influence of Lesné's casino-dependent hometown, would later pose an object lesson for a key question in neuroscience: How do radical rolls of the dice mesh with scientific integrity?

EARLY WARNING

When I first spoke with Vivien in 2022, he described a sobering moment with Lesné twenty years earlier. It changed their relationship forever. He and Lesné and several colleagues had been working on a paper for *Nature Neuroscience*, a leading journal, involving amyloid-beta proteins. Lesné was first author, crediting his role as the primary writer and his deep involvement in the experiment. As principal investigator and guarantor of the work, Vivien was the last author. The stakes were high—a paper in so prominent a publication would be widely noticed.

During final revisions Vivien fielded questions from a peer reviewer about immunostaining images—a way of identifying specific proteins in tissue samples—provided by Lesné. Vivien thought the images looked unlikely. As a precaution, he asked another student to replicate Lesné's findings. The student returned, visibly upset, to report that he could not do so. Vivien said he confronted Lesné, who denied wrongdoing. Although Vivien lacked "irrefutable proof" of misconduct, he said he withdrew the paper before publication "to preserve my scientific integrity," and broke off contact with Lesné.

"We are never safe from a student who would like to deceive us, and we must remain vigilant," Vivien added. "When I had a doubt [about] the integrity of Lesné, I did what I judged I needed to do . . . to stop all interaction with Lesné and people who supported him at this time." Vivien declined to name Lesné's supporters.

Jean-Charles Lambert, a neuroscientist at the University of Lille, verified Vivien's description in an interview. At the time, Lambert told me, another coauthor of the draft paper told him about Vivien's doubts and decision. "I remember it very well, because it's so unusual to learn something like that. It was awful to imagine you cannot trust someone at this level," he said. "This kind of problem may have a strong impact on the life of a researcher and a laboratory. I think that it was just terrifying for [Vivien and his colleagues]." Withdrawing a paper slated for a high-impact journal "also shows strong ethics" on Vivien's part, Lambert added.

In the summer of 2023, I asked Vivien to meet me in Caen for a discussion about his work, his former student, and the world Lesné trained in. Vivien waited outside a hotel restaurant near the university's medical center to greet me as I approached. Dressed in jeans and a T-shirt and sporting a few days of beard growth, the soft-spoken professor exuded an informality I hadn't expected for a scientist of high standing and responsibility. Tucking into a characteristic French lunch of pork loins and *frittes*,

Vivien filled in a few blanks about that episode two decades earlier and the man behind it.

With Lesné, everything had to be perfect, Vivien recalled. He was "always very clean, always very well dressed." His pristine work desk mirrored Lesné's social interactions—unfailingly correct. When he played pickup basketball, typically an informal affair, Lesné insisted that normal rules apply, Vivien recalled.

That ostensibly high-minded strictness extended to Lesné's descriptions of his work. He always maintained a tone of meticulous certainty. Lesné's lack of humility gave Vivien pause, he told me. Given biology's inherent complexity, Vivien said, "You always have to keep it conditional. Maybe Sylvain did not accept that [the science] was not as perfect as he imagined."

The images Lesné produced for *Nature Neuroscience* seemed "too beautiful" to believe, Vivien said. Ensuing events proved painful for Lesné and his collaborators, who had spent years working on the project, Vivien added. Some wanted to revise rather than withdraw the paper, excising apparently tainted images like a cancer surgeon would remove a tumor. Vivien said he insisted that if one image was doctored, nothing could be trusted.

In the aftermath, Vivien set up an audit system for his lab—a way for collaborating students and scientists to cross-check each other's results. (To safeguard his own work from possible misconduct and to prove that results can be reproduced, Lambert said he insists that each experiment be repeated by more than one person.) Then Vivien buried the unpleasant experience and moved on. He spoke to almost no one at Caen or in the wider scientific community about his suspicions about Lesné. Vivien said he never warned Docagne or Buisson.

For obvious reasons, Vivien said, Lesné never asked him for a reference after he finished his PhD and hunted for jobs. But he landed well. Karen Ashe, an illustrious physician and neuroscientist at the University of Minnesota, and an acclaimed Alzheimer's innovator, hired Lesné as a postdoctoral fellow in 2002. It was a plum job, particularly for a young

PhD from a non-elite university. When asked, Ashe told me the hiring took place without ever speaking with anyone from Caen about Lesné or his work. His letters of reference were taken at face value.

From a distance, the choice looked wise. Lesné seemed a perfect fit for an ambitious lab in politically progressive Minneapolis, as his Twitter feed would later validate: fun-loving yet serious, creative and organized, environmental advocate and Donald Trump critic, gourmet cook and dog lover, gun-control backer and Minnesota Vikings football fan. All in a fastidiously groomed package suffused with charm and confidence. And Lesné's penchant for achieving perfection in all things might have appealed to Ashe's own relentless determination to rise to the top.

His whimsical Twitter handle, in its cryptic way, would later seem more revealing than Lesné's tweets or anything he said in public: "Neurobiologist, Biochemist, International man of mystery and Tech addict. Sums it up good."

His fate and Ashe's soon became entangled in ways that would, years later, shake each of their careers—and Alzheimer's research—to the core.

Chapter 5

Prodigy Meets Genius

San Francisco and Minnesota
1970–2005

*"I was astonished. I didn't believe the results when I saw them.
When I saw the memory getting better I actually thought I had
done something wrong in the experiment."*

—KAREN ASHE, UNIVERSITY OF MINNESOTA NEUROSCIENTIST

Sylvain Lesné had landed a dream job in one of the most exciting settings a capable and curious young neuroscientist could hope for. Karen Ashe, a budding superstar in Alzheimer's research, would be his mentor.

Ashe's pedigree began with her parents, themselves high-achieving Chinese immigrants. Her mother, Joyce Hsiao, was a biochemist. Ashe's father, the late Chih Chun "CC" Hsiao, was a highly regarded aerospace engineer—with roots in both industry and academia, and special expertise in the properties of polymers such as plastics. He preceded his daughter as a University of Minnesota (UMN) professor. (Early in her career, Ashe published under her family name, Karen Hsiao.) With his degrees from Yenching and Tsinghua University in China, and the Massachusetts Institute of Technology (MIT), CC was a globally sought-after speaker who forged links with Chinese scientists during a period of US rapprochement. Before Ashe's father died from Hodgkin's lymphoma in 2009, he had unfortunately joined the multitudes of Alzheimer's patients, reinforcing his daughter's resolve to cure the illness.

Ashe grew up in Arden Hills, a small, leafy, lake-dotted suburb of St. Paul. She told a journalist that as a young child she had wanted to become a scientist—even then, bringing extraordinary focus to whatever she attempted. Karen "could close off the rest of the world and be very happy," her sister said. At age nine, a newspaper profile noted, "Ashe wrote a school project on how the brain works, then took scissors and carefully trimmed it into the shape of a brain."

And she showed trailblazing talent early on. In the 1970s Ashe became the first Asian American to attend the prestigious St. Paul Academy prep school—whose illustrious students included the author F. Scott Fitzgerald, explorers, members of congress, and professional athletes. (The school inducted Ashe into its pantheon of "distinguished alumni" in 2001.)

She excelled at science and math. One of her math teachers assumed Ashe would need help to keep up with the boys in an advanced course, she reminisced many years later. "He said, 'In the whole history of the world, there hasn't been a good female mathematician.'" Ashe soon outperformed all of her classmates.

Her steely high school portrait seems to reflect that seriousness of purpose. Before graduating from St. Paul, Ashe gained recognition as a scholar, gymnast, and pianist—a prodigious talent and emerging renaissance woman. As a university professor, she could still play Beethoven sonatas with elegant finesse.

Ashe entered Harvard University as a sophomore in 1972 at age seventeen, and within a decade had completed a medical degree there and a PhD from the department of psychology (now the department of brain and cognitive sciences) from her father's alma mater, MIT. She seemed primed to change the world. It wouldn't take long.

HISTORY-MAKING START

During her medical residency at the University of California San Francisco during the 1980s, Ashe worked under Stanley Prusiner, a scientist with unconventional ideas about the cause of certain neurological dis-

orders in animals and people. He studied bovine spongiform encepha-
lopathy, known as mad cow disease. Afflicted animals become unsteady
on their feet, extremely skittish, or even violent. People can contract Vari-
ant Creutzfeldt-Jakob disease—a terrifyingly fast-moving condition that
devastates muscle coordination, causes dementia, and invariably ends in
death—from eating infected cattle.

Prusiner postulated that an abnormal, infectious protein, which he
dubbed "prion," caused mad cow disease. Ashe contributed to his body of
work by obsessively studying a family with Gerstmann-Sträussler-Scheinker
disease—a genetically linked neurological ailment that can cause slurred
speech, involuntary movements, and vision problems. It's another incurable,
ultimately deadly disorder. She was trying to find a specific gene connecting
the disease and Prusiner's prion hypothesis.

At the time, Ashe was about to give birth to her second child. The baby
slowed her down for just a few days before she leapt back into the lab. Testing DNA from the donated brains of deceased patients provided the solution. Ashe found a genetic mutation that caused overproduction of prions
in Gerstmann-Sträussler-Scheinker patients. She validated the finding by
re-creating the disease in transgenic mice. Prusiner's prion discoveries—
with Ashe's essential contributions—won him the Nobel Prize in 1997.

She was just getting started. Ashe returned home in 1992 to join the
UMN Medical School faculty with a focus on Alzheimer's. In the mid-
1990s, after three years of painstaking efforts to place the right human
gene into mouse eggs, she created transgenic mice that churn out human
amyloid proteins, forming toxic deposits in the animals' brains. The mice
had previously learned to find a submerged platform in a water maze—
a well-established memory test. Ashe called it "the mouse equivalent of
finding your car in the parking lot." After their amyloid transformation,
Ashe's mice could no longer easily find the platform. In effect, they showed
dementia-like symptoms, akin to those faced by Alzheimer's patients.

Ashe's mice became a favored model for Alzheimer's labs around the
world and vaulted her to elite status in her field. At one time biopharma
companies paid up to a million dollars for breeding pairs. Ashe's 1996

paper in *Science* about the miracle mice became her first to be honored with a plaque in the UMN Medical School Wall of Scholarship—a high honor reserved for the most influential articles that gain at least one thousand citations in scholarly journals.

GENIUS AND LAB ACE SYNERGY

By appearances Lesné aspired to experimental perfection, working with drive and creativity. He also developed expertise on how to identify and isolate soluble amyloid proteins called oligomers, widely considered more toxic to brain cells than the sticky, plaque form of the protein.

The team of Ashe and Lesné proved electric. He fed off Ashe's intensity and augmented her scientific brilliance with his flash and charisma. Lesné displayed bench-science talent to help speed and reinforce ideas that Ashe felt confident would make a new mark, extend her influence as a scientist, and move the world, step by step, closer to a cure for Alzheimer's disease. (Years later he would impress US Senator Amy Klobuchar—a key booster of Alzheimer's research—when she visited UMN.) At meetings of her peers, Ashe began to talk up Lesné as a "brilliant" experimentalist.

Ashe's next dramatic triumphs came in 2005. She worked with colleagues including renowned Harvard scientist Dennis Selkoe, and Dominic Walsh, a University College Dublin scholar who would later teach at Harvard and become vice president for Alzheimer's research at the biopharma giant Biogen. Their groundbreaking paper suggested that amyloid oligomers can disrupt cognition in rats. It would become her second entry on the Wall of Scholarship.

The same year, Ashe directed a team working with new transgenic mice she engineered to generate human tau proteins. Toxic tau "tangles," commonly thought to be stimulated by amyloids, form inside brain cells. In their early months of life, the mice easily learned how to navigate the standard water maze to find a hidden platform. But as they aged and tau accumulated, the mice grew forgetful—akin to what might happen in human dementia. Then Ashe found a way to inactivate the gene responsible for tau production. In effect, she shut off the tau spigot. The researchers hoped that the mice would experience no further memory loss. Instead, they witnessed a stunning outcome: The transgenic tau mice *improved*. Their water-maze performance did not merely show signs of slowed regression, a notable achievement in itself. In effect, the mice appeared to regain their memories.

"I was astonished. I didn't believe the results when I saw them," Ashe said at the time. "When I saw the memory getting better I actually thought I had done something wrong in the experiment."

An editorial in the hometown *St. Paul Pioneer Press* titled "Alzheimer's stood on its ear" said that the study "strongly suggests that human Alzheimer's patients have the ability to recover from the disease," moving scientists "closer to a cure." Ashe's paper on the experiment, again in *Science*, became her third Wall of Scholarship entry—among the most for any UMN scholar. That year, she won the $250,000 MetLife Foundation Award for Medical Research in Alzheimer's Disease.

"My dream is for the [UMN] to take the lead in developing guidelines that ensure that Alzheimer's prevention is a reality by the year 2020," Ashe said soon after. In service of that goal, in 2005 she founded a new Alzheimer's center to combine research and patient care. A recent official UMN photo shows Ashe elegantly dressed in a quilted Chinese jacket with a mandarin collar; a Mona Lisa smile and round Harry Potter glasses completed the ensemble. It seemed a perfect image of her progress. She had become her own kind of enigmatic wizard.

Meanwhile, Lesné was coming up to speed as he and his mentor together explored toxic oligomer forms of amyloid and their impact on Alzheimer's disease. Ashe trumpeted Lesné as a bench-science prodigy just as she was hungering for her next big discovery. Soon after, his magic hands would deliver her biggest triumph yet—an experiment that seemed to cement her place in the pantheon of great neuroscientists, helped her raise enormous sums for her new center, and elevated Lesné to his own substantial fame and success. First for better—and ultimately, tragically, for worse—it would become the experiment of his lifetime.

Chapter 6

One Hundred Years of Solitude

Germany, Minneapolis
1906–2006

"O, let me not be mad, not mad, sweet heaven
Keep me in temper: I would not be mad!"
—WILLIAM SHAKESPEARE, *KING LEAR*

"That was a really big finding that kind of turned the field on its head."
—DONNA WILCOCK, EDITOR, *ALZHEIMER'S & DEMENTIA*

Alzheimer's dementia has haunted humanity for millennia. In the seventh century BC, the Greek sage Pythagoras said that after age eighty, "the scene of mortal existence closes . . . where the mind is reduced to the imbecility of the first epoch of infancy." He viewed παραφροσύνη ("derangement" or "insanity") as a natural condition of very old age.

A few centuries later, Aristotle, another towering Greek intellect and astute observer of the human condition, also declared mental decline in the elderly, ruinous to memory and judgment, as inevitable as the body declines. "The incapacity of old age is due to an affection not of the soul but of its vehicle, as occurs in drunkenness or disease . . . When this vehicle decays, memory and love cease; they were activities not of mind, but of the composite which has perished," he wrote.

More than one thousand years later, Shakespeare placed the burdens of dementia into one of his most famous soliloquies, uttered by Jaques in *As You Like It*:

All the world's a stage,
And all the men and women merely players . . .
Last scene of all,
That ends this strange eventful history,
Is second childishness and mere oblivion,
Sans teeth, sans eyes, sans taste, sans everything.

Alzheimer's-like symptoms caused the downfall of the bard's *King Lear*, one of the great tragic literary characters. The king famously captured his own undoing in a flash of terrifying insight:

O, let me not be mad, not mad, sweet heaven
Keep me in temper: I would not be mad!
I am a very foolish fond old man,
Fourscore and upward, not an hour more or less;
And, to deal plainly,
I fear I am not in my perfect mind.

But it wasn't until the early 1800s that doctors and scientists began to define senile dementia not just as a mysterious affliction of the brain and soul—but as a disease that might someday be cured or prevented if studied with care and precision.

Their efforts were modest compared to many other diseases, however, due to senility's relative rarity—a function of simple demographics. In centuries past, like today, few people showed Alzheimer's symptoms until after age sixty-five. Far fewer grew older than eighty, when the disease commonly takes hold. So dementia remained a footnote to medical history.

That began to change markedly after the industrial revolution and increasingly sophisticated public health and medical systems sharply improved life expectancies in much of the world. By 1900 people older than sixty-five comprised nearly 4 percent of the US population, and seniors over seventy-five—nearing the prime age for Alzheimer's onset—finally topped 1 percent. By 2020, nearly twenty-three million Americans were seventy-five or older, about 7 percent of the population. The elderly in Japan and many European nations comprised even larger proportions of their overall populations.

DARK ORIGINS

Alois Alzheimer, a German physician born in 1864, was a cigar chain-smoking, swaggering man of his times. Like his namesake disease, he embodied a jumble of complicated traits. A serious medical student, Alzheimer joined the boisterous fraternity Corps Franconia, known for pranks and sword fights fitting a society steeped in martial values. He earned a saber scar—a badge of honor for German men from the early 1800s through World War II—on his left cheek.

Alzheimer's darker side included vocal support for German aggression in World War I. He was also an early member of the German Racial Hygiene Society. The group, which influenced the later formation of counterparts in the United States and other nations, studied the purported genetic basis for mental and physical disorders, and various social ills and depravity. "Moral decadence, social deviancy, tuberculosis and venereal diseases were all seen as symptoms of hereditary degeneration. Alzheimer appears to have shared many of these views," and lectured about the brain before the society's Munich chapter, according to biographers Michel Goedert and Bernardino Ghetti.

The organization became a leading and powerful supporter of eugenics—the idea of improving civilization by increasing the number of people with desirable heritable traits and sterilizing those who might have genetically linked disabilities or mental illness.

Alzheimer's mentor, Emil Kraepelin, gained fame as a leading figure in the history of classifying psychiatric syndromes. He also wielded wide influence as a theorist for crackpot eugenics theories meant to preserve the vigor and purity of the German "volk." Antisemitism suffused his teaching. He described Jews as the products of a culture bred for intellectual skills at the expense of physical abilities and "free will," resulting in a "strong disposition towards nervous and mental disorders."

A close colleague of Alzheimer and Kraepelin, Ernst Rüdin, co-founded the Racial Hygiene Society. He went on to become an author of policies that led to industrial-scale, Hitler-era programs to sterilize or murder psychiatric patients, Jews, gay people, and others deemed defective or racially inferior. Rüdin's work was funded, beginning in 1940, by Hitler's SS, and colleagues began to call him "Reichsfuhrer for Sterilization."

A doctor at the heart of Alzheimer's great namesake discovery, Hermann Paul Nitsche, was executed for war crimes in 1948. Under Hitler, he had overseen the "euthanasia" of thousands of psychiatric patients.

THE DISCOVERY

After medical school, Alzheimer began a dual career as a clinician and pathologist. In an effort to link mental illness with concrete signs of brain abnormalities, he became a top expert in examining brain tissues from deceased mental patients.

In 1901 Nitsche was a junior doctor at the Frankfurt Municipal Asylum for the Mentally Ill and Epileptics, where Alzheimer served as assistant director. Nitsche oversaw the care of Auguste Deter, a woman in her fifties who suffered from pronounced cognitive decline. She became confused easily—imagining herself back in the town of her birth. With her memory failing, she developed paranoid ideas about friends and her husband.

Alzheimer kept a close eye on Auguste until he followed Kraepelin to take positions in Heidelberg and ultimately Munich, where he directed the anatomical lab of the Royal Psychiatric Clinic at the University of Munich.

But via Nitsche, he continued to track Auguste's dismal progress. When she died in April 1906, Alzheimer arranged to have her brain sent to him for examination. After six months of study, he spoke about the case at a psychiatric conference in Tübingen, Germany, describing his findings: copious, chunky plaque deposits between neurons, and tangled protein fibers within the cells. His meticulous, hand-drawn illustrations added sharp detail. Both deposits had previously been described by other scholars, but Alzheimer was the first to bind them together as the cause of mental decline. They became defining characteristics of the most common dementia.

The assembled doctors—meeting when no other patients like Auguste had yet been documented—greeted Alzheimer's momentous discovery with mild interest. His revelations gained currency four years later when new cases came to light. Kraepelin named the disease after Alzheimer and institutionalized the name in his own acclaimed texts on psychiatry.

Alzheimer died in 1915 at just fifty-one from kidney disease and heart failure. He never knew that he had made one of the most influential findings in the history of neuroscience.

That's partly because Alzheimer's disease remained a black box for decades. No drug or therapy could slow or halt its dire symptoms, let alone offer a cure. The creeping, dreadful solitude of patients continued unabated, decade by decade, with no relief. No one understood how the brain forms an increasingly dense wall against cognition and human connection. What plaques and tangles meant, what composed them, and how the disease process unfolded remained persistent enigmas.

RESEARCH RENAISSANCE

In 1974, the US government created the National Institute on Aging. Around the same time, scientists recognized Alzheimer's as the primary cause of dementia. Research funding to understand the disease vastly increased.

In the early 1980s, many scientists subscribed to the cholinergic hypothesis of the disease. That idea blamed problems in the operations of acetylcholine, an essential chemical for transmission of nerve impulses. Years later, the Food and Drug Administration (FDA) approved drugs to increase the chemical—the first sanctioned Alzheimer's medications. Still in use today, they offer modest, frustratingly short benefits for memory and quality of life for some patients, without affecting the root causes of the disease.

Despite a dearth of Alzheimer's treatments, during the 1980s scientific discoveries contributed to enormous excitement that its complexities could be unraveled and understood.

University of California San Diego pathologist George Glenner isolated the main component of plaques in 1984 and detailed its properties at the molecular level. He had discovered the protein amyloid-beta. Glenner's findings formed the scientific genesis of the amyloid hypothesis. (In a bitter irony, he died in 1995 of systemic senile amyloidosis, a rare disease that can cause fatal heart problems, linked to the same protein.)

In the early and mid-1980s, Harvard's Dennis Selkoe and colleagues, along with three other labs at about the same time, made a new discovery about what was affecting brain cells in Alzheimer's. When I met with him in his lab in 2023, Selkoe said that he and others had wondered, "Which way did the toxicity go?" Did it come from amyloid plaque clumps seen outside the brain cells, or from tangles inside the cells, or both? He pulled down a mounted, highly magnified photo of a tiny section of brain tissue from a deceased Alzheimer's patient. It came from one of his early papers on the topic. Selkoe pointed to dead or dying brain cells, frozen in time. "[Those] dark brown or black cell bodies [are] the tangles . . . which we discovered were made up of a protein called tau." Selkoe said he learned that similar tangles had been linked to rare cases of brain damage in children after a bout of measles or German measles. They also seemed to play a role in other neurological ailments.

The idea that amyloid clumps caused damage from outside the neurons, and tangles made up of tau from inside, began to seem irrefutable, Selkoe said.

Soon after, amyloid-beta was shown as toxic to neurons in lab experiments. At around the same time, scientists found genetic mutations linked to increased amyloid production—and to a higher likelihood of developing the rare, particularly cruel form of Alzheimer's that sometimes strikes before age sixty-five.

That combination of findings—amyloid-beta and proof of its toxicity, genetic links between abundant amyloid and early Alzheimer's, and the nature and role of tangles—suggested a coherent framework for comprehending the disease process.

UK neuroscientist John Hardy—like Selkoe, an illustrious scholar at the forefront of Alzheimer's research—and his American colleague Gerald Higgins articulated that framework in one of the most famous papers in neuroscience history, published in April 1992 in *Science*: "Alzheimer's Disease: The Amyloid Cascade Hypothesis."

Hardy and Higgins argued that amyloid-beta sets off a chain reaction of biological effects that give rise to tau tangles and the death of neurons. The "cascade" of damage and devastation causes dementia. It was soon adopted by most researchers and funders as the most plausible explanation for Alzheimer's. Interrupting the cascade by somehow removing the malevolent plaques became the obvious solution.

Selkoe and others had been working to validate and extend the amyloid hypothesis by showing that oligomers—a form of amyloid-beta protein that, unlike sticky plaques, dissolves in cerebrospinal fluid—disrupt nerve cell connections essential to memory. "Toxic oligomers," considered more pathogenic than plaques, began to gain currency by the early-to-mid 1990s as a possible chief culprit for Alzheimer's.

Research got another big boost in 1996, when Karen Ashe created her transgenic, University of Minnesota (UMN) mice that produced copious volumes of human amyloids and showed signs of cognitive decline. She created a kind of mouse Alzheimer's. Labs all over the world tested new drugs designed to reverse amyloid buildup in the Ashe animals and similar mouse models. Soon after, immunotherapies— vaccines and lab-created antibodies—showed promising results in mice, and cognitive decline was shown to correspond with the presence of oligomer proteins.

From the 1980s, the funding and influence of amyloid-beta work dominated Alzheimer's research. By the mid-2000s, Selkoe, widely regarded as the foremost advocate for the amyloid hypothesis, became the most cited scholar in the field by a wide margin, according to a landmark analysis by life-science data specialist Aaron Sorensen. And seven of the ten most influential scholars focused on amyloid or closely related tau research.

Meanwhile, medical research beat back other relentless assassins, such as cancer, heart disease, and stroke. A wide range of treatments shared credit: surgery, medicines, radiation, genetic therapies, and healthful habits. Between 1999 and 2015, rates for the top three causes of death in the United States fell sharply. But in an aging population, Alzheimer's rates and fatalities went in the opposite direction.

Year after year, drug candidates that seemed promising in mice failed in trials with Alzheimer's patients. Decades of research yielded no anti-amyloid preventives or cures—or even remedies that could provide modest relief. In clinical trials—human experiments required before federal approval of a drug—failure followed failure. Some anti-amyloid vaccines and drugs proved useless. Others caused harmful side effects that scuttled the experiments. Pessimism began to mount that any anti-amyloid therapy could temper, halt, or reverse the devastating symptoms of the disease. The amyloid hypothesis faced mounting skepticism.

By 2006, the centennial of Alois Alzheimer's epic discovery, at least forty-three drugs—many designed to attack amyloid deposits—had failed to gain FDA approval. Exploitive pseudoscience and snake oil cures tried to fill the gap. Hundreds of "brain boosters" or "genius" nutritional supplements hit the market to entice desperate patients and family members.

Doctors, and patients and their loved ones, looked back with bitter frustration at the decades of therapeutic letdowns spawned by the amyloid hypothesis, despite billions of dollars in grants and investments. Its contradictions—such as the presence of massive amyloid and tau deposits found in the brains of many deceased patients who had endured no cognitive decline—have long exasperated critics and raised eyebrows even among supporters.

A growing cadre of skeptical scientists wondered aloud whether the field needed a reset.

BREAKTHROUGH

Then Karen Ashe and her protégé, Sylvain Lesné, delivered a breathtaking experiment. They produced a singular moment that captured the imagination of an entire field.

In the brains of Ashe's transgenic mice, Lesné discovered Aβ*56 (pronounced "amyloid-beta star 56"), a previously unknown amyloid-beta oligomer species distinguished by its relatively heavy weight compared to most other oligomers. They purified that star protein from mouse brains, then injected it into rats. Almost instantly, the animals could no longer recall simple learned information, such as the location of a hidden platform in a water maze. The results, which seemed like a smoking gun for the amyloid hypothesis, appeared in *Nature*, a top scientific journal.

Ashe touted Aβ*56 on her website as "the first substance ever identified in brain tissue in Alzheimer's research that has been shown to cause memory impairment." An accompanying *Nature* editorial called Aβ*56 "a star suspect" in Alzheimer's. Alzforum, the preeminent online forum for scholars of the disease, titled its coverage, "Aβ Star is Born?"

Alzforum wrote, "In a clever bit of sleuthing," Ashe, Lesné, and colleagues "appear to have solved the case of the mysterious memory loss in young mice engineered to express a mutated form of the human amyloid . . . [S]he has already determined that patients with Alzheimer's disease have detectable amounts of Aβ*56, while people without AD do not . . ."

The revelatory findings delivered long-sought hope. Ashe wanted it, the scientific community hoped for it, patients desperately craved it. Lesné, with his magic hands, delivered. The ambitious staff scientist, still early in his career, entered the spotlight. The boy from Luc-sur-Mer suddenly became a globally noted expert.

"That was a really big finding that kind of turned the field on its head," partly because of Ashe's impeccable imprimatur, Donna Wilcock, editor of the journal *Alzheimer's & Dementia*, told me. "It drove a lot of other investigators to . . . go looking for these [heavier] oligomer species."

The paper provided an "important boost" to the amyloid and toxic oligomer hypotheses in the face of rising doubts, Stanford University Nobel laureate and Alzheimer's expert Thomas Südhof said in an interview. "Proponents loved it, because it seemed to be an independent validation of what they have been proposing for a long time."

Indeed, those proponents seized on the Lesné-Ashe paper. "It's clearly a key finding in the field," said Ronald Petersen, director of the Mayo Clinic Alzheimer's Disease Research Center in Rochester, Minnesota. "The hopeful sign of this is that [Alzheimer's] may be reversible."

Sam Gandy, a leading neurologist and advisor to the nonprofit Alzheimer's Association, predicted that the finding would have wide influence on research. "It changes the focus," he said. "This now will be the target."

Soon after the Lesné-Ashe paper appeared, Selkoe and University College Dublin research titan Dominic Walsh described it in a landmark overview of the field, "Aβ Oligomers—a decade of discovery," in the prestigious *Journal of Neurochemistry*.

Again, Ashe bested enormous competition. Again, she elegantly defied crushing scientific complexity. Again, her latest innovation seemed poised to change the course of Alzheimer's research and the hunt for a cure.

The rewards began to pour in. Less than two weeks after the paper appeared, Ashe won the $100,000 Potamkin Prize, promoted as the Nobel of neurology, partly on the merits of her star protein. It put her in the pantheon of Glenner, Hardy, her mentor and Nobel laureate Stanley Prusiner, and a handful of others at the top of the field. The rumor mill began to circulate Ashe's name as a candidate for the actual Nobel.

The following year, Beverly Grossman, widow of Alzheimer's sufferer Bud Grossman—part owner of the Minnesota Vikings football team—

donated $5 million to a new research center run by Ashe. The *Nature* paper would soon join her other plaques along the UMN Wall of Scholarship and became Lesné's first.

With Aβ*56, Ashe's star burned more brightly, and Lesné's rose along with it. UMN elevated him to assistant professor, and he opened his own National Institutes of Health–funded lab. He was living the bioscience researcher's dream.

A frenzied search for oligomers, their properties, and how drugs could be built to attack them took over much of the effort in basic research, and in drug development at biopharma companies. That was by no means due only to the Ashe-Lesné findings. But their paper made skeptics seem like malcontents and reinforced the primacy of the amyloid hypothesis.

Yet, another sixteen years would pass before an anti-amyloid drug hit the market. One called Aduhelm finally crossed the finish line: It would prove to be more a symbol of desperation shared by patients and their loved ones, doctors, and regulators, than real progress.

Chapter 7

Drug of Choice

Washington, DC; Nashville
2020–2022

"This was a disgraceful decision, and we're all going to be dealing with the consequences of it for years to come."
—DEREK LOWE, DRUG DEVELOPMENT CHEMIST
AND BLOGGER FOR THE JOURNAL *SCIENCE*

Ashe and Lesné's historic finding gave pharma companies a new white whale to chase down in a field beset by decades of unmet promises. Billions upon billions of dollars were redirected toward research on soluble oligomer amyloids for drug development and trials. But that pivot proved technically difficult. Oligomers are shapeshifters that gradually reform into heavier, intermediate "fibrils," and eventually sticky plaques. They are hard to measure precisely in brain tissue and harder to selectively target with therapeutic antibodies. It's like using a net to catch only trout in lakes where they swim with walleye, bass, and perch.

So some new anti-amyloid drugs continued to take a conventional approach. They primarily targeted fibrils and plaques in the brain, mopping up some oligomers in the process. A promising entry came from Biogen—among the first storied companies to emerge from the biotech boom following the 1970s genetic-engineering revolution. Company founder Phillip Sharp won a Nobel in 1993 and Biogen had already used gene-splicing to create blockbuster treatments for multiple sclerosis, cancer, and hepatitis.

The company's Alzheimer's drug received the generic name aducanumab. The immune system builds and deploys antibodies that specifically target a threat—such as a flu virus—to kill or neutralize it. Aducanumab is a *monoclonal* antibody—a lab-created antibody that doctors infuse into a patient's vein—signified by the "mab" ending.

The company faced a daunting problem. Aducanumab targeted amyloid plaques between neurons but couldn't avoid affecting blood vessels in the process. Most Alzheimer's patients have cerebral amyloid angiopathy (CAA). About half experience moderate or severe cases, in which plaques replace the smooth muscle that supports blood vessels nourishing the brain. Stripping plaques away from blood vessels or damaging those vessels while removing amyloids from between nerve cells can cause sometimes-fatal swelling and bleeding. Drug makers and many scientists refer to those side effects with a benign-sounding euphemism that sounds like a night at the opera: ARIA—amyloid-related imaging abnormalities. ARIA seems to fault the images rather than the drug. (The name was changed in 2011 from the scarier sounding and more accurate "vasogenic edema," a type of brain swelling.)

With its affinity for amyloids (including sticky plaques) at large, rather than toxic oligomers in particular, aducanumab seemed reminiscent of the old joke in which a police officer encounters a drunk man searching without success for his keys under a streetlight. The officer asks if he's sure he lost them in that spot. The man replies, "No, it was in the park, but the light is better here." Despite a history of costly failures, plaques were relatively easy to target and remove. Selectively stripping out oligomer amyloids is a chancier proposition. Given Biogen's massive sunk costs, the company seemed reluctant to wean itself from what had seemed the obvious target for so many years.

Still, Biogen's formidable track record with other drugs fueled optimism—enhanced by its partnership with Eisai, a respected Japanese company known for anticancer medicines.

Impressive results in early experiments on mice suggested that aducanumab might validate that optimism. It sharply reduced sticky plaques that occupied the spaces between the animals' brain cells without disturbing plaques that encase blood vessels—in theory, reducing the risk of dangerous brain swelling and bleeding. (Oligomers also move in the spaces between neurons, dissolved in the brain's cerebrospinal fluid.) Such bleeding began only after mice got 167 times the dose needed to clear the plaques from between brain cells.

If similarly safe and even modestly effective in people, aducanumab could become the breakthrough sought by amyloid-hypothesis advocates for decades. Initial safety testing with a few Alzheimer's patients looked promising. Side effects were minor. Biogen began infusing large numbers of patients experiencing early-stage Alzheimer's. After a year their brain scans showed that amyloid levels had plummeted to nearly undetectable levels. So far so good.

But in March 2019 the high hopes were dashed. Biogen pulled the plug on aducanumab while the major trials were still in midstream. The technical term in such cases is "termination for futility." Despite clearing plaques, the drug demonstrated no significant impact on cognition based on reports from caregivers and patients—yet another anti-amyloid flop.

Seven months later, the company returned to the research community with a bold approach: If results look bad, reanalyze. In a fresh look at the terminated studies, one large trial still showed no benefits. But the other provided an abrupt reversal of fortune. Aducanumab hadn't cured Alzheimer's or improved cognition. But compared to patients who got the placebo, on average, those on the highest dose experienced slightly slower cognitive decline. (Cassava Sciences might have learned from Biogen's about-face, when a year later, it similarly reassessed disappointing preliminary trial results on simufilam.) Aducanumab jumped back on track.

Biogen used the Clinical Dementia Rating-Sum of Boxes (CDR-SB) test. It relies on interviews with patients and caregivers about such factors as memory, problem solving, and personal hygiene. Subjectivity makes the CDR-SB inherently sensitive to bias. And because Alzheimer's patients' memory and ability to manage everyday tasks fluctuate day by day—it can't offer a clear reading of ongoing cognitive status. Still, many researchers consider the test reasonably reliable and among the best of such exams. It rates cognition on a scale of 1 to 18.

At a glance—the level at which patients and most media reports are generally willing or able to go—the impact of aducanumab sounded dramatic. Patients who received it declined 27 percent to 30 percent more slowly over eighteen months. For the first time, a major anti-amyloid trial showed a statistically significant apparent benefit.

But in a deeper look, the results seemed less compelling. The slower pace of Alzheimer's dreadful impacts amounted to only about four-tenths of a point on the 18-point CDR-SB scale. Dementia research has shown that clear benefits can be seen only after a full point difference. Many neurologists viewed aducanumab's purported advantages as imperceptible to most patients, their loved ones, or doctors.

Meanwhile, frequently painful brain swelling or bleeding afflicted more than four in every ten trial participants. Some scientists say that the symptoms, which can last more than twenty weeks, rarely cause long-term damage. But such drugs are so new—none had ever been approved or used for extensive periods—that no one understands the long-term effects of ARIA. Neurologists disagreed about whether the modest possible slowing of cognitive decline in certain patients was worth the risk.

HISTORICALLY OUT OF SYNC

The company asked the US Food and Drug Administration (FDA) to approve aducanumab for sale. The agency called on a handpicked expert advisory panel to review thousands of pages of company and FDA data and analyses and render their opinion.

When the eleven experts met November 6, 2020, they delivered a stinging rebuke. For approval of the drug, ten voted no, and one voted "uncertain." All cited weak evidence, at best, that the drug could help patients while posing no more than reasonable risks of serious harm. The advisors were so underwhelmed that they reached for humiliating metaphors.

"This analysis seems to be subject to the Texas sharpshooter fallacy, a name for the joke of someone first firing a shotgun at a barn and then painting a target around the bullet holes," quipped Scott Emerson, a physician and biostatistician at the University of Washington.

"It just feels to me like the audio and the video on the TV are out of sync," said an exasperated Caleb Alexander, a physician and specialist in drug safety and effectiveness at the Johns Hopkins Bloomberg School of Public Health. "For every point that you can find suggesting support [for aducanumab], there is another point or two that raises concern."

Yet pressure from amyloid hypothesis boosters and patient advocates—understandably desperate for a drug that shows even hints at slowing Alzheimer's inexorable ruin—helped force a move that shocked many scientists: The FDA sided with the company. It approved aducanumab under its "accelerated" process that required only the removal of amyloid as a biological marker for the disease, plus some sign, albeit meager, of clinical benefit.

The drug's supporters were ecstatic. Stephen Salloway, a leading researcher, physician, and Biogen consultant, said, "The totality of the evidence favors approval, and FDA approval will open the door to a new treatment era for Alzheimer's disease that we can build on."

"This historic moment is the culmination of more than a decade of groundbreaking research," then–Biogen chief executive Michel Vounatsos crowed. "This first-in-class medicine will transform the treatment of people living with Alzheimer's disease and spark continuous innovation."

The "historic" label was certainly true. Aducanumab became the first approved Alzheimer's therapy since 2003. It was the first approved drug said to actually slow cognitive decline, ostensibly by interrupting the biological basis of the disease rather than just treating symptoms such as anxiety or insomnia, or transiently damping down confusion among Alzheimer's patients.

Brand-named Aduhelm after approval, the first-to-market "disease-modifying" remedy also looked poised to be historically lucrative. The day of the announcement Biogen's stock surged nearly 40 percent, increasing the company's market value by $16 billion. That gain seemed tiny compared to unprecedented, anticipated revenues—which terrified health care experts.

Biogen priced Aduhelm at $56,000 per patient per year. Just 130,000 prescriptions—a tenth of the possibly eligible patients—would make it the company's top revenue-producing product. Aduhelm seemed poised to become one of the most profitable blockbusters in pharmaceutical history. Brain scans needed to monitor for swelling and bleeding would sharply boost costs. Medicare could face bankruptcy if one million prescriptions were written for an estimated 1.3 million Alzheimer's patients with mild symptoms. The $56 billion price tag would nearly quadruple Medicare spending on any other drug.

The approval was based mostly on the reduction in the amyloid plaques "biomarker"—rather than any clear benefits for Alzheimer's symptoms. Amyloid hypothesis advocates quickly embraced it as a regulatory template—assuming that the Centers for Medicare & Medicaid Services (CMS) would sign off on funding. The agency is the top insurer of all medicines used by US seniors. If CMS said no, only the rich would be able to afford Aduhelm.

A who's who of prominent amyloid supporters—including Dennis Selkoe, Paul Aisen of the University of Southern California, and Jeffrey Cummings from the University of Nevada—joined Salloway to promote Aduhelm as effective. Those four and six colleagues wrote the widely circulated "Appropriate Use Recommendations" for the drug. All ten were paid consultants for Biogen, Eisai, or both. (Those conflicts were duly noted in fine print at the end of the published recommendations.) The scientists have denied that financial conflicts have any bearing on their views. Biogen cited writings from some of those famous supporters while lobbying CMS, without bothering to note its payments to them.

Patient advocates, including the Alzheimer's Association, found people who offered heartrending tales. They pleaded for any drug that could offer hope, pressing influential lawmakers who followed suit with CMS. Eisai and Biogen had poured as much as $1.7 million into the Alzheimer's Association treasury in the run-up for the agency's decision.

Derek Lowe, a drug development chemist and influential blogger for the journal *Science*, summed up critics' view of the FDA's approval and its implications with blunt clarity: "This was a disgraceful decision, and we're all going to be dealing with the consequences of it for years to come." He later added: "Watching these trials feels to me like watching someone trying to put out an oil well fire by dumping duffel bags of money onto it from helicopters. Hell, that would probably be cheaper. I don't know what the answer to Alzheimer's is, but at this point, as far as I'm concerned, it isn't amyloid."

OUTRAGE

Three of the FDA's Aduhelm advisors resigned from their committee posts in protest. "Accelerated Approval is not supposed to be the backup that you use when your clinical trial data are not good enough for regular approval," said one of them, Harvard Medical School Professor Aaron Kesselheim. In a scornful resignation letter, he called the FDA's action "probably the worst drug approval decision in recent US history." Kesselheim predicted that it would "undermine the care of . . . patients, public trust in the FDA, the pursuit of useful therapeutic innovation, and the affordability of the health care system.

"At the last minute, the agency switched its review to the Accelerated Approval pathway based on the debatable premise that the drug's effect on brain amyloid was likely to help patients," he added. Yet the agency had explicitly excluded the amyloid issue from the committee's debate. "'We're not using the amyloid as a surrogate for efficacy,'" Kesselheim quoted agency officials as having said. He effectively accused the FDA of duping its own advisors.

With Harvard colleague Jerry Avorn, Kesselheim castigated the agency for approving Aduhelm for the full spectrum of Alzheimer's dementia, although it had only been tested in patients with mild symptoms. Backlash on that broad authorization forced the FDA to rein in Aduhelm's approved prescribing information, limiting its use to mild Alzheimer's—although doctors remained free to prescribe it for any level of dementia.

"The agency gave Biogen a full nine years to complete another trial" to demonstrate safety and efficacy in the Alzheimer's population at large, Kesselheim and Avorn added. "Millions of patients will have been treated and billions of dollars passed along to Biogen before we know whether it really works."

Another panel member, National Institute on Aging (NIA) neurologist Madhav Thambisetty, noted an eerie side effect that no one had addressed in the approval process: Anti-amyloid drugs, including Aduhelm, have been directly tied, over and over, to brain atrophy. In plain English: Such drugs cause the brain to shrink—typically a sign of advancing Alzheimer's.

Nick Fox, a neurologist at University College London and a Biogen consultant for the drug, has studied brain atrophy closely. "I do not think this excess volume loss is associated with any . . . cognitive deficits and do not think it portends future deficits," he said.

Scott Ayton, a dementia expert at the University of Melbourne, is a rare Eisai consultant willing to go public with a contrary view. "Brain volume changes consistent with atrophy are consistently reported in anti-amyloid trials, but for more than a decade they have been dismissed or rationalized," he said. "Our analysis found that people [with mild impairment] taking anti-amyloid drugs would have brain volumes approximating that of Alzheimer's disease eight months earlier than if they were not taking the drug," he said. The study by Ayton and colleagues examined data from trials involving some ten thousand patients. He added: "This adverse finding has been swept under the carpet."

Critics increasingly focused on whether potential conflicts of interest infected the Aduhelm saga. Patrizia Cavazzoni, a former executive at giant drugmakers with anti-amyloid drugs in the testing pipeline, headed the FDA Center for Drug Evaluation and Research and led the agency's Aduhelm approval. She represented a vivid example of the revolving door between industry and the agency that I described in *Science* in 2018.

I looked at what happened to FDA medical examiners for twenty-eight recently approved drugs. Of the sixteen officials, eleven had quickly decamped to the drugmakers they previously shepherded approvals for—spiking their salaries, given government-pharma differences. And recent FDA commissioners took lucrative board positions with regulated companies soon after leaving office.

(Similarly, I documented that many members of the FDA advisory committees earn hundreds of thousands of dollars in consulting fees and perks from companies whose drugs they previously voted to approve, and from their competitors.)

Cavazzoni was unrepentant. "We believe [Aduhelm] serves as a model that we hope can be replicated with neurodegenerative diseases," she said, and proposed radical reform to the FDA advisory process: Relax already-weak FDA rules designed to prevent conflicts of interest among advisory panelists. That would make it easier to get required expertise, and "remove some of the increasingly evident emotional undertone or overtones" that sway advice "in the face of very hard facts to the contrary."

AN "UNANTICIPATED PROBLEM"

The controversy washed over Biogen and the FDA until that fall, when media coverage of the alarming death of a seventy-five-year-old Canadian woman unexpectedly disrupted public perceptions. The report, prepared by her physicians and later presented to the FDA by Biogen itself, recounted a harrowing series of events. After ten Aduhelm infusions, the woman appeared confused and had trouble speaking—followed by sudden convulsions. She was rushed to the hospital. A brain scan showed severe swelling—ARIA. Steroid treatments to reduce the swelling failed, and she soon died. The report noted that the woman had brain swelling and bleeding in a prior clinical trial—but was still allowed to take Aduhelm.

"The cause of death remains under investigation, pending the death certificate and hospital records . . . Based on the information currently available in this case and in the overall program, no changes to the known benefit-risk profile of [Aduhelm] or to the conduct of clinical trials are warranted at this time. This event does not constitute an 'unanticipated problem,'" Biogen responded. Those words sounded hollow in 2023, when the coroner concluded that the woman "died following a prolonged and refractory epileptic seizure probably caused by cerebral edema caused by the administration of a drug at the experimental stage, aducanumab."

Biogen's dry defense was followed by a succession of developments that rapidly unraveled Aduhelm's prospects.

The European Medicines Agency rejected a licensing request, noting "that although Aduhelm reduces amyloid beta in the brain, the link between this effect and clinical improvement had not been established." The agency also cited the risk of dangerous brain swelling and bleeding. The UK Medicines and Healthcare Products Regulatory Agency followed suit without comment—as did authorities in Japan, and every other country Biogen tried except the tiny United Arab Emirates. In the first quarter after the FDA approval, Biogen made a paltry $300,000 from sales of the drug for little more than one hundred patients. In a seemingly desperate move to turn the tide in the US market, Biogen and Eisai slashed the drug's price by half. But in May 2022, Medicare declined to pay for Aduhelm except for patients participating in clinical trials. That sounded the drug's commercial death knell.

A scathing investigative report by the US House of Representatives followed in December 2022. Given the enormous doubt about Aduhelm's efficacy and safety, it cited the FDA's approval process as "rife with irregularities," such as undocumented, private meetings between regulators and Biogen.

"Biogen internal documents mentioned a 'high-touch engagement strategy with regulators,'" the *Washington Post* editorial board noted. "High-touch indeed: A presentation to an FDA advisory committee about Aduhelm was written jointly by Biogen and the FDA."

In a written statement, Biogen said it "stands by the integrity of the actions we have taken."

In January 2024, the company discontinued all efforts to develop and commercialize Aduhelm and terminated an ongoing clinical trial. In so doing, it shed the expense to fully analyze the effect of the drug on brain shrinkage—an ethical lapse that insults the trial volunteers' sacrifices, according to the NIA's Thambisetty.

Aduhelm had become a medical failure and financial debacle. But the obsession with amyloid lived on. Regulatory and scientific experts said Aduhelm had still set a malign precedent.

"Now that the bar has been lowered, other companies are likely to seek similar pathways to approval," Harvard's Kesselheim emphasized. "Approving a drug that has such poor evidence that it works and causes such worrisome side effects is not the solution."

George Perry, University of Texas San Antonio neuroscientist, amyloid skeptic, and editor of the *Journal of Alzheimer's Disease*, called it emblematic of the pervasive, pernicious influence of the amyloid hypothesis. "If the amyloid thing continues the way it is, it'll take ten to twenty years, at least, of people just going around and around and around," speaking of the lack of progress the crisis would likely lead to. "This is not science."

ON THE CASE IN NASHVILLE

Watching the Aduhelm debacle unfold from his post at Vanderbilt, Matthew Schrag fretted about what he could do. After all, he was virtually unknown outside relatively narrow professional circles and doubted that he could exert much influence. "[Aduhelm's approval] isn't the turning point in the fight against Alzheimer's disease, in fact, I am very concerned that it may be a major setback. For the safety of our patients, we should proceed with great caution," he wrote on his lab's blog.

Schrag was shocked when his sober, normally obscure status launched him into the national spotlight. Given his deep background in the relevant science, the media, including major newspapers, *CNN*, and *National Geographic* magazine began calling.

"I don't like it," he told a business publication, about the FDA's approval of Aduhelm. The story used that quote in its headline, and Schrag's wife, Sarah, would later nervously tease him about how far he was sticking his neck out in criticizing Biogen, a powerful pharma company, and the federal government. Within a year, that comment would seem trifling next to Schrag's public positions on a wide range of Alzheimer's research.

Other media began to seek Schrag out as a fresh face among neuro-scientists willing to speak directly about the central issue in the Aduhelm debate—that the FDA had favored the amyloid hypothesis despite de-cades of flops in tests to cure Alzheimer's. "We had been hoping for a recalibration of the field," Schrag told the *Washington Post*, adding that he feared the pharma companies would use the approval as a reason to redouble investments into a "dead end."

"Even if amyloid does cause Alzheimer's disease, it does not necessar-ily mean you can cure the disease by removing it," Schrag said. "If some-one came to the emergency room with a stab wound, just removing the knife wouldn't cure them either."

Schrag had to adjust deftly and quickly to his new stature. That kind of notice can raise eyebrows among bosses, funders, and journal editors—particularly for a young scientist still establishing his career. Doubts creep in: Can an outspoken critic be trusted as a loyal soldier?

Soon, what seemed like fifteen minutes of fame would spark a new phase of Schrag's career: whistleblower on the powerful amyloid estab-lishment. It would begin with a fight about another drug that the FDA had recently greenlit for phase 3 trials, final tests before possible approval. For all its weaknesses, overly optimistic bragging, ties to regulators, and dangers, no one had ever accused Biogen of actually faking Aduhelm data. But those claims soon would surface about a different treatment, still making its way through the testing pipeline: Cassava's simufilam.

Chapter 8

Image Problem

Nashville

2021

"If you cheat, cheat professionally.
You cannot be so lazy."

—ALENA KOZUNDA, MATTHEW SCHRAG'S LAB MANAGER

The news was dramatic: After more than a century of failure an effective treatment for Alzheimer's disease—or even a cure—had finally been found, surprisingly, by a small biotech company that previously specialized in opioid painkillers. Cassava Sciences had never taken a drug to market in its fifteen years of existence. Yet it claimed to have discovered a new molecule that stabbed the dark heart of the terrible illness.

Back in 2012—nine years prior to the big claims about Aduhelm—Cassava (then-named Pain Therapeutics, before it rechristened itself in 2019) announced that its experimental compound, code-named PTI-125, "can dramatically suppress the toxic effects of amyloid-beta. Results were demonstrated in a mouse model of [Alzheimer's], and remarkably, in brain tissue from deceased Alzheimer's patients." It added, optimistically, "These novel findings suggest PTI-125 may improve cognition . . . raising hopes for a treatment to combat cognitive decline."

Indeed remarkable, and truly historic. If true. Cassava later offered a proof-of-concept based on tests of frozen brain tissue that a critic later dubbed "zombie science." It claimed discovery of the true cause of Alzheimer's, a "misfolded" form of the protein filamin A, which normally provides a kind of cellular scaffolding. When inexplicably reshaped into a twisted form, it supposedly leads to inflammation and the buildup of deadly tau and amyloid-beta proteins, among other problems, the company claimed.

Within a few years, Cassava abandoned its moribund opioid business, dumped its Pain Therapeutics moniker, and transformed itself into a one-drug Alzheimer's company. Biogen's Aduhelm was approved in June 2021 on the strength of weak data that the drug giant said had very slightly slowed the rate of cognitive decline in Alzheimer's patients. PTI-125, renamed simufilam, had already traveled much further by then, Cassava claimed. Patients were getting better. They remembered more. They experienced greater mastery in life, and less anxiety. In effect, simufilam was the holy grail, the dream drug that generations of researchers had searched for in vain.

"Is [simufilam] a drug that you would stay on for the rest of your life . . . to stop the progression of Alzheimer's?" Cassava CEO Remi Barbier said on a 2021 webcast, *Being Patient*, hosted by a patient advocate. He was replying to a softball question that pharma execs dream of when speaking to the precise audience they want to convince. "Absolutely," Barbier asserted. "My vision is that as soon as [a] patient has evidence of this misfolded protein, don't wait. Start to improve your life, start to exercise, start to lose weight, eat properly, and take simufilam early on."

That evidence would come from a proprietary test Cassava developed, SavaDx, that it said could find misfolded filamin A in blood plasma, even prior to any noticeable Alzheimer's symptoms. From a corporate finance perspective, it was a masterstroke: Create a seamless process for patients to need the drug for decades, once approved by the Food and Drug Administration (FDA). And decades of treatment, for both Alzheimer's patients and the symptom-free "worried well" could mean decades of stratospheric profits.

In the same webcast, Barbier described how his drug worked. "Think of a brick house or brick building. If you remove one brick, so what? A few flies get in, right? You remove a dozen bricks, you know, maybe no big deal. You start removing fifty bricks, a hundred bricks, something's gonna give. Eventually, you remove a thousand bricks, and the whole scaffolding folds. Something similar may be happening in Alzheimer's," he said. "There's an altered form of filamin A. When it's altered, it loses its function, [and] it loses its shape. You're taking bricks away from the house, eventually, you take enough bricks away and the whole thing collapses."

His meandering analogy reflected the challenge to describe the drug's purported effects within a grab bag of Alzheimer's hypotheses. It fights sticky amyloid-beta plaques and toxic, soluble forms of the protein. It attacks deadly tau proteins inside nerve cells and reduces inflammation. It improves the brain's blood-sugar regulation—helping kick off a research trend positing that Alzheimer's might be caused by a kind of diabetes of the brain. With that laundry list of benefits, simufilam does the unprecedented, according to the company. It reverses cognitive decline—tantamount to a cure.

Such claims, based on preliminary clinical research involving a handful of patients, grabbed mindshare among some patient groups and retail investors. Yet not one independent study cataloged on PubMed—the National Library of Medicine's compendium of research—had confirmed the scientific claims generated by Cassava advisor Hoau-Yan Wang of the City University of New York Medical School; Lindsay Burns, Barbier's wife and Cassava senior vice president for neuroscience; and their collaborators. If misfolded filamin A was the long-sought key to Alzheimer's, why hadn't anyone else directly tied it to the disease?

MARKET GYRATIONS

In February 2020, Burns announced early results from a clinical trial that she said supported simufilam "as a new and potentially disease-modifying drug treatment for Alzheimer's," shown by improvements in biomarkers that signify disease severity. The results, she said, "imply a slower rate of neurodegeneration or a suppression of disease processes."

Institutional investors—such as finance titans who represent pensions, endowments, and hedge funds—literally weren't buying it. They have rarely owned more than one-third of Cassava shares, a fraction of the norm for publicly traded companies. At the time of this writing, the only institutions with any significant investment in Cassava are hedge funds or index funds that bundle a broad basket of stocks across a business sector. Dedicated biotech funds—the industry cognoscenti—have stayed away.

Yet, when the FDA approved Aduhelm based on thin data, it "opened up a market frenzy for Alzheimer's-focused companies," some with similarly big claims based on meager data, a leading trade publication noted. Cassava's stock took off like a proverbial Wall Street rocket. By late July 2021, the tiny biopharma company that outsourced most of its lab work, development, manufacturing, and testing was suddenly worth $5.4 billion.

Cassava executives held on to most of their shares. But huge bonuses were tied to the rising share prices. The bonus program kicked in less than three weeks before Cassava announced favorable results in a simufilam trial—a rejiggered data analysis that contradicted earlier pessimistic findings. (Years later, the FDA and other federal agencies would reveal that the new data were based on improper research practices.) Investors filed suit against Barbier and others, describing the program as tied to short-term stock bumps expected when Cassava issued upbeat press releases. Plaintiffs called it "a plan to overcompensate themselves through the back door." (In 2024, the company agreed to settle the suit out of court; the terms were not disclosed.)

Activist investors, who called themselves "SAVAges" after the company's SAVA ticker symbol, promoted the stock relentlessly on Twitter and Reddit. In one of many such pitches, YouTube investment promoter Joe Springer called it "our best stock of the year," part of a push that made SAVA a hugely popular meme stock—with large share volumes bought and sold daily as small-fry retail investors placed their bets.

Short sellers also have controlled several times the normal number of shares during much of the company's history, making it one of the most shorted stocks on the market. That combination of retail investors and shorts fostered immense volatility. SAVA's daily share price fever chart often resembles the jagged polygraph readout of an inveterate liar, even when no news affects the company.

Whether SAVAges are true believers or pump-and-dump stock manipulators, they understand something very real: desperate Alzheimer's patients and their families long for any good news. Given Cassava's bold claims during a period when the FDA was seen as increasingly permissive in approving new drugs, such traders considered simufilam a future blockbuster.

SIMUFILAM SKEPTICS

As SAVA approached its peak, Matthew Schrag became central to exposing doubts about the company's science.

Two neuroscientists who said simufilam was based on false research, or even fraud, had been working on a complaint to the FDA. If they were right, simufilam might be akin to farfetched cures or preventives offered by the likes of Dr. Oz or Gwyneth Paltrow.

The neuroscientists felt convinced that they could mount a powerful case against Cassava. As short sellers, they might make money for themselves in the process. But they needed someone with expert technical and medical knowledge to interrogate published images in papers about lab research behind the drug.

John Smith, a neuroscientist and friend of one of the would-be petitioners, knew someone with elite image-analysis skills, honed over years of preparing his own scientific images: Schrag. As a physician treating Alzheimer's patients, Schrag could also place the research in its disturbing human context. And after his outspoken criticism of Aduhelm, Smith figured that if Schrag found apparent misconduct, he'd have the guts to expose it. (Smith is a pseudonym. He wanted his name out of the rancorous professional, legal, financial, and social media disputes that surround Cassava.) He called Schrag to ask if he would talk with Jordan Thomas, an attorney representing the neuroscientists.

"My response was, 'You think I'm stupid enough to do that?'" Schrag recalled, then added ruefully: "Apparently, I was. He showed me the extent of what was known at the time. I thought, 'This company should not be allowed to go into phase 3 clinical trials.'"

Cassava said it had spent more than $100 million in investor funds to develop simufilam since its 2012 announcement. If based on sham data, that represented waste and fraud on a staggering scale.

"In addition to the enormous financial investment," Schrag said, "the drug had already reached patients. Potentially thousands of people were going to be exposed to it," he added. "That's clearly a piece of work that has attained a very high degree of influence." He was worried that if research data on simufilam had been doctored, volunteer participants in clinical experiments faced possible side effects with little or no chance of meaningful benefits.

So he agreed to work with Thomas. "It would be a substantial investment of time to do this properly, and at so high a level that I would be willing to stake my reputation on the findings. So I asked to be compensated," Schrag said. They agreed to an $18,000 fee. That would prove a token payment, given the time he spent analyzing images in papers by Wang and Burns, independently of his day job at Vanderbilt. Schrag said he has never shorted Cassava stock or earned other money for those efforts.

"I started putting together material to go to the [National Institutes of Health] and the team behind the petition requested that I consult with them. I provided them a packet of material. And they sent me a draft of the citizens' petition. It wasn't good quality. So I helped them put together something that would land harder."

As he dug in, Schrag's thoughts traced back to his teenage years in rural Washington, volunteering in the nursing home where bewildered Alzheimer's patients seemed profoundly vulnerable to harm or exploitation. They needed vigilant protection. Now, as a doctor treating dementia sufferers, Schrag felt that sense of responsibility intensely. He knew that few patients among the hundreds already enrolled in simufilam trials could discern whether they were being helped or callously used in the service of profit. He felt he had to look out for them.

While Schrag reviewed the Cassava data, retired New Jersey building contractor Stephen Price was signing revised consent forms to renew his service as a simufilam trial volunteer. With the help of his son, Matt, a global health epidemiologist, Stephen was grasping for a literal lifeline, Matt recalled. They had to get a drug that would arrest or reverse his dad's worrisome cognitive decline fast. Simufilam was the only trial they could get him into.

Matt worried about the science behind the drug and the way the trial was conducted. For example, qualifying patients to participate involved a type of dementia screening widely regarded as less reliable than many other tests in common use, but faster and cheaper to administer. And Cassava's trial included patients with no sign of impairment all the way up to those with moderate dementia. So broad a range makes data harder to interpret. A company with no track record of success can have trouble enrolling patients to take an experimental drug; recruiting people farther along on the desperation scale made it much easier.

Stephen, who had moderate impairment, had been rejected by other trials; most accepted only patients with early Alzheimer's. He and his family ultimately conceded to the imperative of powerlessness that so many others face: What choice did they have?

DOPPELGÄNGERS AND GHOSTLY HALOS

Schrag guided me through a tutorial on the creation of the western blot images used to support Cassava's ideas. Ground-up brain tissues are loaded into tiny reservoirs at the top of a plastic housing that holds a filtering gel. The gel acts like a sieve that traps proteins, such as amyloid-beta. A digital photography device turns the results into images that resemble stacked bands, sorted by molecular weight, identifying the type and relative amount of each protein. Thousands of scientists use western blots to test experimental hypotheses.

Like any photographic image, the blots can easily be doctored with software such as Photoshop. Bands can be copied and pasted. Their shapes can be subtly stretched or flipped. Their intensity—signifying how much of a particular protein was found—can be adjusted higher or lower with a few clicks. Backgrounds that help confirm the authenticity of an image can be cloned and inserted within or across images to obscure unwanted features. (Before digital imaging, some of those manipulations were done as manual cut-and-paste jobs.)

This isn't rocket science—not even biomedical science. "People who don't have a scientific background have done pretty well in this image-integrity space," Schrag said. "I tagged along with my sister-in-law, who is a wedding photographer, and worked with a professional photographer friend to try to learn something, just for fun. I realized that a lot of what happens is on the back end—how you handle images, how you process them. Watching professionals do that with image-editing software, you see how an image changes as it's polished. Those who doctor scientific images use the same tools. Add to that the experience of seeing thousands of western blots over your career. You learn what to expect, what's normal." He developed an eye for what seems phony.

Schrag recalled the first days of his Wang and Burns analysis. He turned his attention to the original 2012 claim that simufilam "can dramatically suppress the toxic effects of amyloid-beta." That paper in the *Journal of Neuroscience* helped spark the company's reinvention. It originated the idea that dead, frozen brain tissue dosed with simufilam demonstrated its startling effects.

First, Schrag sharpened the contrast and magnified published images at the heart of that experimental "proof." Peculiarities immediately seemed apparent: Oddly shaped bands that were doppelgängers for others in the same paper. Ghostly halos. Clip marks—unnatural-looking sharp edges or appendages to a rounded band. Abruptly varying background sections in the same image. That paper helped lay the foundation for experiments on thousands of patients. How could it be trusted, given such obviously suspect images? he wondered. And what did it mean for unsuspecting volunteers in clinical experiments?

Over two weeks in August 2021, Schrag labored around the clock, poring over study after study in his cramped Vanderbilt office. A few feet away, an antique microscope provided a constant reminder that valid research demands discipline and exactitude. Hours blurred into days. He used ImageJ and MIPAV, software developed and endorsed by the NIH, to deconstruct images, turning his computer into a digital microscope. Wang coauthored all thirty-four papers that directly or indirectly provided the scientific basis for simufilam's development and related science. He was a principal author on eighteen. It established him as the intellectual and scientific throughline—the only person who touched every experiment. Burns coauthored six and was a principal author on five, making her contributions integral to the basic proof behind Cassava's drug.

Suspect examples immediately became visible in image after image, paper after paper. Beyond western blots, Schrag saw micrographs—magnifications of microscopic features of brain tissue—that seemed obviously cloned. Yet they were presented as findings for different experimental conditions. Of course, innocent mistakes happen in science. But the litany and pattern of apparent defects seemed hard to pass off as simple errors.

"How could this be?" Schrag remembered thinking. "Traditionally, we don't view something as replicated unless it's been done three times—and really, five, ten, many, many times. Especially if it's important. If you can't get a good quality image in one of the many replicates that you ran, you have to ask: Why?"

Alena Kozunda, Schrag's lab manager and confidant, sitting at a workstation for tests on mice, shook her head in puzzled disapproval. If fake, the images belied a sloppiness or impunity she found hard to fathom. "If you cheat, cheat professionally," she sarcastically admonished. "You cannot be so lazy."

In experiment after experiment, Schrag found apparent misconduct at the core of Cassava's conclusions. If those experiments were the products of fraud, they would decimate the scientific basis for simufilam. But Schrag never makes accusations of "fraud."

"I focus on what we can see in the published images, and describe them as red flags, not final conclusions. The data should speak for itself," he said, never claiming to have "proven" misconduct. That would require comparing the images to the original, uncropped, unpublished source blots and micrographs. Wang and Burns rarely have made those public, and in some cases Wang said he had often discarded the originals requested by journal editors or others. Fraud is also a term fraught with legal implications. It speaks to intent. Without reading minds, intent can be nearly impossible to determine even if improper tampering seems evident. That's the mystery: What were Wang and Burns thinking? I tried to ask many times and was always rebuffed.

During the Aduhelm episode, Schrag couldn't live with himself without speaking out. This time, he kept his name out of the FDA petition. He made no public comment on Cassava. Schrag wasn't ready to become a social-media target of disgruntled shareholders who had previously lived up to their SAVAges moniker by trolling and even doxing simufilam's critics. He was leery of jeopardizing his family's privacy and security—or facing legal complications.

Schrag's findings supported the core of the citizen petition filed to the FDA on August 18, 2021. He provided forensic street cred. In a cover letter to the agency, attorney Jordan Thomas made the stakes clear: "Cassava Sciences apparently didn't get the Theranos memo. Their desire to do groundbreaking scientific research doesn't give the company and its executives a get out of jail free card from regulators, patients, or investors." He asked the FDA to pause the phase 3 clinical trials of simufilam. The petition claimed some science behind the drug might be based on fraud, making the trials a cynical exploitation of a projected 1,800 participants.

FDA accepted the complaint with no immediate comment but posted the petition and supporting documents to its website. For Cassava, it went off like a bomb. Shares in Cassava Sciences crashed. In less than a month, the stock plummeted nearly 60 percent from its peak value. It has yet to return to the financial stratosphere.

Chapter 9

Doctored

New York, Nashville, Austin

2021

"They're saying they did things that cannot be done."
—MATTHEW SCHRAG

The petition described doctored images in seven papers at the heart of simufilam's purported viability as an Alzheimer's treatment. "It is not conceivable that features in the images [such as apparent duplications] arose due to coincidence or accident, leaving the only plausible explanation being that the images were deliberately falsified or fabricated," said David Vaux, a leading Australian science ethicist, among the first of many authorities to weigh in.

The petition featured only a fraction of the suspect images in papers that formed the bedrock of simufilam's science. Matthew Schrag—the then-unnamed forensic detective who uncovered most of the alleged, egregious flaws—had examined dozens of papers by Cassava contractor Hoau-Yan Wang and the company's chief neuroscientist, Lindsay Burns. Over several months after the petition was filed, Schrag described many of those anonymously—with original or incremental contributions by the well-known forensic image sleuth Elisabeth Bik and others—on PubPeer, the discussion website for concerns about doubtful experiments.

Schrag's analysis snared some illustrious collaborators. Notably, Harvard University neurologist Steven Arnold, who has served for years on Cassava Sciences' advisory board and coauthored several publications. Arnold, Wang, and Burns all went to ground, making no public comments.

"Let me be very clear," Cassava CEO Remi Barbier said, after weeks of stock-market carnage. "We intend to vigorously defend ourselves and our stakeholders against false and misleading allegations." (Months afterward, I provided Barbier with Schrag's complete findings, including unpublished images. He said in an email that they were "generally consistent with prior allegations about our science . . . such allegations are false.")

For Wang—who was integral to simufilam's scientific basis and testing—the drug had offered a shot at research fame and commercial fortune. Burns wrote some of the key papers, reviewed and approved images and data, raised money off the findings, and took credit. As Barbier's spouse and a Cassava executive, her reputation and livelihood were inextricably tied to the drug's success. Whether Burns knew about or had a hand in the apparent fabrications seemed unclear, but it was hard to see her as naïve.

The *Journal of Neuroscience* paper in 2012 unveiled what Wang and Burns described as the protein filamin A's central role in Alzheimer's disease and simufilam's dramatic benefits. It formed the basis for Cassava's resurrection after its opioid fiasco into an aspiring dementia-drug powerhouse. Nine images in that article appeared to have been the product of some combination of gross errors and misconduct.

"Initially, I thought that Wang and Burns probably believed their own core argument, and started by possibly fudging results to make things look more perfect," Schrag said. "I thought I saw a slippery slope, where things seemed more and more brazen, more and more outlandish as time went by. It's a long piece of science, spanning more than a decade," he added. "You have to show continued development to continue to get funding."

Schrag was referring to dozens of studies before and after that trailblazing paper. Apparently blatant falsification in paper after paper, year after year, suggested that he wasn't flagging innocent glitches or pointing the finger unfairly. Even so, Schrag proceeded cautiously. "I'm not a lawyer, and it's not my job to decide if it's fraud. My job as a scientist is to decide, 'Is it right or not? Is this data reliable?'" he said. "The consequences of making an allegation are so high that you really have to err on the side of saying, either it's not a problem, or I'm not sure," Schrag added. "In those cases, you're not going to act."

The "zombie science" concerns, described in detail in the FDA petition, strengthened his certainty, and not his alone. Schrag's analysis had been adopted by the two neuroscientists—Cornell University's Geoffrey Pitt and former drug company executive David Bredt—for whom the petition was prepared.

"To the best of my knowledge, nobody else anywhere has gotten that frozen-brain technique to work," Schrag said. "Some of it is very simple stuff that alerted me. Like the notion that they used the McIlwain chopper. That's a little gadget that has an arm on a spring with a razor blade. It just goes 'chop, chop, chop, chop,' and minces up tissue. Wang's saying that he's chopped frozen human brain with that. It would just bounce off if it was frozen. Anyone who's handled this equipment knows that's just not how the machine works." Technical descriptions from lab-equipment companies supported his comments.

Schrag's doubts went further. Wang and Burns claimed that they treated the revivified brain tissue with beta amyloid protein for an hour, sparking a burst of chemical changes that promoted tau protein "tangles" within the neurons. Tangles represent a key element of the amyloid hypothesis. Then they treated the tissue with simufilam. The scientists said the drug quickly arrested those tau changes. If true, it effectively monkeywrenched tau's role in degrading brain cells—a revelatory achievement.

In the FDA petition, Pitt and Bredt maintained that it was unlikely that various essential brain enzymes—proteins that speed up biochemical reactions—could have survived after having been frozen at -112 degrees Fahrenheit without using any special cryopreservation techniques. Even if they did survive, the claim that enzymes operated correctly after having been thawed to barely above freezing, as described in the experiments, defied belief. Nor was it likely neurons could survive and show robust reactions as the Cassava scientists showed.

"Neurons in the human brain do not survive extended postmortem intervals and long-term freezing. The complex, multistep cellular processes the authors claim to observe in tissue that has been dead for a decade are contrary to a basic understanding of neurobiology," noted the petition. "Claims of this magnitude require extensive, detailed verification, but the authors provide no evidence of tissue viability."

Cassava formally responded a year later, in a lawsuit against Pitt, Bredt, and other short sellers. The filing noted that Wang used standard practices and that research using frozen postmortem brain tissue is routine. It cited ten articles showing how other researchers had coaxed chemical reactions from postmortem samples. Those arguments were correct, as far as they went. But Cassava's detractors weren't disputing the obvious—that frozen brain samples are used in research. They were saying that the specific claims made by Wang and his colleagues didn't make sense scientifically. For the experiments described, the brain cells would need to remain intact. Frozen, partly thawed, chopped brain cell membranes would break apart and lose the kind of biological functions that the Wang experiments purported to discover, according to Schrag.

Comparing the Wang experiments to "a Rube Goldberg machine," Schrag said, "The results that they're talking about haven't been fudged to look a bit better. They're saying they did things that cannot be done."

If he's right, the zombie-brain studies unduly swayed Alzheimer's research well beyond any support they might lend to simufilam. That's because Wang, Burns, and their coauthors argued that the same studies showed that by reducing resistance to insulin, the drug could treat Alzheimer's as something like brain diabetes. Interest in that idea surged after the 2012 *Journal of Neuroscience* paper and a related Wang-Arnold study in the respected *Journal of Clinical Investigation* that year. It would become a highly cited, influential piece of work.

Concerned that such influence might be steering scarce resources in the wrong direction, just before the FDA petition was delivered Schrag independently submitted a scorching report to the NIH concerning the noted papers and others by Wang, Burns, and their collaborators. He cited "serious concerns of research misconduct." Schrag asked the agency to safeguard his identity as a whistleblower. NIH wouldn't say what, if anything, it would do. But soon after, Wang's employer, the City University of New York (CUNY), launched an investigation.

Between treating patients and running his own lab, Schrag continued to chip away at other papers by Wang or Burns. He worked late most nights after his young daughter went to sleep, examining hundreds of scientific images—identical-looking western blots, apparently duplicated micrographs of brain tissue, and tables of improbably similar numbers. Schrag assembled a hundred-page dossier, replete with piece-by-piece views of what looked like fakery. It included more than 170 images that looked to be improperly altered or duplicated. The document has never been made public in its entirety—although Schrag eventually posted most findings on PubPeer. It amounted to a devastating indictment of the entire body of work.

SAVAGE BATTLES

The FDA petition ignited a social media firestorm. Legions of Cassava critics and SAVAges engaged in the Twitter equivalent of hand-to-hand combat.

"Warning: The $SAVA fight has escalated into dangerous territory," tweeted Adam Feuerstein, a veteran biotech journalist with the medical website STAT, Cassava skeptic, and frequent target of the SAVAges. "@JoeSpringer, ringleader of the Cassava retail investor mob, is using Twitter and YouTube to disclose the home addresses, phone numbers, and other private info of people critical of Cassava . . . Take the harassment seriously. Report him to Twitter and YouTube. His rhetoric has become increasingly threatening," Feuerstein wrote.

"It's just the start, enjoy your last days of fresh air," replied @nabster88, one of the legion of anonymous SAVAges who jumped into the fray.

Four aggressive short-seller scientists mocked Cassava and simufilam in a slide deck titled "Cassava Sciences: A Shambolic Charade." They appropriated Barbier's intemperate outburst against the FDA's "shambolic regulations" that he claimed had improperly sunk a previous golden ticket, an opioid pain treatment that failed FDA scrutiny in 2019. Eschewing subtlety, it described Cassava's efforts as "an astonishing story of sleazy drug development that potentially endangers [Alzheimer's] patients," involving "a web of shady characters and cronies, nefarious development, fabrication & manipulation of data, and excessive unsubstantiated claims . . . [that] outdoes the greatest biomedical dumpster fires." Behind the snark, the critique provided sophisticated detail. (The Cassava lawsuit named the "Shambolic Charade" authors as defendants, along with Bredt and Pitt.)

Barbier resolutely denied any misconduct and strongly supported the work by Wang and Burns. Barbier's "fact" vs. "fiction" rebuttal of the petition began with the statement that key biomarker data showing how simufilam affected tau protein levels in blood plasma "was generated by Quanterix Corp., an independent company." That rejoinder lost its punch two days later, when the analytics firm flatly refuted Barbier's claim. The news sent SAVA shares into a new nosedive.

As bad news mounted, Barbier privately asked CUNY to investigate the charges—after the university had already initiated a review of Wang's work. In a letter to CUNY research provost Rosemarie Wesson, Barbier's "support" for Wang took a tone of uncertainty compared to his full-throated public defense. "I believe the allegations are false and misleading as they pertain to Cassava Sciences," he told Wesson. "Absent hard evidence, we think it is not credible and not fair to accuse Professor Wang of a long-term, widespread pattern of scientific fraud." Two months later CUNY changed its initial inquiry into a formal misconduct investigation.

Schrag also sent his findings to most of the journals that had published the suspicious Cassava papers. In December, Wang, Burns, and co-authors of the seminal 2012 paper in the *Journal of Neuroscience* issued a correction involving one of the nine challenged images. They denied that the error affected the study's conclusions about simufilam's effects. They also provided purportedly original, unedited western blots in three other cases. A flurry of rejoinders by Bik, Schrag, and others followed on PubPeer. They showed that the newly produced blots contained their own apparently clear signs of doctoring.

A month later, the journal editors issued an "expression of concern" about the images and said they would "await the outcome of [CUNY's] investigation before taking further action."

Corrections and notices of concern from editors of the other journals began to pile up. Seven retractions followed. Other journals that published suspect Cassava-related papers kicked off a seemingly endless stream of investigations that remain pending more than two years later. It would become a prime example of the often-self-serving, sluggish response to possible misconduct too typically seen in the academic press. Their languid, deferential approach to the home institutions of the accused scholars would let questionable Alzheimer's research remain quietly in place for years to come.

In August, Cassava shareholders filed a class action lawsuit seeking remuneration for an alleged "fraudulent scheme" by management. The suit accused the company of making false claims about simufilam's seemingly miraculous benefits to sell company shares at an inflated price. In effect, according to the complaint, this fleeced unsuspecting investors—who saw their investment evaporate when the stock plunged on news of the petition to the FDA.

In November, the evolving simufilam controversy finally received attention from mainstream media. The *Wall Street Journal* reported that the US Securities and Exchange Commission (SEC) had launched an investigation into concerns that Cassava's management "manipulated research results," and also surfaced a separate investigation underway at the NIH. A month later, the Federal Bureau of Investigation began inquiries. In the months that followed, the *New Yorker*, the *New York Times*, and others weighed in with skeptical reports about Cassava and simufilam. None of those publications knew that Schrag's insights provided a basis for those probes.

Cassava finally got some good news in February. The FDA decided not to act on the citizen petition. The rejection was signed by Patrizia Cavazzoni, director for the agency's Center for Drug Evaluation and Research, who had drawn the ire of many scientists and clinicians when she approved the controversial anti-amyloid drug Aduhelm. But Cassava's victory fell short of a vote of confidence. In essence, Cassava got off on a technicality. Cavazzoni said that petitioners lacked legal standing to request that her agency impose a hold on the simufilam trials. "We take the issues you raise seriously," she wrote to the attorney representing Bredt and Pitt. "Your Petitions are being denied solely on the grounds that your requests are not the appropriate subject of a Citizen Petition. This response does not represent a decision by the Agency to take or refrain from taking any action relating to the subject matter of your Petitions."

While declaring victory in public, Cassava Sciences acknowledged anxiety in a filing to the SEC a few weeks later. "The FDA or other regulatory agency may put a clinical hold on our clinical studies and our business will suffer. A clinical hold is an order issued by FDA or other regulatory agency to suspend an ongoing clinical trial, typically due to newly identified deficiencies with our studies or our drug candidate," as it recently had for Alzheimer's drugs from other companies. Cassava added that "a clinical hold may require us to spend significant resources over many months to address the root causes of FDA's concerns. We may not find and successfully address such root causes . . . If we are on clinical hold for 1 year or longer [it] may result in termination of the clinical program for simufilam."

The company would later acknowledge that NIH funding, key to the credibility of its work during simufilam's early development, had dried up. To some important partners, Cassava had become a scientific pariah. Nonprofits including the Alzheimer's Association shunned Cassava's sponsorship in their own fundraising. Nine clinical research sites—the testing centers for human studies of simufilam—walked away, slowing down the company's trials. The researchers were trying to escape association with "a toxic environment" for Cassava, caused by short seller claims on social media and the citizen petition, according to the company.

Cassava provided "nearly one hundred thousand pages of documents to an alphabet soup of outside investigative agencies," Barbier told me in a 2022 email, nodding to the investigations by the SEC, NIH, and apparently a criminal probe by the US Department of Justice. He said the CUNY investigation of Wang "has yielded an important finding to date: there is no evidence of research misconduct." Actually, facing the prospect of massive institutional embarrassment, CUNY had said nothing whatsoever about its findings.

Schrag felt satisfied that his efforts to expose research misconduct were gaining traction, but the episode left him apprehensive. He had just uncovered dozens of almost certainly doctored papers supporting a major drug development effort, published in mainstream, respected journals. How had those problems gone unnoticed for years or even decades? He wondered nervously: What other Alzheimer's research should be reconsidered with skeptical eyes?

To his shock, it didn't take him long to uncover a far bigger and more important body of questionable research. Almost by accident, Schrag detected another case of magic hands behind what appeared to be the most consequential misconduct in the history of the disease. His findings would shatter the Alzheimer's world.

Chapter 10

"Biology Doesn't Care"

Nashville

2021–2022

"You can cheat to get a paper. You can cheat to get a degree.
You can cheat to get a grant. You can't cheat to cure a disease.
Biology doesn't care."

—MATTHEW SCHRAG

In late November 2021, my *Science* colleague Meredith Wadman reached out about a story. Wadman—a physician and Rhodes scholar turned journalist—had recently rocked the scientific community with shocking stories about sexual harassment at the Salk Institute, the National Institutes of Health, and other august scientific institutions. She was swamped with stories and couldn't follow up on a tip from John Smith, a neuroscientist and fan of her work who claimed to have inside information about the Cassava Sciences controversy. Wadman didn't want to put him off and lose what sounded like a tantalizing opportunity and asked if I'd like to follow up.

Unfortunately, I was equally stretched. She had reached me during the last weeks of a six-month investigation on a Canadian botanist who had engaged in a jaw-dropping succession of seemingly obvious fabulism and misconduct that upended the nutritional supplement industry and brought in millions of dollars for his pet projects and companies. I was gearing up to put the finishing touches on the piece through the holidays, something my wife was not excited about. I wasn't looking for a distraction.

I get a lot of tips that don't end up as stories. Some are too parochial for the magazine's global audience. Others don't have a research angle that *Science* usually needs. Many interesting ideas are just not important enough to justify the time and expense required to report them out. And some claims seem persuasive but lack essential documentation. In any case, it would have to be big—and exclusive—for me to jump on after recent coverage by the *Wall Street Journal*.

But as a noted neuroscientist, Smith seemed credible. And I rarely give a hard "no" before exercising some due diligence. I'd heard of Cassava but hadn't paid close attention to the controversy and asked him to send me a few links to get me up to speed. To set expectations, I warned Smith that I was enmeshed in a major project and would be busy for a few weeks. And I asked if he could say more about the NIH and FDA whistleblower who uncovered the raft of suspect images that led to Cassava's crisis. I knew that the whistleblower would be key to advancing the story and uncovering additional misconduct.

Smith sent some links, but instantly turned prickly. "The NIH whistleblower is unnamed, and you are going to have to show some interest and engagement if you want the name because you could have googled what I gave you in 3 minutes," he emailed.

"I should have been a little more clear," I replied. "The *WSJ* is very good at this sort of thing and is on it with a substantial head start. They might just stop now, but almost certainly are turning over rocks as we speak. I dig deep and spend a lot of time on each project. To justify that time, effort, and expense to my editors on a competitive story like this one obviously is, I need to be able to report out original and important angles that are for whatever reason being neglected by other media—or that I can get to first via sourcing or smarts."

This was normal. Investigative reporters have to skeptically triage what comes over the transom. Many tipsters are well-meaning but naïve. They might have hidden interests that skew their judgment or can't add anything substantive to the mix. Others have insider documents or sources that can turn a loose thread into my new obsession. I asked Smith: "Which of those two are you?"

He was the latter type and connected me with Matthew Schrag. That was the genesis of this book.

"WHY YOU?"

I first spoke with Schrag on December 22, 2021. He took a polite, businesslike tone, a touch guarded. I learned later that he had shoehorned me in, despite trying to focus on the upcoming holidays and nesting with his wife, Sarah, then pregnant with their second child, and their eighteen-month-old daughter. Schrag, thirty-seven at the time, later called himself an "old dad" who needed to marshal his reserves of stamina. He'd been burning the candle at three ends—running his lab, seeing patients, and sleuthing for misconduct—since the summer.

Schrag often worked long hours, but there was never enough time. When Sarah and their little one went to sleep, Schrag later told me, he sprawled on the living room couch with his laptop or retreated to his "home office"—a corner of the basement at their modest house on a tiny ranch outside Nashville. He works at an antique writing desk. Navajo pottery fired with horse hair on the surface to make elaborate swirls—a token of Sarah's lifelong passion for her equine charges Velvet and Red Robin—tops tall, glass-doored shelves. Inside a case, "Leo"—the neuroanatomy skull that saw Schrag through med school—looks down inscrutably.

He pulled out *Archives of Neurology and Psychiatry*, a bound volume drawn from treatment of patients in asylums near London more than a century ago, ages before MRIs and PET scans began to dominate his field. "A lot of this volume is focused on trying to understand why people develop dementia—before Alzheimer had done his work. They were observing that the brain shrinks in various forms of dementia," Schrag said, pausing a beat. "We've come a long way."

My first question was, "Why you?" Why would an obscure junior professor at Vanderbilt blow the whistle on a rising drug company to the Food and Drug Administration (FDA) and the National Institutes of Health (NIH)?

"This is my scientific space," he replied. He wanted to play a role in curing Alzheimer's and had the medical and forensic chops to learn if the Cassava work might be a harmful distraction. "Our understanding of the neurobiology of this disease is growing. We're nearing a moment of discovery on Alzheimer's. But there's this potential for people to jump the line and compromise standards."

Schrag said that as a scientist who treats dementia patients, he found many technical images at the core of studies behind simufilam offensive. "There are massive and egregious red flags," he said. "Some changes to scientific images appear fairly crafty. It's hard not to view them as intentional." Most alarming to Schrag: A drug based on apparently tainted studies was already being taken by hundreds of human guinea pigs.

He also felt concerned that prestigious, high-profile collaborators of Hoau-Yan Wang and Lindsay Burns—such as Alzheimer's research heavyweight Jeffrey Cummings of the University of Nevada, and Steven Arnold of Harvard, both members of Cassava's paid advisory board—provided a patina of prestige for the company and simufilam. Arnold was an important player on six doubtful papers, including work behind "diabetes of the brain" that exerted influence well beyond the development of Cassava's drug. Elite collaborators can prompt editorial boards to wave through studies so far outside the mainstream that they should provoke acute skepticism.

Even if simufilam never came to market, suspicious work can pollute the scientific record indefinitely. Schrag said he had to act. He sent four complaints to NIH—against Wang, Cassava, Arnold, and a more general file about the brain-diabetes studies. He labeled them "RIO 1" through "RIO 4," after the NIH term "research integrity officer." Schrag told me that he did so as soon as the short sellers' lawyer filed the FDA petition. "I was led to believe that the Wall Street Journal was going to publish an exposé, and I had made up my mind that I needed to go to the NIH about this before it went to the media or anywhere else." The move fit Schrag's plan to operate above reproach, making sure the proper authorities heard it from him first.

He also sent the NIH some details of undisclosed, incestuous relationships between journal editors and Cassava-linked scientists. My ears perked up. I had for years been writing about such hidden conflicts and their often-pernicious effects on science. It was the start of my look at the self-serving role the scholarly press plays in responding to bogus or dubious studies.

"Dr. Wang was integrally involved in all of the works that we have complained about. But Dr. Arnold was the supervising investigator of a large number of trials, and was on the scientific advisory board for Cassava," Schrag said. "Quite a number of papers that were unaffiliated with Cassava but that involve Dr. Wang and Dr. Arnold appeared to have similar patterns of what we perceive as manipulations. And they have the potential to compromise very important fields of study. One of them, in the *Journal of Clinical Investigation*, has been cited 1,600 times. [The total would eventually rise to nearly 1,900.] It was accompanied by an editorial about its importance to the field." (When I later approached Arnold, he declined to comment.)

But Schrag soon had to confront the agonizingly slow approach and excruciating passivity federal authorities would show to CUNY. The university's investigation into Wang would go on for many months before reaching any conclusion. In the meantime, the papers were still cited as precedents for new studies and funding. And Cassava's clinical studies with human guinea pigs continued apace.

Just before the new year, Schrag sent me the four RIO documents and then gradually shared revisions and supplements as he found more examples and refined his earlier analyses. At that point, every document was confidential, every talk off the record. He was showing what he had, gauging my interest. He was selling me on his credibility. I was selling him on mine.

The material moved well beyond the FDA petition. It offered a powerful indictment of the research, and much more. Schrag's diagrams and notes suggested lax vetting of work largely funded out of the highly competitive federal grants. It supported the concern that some journals published papers without adequate review. I no longer wondered if there was a solid incremental tale to be told about Cassava. This looked deeper and more profound. I resolved to trade up—to write as comprehensive an investigation as the materials warranted.

On January 2, I briefed my editors, John Travis and Tim Appenzeller. They oversee the journalism side of *Science*, which operates independently of the scholarly part of the magazine—although Appenzeller, who leads news coverage, reports to Editor-in-Chief Holden Thorp. I was careful not to put Schrag's name into an email. I needed to protect his identity and planned to switch to encrypted messaging if I needed to reveal sensitive information in writing.

FLAT-BOTTOM SMILES

To no surprise, Matthew Schrag spent the day before our first meeting in the lab. He'd been running computer-imaging experiments to refine his work on the Cassava dossier after an extended examination of other studies on PubPeer, a website where technical gumshoes post deconstructed western blots, displaying telltale clip marks, halos, and shadows—signs that suggest copy-paste misconduct, such as the removal of a band from an image before publication, or insertion of another where it doesn't belong.

Schrag was looking to pull random examples of doctored blots in Alzheimer's research to test out a new detection technique he was tinkering with. He wanted to quantify just how similar the suspect blots he'd collected for his Cassava dossier were to one another. Wary of injecting "expectation bias" into the test, he'd sought out random examples first rather than try out his method of identification on images that he already thought were probably improper.

The first article on the results list, recently flagged by a pseudonymous critic, had appeared in the *Journal of Neuroscience*. The lead scientists on the paper were French researchers whose names were unfamiliar to Schrag. The experiment examined chemical transmissions in postmortem brain tissue to understand how acute brain injuries might be a risk factor for Alzheimer's disease. The topic was of growing interest in the field, and the findings provocative—a link to how brain trauma might promote amyloid-beta production. It raised his eyebrows for another reason. One of the coauthors, Charles Glabe, was a noted Alzheimer's researcher from the University of California at Irvine. His role had been relatively minor from what could be gleaned from the publication, but his name lent credibility. Sets of bands in two separate western blots presented in the paper looked strikingly similar, if not identical, yet were said to represent different experimental conditions. The likelihood of such twinned bands is remote. The images offered an ideal test case for his new technique.

The dark bands on white backgrounds looked like silhouettes of flat-bottom smiles. First Schrag matched the two sets for size and contrast, ensuring an apples-to-apples comparison. To compare every detail, he colored one a brilliant fluorescent red, and the other green. Using NIH-approved software, Schrag merged the colored bands, displaying precisely overlapping areas in bright yellow. Areas that didn't overlap would retain their red or green hue. To the naked eye, the merged bands looked 100 percent yellow. An identical match. Then to quantify his findings, Schrag calculated a correlation coefficient by tracking the similarity of every pixel—each tiny dot of the image. With thousands of such comparisons, he could calculate the strength of the overall relationship between the merged bands. Identical images—pixel-perfect—would show a correlation of 1.0. For genuinely different bands, a correlation above 0.7 or so would be rare. In this case, the bands showed a 0.98 correlation. Schrag's years of experience and the logic of the science told him that identical-twin bands virtually never occur by chance. In his typically understated way, he called the correlation "remarkably high."

That was December 21, one day before we first spoke. Schrag didn't mention the test during our conversation. We were just getting started, after all. He wasn't ready to share the first hints of the scandal of a lifetime.

As Schrag pored through the PubPeer list, he noticed that some of the same authors came up a few times. He tugged on that string, searching for the first and last authors on a couple of the papers. The first author usually does most of the writing, while the senior scientist—often a mentor or principal investigator for the experiment—normally takes the last slot. A throughline—the single name that appeared on every paper—floated to the surface. Schrag hadn't heard of him among the multitudes of Alzheimer's researchers. But then he noticed that the scientist was lead author on one of the most cited papers in many years. This was an ascending neuroscience talent: Sylvain Lesné at the University of Minnesota.

"CHEATERS CHEAT, RIGHT?"

During the five months he had spent refining his Cassava dossiers, Schrag's thoughts returned over and over to a central worry that he gradually realized he'd need to face: Could this be more than a single set of bad papers, a lone bad actor, or a wayward lab? Could there be many more lapses and fakes in Alzheimer's research that few in the field wanted to acknowledge, let alone confront? If so, important research might be based on wobbly foundations. Just as bad, research might be detoured into costly dead ends.

"Everybody thinks that scientific integrity issues are very, very rare. I can't say I've ever been asked to review a paper where I went into it saying, 'I don't trust these guys. They're gonna cheat on me,'" Schrag said, conceding that the apparent misconduct had left him unnerved. "I don't think that's how people think about scientists," he added, sounding more hopeful than convinced. For the first time, Schrag found himself questioning a bedrock assumption about his chosen profession. He knew that the alternative—a breakdown of trust—could taint an entire research direction. Did the Lesné articles rise to that alarming level, possibly more alarming than Wang's seemingly blatant doctoring? It was too soon to tell.

The detection of phony images is part art, part science, and not always clear-cut. But even when some doubtful western blot or micrograph doesn't quite meet the threshold that demands public exposure, prudent scientists would steer around dubious work to avoid investing efforts in the wrong places. If they knew about it.

"Knowing where the land mines are can keep you out of trouble," Schrag said. He couldn't stop thinking that Alzheimer's research needed one of their own to turn the microscope around, to get a clear focus on what corrupt scientists might be up to. *Bring it on*, he thought. As he said to me during our very first conversation, he wanted to protect "my scientific space."

It also became clear that, almost like an investigative reporter, Schrag seemed to find thrills in the hunt; a chance to right a disturbing wrong—even if the implications for the field disturbed him.

"Cheaters cheat, right?" he said during our next conversation. "So, when I pulled up Lesné's name on PubPeer and three or four other papers came up, I started to wonder. If somebody might be cheating three or four times, there's likely to be a ton of stuff here for me to work with." As Schrag began to check other Lesné writings that hadn't been flagged on PubPeer, land mines exploded everywhere. "Within a day or two, I found out that ton of questionable stuff [had appeared] in *Brain* and *PNAS* and *Nature*," among the world's leading journals.

Schrag had stumbled upon the seminal *Nature* paper in which Lesné and his mentor Karen Ashe, a top neuroscientist, unveiled their star protein, amyloid-beta star 56 (Aβ*56). Since it appeared in 2006, that study had been cited thousands of times by other scholars, some of them the top names in the field, including Harvard's Dennis Selkoe, a chief progenitor of the amyloid hypothesis; his UK counterpart John Hardy; University College London luminary Bart de Strooper; and University of Zürich's Adriano Aguzzi.

Lesné, first author of that study, Ashe, and their colleagues seemed to prove that when Aβ*56 was injected into rats it caused something like Alzheimer's dementia. The study's emergence came at a moment of discouragement—even despair—for the amyloid hypothesis and placed it back at the center of the patients' and the pharmaceutical industry's focus. The *Nature* paper offered strong support for a new organizing principle: If old, failed drugs targeted sticky amyloid-protein plaques, new ones should try to attack, as much as possible, the elusive oligomers floating in the cerebrospinal fluid—even if removing plaques remained a concurrent goal. Drug developers saw new opportunities, and federal funders soon lavished vast sums on oligomer research.

Lesné soared in the aftermath, becoming an assistant professor at UMN with his own NIH-funded lab in 2009. Aβ*56 remained a primary research focus. And in May 2022, Lesné received a coveted R01 grant from the agency, securing him up to five years of support. (The NIH program officer for the grant, Austin Yang, coauthored the 2006 *Nature* paper. When I reached out to Yang later, he declined to comment.)

If Schrag's doubts were correct, Lesné's findings were an elaborate mirage.

Schrag quickly identified twelve other papers that directly concerned or described Aβ*56 that appeared to have been doctored. Lesné's fingerprints were all over them. Ashe had coauthored five. (He also found other deeply suspect Lesné papers, written without Ashe, on related or different issues.)

Schrag had reached a crossroads. If he was right, he would have to cast serious doubt on a key advance in his field. Sham experimental results had been treated as established fact with enormous influence. If he exposed the case, Schrag realized, fresh doubts about the amyloid hypothesis would surely burst into view. His findings could set back—or even provide ammunition to derail—the dominant view of how to cure one of the most terrifying diseases of our time.

"It became clear to me very quickly that not only was this going to be a case for me to practice this technique on and make sure it was working," Schrag told me months later. "I was going to have to tell the NIH that this was an issue. The journals were just too big. The papers, the concepts were too big."

"YOU CAN'T CHEAT TO CURE A DISEASE"

Schrag couldn't shake the feeling he first experienced at the beginning of the Cassava investigation. He remembered reeling at the idea that a billion-dollar company might be testing a drug based on faked data. Even if the drug failed—as seemed almost certain to him—it could needlessly endanger or exploit patients. The Lesné case was different. Image by image, he had opened a window into seeming misconduct that could dwarf Cassava and wreak havoc, not just in the rarefied warrens of bioscience labs, but the entire world of Alzheimer's research and treatment.

If the work was false, it would cast doubt on decades of research and raise questions about billions of dollars reserved for or already spent on doomed therapeutic strategies.

Schrag treaded carefully as he composed a dossier on his findings on Lesné, titled "RIO 5." Like Wang and Burns, the French scientist with magic hands and his illustrious mentor had attracted respected collaborators who almost certainly assumed that images in complex, multifaceted experiments had been constructed properly. Glabe appeared again in the *Nature* paper. "It's such a collaborative business," Schrag said. "A lot of people can get pulled into things, you know. They do one little piece and they're responsible for their zone," he said.

In early January, his mind racing with scenarios about how his findings would play out, Schrag sent me a first pass at the new dossier. It was by the book, like all his other work. No accusations of "fraud," but page after page of clear, apparently damning evidence that images had been tampered with. As with some of the Cassava papers, he had trouble seeing how the whole thing might have been an accident or the result of careless mouse clicks in the editing process. Some of the changes seemed elaborate and calculated.

Schrag was ready to talk it over, and finally, on February 1 we had our first substantive discussion about the Lesné materials.

"The quality of the images is quite high," he explained to me, reducing the possibility of innocent glitches as explanation for the clear pattern of fabrication throughout Lesné's work. "This is what the whole story is about," Schrag added, his voice rising as he pointed out a figure in the *Nature* paper. "Everything else is downstream of this image."

"If the images are doctored, does it mean that the experiments have to be false?" I asked. Could readers be confident in any part of the findings? Who could know what the rats had been injected with? And the second half of the experiment—the way the rats forgot how to navigate a maze—therefore couldn't be relied on either.

"You can't interpret the results," Schrag agreed.

As we spoke and our words teased out the *Nature* study's implications, Schrag and I lapsed into a moment of stunned silence. If the Lesné/Ashe paper was false, it could place doubts on not just one of the most influential Alzheimer's studies in decades, but a sizeable body of subsequent work that relied on the article's conclusions as a sound footing.

"Has a lot of the stream of Alzheimer's research been corrupted by people who are using possibly disingenuous or fraudulent methods?" I asked.

"I think so," Schrag replied. A more tentative quality had crept into his voice. "I don't know how widespread this is. But I'm startled by how easy it is to find."

That was the moment everything changed for me. This was not just about Cassava, or even the University of Minnesota lab that produced these faulty papers. The entire field of Alzheimer's seemed to need a close look.

"Multiple structures meant to protect the research record look like they broke down. Would you agree?" I said to Schrag.

"I would have dismissed that not very long ago. I would have said: 'This is rare,'" Schrag replied. "I still think it's rare. But if false information is inserted into key nodes in our body of scientific knowledge it can warp our understanding. I don't know how much fraud the field can tolerate before it really creates a murky research environment."

In the long run, Schrag said he had no doubt that his chosen field of study and care would find a way past misconduct, obscure or flagrant. "You can cheat to get a paper. You can cheat to get a degree. You can cheat to get a grant. You can't cheat to cure a disease," he told me. "Biology doesn't care."

Schrag had done honorable, yeoman's work to make things better, but was his overall optimism misplaced? Scientific progress might be inexo-rable. But it can be derailed for years or decades—at a horrific price in missed opportunity, wasted resources, and human suffering—when the scientific enterprise puts too much faith in often-feeble, glacially slow sys-tems of "self-correction."

In that moment on February 1, 2022, Schrag seemed to cross into a new world. He was going to have to stop relying on institutions to correct the record. He would assume personal responsibility to expose corrupt practices that divert the desperate race to cure Alzheimer's.

Chapter 11

Trust but Verify

Nashville

2022

"I've got a lot of advisors.
I haven't found a single one who thinks this is a good idea."
—MATTHEW SCHRAG

Matthew Schrag knew he had to alert the scientific community and the world about the Sylvain Lesné affair. He thought I might help him do that, but sensibly proceeded cautiously. In December 2021 we had no history together. He wasn't ready to take the leap of faith that *Science* and I would provide the power, reach, and credibility needed to rise above the din of other news without unduly jeopardizing his career—or worse.

"At the moment, I don't want to be a source on the record," Schrag said. "I'm happy to comment on what's publicly available and provide some insights."

I didn't immediately say so, but I knew as a journalist I could not put his materials into the public domain or reference those he placed on Pub-Peer, then quote him commenting on his own work, without naming him as the source. "Let's take it a step at a time," I said.

I warned him that a complex tale like this one, raising questions of ethical lapses involving many millions of dollars and years of research—a story that could destroy careers—had to proceed briskly but with methodical care. "To justify the time and get the full support of my editors, I'm asking that you not also have this conversation with, say, the *Wall Street Journal* or the *Washington Post,*" I said.

"Okay," he replied tersely, "so long as this is progressing."

I asked Schrag to share anything and everything he had, including deconstructed scientific images, emails with regulators and scholarly journals, and papers that helped explain how doctored images might have skewed scientific thinking. I needed to understand his analysis deeply. He began to feed me a stream of dense materials confidentially, but with the understanding that once he finalized his documents I could use them for a story.

We were feeling each other out. He seemed to want to see if I could catch on quickly and would make the story a priority. I needed to verify that his big claims about two separate lines of influential research—from Cassava, and Lesné and Karen Ashe—were credible, first to me and my editors, then to world-class experts.

I knew from the start that a dry recounting of possible scientific error or even fraud could fall flat. "I'm more and more convinced that it's a bigger story about the credibility of Alzheimer's research," I told him. "You're the guy who has turned over those rocks. I need to place readers inside the intense process of discovery that might raise scientific havoc," I told Schrag. "To jolt people awake, I want to show it through your eyes. That's how to have the kind of impact we both want. I'm asking you to think carefully about it."

"I'm really reluctant to be named," he said. "I see a massive downside."

"You are wise to be cautious," I replied. "The history of whistleblowing is littered with . . ."

Schrag cut me off with one word:

"Corpses."

"TWO COURSES OF ACTION"

Whistleblowers actually have been murdered—although very rarely. More have seen their careers derailed, even when the claims proved true.

In the 1990s, Nancy Olivieri, a hematologist at the University of Toronto, conducted a clinical trial of an experimental drug to treat the life-shortening blood disorder thalassemia. After uncovering that over time the treatment lost its benefits, Olivieri violated her confidentiality pledge and published the result—becoming a muse for John le Carré's novel about the perils of calling out drug-company greed, *The Constant Gardener*. As University of Minnesota medical ethicist Carl Elliott recounts in his landmark book on whistleblowers, *The Occasional Human Sacrifice*, Olivieri "was not only fired from her administrative position but forced to endure years of harassment, threats, smears, litigation, and professional marginalization."

Or John Pesando, who leaked the story of a scandal at Seattle's Fred Hutchinson Cancer Research Center, in which researchers used experimental bone marrow transplants instead of proven treatments known to sustain life in many patients suffering from leukemia or lymphoma. Pesando tried for years to get officials to listen to his concerns. By the time the *Seattle Times* exposed the case with his help, nearly all trial volunteers had died. As Elliott wrote, "It's hard to put a hopeful spin on the story of John Pesando's struggle . . . His is a bleak, demoralizing story of defeat."

The *Times* reporting and subsequent litigation changed nothing, Elliott added. "It was astounding that nobody gave a damn," Pesando told him. "That was probably one of the most shocking things, that nobody really gave a shit. And I wasn't prepared for that."

Elliott would find Schrag's instinct to exercise caution sensible. "Some people manage to blow the whistle without being fired, demoted, disciplined, or sued," Elliott noted. "Yet many of those same people still emerge from the experience deeply scarred. Their view of the world has been irrevocably altered, like a soldier returning from a combat zone. Often their scars remain unhealed for years, even if they succeed in their mission and find public vindication."

Schrag's eyes were open. But I had to be sure he knew my approach to high-stakes stories. "I can't predict your future. But I guarantee that every word I write will be checked, rechecked, and triple-checked. Errors won't haunt you," I said. "And I'll write a story as tough as the facts warrant. I'm going to send you the article I just published." It was my piece on a Canadian botanist who had faked and blustered his way to fame and fortune. It challenged several private companies the scientist founded or worked for. I added: "We didn't pull any punches, because I made sure that everything was true, and proved it to my editors and our lawyers."

Later that day, I told my editors, Tim Appenzeller and John Travis, that I was making progress. They knew Schrag's identity—the only people I had shared it with—but as a precaution I still didn't mention it via email. I sent them a snippet from my haunting interview with Schrag:

Me: Has a lot of the stream of Alzheimer's research been polluted by people who are using disingenuous or fraudulent methods?

Whistleblower: I think so. I don't know how widespread this is. But I'm startled by how easy it is [to fake images and find fakes] . . . I don't know how much [possible] fraud the field can tolerate before it really creates a murky research environment.

By early March in 2022, more than six months after the citizen petition had been filed to the Food and Drug Administration (FDA), it dawned on Schrag that for all of his scientific sophistication, he had a lot to learn about twenty-first-century capitalism. "Initially, I really expected Cassava to collapse, because the apparent problems were so crystal clear that I didn't think any investor would touch them," he said. "I've been a little surprised." Despite its down-trending share price, the company held plenty of cash and die-hard, meme-stock investing SAVAges were betting that Cassava would survive the scandal in one piece.

Schrag was also becoming unsettled by sluggish, at best, reviews of his findings sent to dozens of scholarly journals. Just one suspect Hoau-Yan Wang paper had been retracted by then. Many other editors had been sitting for months on what Schrag saw as a mountain of convincing evidence.

And he worried that some of the editors might purposely or accidentally out him publicly. Schrag hadn't initially noticed that two powerful
editors he contacted—Rexford Ahima of Johns Hopkins University, then
chief editor of the *Journal of Clinical Investigation*; and Bruno Vellas of
Toulouse University Hospital in France, then cochief of the *Journal of
Prevention of Alzheimer's Disease*—had coauthored papers with Wang in
other journals.

"Two courses of action make sense to me," Schrag said. "One is to stay
as anonymous as I can, as disconnected as I can. Or to own it."

Schrag worried that if he went public he would alienate powerful people in his field, risking support that a junior professor needs for academic
success or survival. Anyone who distrusts a whistleblower or has something to hide could hold him at arm's length. He had grant proposals in
the pipeline. Backroom lobbying by new enemies might scuttle those. The
dilemma weighed heavily. Schrag also continued to fear that he could tar-
nish the reputations of scientists whose chief offense had been that they
were too trusting—duped by apparent fabricators.

"There are people in this process who are lined up to become collateral damage," he said. "I could help them get ahead of this and limit some
of that damage by talking to them."

Schrag meant collaborators on the Wang, Burns, and Lesné papers.
People like David Bennett. That globally known neurologist heads an
Alzheimer's institute at Rush University and leads the Religious Orders
Study. More than 1,100 priests, nuns, and other clergy members participated in medical and psychological testing for years and agreed to donate
their brains after death. As primary gatekeeper for a large brain bank,
Bennett provides tissue to qualified scientists. By contract, he becomes a
coauthor of many studies using the tissue—comprising a big share of his
nearly 1,900 scholarly papers.

In that way, Bennett coauthored six questioned Wang papers—
including the one retracted a month earlier, and five others with Lesné.
Bennett and a close colleague at Rush were the only scientists who over-
lapped on papers with both sets of problematic researchers. Although he

wouldn't have had a hand in creating dubious images, in principle Bennett would have scrutinized and approved each image before publication. Perhaps he waved them through, trusting collaborators to operate in good faith. (When I later approached him, Bennett declined to comment, deferring to official reviews by Rush or others.)

All researchers should exercise due diligence when their names go on papers. But Schrag especially worried about harming credulous junior scientists who might have been in the wrong place at the wrong time. Maybe they squelched their own doubts, assuming their bosses knew better. As for outing senior scientists on tainted studies—they could become powerful enemies. Should he offer them advance warning of unwelcome news, or withhold it? It wasn't obvious which path created a bigger personal risk.

Schrag also fretted that by issuing such courtesy warnings, he might blow up my story. The more people he talked to, the more likely misconduct concerns could leak into the public domain drop by drop and dissipate without the authoritative context and reach a large story in *Science* could bring. For now, Schrag said, he'd hold off and ponder the matter.

DIGGING OUT THE GEIGER COUNTERS

At the start, Schrag realized that his findings cried out for better regulatory oversight. So he considered his reports to the National Institutes of Health (NIH), primary funder of much of the suspect work, as his first, most vital, and maybe only real duty. "[The Lesné] dossier is a fraction of the anomalies easily visible on review of the publicly accessible data," he wrote to the agency integrity officer in January 2022. That group of studies, he added, "not only represents a substantial investment in [NIH] research support, but has been cited . . . thousands of times and thus has the potential to mislead an entire field of research."

Schrag admitted frustration about NIH follow-up. By policy, the agency off-loaded examination of his complaints to another federal agency, the Office of Research Integrity, which passed the buck to City

University of New York and the University of Minnesota—Wang's and Lesné's employers, respectively. That standard process is freighted with weaknesses. Among them, universities naturally fear reputational damage if their internal investigations confirm wrongdoing.

Meanwhile, Schrag waited impatiently about whether NIH would fund his own proposals. He needed that money to build on his own work. And because the apparently altered images appeared in scores of articles across dozens of scholarly journals, going public could embarrass many of the most influential and powerful editors in his field. Those gatekeepers might resent him calling out breakdowns in their quality control, or tagging their conflicts of interest. They could quietly try to handicap his career. If editors or the NIH turned against him for his work to out misconduct, Schrag feared being placed on an informal blacklist.

Schrag also worried about personal attacks—or being doxed—by Cassava defenders as had happened to some of the company's detractors. His pregnant wife, Sarah, already had understandable doubts about her husband's research-integrity side gig that seemed to be growing into a second career.

As a nontenured faculty member, he also feared angering his risk-averse employer. Like most academic institutions, Vanderbilt wanted to avoid controversy. Even his close colleagues there wouldn't talk to me or would only do so off the record. Schrag wasn't quite radioactive. But people had dug out their Geiger counters just in case.

Vanderbilt already faced a tense moment. As Schrag considered going public, the university was weathering a medical breakdown and public relations debacle. That March, a nurse at the university's medical center was tried for negligent homicide. An elderly woman in her care died after being given the wrong medicine. The case made national news as nursing organizations worried that it would criminalize medical mistakes. During the trial, federal authorities accused Vanderbilt of failing to properly report the fatal misstep. The nurse was convicted and sentenced to probation.

"I have spoken with people who outrank me by a very, very long way. There were lots of uncomfortable conversations about how this was going to be handled," Schrag said. To their credit, higher-ups never asked him to abandon the research-integrity work. But they asked Schrag to disassociate Vanderbilt from views he shared with reporters. (Vanderbilt asked him if I would let them review his quotes before publication, "to assess the impact on the medical center." I told him that would never happen.) And they advised him to find a lawyer.

The lawyers he consulted advised him to avoid reporters. "They said, 'You're going to be on the record for a long, long time. To keep everything straight and boring is very hard. You're gonna say something clever and wish you hadn't.'"

Schrag kept a sober tone, but otherwise rejected that counsel. "I think so long as I'm anonymous, I'm reasonably safe. Is that foolish?" he asked me. It wasn't a rhetorical question. He was not naïve, but this was all new to him. He didn't exactly ask me for advice, and I didn't exactly offer any. But I had wrestled with such questions from whistleblowers often.

It was time to have a more formal talk about where our interests converged and might diverge, for ethical and practical reasons. I needed to sleep at night. I also needed him to be fully on board, to trust me, so I could write a story that might force the world to take notice.

"I've always seen you as taking two major risks," I said. "One is your job. The second is an expensive harassment lawsuit." We both knew that there was at least a small chance he could lose his little ranch in all this. He understood that a lawsuit, no matter how frivolous, might result in bankruptcy-inducing legal fees and *Science* could never backstop him legally; that would be a conflict of interest. I suggested that he look at pro bono attorneys who would be interested in a fairly high-profile client—a path other sources of mine had explored.

Within two or three weeks, I'd have a reading on what independent Alzheimer's experts and forensic image analysts are going to say, I told him. It was crucial due diligence. I had to ensure that Schrag knew what he was talking about—that his dossiers were credible, well constructed, and as important as they seemed.

"I'm going to have a conversation with my editors," I said. "We're gonna say, 'How do we build a story that grabs readers from the start and holds them to the end? What's the narrative thread?' And it will be obvious: Tell it through your personal journey of discovery. But I can't center a whole story like this around an anonymous person. It would lack strength and authenticity. So, you would be named. I know you haven't agreed to anything. I know you're thinking about it. I'm just keepin' it real here.

"If you decide to remain anonymous, I won't judge you. I'm not totally sure what I'd do in your position," I added. "But it's worth considering how much impact the story could have. And I think we share the goal to reach for something important."

"Well, I've got a lot of advisors," Schrag replied. "I haven't found a single one who thinks this is a good idea."

VETTING THE FINDINGS

A few days later, I heard back from two leading forensic image analysts with whom I shared Schrag's complete Cassava and Lesné dossiers. Elisabeth Bik reached me first over email. A well-known advocate for scientific integrity, Bik had been profiled often in leading media, including *Science*:

> *"Combined, these issues paint a picture of two independent research groups working in very similar fields that both appeared to have composed figures by piecing together parts of photos from different experiments . . . These papers raise the concern that the obtained experimental results might not have been the desired results, and that data might have been changed to better fit a hypothesis."*

In short: authoritative confirmation.

Soon after, I heard from Jana Christopher, another expert. She mostly agreed with Schrag and judged his body of work credible and compelling. Christopher also identified several other ostensibly cloned sections of images that Schrag missed in his analysis—identical backgrounds in blots and micrographs that seemed impossible as a chance occurrence.

I turned my reporting to other well-known experts in Alzheimer's disease who could scientifically validate Schrag's findings, beginning with a list of forty-five experts culled to exclude close collaborators of scientists whose work had been challenged. Loyalty could undermine credibility, and perhaps, even worse, make them more likely to disclose Schrag's dossiers to the scientists at the core of his findings before I was ready to ask the right questions.

Views about amyloid also seemed crucial. A mix of boosters and skeptics could indemnify me against accusations that I cherry-picked critics prone to see problems. This was "a big ask." The experts would need to review about 175 pages of image analyses and the full papers those images had appeared in. And I needed people who would go on the record about possible misconduct that implicated or entangled prestigious scientists such as Ashe, whom they might know professionally. They would need to weigh in on whether influential studies might have been based on fraud— a risky stance.

(I'd learned to expect a lot of refusals. Years earlier I wrote a series about technical defects on the newly built San Francisco–Oakland Bay Bridge. I soon learned that Caltrans, the state agency responsible for the multibillion-dollar structure, was the second-largest source of construction funding in the country. Experts fell into two basic categories: Caltrans contractors, and wannabe Caltrans contractors. For one story, I had to contact one hundred top US and European engineers to find a handful who would speak on the record.)

Over two months I reached out to a dozen experts. Some said they were too busy (or too fainthearted, it seemed) to help. But anyone who examined the package I sent found the Cassava case alarming. A leading independent image analyst and several top Alzheimer's researchers— including George Perry, editor of the *Journal of Alzheimer's Disease*; and Donna Wilcock, then an Alzheimer's expert at the University of Kentucky who would later become editor of *Alzheimer's & Dementia*—

reviewed most of Schrag's findings at *Science*'s request. They concurred with his overall conclusions, which cast doubt on hundreds of images, including more than seventy in Lesné's papers.

Some images showed "shockingly blatant" signs of tampering, said Wilcock. Stanford University neuroscientist Thomas Südhof, the Nobel laureate, told me: "The immediate, obvious damage is wasted NIH funding and wasted thinking in the field because people are using these results as a starting point for their own experiments."

I told Schrag that I was going to have on-record comments from illustrious researchers. He was encouraged, but clarified: "Candidly, I'm struggling. It's not my nature to stay anonymous. I really want to do this in an aboveboard way. But I also feel like the data should speak for itself. It's so easy for people to get hung up on what's the motivation of the people raising the concern. What did they have to gain? Who are they and why are they doing this?" Schrag paused a beat. "I don't want you to be shocked if I can't do what I know you want."

To lighten the mood, I offered a lame joke: "If you do go public, and this neuroscience-university-professor thing doesn't work out, you could always fall back on being a forensic image analyst." He laughed. "I'll be a doctor in a nice little country hospital and retire to a house on a lake," Schrag said, only half joking. "I'll be fine."

Then he took a leap: "I'll put my name on the Lesné piece in a heartbeat." It was the safer part of the story, involving no deep-pocketed, potentially litigious company.

I felt elated. We were halfway there. But the narrative, the story of discovery, was integral to his having found the Lesné materials. Without Cassava that narrative fell apart. And as we talked it through, Schrag slowly concluded what I suspected—hoped—he would from the beginning: Going fully public was the only way to force the reckoning that his field must face.

"It's okay. It's okay to say, 'We did this,' and tell the story. It's okay," he repeated to himself, like a mantra, as he steadied his nerves. "I want to solve this disease. I've got to be willing to take the next step. These studies are barriers to the field getting to where it needs to go, to have a better shot at solving Alzheimer's. Once you get a certain depth, you can't let it go. You've got to finish the job."

For the sake of his overarching life goal, he added simply: "So I'll do it."

GROUND TRUTH

Soon after, I flew to Nashville to try to understand Schrag better as a person and a scientist, and to see each other face-to-face after dozens of calls and video conferences. The tiny medical "museum" in his cramped office, the evident mutual respect with his lab colleagues, his comfort with the science and the technique of deconstructing western blots—all nourished my confidence that Schrag was for real. It was time to move to the endgame.

"The story will hit hard," I told him, previewing my approach to the web of implicated researchers to be interviewed next. "But we'll let the readers draw their own conclusions."

For Ashe and Lesné, it was sure to be a moment of personal devastation and possible professional catastrophe. But first, I had to check with one more source. An amyloid true believer with so much prestige, brilliance, and influence in the field that some researchers privately spoke of him as the godfather of the "amyloid mafia."

Chapter 12

The "Amyloid Mafia"

Cambridge, Massachusetts; San Francisco; Nashville

1982–2022

"He recalled something that [Thomas] Kuhn had written
about [Joseph] Priestley—that a scientist who continued to resist after
his whole profession had been converted to a new paradigm might be perfectly
logical and reasonable, but had ipso facto ceased to be a scientist."

—KIM STANLEY ROBINSON, *GREEN MARS*, 1993

"I'm on the right side of history."

—DENNIS SELKOE, 2022

In November 2022, Dennis Selkoe, a Harvard professor of neurologic diseases and among the most celebrated and prolific Alzheimer's researchers, chastised me over lunch.

I had just broken a story in *Science* about the horrific death of a volunteer in a trial of lecanemab, another new anti-amyloid drug to treat Alzheimer's. The woman suffered a massive cerebral hemorrhage. A pathologist said it was like "her brain exploded."

Leaning over a plate of pasta and sipping a Pepsi during lunch at an upscale San Francisco hotel, Selkoe pressed me to concede that some in the media are far too pessimistic about such drugs. We owed greater deference, he said, to doctors "who have taken care of hundreds of patients with Alzheimer's and have been through this long journey."

Selkoe was shrewd. I was skeptical about lecanemab, which minutely slows cognitive decline among some patients with mild Alzheimer's symptoms, costs tens of thousands of dollars per patient annually, and poses deadly risks. And the drug's benefit, although a minute improvement on its troubled predecessor, Aduhelm, likewise seemed so subtle as to be imperceptible to doctors, patients, and caregivers. But Selkoe must have surmised that I didn't want to seem like a cynic or iconoclast to a deeply committed doctor and world-famous scientist like himself. He implied that only misguided contrarians could dispute that lecanemab established the amyloid hypothesis as fact, and that such drugs *would* illuminate the path to solve the Alzheimer's puzzle.

That notion of consensus was absurd, as was his description of the media coverage. As a rule, news reports tilt to fawning approval of any treatment that offers a glimmer of hope, however dim. But Selkoe was persuasive; known as much for his verbal acumen as his prodigious scientific output. He was adamant, telling me he had waited decades for the arrival of this, the first "objective evidence" (his words) that reducing amyloid in the human brain produces better cognitive outcomes. "I'm on the right side of history," he said. His skill as a talker helps explain why the field often has followed his lead. "I am a good speaker. I make a good point," he would tell me another time, unabashedly.

Lecanemab had received a first-of-its-kind accepted description as "disease modifying" from credible voices in neuroscience—slowing cognitive decline by flushing many amyloids, the reputed cause of Alzheimer's, from the brain.

"Success has many fathers," he told me later, noting a groundbreaking 1992 paper by neuroscientists John Hardy and Gerald Higgins—"the most influential paper in contemporary research into Alzheimer's disease," according to medical ethicist Timothy Daly—had been built on the backs of two others, his own and another by UC-San Diego pathologist George Glenner.

If we didn't have patience with intermediary steps, he seemed to argue, we'd lose a great deal of progress overall. I wondered if sluggish intermediary "progress" of the amyloid hypothesis had been crowding out healthy scientific competition.

Selkoe's pasta grew cold as he provided technical support for his views in a filibuster suffused with charm, and the occasional (and contradictory to his overall intent) soft flattery. "I always said you were absolutely doing the right thing, and you have done it with other articles," he told me, although a few months earlier he'd publicly attacked one of my Alzheimer's investigations. "I think you're on the right track."

The scientific conference that had brought us both to San Francisco to have this lunch would turn out to be a lecanemab lovefest—a victory lap for Selkoe and his allies. The antibody drug was heralded as a breakthrough despite its meager benefits and some ghastly fatalities and brain injuries among trial volunteers.

In short, the silver-haired, slim, and fit Selkoe—armored with his trademark quarter-zip, mock-neck sweater, calm vigor, and gravelly voice that only slightly betrayed his seventy-nine years—had won the day.

Not entirely reductive in his thinking, during our discussions the following year Selkoe would at least portray an openness to the idea that the amyloid hypothesis couldn't *fully* explain Alzheimer's disease. Viral infections might "contribute in some way" to the cascade of pathology that amyloid proteins cause, he would admit.

Nonetheless, his central role in strong-arming the field to favor a focus on amyloids above all else—"the scientific equivalent of the Ptolemaic model of the Solar System," the ancient idea that the Sun and planets rotate around Earth, said one scientist I spoke with—was beyond debate. He was certainly a key member of what some have described as a "cabal" or "mafia" whose influence, prestige, networking, and prolific writings work to enforce a singular scientific and commercial vision.

Others went so far as to suggest a moniker even more likely to rankle seemingly committed rationalists: A "Church of the Holy Amyloid," with Selkoe among its high priests.

In his book about the pioneers of CRISPR—a gene-editing technique that has revolutionized genetic research—Walter Isaacson described the constant dialectic of competition and cooperation that leads to world-changing breakthroughs. But what happens when one big idea impedes progress on others for decades? Farmers rotate crops to enrich the soil.

Skeptics argue that the amyloid mafia fostered the equivalent of a scientific monoculture that depleted the research landscape around it.

ASCENDING PATH

Selkoe and I grew up in neighboring Illinois towns—Selkoe in Glencoe, a small northern suburb along the shore of Lake Michigan and an affluent breeding ground for hard-driven professionals and business executives. I hail from the next town north, giving me an inkling of how he became who he is.

Selkoe's father, a successful salesman of towels and linens to department stores, was among the first owners of a car phone—an early adopter ethos that the son would embrace. Selkoe's maternal grandmother was a concert pianist who performed for Tsar Nicholas before he was toppled in 1917 during the Russian Revolution. His mother, also a musician, accompanied Selkoe's chorus at New Trier, among the nation's top public high schools. He later sang with Columbia University's Glee Club. Selkoe lacked the talent or interest to live up to that musical pedigree, he said. But performative training endowed his influence in new realms.

Even as a kid, Selkoe wanted to be a doctor. "It wasn't really about the science then. It was just the view of what physicians did and that they were also helping people who were suffering greatly," he said. His first exposure to science came in biology class as a high school sophomore, when he dissected a fetal pig. "My lab partner wasn't terribly fond of it. I thought it was really cool."

A top student, Selkoe graduated from Columbia University in 1965 and attended the University of Virginia School of Medicine. He trained in neurology at Boston Children's Hospital and Brigham and Women's Hospital. By 1978, he was a Harvard professor with his own lab.

These days, Selkoe works from the tenth floor of an ultramodern lab building where he accepted my request to visit him on a sparkling March day in 2023. His majestic corner office offered sweeping views of Boston's Mission Hill area and nearby Harvard research buildings. Shelves held trophies of fame and accomplishment—photos of award ceremonies and magazine covers. The environment exudes success and optimism, reinforced by a stream of students and well-wishers greeting the great man with personal news or questions.

Selkoe shares a floor in the Ann Romney Center for Neurologic Diseases—named for the spouse of Utah Senator Mitt Romney, former governor of Massachusetts. A person who lives with multiple sclerosis, her donations helped start the center, which Selkoe cofounded and directs with neurologist Howard Weiner. It boasts more than three hundred researchers in twenty-five labs. A bobblehead of Selkoe and Weiner honoring forty years of partnership occupies a prominent spot on his shelf.

Selkoe generously introduced me to Weiner as "my friend." Had I charmed him a little, or was it tactical, more soft flattery? I couldn't tell.

As we ate sandwiches in his office, Selkoe removed a framed photo from a place of honor above his desk. It appeared in the 1991 paper that laid out his vision of the amyloid hypothesis. I took in the striking image. It showed a greatly enlarged slice of brain from a deceased man who had suffered from dementia. At the center, a halo of damaged nerve tissue surrounds a bright orange supernova consisting of amyloid plaques. The jagged blob floats amid altered nerve cells that resemble burned-out stars in a dying microscopic galaxy.

SCIENTIFIC HEGEMONY

The amyloid mafia is not a real organization, of course. But it aptly characterizes power figures who some say steer grants and career opportunities away from those who suggest alternatives. "It became gradually an infallible belief system," said Zaven Khachaturian, former director of Alzheimer's research at the National Institute on Aging (NIA), part of the National Institutes of Health (NIH). "Everybody felt obligated to pay homage to the idea without questioning. And that's not very healthy for science when scientists . . . accept an idea as infallible."

That influence seemed apparent in the years that followed the famous 2006 experiment by Sylvain Lesné and Karen Ashe that tied cognitive decline to that amyloid-beta protein dubbed Aβ*56. A surge of research about that class of soluble protein—"toxic oligomers"—became central to the evolving amyloid hypothesis. Selkoe often cited the 2006 *Nature* study and saw his own oligomer ideas ascend.

Oligomer funding from NIH skyrocketed from near zero in 2006 to more than $333 million in 2021 alone. Projects that mentioned amyloid proteins hit about $1.5 billion that year out of a total Alzheimer's budget of about $3 billion. Since 2002, the majority of clinical trials beyond small phase 1 projects have focused on how to fix the amyloid problem—including most major drug studies that can cost hundreds of millions of dollars. Such spending exasperates skeptics who view it as a sign that other ideas have been crowded out to the detriment of patients.

"You can't look at brain tissue and believe beta amyloid has nothing to do with it. It's absolutely everywhere. But we've got lots and lots of patients who have tons of amyloid and tangles with normal cognition," said Matthew Schrag. "Biology is trying to tell you that there's clearly more to the story. A lot of things that make perfectly good sense are perfectly wrong. I'm not saying that happened with the amyloid hypothesis. But there is receptivity to certain amyloid findings and some hostility to other things reflected in the scientific literature."

With clinical trials failing to show more than scant benefits, he added, "You've got to be willing to ask, 'Does the hypothesis need to be reconsidered, even if it's a good hypothesis?'"

Selkoe disputed the apparent dominance of the amyloid hypothesis. He cited a 2022 review of Alzheimer's clinical trials, authored by Cassava advisor Jeffrey Cummings and colleagues, showing that the research community explores a host of other ideas. His annual list of trials shows each treatment's "mechanism of action"—how it attacks the disease. Cummings concluded that amyloid-targeted therapies comprise only about a fifth of trials.

A closer look shows cracks in that analysis: Many trials that Cummings and colleagues said target inflammation, the microbiome, ways to protect neurons, or other factors, also go directly after amyloids or include reducing amyloid levels as central to measuring their effectiveness.

Even studies that would not appear to have accepted the amyloid hypothesis accede to it.

When I examined records in ClinicalTrials.gov, the highly detailed federal database, I found that for all human experiments meant to improve cognitive performance or delay cognitive decline—"disease-modifying" therapies, rather than merely treating symptoms such as agitation or insomnia—nearly two-thirds targeted amyloids. Anti-amyloid trials enrolled or targeted about fifty-two thousand trial participants, three in every four volunteers in all Alzheimer's trials.

And big pharma companies—which spend most of the money to bring major drugs to market—dedicate the lion's share of their Alzheimer's development spending to studies in which amyloids are the primary or secondary target. Such trials sponsored by the top one hundred pharma companies comprised thirty-eight thousand participants, or 83 percent of the companies' efforts for any potentially disease-modifying Alzheimer's drug.

Parsing each trial requires nuance, but the bottom line does not: The amyloid hypothesis remains dominant. And an entrenched idea can be extremely difficult to dislodge.

LECANEMAB "BREAKTHROUGH"

"To be blunt, [amyloid] lowering seems to be an ineffective approach, and it is time to focus on other targets to move therapeutics for Alzheimer's disease forward," said Mayo Clinic neurologist David Knopman in 2019. For decades, Knopman was a top researcher and advocate of the hypothesis, and an investigator for Aduhelm. "The hope was that amyloid removal would have the same therapeutic benefits that vitamin C has for scurvy—you introduce a treatment and you get a cure," he added later. "Amyloid lowering doesn't come close to that."

When the FDA approved Aduhelm in 2021, Knopman was a member of its advisory committee that recommended rejecting the drug. He resigned in protest and emerged as a pessimistic outlier among longtime amyloid-hypothesis boosters.

Alberto Espay of the University of Cincinnati compiled a chart describing all fifty-one anti-amyloid trials conducted since 2002. Although 80 percent had successfully reduced amyloid-beta deposits, by 2022, the treatment had outperformed the placebo only in the dubious Aduhelm case.

That year lecanemab—the next great hope—neared the end of clinical trials. Preliminary results suggested minimal effectiveness. Then that fall a confidential source reached out to me about a horrific death in the trial. A sixty-five-year-old woman who received lecanemab infusions entered Northwestern University Medical Center in Chicago with an apparent blood clot–induced stroke. She was given a common, often life-saving intervention, the powerful clot-busting medicine tissue plasminogen activator (tPA). Substantial bleeding throughout her brain's outer layer instantly followed.

"As soon as they put it in her, it was like her body was on fire," the woman's husband later told me. "She was screaming, and it took, like, eight people to hold her down. It was horrific. Everybody's running in and [asking], 'What the hell is going on?'" His wife was sedated and moved into intensive care, he said. A priest came to deliver the "Anointing of the Sick" prayer. Soon the woman suffered seizures and was placed on a ventilator. After a few days the family approved disconnecting the device, and she died. Her doctors said they had never before seen a case of similarly massive bleeding.

My report in *Science* on the death—the second known fatality of a trial patient who was given blood thinners—quickly became the subject of global headlines: The most promising anti-amyloid treatment was also a killer.

Less than a month later, a new source came forward to tell me that her mother, another lecanemab trial participant, died after hideous brain swelling and bleeding, and violent seizures. The daughter sent me brain scans and medical records for her seventy-nine-year-old mother, Genevieve Lane, a car-rental company retiree. Multiple neurologists I spoke with tied lecanemab inextricably to the death—this time without any significant involvement of blood thinners, and in a woman who, other than signs of early Alzheimer's, enjoyed good health for an elderly person and faced no near-term life-threatening conditions. I would report that Eisai had changed its consent form late in the trial to reflect the deadly risk, but it took months for the warning to filter down to many of those taking the drug—too late to reconsider their participation.

Knopman, among others, began to place the lecanemab "success" in sober context. "We may have reached the limit of what amyloid lowering can do," he said. "We therefore need to be thinking about alternatives."

As with Aduhelm, the raw percentages produced in trials (a 27 percent reduction in rate of cognitive decline compared to a placebo) looked less impressive upon closer inspection. When brought to ground level, results from tests versus the 18-point dementia scale used in the experiment were only slightly better than Aduhelm's. By even the most modest standards used in science, lecanemab fell short of clear benefits in the daily lives of patients.

And as the drug swept amyloid plaques from participants' brains, like Aduhelm it induced brain bleeding or swelling—amyloid-related imaging abnormalities, or ARIA. Dozens endured painful symptoms, and at least five, including those I wrote about, died or suffered serious brain injuries. No one knows whether ARIA, which can last more than twenty weeks, causes long-term damage. More than one in every one hundred trial participants had serious reactions to the infusion of the antibody into a vein. Seven required immediate intervention, emergency care, or hospitalization after infusions for symptoms including fevers, vomiting, loss of consciousness, rapid heart rate, and blood pressure spikes. One almost died, according to Eisai. All withdrew from the trial.

Also like Aduhelm, lecanemab shrank the brain rapidly—more rapidly than Alzheimer's itself. Scientists have no clear idea what that might mean over the long run—and it will be impossible to deduce from the key study of the drug. That's because of the "data sharing plan" for that study: Data will be kept secret. No independent experts will be able to examine the details on what happened to patients' brains or follow what happens to them in years to come. (The New York Times reported in 2024 that the makers of the drug also didn't disclose added risks to trial participants whose genetic predispositions made serious brain bleeding more likely.)

NIA's Madhav Thambisetty and others have pointed to another key doubt about the trial's marginal data that were affected by ARIA: "functional unblinding." The most reliable experiments use a double-blind approach. Neither doctors nor participants have any idea if they are getting the drug or the placebo—a hedge against expectation bias that can skew results, particularly when outcomes are measured using subjective scoring.

Severe adverse events were much more common among those who received lecanemab. When a trial volunteer dropped out or paused participation to recover, it became clear to everyone that the person was probably on the drug. The trial used normal saline—salt water—as a placebo, rather than the long-understood approach of using a placebo meant to closely resemble the treatment. With reliable blinding lost, Thambisetty told me, the narrow benefit of lecanemab looks even more dubious.

Lecanemab offered the amyloid hypothesis as a promise to millions of patients and families: *We have solved the Alzheimer's mystery. We follow the one true path to relieving your misery.* That promise has never decreased symptoms for a single patient, let alone cured anyone. So, to many doctors, it looked like a cruel charade.

Yet the FDA bought the amyloid hypothesis in full. It provisionally approved lecanemab even before seeing the major trial results. In July 2023, it delivered full approval. The agency ignored requests for a Risk Evaluation and Mitigation Strategy (REMS), as advocated by neurologist Jason Karlawish, who codirects a memory center at the University of Pennsylvania and has investigated drugs for Eisai and Biogen. A REMS would have required educating patients and doctors, and monitoring outcomes to contain risks such as deadly brain bleeds.

European regulators have taken a more cautious approach—with a key committee of the European Medicines Agency recommending in 2024 against approval of lecanemab—likely spelling the agency's final decision. UK authorities approved the drug, but the National Health Service (NHS) won't pay for it, so few patients will get lecanemab. The high cost of treatment and necessary brain scans for diagnosis and safety—particularly given the drug's minimal benefits and clear dangers—could have placed enormous new burdens on the desperately overstretched NHS.

Critics objected that the amyloid lobby—pharma companies and the patient advocacy groups, famous doctors, and researchers they underwrite—had gone too far. Advocates of lecanemab countered that individuals with a deadly disease and their loved ones are entitled to judge the risks and benefits. In any case, scientists agree that carefully screened trial participants face lower risks. Deaths and brain damage will almost certainly rise sharply if lecanemab reaches tens of thousands of patients who demand it from average doctors all over the country.

That worry led to a surprising development: The FDA required a "black box warning" on the approved lecanemab product label. That denotes risk of death—the strongest warning the agency provides to doctors. The FDA's hand might have been forced by my widely cited coverage of deaths tied to the drug, and a detailed case report by Schrag and colleagues showing that massive brain bleeding led to the death of Genevieve Lane.

The black box seemed to alter the trajectory of lecanemab. Every doctor who prescribes it has to ask a sobering question: Am I prepared to face the moral, legal, and financial liability if my patient suffers brain damage or dies from this drug? By early 2024, only two thousand patients had been treated with lecanemab, now using the brand name Leqembi—fewer than the number that participated in clinical trials.

The FDA was expected to wave through Eli Lilly's look-alike antibody donanemab in 2023 but decided to hold an advisory committee meeting first. That drug poses slightly greater risks of death or brain injury, and similar brain shrinkage. It offers similar benefits, slowing cognitive decline to a statistically significant degree that many neurologists say would be imperceptible. A recent meta-analysis examined results from many studies of anti-amyloid drugs. None met the standard of "minimal clinically important difference," defined as "the smallest change in a scale measuring cognition or function that is noticeable by the patient or their caregiver."

The advisory committee, this time packed with boosters of the amyloid hypothesis, gave donanemab a green light. Soon after, the FDA approved it under the brand name Kisunla, requiring the same kinds of warnings as for Leqembi.

Lon Schneider, an Alzheimer's researcher at the University of Southern California, studies amyloid vaccines and takes fees or grants from the top makers of anti-amyloid drugs. He's hardly an amyloid hater. Schneider noted that most Alzheimer's patients get the terrible diagnosis late in life. "So much of the amyloid world is built on an almost biblical end-of-times story," he said in an interview. "But half of the people who get Alzheimer's after age eighty-two, frankly, don't have that much of a problem with its slow progression. Many die *with* it, not *from* it," a very different disease than the tragic, rare cases of younger people featured in the media.

"Lecanemab offers just a tiny effect after eighteen months. But its advocates use dream statistics to project forward," Schneider said. "'We will see a bigger effect,' they say. Then the message becomes 'proof' that people benefit for years, and many will be 'survivors.' The study wasn't designed to show long-term outcomes, beyond eighteen months. But if you say it long enough, you will believe it." He added in a comment on Alzforum, the popular website for scientists, "Optimism is good but not if it hurts others."

COSTLY DREAM

When the FDA fully approved Leqembi, the US Centers for Medicare & Medicaid Services approved payments. To its credit, the agency mandated doctors to submit data on each covered patient. Registries would gather brain swelling and bleeding events, and the results of cognitive testing if available.

With pricing set at $26,000 annually, Eisai and Biogen expect to earn more than $10 billion a year on the drug by 2031, assuming that demand develops notwithstanding predicted deaths and brain injuries, and that infusion centers can meet that demand—big ifs. Medicare will also cover costly brain scans for diagnosis and safety monitoring that could run the bill to as high as $90,000 per patient year, according to Schneider, and boost overall costs above payments for any other drug covered by Medicare. And many recipients would owe $6,600 in copays, a substantial portion of the $50,290 median annual household income for seniors, making the drug unaffordable for many who would ostensibly benefit from it. If widely adopted, it would almost certainly spike drug premiums for all Medicare recipients, as seen with Aduhelm.

I asked Selkoe if he worries about that high price tag. He said he wishes the drug cost less. But if Leqembi works as described, he added, it would partly offset Medicare spending on nursing care by keeping people in their own homes a bit longer. If he's right, most of those costs would be pushed to family caregivers, who would also pay for transportation and managing the common side effects for the twice-monthly infusions.

Then I asked Selkoe what he makes of the amyloid skeptics. He said they were ignorant of the facts. He seemed disdainful of those who disagree with his glass-half-full philosophy.

"Having actual therapies that even have a small beneficial effect is positive and great for patients," said one such skeptic, Stanford's Thomas Südhof. "I wouldn't call it a breakthrough, though. I find the contrast between getting rid of all plaques and having only a very small incremental benefit for the patient disappointing, disturbing, and worrisome." He doubts lecanemab's results warrant widespread use, given that the drug shows little evidence of long-lasting effects, is "insanely expensive," and poses life-threatening risks.

To Südhof, rather than proving the amyloid hypothesis, lecanemab does the opposite. It proves that plaques can't cause the disease, because after removing them symptoms of dementia still steadily worsen.

"I am not sure that the approval of the antibodies is actually a positive thing," Südhof said. "I worry that they might actually slow down the field by providing a commercial impediment to developing advances that might provide a bigger impact."

I asked Selkoe if he foresees a day when better and better anti-amyloid drugs will go beyond minutely slowing the progression of Alzheimer's. Will they improve cognition or even cure the disease? His downbeat answer surprised me: "I doubt it."

MEDICATION FOR LIFE

Such drugs are not delivering on all they claim, but there is another untested hypothesis that these or similar drugs might someday prevent Alzheimer's: What if we were to give the drug to healthy people? At age fifty-five or sixty, such a drug might head off amyloid plaque deposits before they cause cognitive symptoms. Give them a drug for a year or longer, maybe for decades, and that might disable the amyloid device of destruction. It's a drugmaker's dream—the potential for millions of people to take a costly product for decades. And Eisai is underwriting just such a trial for lecanemab.

In essence, Selkoe believes scientists are on a clear, albeit long glidepath to targeting the right amyloid proteins in the right way to treat or prevent Alzheimer's. "Something that would not be as crude as fishing the amyloid out of the brain," he said. "More of a surgical strike."

(Cassava Sciences CEO Remi Barbier agrees. Symptom-free younger adults should take his drug for decades, he said, if Cassava's proprietary test detects a misfolded brain protein.)

An Eisai competitor has started a trial targeting amyloid deposits in patients as young as eighteen who have or might have genetic markers that make them susceptible to Alzheimer's. Some scientists and clinicians challenged the ethics of administering such drugs to asymptomatic people based on the presence of biomarkers showing that they might someday develop Alzheimer's.

"'Not treating early enough' is why [companies] are targeting young adults," Espay told me. "As we cannot conceive of any alternatives to the 'amyloid is toxic' idea, after this fails (which it will) we will move to a primary prevention trial targeting children."

He might have been only half serious. But consider "prediabetes"—the most common chronic "disease" after obesity. Prediabetes was born as a public relations catchphrase. The American Diabetes Association (ADA) needed a pitch to persuade complacent doctors and the public to take seriously slightly elevated blood glucose, which might signal heightened diabetes risk. Raising an alarm wasn't easy, given the condition's abstruse name, "impaired glucose tolerance," and lack of symptoms. So "prediabetes," was born. Less than a decade after the ADA created the pre-disease the number of US patients rose from about twelve million to eighty-four million.

Many people face psychological and financial burdens trying to address a prediabetes diagnosis. Billions of tax dollars are spent on research, education, and health improvement programs, generally focused on weight loss and exercise. They have generated lackluster results. Richard Kahn, the ADA's former chief scientist who invented the term "prediabetes," told me that spending vast sums of public money on such programs "has nearly the same effect as burning it in a fire . . . [it's] a terrible waste of money."

To address its self-generated crisis, the ADA advocated more aggressive measures: prescription drugs for weight loss and blood-sugar control. The group is funded by the makers of such drugs. The UK government's National Institute for Health and Care Excellence recently endorsed the new weight-loss drug liraglutide (sold as Wegovy and other brands) to treat prediabetes. Given the massive dubious spending and wave of anxiety it unleashed, Kahn calls his invention of prediabetes "a big mistake."

Similarly, the term "preclinical Alzheimer's" has come into play, affecting an estimated 315 million people globally. It was codified in a major study underwritten by Alzheimer's drug makers Hoffman-La Roche and Biogen. A younger market for anti-amyloid therapies understandably excites such companies—and infuriates skeptics.

Schneider wrote on X (formerly Twitter): "Once upon a time a pathologist saw plaques & tangles in a person with abnormal behavior; ergo, 'Alzheimer disease dementia.' By 2017 behavior is not required. New definition: AD = plaques + tangles. Now: 40 percent of older folk have AD. It's a virtual plague!"

A 2024 Los Angeles Times exposé detailed plans by the FDA, leading academics, and the Alzheimer's Association to promote treatment of young people with no signs of dementia but with biomarkers sometimes associated with Alzheimer's. A sixty-year-old who tests positive for amyloid and tau biomarkers, for example, faces a less than one in four lifetime risk of developing dementia—yet would be considered a candidate for drugs that can have lethal side effects.

Mordant critics suggested that Alzheimer's treatments in the womb would be next.

POWER PLAY

George Perry retains the relaxed informality of the boy who got his start on an isolated ranch on Point Conception, near Santa Barbara. Son of a tenant farmer, Perry grew up on that rugged, windswept coastal headland with some thirty residents on twenty thousand acres. "My father grew lima beans for twenty-seven years," Perry said. "I had no playmates because I was too far from everybody. I had a lot of free time. So I did a lot of reading and maintained a bunch of scientific collections"—skulls from every bird and mammal in the area, thousands of local insects, along with marine life samples, all classified and labeled. His bedroom became a miniature lab. Some of his work was adopted by the Cleveland Natural History Museum.

Perry's PhD in marine biology, from the Scripps Institution of Oceanography, is unusual for an Alzheimer's researcher, particularly one so prolific and widely respected. The University of Texas at San Antonio scientist founded and edits the *Journal of Alzheimer's Disease*. Maybe due to his remote upbringing he never fully learned to play nicely with others; Perry refused to mince words when we spoke about prominent boosters of the amyloid hypothesis. He called Selkoe a "sophist," someone who advances specious science with consummate skill and apparent logic.

Perry's journal publishes many articles about amyloids. He has written often that they play a role in the disease, although one that has been extravagantly hyped. And he has criticized the undue influence of the amyloid mafia for decades, sometimes with a polemical blade.

"The amyloid hypothesis has a very simple story. We get rid of this evil thing, and things go back to normal. But that didn't happen," Perry told me. "So now they say, 'Patients won't decline as fast. They will eventually get better. Maybe we'll start treating earlier. How scary is that, when you start treating fifty-year-olds with something that causes cerebral bleeding?

"The major goal of these people is to win—if it isn't the Nobel Prize, it's God's glory. To be acknowledged that they really did something great," Perry said. "They don't want the amyloid hypothesis to die, because then they have no legacy."

(Schneider described ideas espoused by key supporters of the amyloid hypothesis like this: "'If one anti-amyloid approach doesn't work, try another.' It's iteration, not science." He noted that many scientists produce an avalanche of amyloid-related scholarly writings, flooding the zone for funding. "Amyloid in rats, amyloid in mice, amyloid here or there, how to change it, how to measure it. When you create that large volume of work in one area, it drives out other stuff," Schneider said. "Others tell funders an idea about how microglia [immune-system cells in the brain] can affect nerve degeneration in Alzheimer's, and you write your grant proposal based on less prior work. It competes with proposals that say, 'We want to show how amyloid early in development does this, that, and the other thing. And here are five hundred amyloid references to back it up.' The reviewers will be overwhelmed and rank the amyloid-centric proposal very highly.")

Investors and funders revere Selkoe, Perry said, because "It's like buying IBM and General Motors back in the day. It's safe to fund Dennis Selkoe. He's gonna do good work that will be published in good journals. And he's very presentable. But is that really going to advance things? That's what I see as the whole problem. Everybody's trying to minimize the risk."

Selkoe countered that he gets plenty of rejections from top journals and funders. Yet, he's collected $250 million in research funds (including some shared with colleagues), not counting vast amounts provided by private philanthropists or corporations. He has published in *Science*, *Nature*, *Cell*, *Neuron*, and other leading journals dozens of times.

For his part, Selkoe calls Perry—who edits an influential Alzheimer's journal—a contrarian who "is not deeply knowledgeable about the biology of the disease." Not everyone agrees. A poster for a major international meeting for the 2006 centenary of the discovery of Alzheimer's hangs in the corridor near Selkoe's office. It features him as a scientific advisor—along with Perry.

I asked Selkoe, are amyloid skeptics intellectually dishonest? Maybe not, he said, but they don't understand the science. "They don't feel it the way that I have felt for forty years," Selkoe said. "It's fine to bring up the specifics about price, danger, and degree of meaningful benefit. But we should put aside the notion that the science behind this hypothesis has not gelled, has not been sufficiently validated." Flipping their script, he compared skeptics to Earth-worshipping Ptolemaic scholars.

For all the excitement about lecanemab, something comparably effective has been around since 2004. Aricept, which affects production of the brain chemical acetylcholinesterase, has been shown in multiple studies to improve cognitive performance—not just slow decline—over twelve to eighteen months without lethal side effects. It doesn't modify the underlying causes of Alzheimer's, so its benefits taper off over time. Schrag told me that only about one-third of his patients find it beneficial. But unlike lecanemab, it's cheap and safe. So he prescribes it.

When I asked if he ever had doubted the amyloid hypothesis, Selkoe said no. He conceded that "once you get into a line of thinking, I'm sure that for all of us, you're stuck on that line."

NOT JUST BIG PHARMA

Perry has written more than 1,100 scholarly articles about Alzheimer's, which have been cited more than seventy-five thousand times. Yet, in recent years, he's never been invited to speak at a top Alzheimer's meeting. He blames his persistent, vocal doubts about the amyloid hypothesis.

He was one of several scientists interviewed for a seminal article about the "amyloid cabal" by the late Sharon Begley in *STAT*. (Disclosure: Begley, who died in 2021, was my friend, and for a few years we worked together at *STAT*.) She described career-altering obstacles faced by some who bucked the hypothesis. One received whispered advice: At least pretend in research proposals that her work was linked to amyloids. Venture capitalists and major biopharma companies told others who tried to start companies that they would back only an anti-amyloid approach.

Those scientists said that disproportionate attention and money focused on the amyloid hypothesis prevented other ideas from flourishing: "The whole field is governed by an old boys' network," Stanford's Südhof told *Nature Medicine* in 2006. "It needs new blood, new movement, new ideas."

"My program officer at NIH recommended that I include a 'pro-amyloid collaborator' in my grant application," said neurobiologist Rachael Neve of Massachusetts General Hospital, a pioneer of the field who was among the discoverers of the genetic mutations responsible for amyloid production. "I was fortunate to receive sizeable grants in the late '90s from private donors who had no stake in the amyloid hypothesis. Without that funding I would have had to shut my lab down."

Ruth Itzhaki of the University of Manchester in England saw her 1991 alternative explanation—a link between the herpes virus and Alzheimer's—rejected by top publication after top publication. Two decades later a peer reviewer of a funding proposal she'd put together responded, "Very few [of your] papers have appeared in the most highly regarded journals."

"I thought research should be judged on its own merits," Itzhaki told me, recalling the curious history. She never rejected a role for amyloid. She only questioned whether it caused the disease.

The late Harvard scientist Robert Moir faced headwinds for years from funders when he promoted his own version of a microbial basis for Alzheimer's. A 2016 paper on the topic was called one of the top advances of the year by some leading neuroscientists. But it never found the footing needed to generate the kind of following and funding that promotes rapid progress.

Neuroscientist Malú Tansey, codirector of a research center at the University of Florida, showed that a hyperactive immune response can kill brain cells and the connections between them—posing an alternative target for Alzheimer's drugs. But as a young professor, she was shot down by senior scientists who insisted that she refocus on the "obvious" problem: amyloid plaques. Tansey has since shifted most of her efforts to Parkinson's disease.

"We could not get an NIH grant for a long time," she told me. Adding that if the Michael J. Fox Foundation hadn't funded her, "we wouldn't be here."

When I shared this litany of complaints with Selkoe during my visit to his lab, he told me that such critics were dead wrong.

"Just because my lab produced a lot of stuff on amyloid, I'm not demanding that the field pay homage to amyloid," Selkoe added with exasperation. "I'm just not that kind of person. I came out of Glencoe and I did my stuff. I don't have a feeling that I'm an emperor."

Selkoe tried to buttress his reply by saying he had branched out as well, applying for grants on tau proteins and the possibility that microglia-derived nerve cell inflammation was part of the root cause of Alzheimer's. Research on microgliosis has indeed gained more prominence recently. But in his writings, Selkoe describes both tau and microgliosis as direct results of the cascade of trouble that begins with amyloid buildup—another permutation of the hypothesis.

He told me he favors allocating about a third of future basic research funds to amyloids, and equal amounts to brain inflammation and "new ideas." Yet Selkoe advocates publicly only for amyloids, and his words carry weight. Companies listen, the next generation of researchers listens, and those who fall in line have seen the incentive structure pay off in the research funding, grants, and drug trials that make or break a research career.

And there are lucrative side-hustles to be had. Selkoe sits on the board of Prothena, a company that builds drugs to attack amyloids and synucleins, another family of proteins linked to Alzheimer's and Parkinson's. Cummings disclosed in scholarly papers having consulting relationships with forty-three biotech or pharma companies, including Cassava, Eisai and its partner Biogen, Lilly, and Selkoe's Prothena. Brown's Stephen Salloway has taken $173,000 in fees from Lilly, Biogen, Eisai, Roche, Prothena, and others recently, and managed a career total of more than $26 million in pharma grants.

I asked Selkoe if he had ever encouraged government, private, or corporate grant makers or drug developers to shun alternatives to the amyloid hypothesis. "I never gave that advice," he replied, except during private meetings with pharma companies and investors, often behind closed doors. "If companies asked me what do I think they should invest their shareholders' dollars in? I can certainly remember saying that I think that [the amyloid hypothesis] is the best approach." (Later that day, Selkoe drove me to his next appointment, a speaking gig at an investor conference to talk about anti-amyloid antibodies in the development pipeline. He asked if I'd like to attend, but the organizers prohibited journalists from sitting in.)

"Industry loves putting key opinion leaders, scientists, physicians into a conference to talk about their drugs. Then they attribute drug development plans to 'the thought leaders or scientists,'" USC's Schneider said. "That's unfortunately how they make or rationalize many decisions."

Selkoe is right that the amyloid hypothesis never attained an exclusive stranglehold on Alzheimer's research. Science is too vast for any idea to gain a total monopoly. Its dominance derives from shapeshifting, Protean flexibility. "I hate the phrase, 'the amyloid hypothesis,'" said Südhof, who views amyloids as a part of a complex interplay of contributors to Alzheimer's. The general idea has been called the "amyloid plaque hypothesis," the "amyloid-beta hypothesis," the "amyloid cascade hypothesis," and the "amyloid oligomer hypothesis," he noted. Because it continually changes, he added, "You can never disprove it."

Chapter 13

Blots on a Field

Minneapolis, Nashville

2022–2023

"What is more shocking: reading that the discovery of the elusive Aβ*56 oligomer may not have been one 16 (!) years after its publication, or reading repeatedly that this finding was doubted anyway?"

—CARSTEN KORTH AND ANDREAS MÜLLER-SCHIFFMANN,
HEINRICH-HEINE-UNIVERSITÄT DÜSSELDORF

I reached out to several of Sylvain Lesné's and Karen Ashe's current or former lab employees—technicians, managers, and postdoctoral fellows—before approaching them for their side of the story. I needed to find out how they operated as mentors and investigators, and I needed to rule out the possibility that an obscure junior scientist had engaged in unseen misconduct tracing back to Ashe's lab.

Only one former employee responded. Megan Larson, a manager in Lesné's lab before she took a job at a biosciences supply company, had a thorough grasp of how her former boss conducted business. In an early interview Larson spoke fondly of Lesné, calling him passionate and hardworking, fun and brilliant. Lesné's unorthodox, whimsical lab website reflected as much, and showed photos of his team sharing sushi and generally enjoying life. Lesné also displayed a picture of himself surfing.

Larson described a collegial team who ran tests and delivered western blots and other scientific images to Lesné for review. But Lesné alone prepared the final images for publication. When I explained that many of those images seemed improperly adulterated, she paused a beat. "It's both surprising and disappointing," Larson said. Yet her calm tone surprised me. Far from the sense of shock I'd anticipated.

I asked Larson if she had suspected something corrupt had happened behind closed doors. After she left the lab in 2020, Larson said, she visited another former employee who had been a postdoctoral fellow in Lesné's lab after earning her PhD in neuroscience. She left for a fellowship at Columbia University. During Larson's visit, she said that the former employee alluded to some problems with Lesné's work but offered no specifics, Larson said. That former employee never replied to my queries.

Any lingering concern, any possibility that Lesné somehow could have been duped, was washed away by my talk with Larson. Lesné had represented the singular throughline for all the suspect Aβ*56 images: The only person on every paper. The only one with the access, control, history, and incentive to doctor images on a wide scale.

END GAME

Dennis Selkoe acted as my "acid test" for Lesné's apparent misconduct. Prior to our at-times contentious afternoon in his lab, we had initially connected when I asked him to review hundreds of pages of reports about Lesné and Ashe for me, followed by hours of interviews to parse his response.

Schrag's dossier on Lesné's papers looked credible and well supported, he said, adding: "There are certainly at least twelve or fifteen images where I would agree that there is no other explanation" than improper manipulation. A key image in the 2006 Nature paper displaying purified Aβ*56 showed "very worrisome" signs of tampering, Selkoe concluded. If false, it killed the experimental premise. And the same image reappeared, as if new, five years after the Nature publication in a different paper co-authored by Lesné and Ashe—a clear scientific offense, even for a genuine image. He agreed that the dossier cast serious doubts on Lesné's entire body of work.

Like Hoau-Yan Wang's magic hands in zombie science, Lesné had used a unique system to measure amyloid-beta oligomers separately in brain cells, outside the cells, and in membranes that enclose the cells. Selkoe said Ashe had been known to brag about her "brilliant postdoctoral fellow" who devised the novel technique. "All of us who heard about that knew in a moment that it made no biochemical sense. If it did, we'd all be using [the] method," Selkoe told me. At the time, he said nothing publicly.

The 2006 *Nature* paper depended on Lesné's seemingly miraculous process. In the sixteen years that followed, Lesné and Ashe, separately or jointly, published many articles on their stellar protein. Yet long before Schrag happened upon Lesné's work, the scant evidence for Aβ*56 had raised eyebrows. Donna Wilcock, then a neuroscientist at the University of Kentucky, said she had always doubted claims of "purified" Aβ*56. Oligomers are notoriously unstable, she said, converting spontaneously to other molecular structures. Multiple oligomers can be present in a sample even after purification, making it hard to tie cognitive effects—if any actually occurred—to Aβ*56 alone, assuming it even exists, according to Wilcock.

Only a handful of other groups ever claimed to detect Aβ*56, and none had successfully done so utilizing Lesné's approach. Those few papers claiming to have found Aβ*56 have languished in obscurity, deemed unconvincing by all but a few. Many more labs have unsuccessfully tried and failed to find the protein, though almost none published those findings. Journals want to break new ground, and researchers rarely gain credibility or acclaim by contradicting a famous investigator like Ashe.

Given signs of misconduct in the first Aβ*56 papers, the dearth of independent confirmation seemed telling, Selkoe said. "Once you publish your data, if it's not readily replicated, then there is real concern that it's not correct or true. There's precious little clear-cut evidence that Aβ*56 exists, or if it exists, correlates in a reproducible fashion with features of Alzheimer's—even in animal models." He bristled about a 2006 paper he coauthored with Lesné that sought to neutralize the effects of certain toxic oligomers, although not Aβ*56. It includes a graphic later reprinted as if original in two subsequent Lesné articles. Selkoe called it "highly egregious."

He seemed convinced that my investigation was original and important, but he struggled with how to balance my findings' value against the risk of public demoralization. The affair might further undercut trust in science after a frightening period during the Trump presidency and Covid pandemic when attacks on scientists and public health officials had become routine and sometimes violent. But ultimately, he decided, scientists must show they can find and correct apparent misconduct. "We need to declare these examples and warn the world," Selkoe said.

None of this is to say Selkoe's faith in his hard-won amyloid franchise ever wavered. Lesné's works were troubling and had been a problem, it seemed, but human trials of the anti-amyloid drugs lecanemab and donanemab were far down the road toward completion. Selkoe worried that the Lesné episode might dampen their prospects. "I hope that people will not become fainthearted," he said, "as a result of what really looks like a very egregious example of malfeasance."

Getting my article into print had by then become a race against time. Months earlier, Schrag had contacted *Nature* and other publishers of dubious Lesné papers to no avail. This was central to his approach: First give the "self-correcting" system of science a chance—contact institutional authorities like the National Institutes of Health (NIH) and the journals before going to the news media. Journal editors had convinced him to pump the brakes when they told him they would follow up on his query. Months passed with scant evidence of progress. Schrag became as eager as I was to see the matter aired publicly.

In the interim period I came to feel an obligation to get ahead of a possible *Nature* retraction. It would satisfy the field, perhaps, but this was a tried and true method of keeping things "inside the family" of research scientists. A simple retraction might make the system look superficially effective, taking pressure off the bigger question of what retracting the landmark research meant for the field as a whole.

Nature had been sitting on the evidence for four months, since February 2023 with no public comment. But a query from me, a reporter for *Nature*'s chief rival, might force their hand. I held off for a few weeks.

HITTING THE TARGETS

I emailed Cassava's Lindsay Burns, Wang, Ashe, and Lesné the same day I contacted Selkoe. I also reached out to Rush University's David Bennett, who landed in bed with both sets of apparently doctored studies by supplying each group with tissue from his brain bank. He had enabled twelve such studies.

(As with any investigation I write, there would be no surprises. It's a covenant with both readers and subjects. For fairness and accuracy, the scientists deserved an informed chance to tell their own stories. It helps ensure that I never miss a key fact or write a piece construed as unfair. I never want to hear, "I would have talked to you if I'd known . . .")

Bennett was the first to reply, with a carefully lawyered brush-off after I sent him copies of the full Ashe-Lesné and Wang-Burns dossiers: "Opining on the documents you shared, regardless of their authenticity, which I have no way of determining, would not be appropriate. I am unable to say anything that would undermine the review process and/or the reputation of my peers." Bennett didn't respond to my follow-up question about whether Rush had launched a review.

I then sent Schrag's hundred-page dossier of suspect images, with detailed questions indicating what I planned to describe, to Wang, Burns, and her husband and Cassava CEO Remi Barbier. Barbier replied via email that Schrag's "allegations are false." By that time, ten of the questioned articles had been retracted or the journals had posted notices that they were waiting for the results of a misconduct review of Wang by the City University of New York. Barbier added that Cassava had hired investigators to review its work, and they had provided vast numbers of documents to outside investigative agencies. (Cassava later conceded investigations by the SEC and DOJ.)

But Ashe and Lesné were the main act. Lesné did not respond to my queries. A UMN spokesperson also declined to comment, saying only that it had launched a review.

At first, Ashe agreed to talk, then demurred days later. "Several people have asked me to refrain from speaking with you tomorrow to avoid any potential interference with the official processes that the University has initiated to address such matters. [I'm] sorry to have to back out," she wrote. "I can't honestly say I'm looking forward to reading your piece, but hope that on balance it makes the world a better place. Good luck!" She signed the note, "Karen."

"Thanks for your gracious note. I greatly respect your distinguished work, and everyone I've spoken to thinks the world of you," I replied. "I appreciate the awkward position you find yourself in. I hope you'll forgive me for offering a reflection based on my many experiences as someone who asks awkward questions. Institutions almost never want people in your situation to be interviewed. Some version of protecting 'official processes' is usually the stated reason. But people in your situation almost always benefit by talking in a forthright way. It's your chance to get your perspective into the first, most-read, and most-detailed story. It would give readers the biggest picture and help me write the fairest and most accurate article. It's your opportunity to talk about the issues in the most timely way . . . Please reconsider."

"Your note does give me pause about my decision, particularly as I sense you are writing not to bring down but rather to suggest how we might fortify a struggling field. I'm gratified to know that I'm held in high esteem," she replied. "You may be happy to know that you have a good reputation around here, which is high praise coming from administrators who want to avoid being in the news at all costs. I'm afraid it's a hard 'no' this time." (The compliment from Ashe's people surprised me. A year earlier I had caused them considerable heartburn when I profiled a scandal involving apparently deadly lapses in tests of powerful sedatives at UMN's primary teaching hospital, as part of an investigation of lax federal regulation of human experiments.)

I then sent written questions, which Ashe also declined to answer, but not before calling them "sobering." She added: "I still have faith in Aβ*56," citing ongoing experiments. "I remain excited about this work, and believe it has the potential to explain why Aβ therapies may yet work despite recent failures targeting amyloid plaques."

Schrag had conducted a separate spot-check of papers Ashe had produced without Lesné. He found no anomalies—suggesting that Ashe hadn't personally doctored any images.

Nonetheless, Ashe had at the least shown a complacency that invited misconduct. As University of Lille neuroscientist Jean-Charles Lambert put it, Ashe had provided a picture of how high-stakes research goes awry. "It's very difficult to say 'no' to a potentially very big publication" in a top-tier journal, he said. "When you have very strong results, you want to trust people. Even if you may think a problem could occur, you can easily be in a kind of denial." Lambert added: "We have to work on this to not fall into such a trap."

"Ashe obviously failed in that very serious duty" to ask tough questions and ensure the data's accuracy, said John Forsayeth, a neuroscientist at the University of California San Francisco. "It was a major ethical lapse."

After I contacted Ashe, she tried to get ahead of my story with a defense on PubPeer of some images Schrag had previously posted to challenge the *Nature* paper. She included parts of a few purportedly original, unpublished images that lacked the digital copy-paste marks Schrag had detected in the published versions. Ashe said this proved the flagged markings were innocent artifacts created during the publishing process. Yet the originals introduced unequivocal evidence that multiple parts of images, central to the meaning of the experiment, had been duplicated from adjacent areas. (See Illustration, next page.)

It was also unclear if Ashe, Lesné, or someone else produced the images Ashe posted in her defense. But Selkoe called Ashe's impulsive posting of seemingly falsified corrections "shocking," adding: "I don't see how she would not hyper-scrutinize anything that subsequently related to Aβ*56."

How an image sleuth uncovered possible tampering

Vanderbilt University neuroscientist Matthew Schrag found many apparently falsified images in papers by University of Minnesota neuroscientist Sylvain Lesné, including key examples in a landmark 2006 paper in *Nature* coauthored by Karen Ashe and others. It linked a supposed amyloid-beta protein, dubbed Aß*56, to Alzheimer's dementia.

Published image

The below published image in that paper purportedly shows that Aß*56—across the image to the left of the "12-mer" marker on the right axis—can be isolated from other amyloid proteins from the brain tissue of genetically engineered mice. The paper said that this finding helped validate the claim that Aß*56 can be extracted in a pure form—critical to the experimental hypothesis. Schrag saw faint signs of unnatural mottling in the image background.

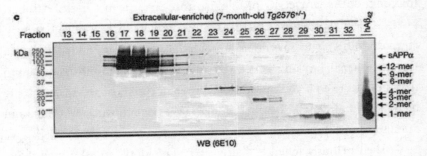

Image with enhanced contrast

To examine the image more closely, Schrag sharpened the details by increasing the contrast, below. It revealed obvious signs of improper changes, including the use of a digital-eraser tool (irregularly shaped white areas). Those changes seemed to delete evidence that contradicted the assertion about purified Aß*56. Lesné did not provide the original images that could have supported his findings and the experiment's validity.

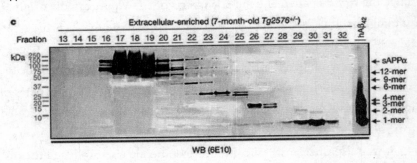

Result: Paper retracted

Ashe and most of the paper's other authors concluded that image doctoring occurred, and re-tracted the paper in 2024. (Only Lesné disagreed. Another coauthor, Austin Yang—who is also the National Institutes of Health program officer for a major Lesné grant—did not respond to an inquiry about the matter from *Nature*'s editors.)

THE SCORE CARD

In all, Schrag or forensic image expert Elisabeth Bik identified more than twenty suspect Lesné papers, including ten concerning Aβ*56. Schrag contacted several journals starting early in 2022, and Lesné and his collaborators posted two corrections. One for a 2012 paper in the *Journal of Neuroscience* replaced several images Schrag had flagged as problematic, writing that the earlier versions had been "processed inappropriately." Even the corrected images showed numerous signs of improper changes or duplications of western blot bands, and in one case, complete replacement of a blot, Schrag and Bik showed in detailed posts to PubPeer.

Extensive corrections also appeared in a 2013 paper in the influential journal *Brain*. Lesné and Ashe were the first and senior authors, respectively, of that study, which showed "negligible" levels of Aβ*56 in children and young adults, with the presence of the protein rising steadily as people aged. It concluded that Aβ*56 might be important in early Alzheimer's. The authors said the correction had no bearing on their findings. Schrag wasn't convinced. Among other problems, one corrected blot showed multiple bands that seem to have been added or removed artificially—substantially affecting the meaning of the experimental findings.

The *Journal of Neuroscience* stood out with five suspect Lesné papers (plus five others by Wang). A journal spokesperson said it follows guidelines on such concerns from the Committee on Publication Ethics trade group, but otherwise declined to comment—although by that time, it had corrected two of the Lesné papers. On June 21, *Science Signaling*, a sibling of *Science*, posted expressions of concern for studies from 2016 and 2017.

No one seemed to notice. My story was in final editing and legal review when I reached out to *Nature*'s editors on July 11, ten days before we planned to publish. Three days later—five months after the journal received Schrag's detailed dossier—*Nature* posted a notice above the article that it was under review for complaints about some images: "*Nature* is investigating these concerns, and a further editorial response will follow as soon as possible. In the meantime, readers are advised to use caution when using results reported therein."

My hunch that *Nature* would "suddenly" take notice of Lesné and Ashe if I contacted them seemed right. But the scholarly press barely noticed, let alone the mainstream media. So far as I could tell, no other reporters had taken up the scent.

My story, "Blots on a Field?—A neuroscience image sleuth finds signs of fabrication in scores of Alzheimer's articles, threatening a reigning theory of the disease," appeared online July 21, 2022. The story was covered widely in the scientific and popular press. The 2006 Lesné-Ashe *Nature* paper—already one of the most cited Alzheimer's research papers— became one of the most discussed articles in recent scientific history, according to the audience-tracking service Altmetric.

The Alzheimer's research community reacted with alarm.

Skeptics of the amyloid hypothesis considered their views vindicated. Many said that Schrag's findings and my article offered a chance to rethink long-standing dogma. They asked the research establishment to take a good hard look in the mirror. Alzforum, the scientific news and discussion website, obtained commentaries about my article from top researchers within days of its publication. Many admitted, after sixteen years of deferential silence, that they could never detect the star protein. "What is more shocking: reading that the discovery of the elusive Aβ*56 oligomer may not have been one 16 (!) years after its publication or reading repeatedly in the comments that this finding was doubted anyway?" asked two German scientists, Carsten Korth and Andreas Müller-Schiffmann of Heinrich-Heine-Universität Düsseldorf.

Grace Stutzman, a respected Alzheimer's researcher at the Chicago Medical School, raised the bigger challenge bluntly: "It makes me question how a protein associated with Alzheimer's disease that has been studied for over thirty-five years, with billions of dollars of research funding and hundreds of scientists dedicated to unraveling its role, has yet to generate a clear answer, or even a consensus. That raises a red flag." Christian Hölscher, a professor at a leading Chinese university, added: "We need to stop this obsession with amyloid-beta. It is time to make room for new ideas and approaches."

Scientists whose careers depend on the amyloid hypothesis were appalled by the apparent misconduct but dropped into a defensive crouch: "Beyond damaging our morale and the standing of scientists, the refutation of Aβ*56 has in my opinion little consequence for the amyloid hypothesis, or the more nuanced oligomer hypothesis," wrote Harvard professor Dominic Walsh, also vice president for Alzheimer's and dementia research at Biogen, maker of the lackluster Aduhelm. Walsh was one of the most consistent and prominent promoters of Aβ*56—citing the *Nature* paper in fourteen of his own articles. In turn, those were cited nearly seven thousand times.

Amid the rush of commentary and media attention that was making him famous, the unflappable Schrag agreed that oligomers might still play a role in Alzheimer's, in part because other investigators have linked them to cognitive impairment in animals. "The wider story of oligomers potentially survives this one problem," he told me. "But the Lesné affair makes you pause and rethink the foundation of the story."

Lesné went silent. He has yet to address the concerns publicly, while UMN examines his work. Days after my story appeared, Ashe told *NBC News* that she wanted to retract the *Nature* study. Then in a mystifying reversal, she blamed Lesné but insisted any possible fakery had no effect on the study or any of her work. Ashe went on the offensive, attacking my article in multiple media interviews.

In a letter to *Science*, Selkoe and Jeffrey Cummings defended the amyloid hypothesis and the role of oligomers. "Lesné's 'star suspect' rapidly became history," they wrote. The vastly increased funding for anti-oligomer lab experiments and drug development that directly followed the Lesné-Ashe findings seemed to refute their comments.

The complaint was contradicted by Cummings having cited Lesné's work repeatedly and favorably as recently as 2021. Selkoe had noted in two papers that he could not find Aβ*56 in human fluids or tissues—so far as I can tell, the only such negative findings ever published. Yet he hadn't hesitated to routinely mention the *Nature* paper as support for his toxic oligomer vision. He was, by far, the most influential promoter of the now-disgraced experiment, naming it in nineteen papers that were cited nearly thirteen thousand times.

I asked Schrag if the Lesné and Cassava cases made him optimistic about fixing the scientific record, and if a more reliable record might lead to a remedy for Alzheimer's. "I hope that the one leads to the other," Schrag replied. "Otherwise, why bother?"

His hopes depend on institutions that respond to lapses in scientific integrity. But their approach might require an overhaul—starting where Schrag turned for help long before I ever met him: federal funders and overseers of biomedical research.

Chapter 14

Federal Failures

Washington, DC

2021–2024

"It is a wonder that the ORI accomplishes much at all.
Its current budget is $12 million per year to oversee work funded by NIH,
a $48 billion agency."

—IVAN ORANSKY, COFOUNDER OF *RETRACTION WATCH*,
AND BARBARA REDMAN OF NEW YORK UNIVERSITY

Most academic bioscientists depend on the National Institutes of Health (NIH) to keep the lights on. In return, many give back by reviewing grant applications in a "study section"—specialists who recommend which researchers propose the most promising experiments in their fields and therefore should be given public funds. The competitive process results in approval for only about one in five applications. Selection as a reviewer is an honor. It signifies expertise to judge the merit of peers. It's also a burden—two days of meetings, two or three times a year, following a review of thousands of pages of technical material.

As the largest biomedical research funder in the world, NIH provided about $37 billion in grants and contracts in 2022, plus funds for agency scientists. About 10 percent went to Alzheimer's experiments. Study sections form the core of how it decides who spends that largess.

Given the agency's profound power to steer biomedical research, citizens should hope and expect that grant recipients meet a certain standard of integrity, but of course some do not. Matthew Schrag said he found an experience in an Alzheimer's study section in early 2022 unnerving. In his review of materials from a group that included a well-established scientist, Schrag told me soon after, "I found cut-and-paste western blots." In one, after he boosted image contrast, a crisp white square appeared atop a blot, something exceedingly unlikely to occur by accident. Schrag reported what he saw to the NIH scientific review officer via a "back-channel" text chat during the meeting. "I did it quietly, because for ethical reasons you're not supposed to discuss possible misconduct in front of the whole group," which seemed logical, he said. "That way, if NIH disagrees with you they can still fund the grant, and you've not altered other people's votes."

What happened next in this instance seemed less logical. NIH deleted Schrag's low score for the grant application and asked him to revise his personal statement to place himself in a conflict of interest with the scientists in question, "even though I'd never heard of those people before," he said. Schrag was excluded from further consideration of the proposal. No one else on the panel was informed about the apparently doctored images. (Bowing to confidentiality rules, Schrag didn't identify to me the doubted researchers or their work.)

NIH forwarded the concern to its own integrity officer and to the Office of Research Integrity (ORI), a tiny investigative arm of the US Department of Health and Human Services. Schrag followed up a few months later with the NIH officer, noting that he had identified more concerns in the grant application. No response. Soon after, NIH funded the suspect proposal.

The City University of New York (CUNY), where a lot of the development of Cassava Sciences' simufilam was done by Hoau-Yan Wang over the years, took in $55 million from NIH in 2022. That year the University of Minnesota (UMN), home to Karen Ashe and Sylvain Lesné, gained $433 million—more than one in every hundred dollars NIH spent, placing it in the top twenty recipients nationwide. Over the years, that agency paid for most of the work on the two scientists' star protein, Aβ*56.

Schrag thought NIH deserved a chance to act forcefully to set things right out of the glare of public attention. So long before his full findings went public via my articles, he sent his dossiers to the federal agency.

DEFER AND DELAY

When NIH receives a concern about misconduct—fabrication, falsification of data, or plagiarism—it conducts a preliminary review. If deemed sufficiently credible, the agency passes the file on to the ORI.

Schrag delivered his Cassava dossier to NIH in August of 2021. He sent his Lesné dossier in January 2022. It's been radio silence since then. The agency would understandably want to preserve confidential due process for anyone accused of misconduct. But Schrag had trouble with that opacity, given that full adjudication can take years. Meanwhile, those who conducted the dubious work can go about their research—including human trials—as if nothing's amiss.

It didn't seem reassuring when five months after Schrag provided the massive Lesné dossier, NIH committed to funding the Minnesota scientist's work for up to five more years. As it happened, the administrator overseeing the grant at NIH had coauthored Lesné's suspect 2006 *Nature* paper about $A\beta^*56$.

Meager resources at ORI invite such things. As of the end of 2023, it had just thirty-seven employees, including only a handful of "scientist investigators." The agency budget amounts to three hundredths of 1 percent of what NIH spends on grants and contracts. "It is a wonder that the ORI accomplishes much at all," Ivan Oransky, cofounder of *Retraction Watch*, and Barbara Redman of New York University, wrote in *Science* in 2024. "Its current budget is $12 million per year to oversee work funded by NIH, a $48 billion agency." And although NIH is ORI's *biggest client*, ORI also oversees research integrity issues for every other HHS agency—including the Centers for Disease Control and the Food and Drug Administration.

It's far from a new problem. In 2014, *Science* reported that David Wright, ORI's director, had delivered a "scathing" letter of resignation. Most of Wright's time was "spent navigating the remarkably dysfunctional

HHS bureaucracy to secure resources and, yes, get permission for ORI to serve the research community. I knew coming into this job about the bureaucratic limitations of the federal government, but I had no idea how stifling it would be," he wrote.

Not surprisingly, ORI normally hands off investigations to whatever university employs the accused researcher. In principle, CUNY and UMN had about six months to report back. In practice, universities almost always gain extensions that drag the process out indefinitely. In both cases, years have passed without resolution. ORI recently floated proposals to tighten deadlines and streamline actions—moves strongly opposed by many universities. The agency caved to that pressure, ending up with a proposed set of rules that effectively relaxed its already weak approach. Eugenie Rich, a lawyer who represents whistleblowers in scientific misconduct cases, called it "further evidence of academic institutions capturing ORI."

Due process delays can be understandable, given that a finding of misconduct can be career-ending. But sometimes universities have bogged down probes in bureaucratic procedures or hidden bad outcomes, according to Susan Garfinkel, who formerly directed ORI's investigative oversight. Garfinkel, who now heads compliance for the Ohio State University, argues that despite conflicts of interest and sometimes a lack of sophistication, universities should be the first examiners of alleged misconduct. Insiders best understand cultural conditions and personal relationships that can affect the outcome of a probe, she added.

If a university finds misconduct and ORI concurs, the agency might ask the scientist to agree not to seek federal funds for a few years, or to work under the supervision of another scientist. In rare cases, HHS debars a scientist from engaging in federally funded studies for a few years. If the accused researcher objects, the case can be kicked up to a higher HHS level to try to enforce such penalties. On rare occasions HHS tries to claw back funds deemed to have been spent fraudulently or launches a criminal prosecution.

The complexity of each case immensely burdens ORI's small staff with a predictable result: Few researchers ever face penalties for misconduct. Only about 360 have been disciplined since the agency's inception in 1992. Of the eighty-seven cases that came to fruition since 2008, just one involved research on Alzheimer's disease. During that period several thousand concerns about doctored Alzheimer's research have been posted to PubPeer, the crowd-sourced website that debates scientific papers. A recent study found that more than two-thirds of PubPeer comments report possible misconduct. (In late 2023, ORI proposed another option: For the first time, it would publicly announce misconduct findings by universities that would otherwise handle the results of its investigations internally. In theory, that would pressure secretive universities to open their process a crack to public scrutiny. The academy successfully quashed the proposal.)

Passivity begets that lackluster record, said Stuart Buck, who heads the Good Science Project, a nonprofit effort to improve research oversight. NIH and ORI don't look for fraud on their own initiative, despite growing evidence on PubPeer and in the media. "Give the scientific integrity official enough of a budget and staff to proactively look for research integrity issues, rather than merely reacting to allegations and complaints," Buck says.

Garfinkel agreed that some expansion of ORI's charge to take on recalcitrant institutions known to conduct ineffective investigations of their own researchers could help. That would require a vast increase in the agency's resources, she added. "I don't know if they would ever be able to get that kind of funding."

COP-OUT ON THE BEAT?

Schrag experienced similar challenges with the FDA. He contributed to the citizen petition submitted to the agency about Cassava's simufilam out of concern that patients are being used to test a drug based on apparently doctored data. In so doing, they foreclose their eligibility for drug trials not shadowed by misconduct concerns.

I was reminded of my 2020 investigation of the FDA's track record overseeing patient safety in clinical trials. I found a light-handed, slow-moving, secretive approach, based on about 1,600 agency inspection and enforcement documents for trials that the FDA said violated rules and law. (Almost all were acquired via Freedom of Information Act requests, including many shared by Redica Systems, a company that tracks the agency.)

Clear corrections of dangerous or unlawful practices were rare, even amid signs that trial participants had been harmed and that data underpinning evidence-based medicine were corrupted. On rare occasions when the FDA formally warned researchers that they had broken the law, the agency often neglected to ensure that fixes occurred. Moreover, the FDA frequently closed cases on the basis of unverified claims by the accused.

Jill Fisher, a social scientist and expert on trial conduct at the University of North Carolina Chapel Hill, noted a particularly alarming problem. When an FDA inspection exposes mistakes, recklessness, or fraud in a clinical trial, neither the agency nor the experimenters are obliged to notify participants. She called that failure to inform "a travesty."

Moreover, I found that the FDA almost always rules that no action is warranted or requests voluntary corrections. And among the 291 cases in which the agency actually required corrections in human experiments over an eleven-year period, only 71 resulted in a clear regulatory end point—such as disqualification of the researcher, or a "closeout letter" certifying that corrections were completed. For the remaining 220, no clear outcomes could be found in public documents or data banks, leaving trial participants and others in the dark. The FDA also deems some violations "not correctable," ending its enforcement with neither compliance nor any form of disclosure. From outside the agency, it's impossible to know how often that occurs.

The FDA told me that it deploys limited enforcement resources on the highest-risk problems. It tries to address clinical trial flaws early in the process, so "an issue that might warrant a warning letter could be resolved before the problem rises to that level." (Officials would not agree to an interview. Spokespeople emailed selective responses to written questions.)

That apparently lax approach sometimes extends to drug approvals.

Critics often fault the "revolving door" phenomenon. Many senior FDA officials have been or soon will be industry executives. For example, Commissioner Rob Califf had millions of dollars in investments in two dozen biopharma companies before his appointment in 2021 and had recently been paid $2.7 million as a consultant for Verily, Alphabet's biopharma subsidiary. His predecessor, Scott Gottlieb, joined the board of directors of Pfizer, the top drugmaker, just after his stint as commissioner.

The phenomenon proliferates down the agency food chain. Writing for *Science* in 2018, I found that eleven of sixteen FDA medical examiners who worked on twenty-eight drug approvals left the agency to become employees or consultants for the companies they recently regulated. (It was a small subset of a common practice.)

In 2009, for example, a panel of independent experts was asked to assess whether the agency should approve AstraZeneca's widely prescribed antipsychotic drug Seroquel for a wider range of conditions. The panel heard expert testimony linking the drug to sudden cardiac death when used with certain other medications. According to the meeting transcript, the FDA's then-director of psychiatric products Thomas Laughren, who shepherded Seroquel and similar drugs through the review process and signed their approvals, challenged the concern and defended AstraZeneca. The committee voted overwhelmingly to advise approval for new conditions, without suggesting that doctors and patients be warned about sudden cardiac death.

Soon after, Laughren left the agency and formed a consultancy to help psychiatric drug makers, including AstraZeneca, navigate FDA approvals. He did not respond to repeated requests for comment. Later evidence showed that the cardiac problems were real. In 2011, the FDA added a warning on Seroquel's label.

Jeffrey Siegel, an FDA staffer specializing in reviews for arthritis drugs, oversaw the 2010 approval of Genentech's arthritis drug Actemra. Months later, he left the agency to join the company and its parent, Roche, as director of the division that includes Actemra. Siegel represented Roche before former FDA colleagues when the company sought approval to promote Actemra for new ailments. He later told *STAT* that the timing of his decision to join Roche and Genentech was coincidental.

Laughren, Siegel, and numerous other former FDA regulatory professionals in similar situations complied with existing federal laws and FDA requirements. Vinay Prasad, a hematologist-oncologist at the University of California San Francisco who has studied the revolving door, said that weak federal restrictions, plus an expectation of future employment, bias drug reviews. "When your No. 1, major employer after you leave your job is sitting across the table from you, you're not going to be a hard-ass when you regulate. That's just human nature."

ALZHEIMER'S TEMPLATE

The story of anti-amyloid Alzheimer's drug Aduhelm offered a prototypical example of how corporate links can muzzle the drug watchdog. Biogen, Aduhelm's maker, donated heavily to patient advocacy groups, which in turn lobbied Congress and directly pressured the FDA to approve the drug. Biogen enjoyed a particularly cozy relationship with the agency, well documented by *STAT*, as I wrote in chapter 7. Billy Dunn, the FDA's top regulator for Aduhelm and other Alzheimer's drugs, had opened a back channel to work closely with the company to get their drug across the approval finish line.

"Regulatory capture has now infiltrated the Food and Drug Administration," concluded the consumer advocacy group Public Citizen.

"It says right there in the agency's charter that its mission is to Give People Hope One Way or Another, right? That its job is to Approve Drugs, which means that you can defer for years the question of whether they actually do any good?" Derek Lowe, a chemist and blogger for *Science* said with derisive snark. "And that if a given drug candidate actually has stronger evidence that it does harm, that this can be canceled out by the amount of Hope Delivered? Billy Dunn . . . can apparently tell you where those parts of the mission statement are, and the rest of us just need to Believe, to Hope, and to Trust. What a beautiful sight it all is."

Soon after, Dunn shepherded Aduhelm's look-alike, Leqembi, through the same process. Then he departed through the revolving door, to hang his industry-consultant shingle and join the board of Prothena, an anti-amyloid biopharma. He received options to buy thirty thousand shares of the company.

Given the often-ineffectual federal regulators, Schrag knew he had to take other measures to stir up the scientific community about simufilam, and to try to correct the scientific record. He approached another key player in fixing corrupt or inept science—the scholarly journals.

Those essential gatekeepers—arbiters of technical knowledge and scientific importance trusted by regulators, funders, scientists, doctors, and the public—claim to uphold the highest standards of scholarship and integrity. As Schrag would soon learn, that trust has been catastrophically betrayed.

Chapter 15

Scholarly Deceptions

Nashville, Prague

2021–2023

"It was one of those roles that never moved on from a title."

—JASON KARLAWISH, UNIVERSITY OF PENNSYLVANIA BIOETHICIST,
FORMER ETHICS EDITOR FOR THE *JOURNAL OF PREVENTION OF ALZHEIMER'S DISEASE*

The *Journal of Prevention of Alzheimer's Disease (JPAD)* seems authoritative and looks prestigious. Its sponsors are Springer, a division of Springer Nature, one of the largest scientific publishers, and the annual Clinical Trials on Alzheimer's Disease Congress—a major, global, scientific meeting. Many doctors rely on *JPAD* when deciding whether to prescribe amyloid-reducing drugs such as Leqembi, or others to fight agitation or anxiety that can accompany Alzheimer's dementia.

Matthew Schrag first raised an eyebrow about the journal in August 2021 while examining possible misconduct in studies behind Cassava Sciences' simufilam for the citizen petition to the US Food and Drug Administration (FDA). The prior year, *JPAD* had published a paper by Cassava's Lindsay Burns and Hoau-Yan Wang that suggested strong potential for the drug. It said simufilam lowered key biomarkers associated with Alzheimer's—particularly tau proteins—in the spinal fluid of patients who were volunteers for the company's clinical trial. That paper helped boost confidence in Cassava and simufilam.

Schrag thought an image central to its experimental findings looked strange. A single band of a western blot depicting the presence of tau seemed to have been copied and pasted into the larger image. He emailed his doubts to *JPAD* editors in September 2021. Bruno Vellas, a French neuroscientist and then coeditor-in-chief, handled the query. He seemed a curious respondent, because Vellas and Wang coauthored a similar 2017 article in another journal. It too showed biomarker benefits from simu-filam. Schrag thought that it too showed strong signs of image doctoring; that paper would be retracted in 2022.

Soon after, Schrag asked ethics administrators at Springer to ex-amine the matter, and coeditor-in-chief Paul Aisen of the University of Southern California took over the complaint. Vellas also stepped down as coeditor-in-chief.

Independently, I confirmed Schrag's findings with image-integrity specialists and Alzheimer's researchers who were not affiliated with *JPAD*. Yet eleven months after Schrag raised his concern, Cassava issued a press release saying *JPAD* had exonerated the paper. Aisen later told Schrag that they had run the images by experts familiar with western blots, rather than a forensic-image analyst. The article helped smooth simufilam's glide path to late-stage human trials.

Schrag noticed University of Nevada neuroscientist Jeffrey Cummings among its editorial board members. Cummings, an authority on Alzhei-mer's trials and amyloid hypothesis advocate, had with Harvard's Dennis Selkoe sharply criticized my 2022 "Blots on a Field?" article in *Science* about the influential study by Sylvain Lesné and Karen Ashe. The same story de-scribed concerns about Cassava's work. As of April 2024, Cummings was a long-standing paid member of Cassava Sciences' advisory board.

According to federal records, Cummings augments his income—by nearly $1 million in personal fees and travel in the last few years alone—consulting for a laundry list of big and small Alzheimer's companies, in-cluding Cassava, Biogen, Eisai, Alzheon, and Acadia.

Other top *JPAD* editors show similar issues. Vellas has received consulting fees from Eisai and others. Aisen has been paid more than

$100,000 since 2016 by makers of anti-amyloid drugs. As head of a clini-cal research center, he has pulled in tens of millions of corporate dollars to test such drugs. Another editor, Brown University's Stephen Salloway, took $170,000 in fees and $25 million in research support. Others on the journal's editorial board show similar figures. Current and former Biogen and Eisai employees have actually served on that board.

Anti-amyloid drugs from those companies and others often have re-ceived favorable coverage in *JPAD* in papers written by Cummings, Aisen, Vellas, and Salloway. Their articles supported the companies' arguments that their drugs enjoyed a sound scientific foundation at critical junctures in the development and regulatory process.

As shown earlier here, Biogen and Eisai's Aduhelm became a fiasco that never achieved full federal approval. Yet *JPAD*'s "'expert panel' pro-duced 'appropriate use recommendations' for aducanumab [Aduhelm] before the clinical trials of [Aduhelm] had even been published," Schrag noted in his analysis. "Five of the six members of this panel were paid by Biogen and/or Eisai," the drug's makers. They included Salloway and Cummings. "This was not disclosed in the abstract or main text, but only in fine print at the end of the article," Schrag added.

Like any normal journal, *JPAD* relies on peer review to ensure accu-racy and scientific relevance. Unpaid, ostensibly unbiased and skeptical experts critique each submission. Peer reviewers nearly always request clarifications or changes to sharpen and improve a manuscript. Such re-views and corrections, required for acceptance of a paper, typically take weeks and can last several months. The delays understandably frustrate authors, but high-quality reviews of complex science take time. The *Nature* journals—among the world's most respected—average 213 days from submission to acceptance. The *Science* journals move at a comparable pace, 202 days. *JPAD*'s "peer reviewed" guidelines for Aduhelm took eight days, including a US holiday.

Schrag wondered how fast *JPAD* generally completed peer reviews, examining the dates manuscripts were submitted and approved. Some cases involving Cummings and his affiliated companies proceeded at an improbable clip. The Cassava biomarker study took seven days. A favorable 2016 study of the anti-amyloid drug tramiprosate, coauthored by Vellas, Cummings, and Serge Gauthier, another coeditor-in-chief, took just six. The drug's maker, Alzheon, paid all three of those scientists for consulting at the time, and they served on its advisory board.

"This casts a shadow on the whole publishing and peer review process," said Donna Wilcock, the Indiana University neuroscientist and chief editor of *Alzheimer's & Dementia*, who examined a dossier Schrag prepared about *JPAD*. "Anytime you get a paper that is accepted within a week of being received, I guarantee it's not been peer reviewed." Wilcock worries about the *JPAD* guidelines for prescribing anti-amyloid antibodies, she said. "That's what all of us are using to guide our clinical programs. If they are not undergoing peer review, as advertised, then you've got to question the robustness of those papers."

Cummings also has described his own credentials in an unorthodox way. The physician prominently notes a ScD degree in his biographical materials—reinforcing his credibility as a researcher. He fails to mention that his undergraduate alma mater, the University of Wyoming Laramie, bestowed the ScD in 2011 as an honorary degree. He replied to my query about this via *JPAD* editor Jacques Touchon, who noted that the university found Cummings's voluminous writings "worthy of an advanced degree."

According to the university registrar, "An honorary degree was given to [Cummings] in 2011 based off his contributions to his profession. Honorary degrees are not noted on official transcripts."

A 2018 *JPAD* article suggested that pimavanserin, a drug to treat psychosis among Alzheimer's patients, was effective. The manuscript cleared peer review the same day *JPAD* editors received it. Public disclosures show that afterward, Cummings—the first listed author—received about $65,000 in various fees from its developer, Acadia Pharmaceuticals. The journal accepted a second paper extolling the benefits of the drug for patients with "pronounced psychotic symptoms" on the day received.

According to Schrag's analysis, *JPAD* published 129 research articles, including expert statements and drug-use guidelines, between 2019 and 2021. When one of the journal's editors-in-chief—including Vellas, Aisen, and Gauthier—coauthored a paper, submission to acceptance averaged about twenty-three days, compared to a still-brisk fifty-two days for other papers.

"It raises questions about whether this journal is a fair and legitimate venue for the dissemination of scientific results, or . . . a personal platform for selected editors and their allies," Schrag noted in his analysis.

I forwarded Schrag's concerns and my own questions to all of the concerned editors. They sent a joint reply that they review quality and police conflicts of interest rigorously. Pharma company leaders, they said, "are among the most knowledgeable experts in the field and contribute important perspectives," and that editors from Biogen and Eisai do not "review clinical trial results due to potential conflict of interest." *JPAD* relies on declarations by authors to avoid such conflicts, the editors said, noting that "statistically, we have good reason to believe that we are in the right." Vellas denied receiving personal compensation from Alzheon, although he disclosed receiving "fees and/or stock options" from the company in the pages of *JPAD* itself within a favorable article, in 2017, about that company's drug tramiprosate. In November 2023, Vellas said he had asked his assistant to put in corrections to his own journal, and to others in which he said he had accidentally disclosed payments from Biogen that were not received. Seven months later, no corrections had been posted.

Regarding the ultrafast peer review process for themselves, they noted, "because the editors-in-chief and board members lead some of the most important clinical and research centers in the field, it is unsurprising that some papers from their teams are of high value and readily judged to be publishable [and] accepted quickly due to their quality, originality, or importance." They added: "We do not give priority to anyone."

Jason Karlawish, an eminent ethicist and Alzheimer's expert at the University of Pennsylvania, and *JPAD*'s ethics editor from its inception through 2020, declined to comment about any of these matters. "My experiences were precisely none," he said about his work at the journal. "It was one of those roles that never moved on from a title."

CHILLING BACKLASH

JPAD's editorial behavior, if extreme, is hardly unique. For example, many editors routinely self-publish in their own journals. Many journals—not just predatory, pay-to-play titles that charge authors exorbitant fees and feature low editorial standards—hide behind high-minded statements of principle while engaging in dubious practices. Journals, like universities, abhor scandal and embarrassment. Even after extreme misconduct seems irrefutable, retractions can take years or even decades, if they are made at all. For example, a study by Elisabeth Bik of 960 papers published in the highly regarded *Molecular and Cellular Biology* found that about sixty had "inappropriately duplicated images." That led to five retractions.

Even when journals retract notorious papers, lazy authors backed by complacent editors continue to cite them. In a notable case in June 2020 a major scandal hit Covid-19 pandemic research. Two prestigious journals—*The New England Journal of Medicine* (*NEJM*) and *The Lancet*—published high-profile studies said to be based on a massive database of patient records compiled from hospitals worldwide by a tiny company, Surgisphere.

The *Lancet* paper claimed that hydroxychloroquine, the controversial antimalarial drug promoted by former President Donald Trump and others as a Covid-19 remedy, could harm rather than help patients. Its publication led to a temporary halt in a major clinical trial and inflamed an already-divisive debate over the drug, which proved useless against the virus. The *NEJM* article corroborated other evidence that people already taking certain blood pressure medicines did not face a greater risk of death if they developed Covid-19.

But questions soon arose about the validity and even existence of the Surgisphere database, and the journals retracted the papers. The affair delighted anti-science culture warriors. Thousands of news articles, tweets, and scholarly commentaries pummeled Surgisphere and the gullible journals, yet many researchers and journal editors apparently remained oblivious. For a January 2021 article in *Science*, I found more than 100 academic articles—many in leading journals—that cited those papers after their retractions, to support related findings.

Ivan Oransky, cofounder of *Retraction Watch*, told me such blunders occur often. Some authors copy and paste lists of citations from similar papers without reading them, and editors wave them through. "It's frightening. It's terrible, but common," he said.

Publishers often rely on guidelines from the nonprofit Committee on Publication Ethics (COPE) to assess possible misconduct. But even prestigious journals seem to hide behind COPE's ponderous procedures rather than using them to enhance and speed policing of suspect articles. COPE guidelines can provide an excuse to do nothing while the accused scientist's employer—which risks reputational harm from public repudiation of a paper—dithers, obfuscates, and delays. The dirty secret: Even top journals tend to suffer editorial paralysis when faced with the need to investigate a paper or concede responsibility for letting damaging errors or fraud enter the scientific record on their watch.

Nature's editors sat on Schrag's analysis of the 2006 paper on Lesné's star amyloid protein for six months, commenting publicly only after I contacted them. After my article on Lesné came out in July 2022—receiving global coverage in the popular and scholarly press—that *Nature* article was cited more than 100 times in other scholarly papers as of March 2024, boosting its total citations to nearly 2,500.

Schrag forwarded elaborate dossiers about Wang's questioned experiments to more than a dozen leading journals. Among thirty-six papers flagged, as of March 2024 only seven had been retracted—five by the journal *PLOS ONE* alone. Six others had been corrected or the journals posted expressions of concern about the results.

The most influential Cassava-related paper that contained numerous suspect images appeared in the *Journal of Clinical Investigation* (*JCI*) in 2012, accompanied by a laudatory editorial. As of March 2024, other papers had cited it a formidable 1,800 times. The study linked insulin resistance to Alzheimer's and the formation of amyloid plaques, using a method Schrag and others said contradicted basic neurobiology.

"If science is conducted with a very low degree of rigor," Nobelist Thomas Südhof told me, "you get bad science. Simple as that. And, of course, it's not possible to reproduce bad science." He was talking in general about Alzheimer's publishing. Many journals, he said, have been edited by people "who operate primarily by networks—who they know and chat with—and don't really understand even what the techniques are. They have no clue what's important."

The *JCI* paper supported the science behind Cassava's simufilam. Schrag provided Rexford Ahima of Johns Hopkins University, then chief editor of *JCI*, his analysis of more than fifteen problematic images in the study, sending them in two groups. At the time, Schrag didn't realize that Ahima had coauthored three suspect papers with Wang and Harvard's Steven Arnold, and shared $7 million in grants with Arnold and another collaborator. Ahima recused himself from looking into the complaints. Other editors rejected the concerns.

Northwestern University cardiologist Elizabeth McNally succeeded Ahima as *JCI* editor after the investigation. She told me that the journal had reviewed high-resolution versions of the first group of images with a software tool and found nothing untoward. I learned later from the software provider that at the time of the *JCI* review, their product lacked the capacity to detect the types of problems Schrag identified. After *JCI* editors could not corroborate his findings in the first set of images, they opted not to review the second set.

"This article was a major part of the foundation of an entire field of research around Alzheimer's disease, 'diabetes of the brain.' It's hugely influential work, and retracting it would materially harm the authors and the journal," Schrag said.

Soon after my 2022 article in *Science* described some of those details, McNally used her editorial soapbox to threaten short sellers who used

Schrag's work to criticize the paper. She called them agents of a "short and distort" campaign—using language Cassava Sciences had deployed earlier. The term refers to efforts to unfairly depress the company's share price for profit. (To reiterate, Schrag told me he had never owned Cassava stock or held any short positions.)

"*JCI* will always take seriously any allegations of misconduct or misrepresentation," McNally wrote. But she added that if allegations are "made for the purposes of stock manipulation, with evidence of misinformation, the *JCI* may elect to express its concern to the US Securities and Exchange Commission or the Department of Justice." She didn't say what evidence would be collected to brand whistleblowers as malicious stock traders.

The *JCI* editorial unsealed "a Pandora's box through which it saddles itself with the role of stock market watchdog," said Alexander Trevelyan, a bioinformatics and genomics software developer and physicist who has written analyses about Cassava. "Will the journal be taking disclosed or suspected securities positions into account when deciding what to review, or how to review it? How do they plan to 'independently seek to verify whistleblowers' potential conflicts' exactly? . . . How exactly do they plan to account for the 'time sensitivity to short selling' if they have no reason to believe that the whistleblowing is illegitimate? By purposefully dragging their feet? Do they take on financial liability for this? Should they? Trust me, these are questions that the journal does not want to answer. That they chose to even raise them in the first place suggests that the situation may be even worse than we perceive."

CHEATERS ARE ALWAYS
ONE STEP AHEAD OF THE DETECTORS

McNally's unprecedented warning—widely viewed as a threat to silence critics of Ahima, herself, and *JCI*'s authors—reflected a radically changing landscape. Whether or not biomedical research misconduct has increased, its discovery has. Publishers and editors can no longer ignore insurgents chipping away at age-old bastions of scholarly power. A small army of image sleuths has risen. Most use pseudonyms to post comments to PubPeer or X. Pattern-matching software has accelerated their work to an almost industrial scale to help people detect signs of doctoring, regardless of their scientific expertise.

Those skeptics—some called "data thugs," a derisive epithet that a few fraud hunters have adopted as a prideful moniker—have made PubPeer a force to be reckoned with.

In July 2023, I attended a small private confab of some of the most prolific and effective image detectives—who collectively have posted many thousands of comments to PubPeer and sparked thousands of corrections and retractions. It was the first face-to-face meeting for most of a group that has become the worst nightmare of button-down editors.

Cheshire, the pseudonymous nonscientist who would later play a key role in helping me assess the extent of apparent misconduct in Alzheimer's research, organized the meeting. The middle-aged American, who sometimes wears a T-shirt emblazoned with the grinning cartoon face of his namesake, the cat from *Alice in Wonderland*—rented a few luxury apartments in Newtown, steps from the Vltava River that runs through Prague's heart, and a few blocks from the historic city center.

He assembled a motley group of about a dozen leading, self-appointed scientific-fraud investigators from Europe, the United States, and beyond for a week of nerdy technical discussions, competitive banter, and strategy sessions—breaking in the evenings to drink *pivo* (beer, in Czech) in a subterranean dive bar down the street.

They included David Bimler, a retired New Zealand perceptual psychologist with a long, wispy beard who resembles a skinny, aging Hell's Angel. His jokey online name, Smut Clyde, came from a porn-name generator (which provides a fake name for self-evident purposes). Bimler said it's a takeoff on the name of his first cat, Smut, a word for chimney soot. "Self-mockery . . . has advantages. I cannot use an argument from authority to assert that my criticisms are correct. They have to stand on their feet," he told *Le Monde*: Bimler is the scourge of "paper mills"—fraudulent services that generate supposedly scholarly papers and sell author slots to desperate or ethically challenged academics. His success earned Bimler a profile in *Nature*—where he outed his true identity.

Sholto David, a young molecular biologist from South Wales who completed his PhD at Newcastle University in the United Kingdom, has written some two thousand comments on PubPeer, making him one of the most prolific image sleuths. Clean-cut and soft-spoken, he betrayed his rebellious nature by pairing a bright red sock with a bright orange partner. At the confab, his polite, low-key, and thoughtful observations about the finer points of policing science contrasted with his comedic YouTube "Science Police" videos. The low-production-value send-ups of allegedly cheating scientists entertain with a serious purpose.

Only a few thousand people view those videos, but in early 2024, David, then thirty-two, became somewhat famous when he blogged about dozens of problematic studies by scientists at Dana-Farber Cancer Institute, the renowned Boston research and treatment center. The concerns were picked up by the *Harvard Crimson* student paper, and soon in dozens of media outlets. Amid the scandal, Dana-Farber scientists quickly retracted six studies, and corrected thirty-one others. For David and others, watchdogging scientists is a labor of love. He estimated that he gets monthly contributions from fans of just over $200 via the donation website Patreon. (He's going to have to get a real job at some point, David told the *Guardian*. He added about his South Wales digs: "I'm just stretching my meagre savings and it's cheap rent out here.")

Nick Brown, a boisterous, loquacious statistics specialist and expat Brit living on the Mediterranean island of Mallorca, knows how to command a room. With psychophysiologist James Heathers, he was among the original data thugs—gaining dozens of corrections and retractions by showing where numbers don't add up. He wore a T-shirt emblazoned with "Russian warship go fuck yourself" on the back, written in Ukrainian. Brown is equally direct, in more erudite fashion, calling out examples of academic error or fraud as "proctologically derived." (Leaning in the direction of the other journalist invited to the meeting, he said in jest,

"There will be moments when we will have to kill you"—if she heard any of their trade secrets. "I prefer not," she replied good-naturedly.)

"Publishers literally do not care if what is in their journals is true," Brown said, showing a half-serious cynicism that characterized much of the discourse. "The only way to get them to care is to make sure the reputational damage is high enough."

Leonid Schneider, a cantankerous, unruly Ukrainian who emigrated to Germany as a teenager, fully subscribes to that approach. The former scientist operates a blog for polemics about researchers whom he accuses of misconduct, backed by investigative findings of his own or others. (He hosted David's work on Dana-Farber.) His penchant for hyperbole—at the meeting, he compared some scientists who might have engaged in doctoring images to Nazi doctor Josef Mengele, and journals to cigarette makers—has enraged his targets.

Schneider, a vegan, prefers large slices of cake to *pivo*. His blog features self-portrait line drawings of his bespectacled, bearded face framed by electric black hair, thick and wild—authentically reflecting humorous self-deprecation as he ridicules his targets. The blog proudly displays a mock wanted poster for himself: "WANTED: For Anti-Science Trolling & Slander of Scientists." Nothing gives him greater pleasure than "humiliating" his targets, he said, proudly introducing himself to a journalist as "Satan."

"I'm a failed scientist and a successful science terrorist," Schneider added, bragging that he has been sued ten times. Schneider expressed intense grievance against PubPeer (whose moderators have rejected some of his posts) and journalists whom he thinks should credit his blog when writing about academic misconduct. He does sometimes beat mainstream journalists to the punch. The Prague crew embraced him as one of their own.

Elisabeth Bik, instrumental in validating Schrag's findings about Lesné and Ashe's work, also attended. The fiftysomething biologist began to uncover corrupt research in 2013 after working as a lab scientist at Stanford University. In 2019, after working for bioscience companies, she pivoted to full-time image sleuthing, blogging for her "Science Integrity Digest." Features in *Le Monde*, the *New Yorker*, *Science*, *Nature*, and elsewhere helped her emerge as a globally known expert. (But not even Bik is getting rich off this work. Her Patreon donations total about $2,300 per month; much in demand for speaking gigs, she also earns honoraria.) Bik became a cause célèbre, supported by more than two thousand scientists in 2021 after becoming the subject of a criminal complaint and the doxing of some of her personal information by a colleague of the controversial French microbiologist Didier Raoult, a booster of hydroxychloroquine for Covid-19. Bik was among the first to challenge his research, now widely discredited. She also faces brutal online attacks from Cassava's SAVAges. Bik counts more than one thousand papers retracted as the result of her observations. Journalists worldwide inundate her with requests.

Tall and brightly dressed, the unfailingly polite Bik delighted in the company of friends and kindred spirits in Prague. She became the unofficial group photographer and contributed her signature Dutch stroopwafel cookies, a trademark of her native Gouda, as a meeting snack. Just like she cleans up the scholarly literature, Bik tidied up the apartments for the boys.

She admits to being obsessed with patterns—can't *not* see them. One evening in a Prague bar, I noticed that she couldn't take her eyes off a detailed art print on the wall, depicting hundreds of people standing in a field of flowers. No one else had noticed that some of the figures appeared on both sides of the print in mirror images of each other.

Bik speaks with modest precision. (Her go-to description of an apparently duplicated image is "unexpectedly similar.") She told me privately that she sometimes worries that Schneider's caustic blog posts might contribute to tragic mental health consequences. "I've been the victim of nasty blog posts. So, I know how that affects a person," Bik said. She usually leaves names and accusations out of her public posts on PubPeer or X, focusing on the images. Bik said she worries about innocent collaborators falling victim to fraudsters—recalling the Japanese scientist who hung himself in the wake of a public scandal after his colleague seemed to have falsified their joint experiments, tainting his life's work.

It's obvious why this crew—in turns tempered or extreme, unwavering, deeply skeptical of institutional authorities—would terrify journal editors. Those editors are losing their exclusive control over standards for their own publications.

The Prague group's efforts have gotten a gigantic assist from artificial intelligence software such as Imagetwin—produced by an Austrian start-up that offers some of those in attendance free accounts. The company's clean-cut young founders—computer scientist Markus Zlabinger and business specialist Patrick Starke—joined the group, mostly to listen and learn about how to improve their product for its arms race against cheats who also deploy evolving software techniques to make doctored images harder to find.

I asked Bik who is winning that arms race.

"The cheaters are always one step ahead of the detectors," she said.

Bik told me she believes in the integrity of the vast majority of scientists and journal editors. She tries to protect them by exposing apparent fraud and error in a culture that can seem willfully blind to corruption. (In fairness, while journals have been slow to react, some prominent ones are changing. *Science* editor Holden Thorp wrote in early 2024 that the journal would use the image-checking software program Proofig, among other measures, to catch problems.)

"It's like the Tour de France when everybody accepted that doping was quite okay. Or like having traffic rules without the chance of ever getting a ticket. Everybody would be speeding," she said. "If there's no regulatory body, then the rewards [for misconduct] are much higher than the chance of any consequences in your career."

In a world of sometimes feckless government officials and arrogant editors, Bik was referring to how people in the Prague meetings have in effect begun to stand in for the third key institution in battling fraud in biomedical research: universities. As he pursued challenges to work by Wang, Lesné, and others, Schrag soon learned that the people running institutions founded on principles of debate and openness, and ideals of fast-moving progress, often work with perplexing lassitude in the shadows.

Chapter 16

Ivory Tower Deceits

Guelph, Canada; Cambridge, Massachusetts;
Stanford, California; and Elsewhere
2012–2024

*"The . . . paper reflects a pattern of deception and academic misconduct.
The university has chosen to stand back for reasons that I don't understand.
I am disturbed to sit in a building where someone has been
running a fabrication mill."*

—PAUL HEBERT, UNIVERSITY OF GUELPH

The federal Office of Research Integrity (ORI) had passed Matthew Schrag's findings on Hoau-Yan Wang and his work with Cassava Sciences to Wang's employer, the City University of New York (CUNY). ORI also asked the University of Minnesota to examine the dossier Schrag prepared on work by its Alzheimer's experts Karen Ashe and Sylvain Lesné. Given the exacting detail he provided on scores of papers, Schrag hoped that those institutions would quickly confirm that wrongdoing had taken place.

But the history of similar cases shows the pitfalls of self-policing by universities.

In 2013, a team led by University of Guelph (UG) botanist Steven Newmaster took a hard look at popular herbal products such as echinacea, ginkgo biloba, and St. John's wort. Their study used DNA barcoding—which identifies species using unique snippets of genetic material—to test if each bottle really contained what was printed on the label.

They found troubling results. Most of the products contained different plants, were larded with inert fillers, or included contaminants that could cause liver and colon damage, skin tumors, and other serious health problems. The paper, published in the journal *BMC Medicine*, received prominent attention in the *New York Times* and other media. The findings "pissed me off," Newmaster told PBS *Frontline*. "I go in to buy a product that I believe in, that I care about and I pay a lot of money for, and it's not even in the bottle? Are you kidding me?" Major retailers pulled products from their shelves or added quality-control measures.

Almost overnight, Newmaster became an authority on validating food and supplement ingredients. He quickly morphed from critic into industry ally. Major supplement makers hired companies he created to certify their products as authentic. In 2017, Newmaster founded a venture within UG to improve certification technologies for supplements. It raised millions of dollars from herbal suppliers.

But in a surprising twist, eight experts in DNA barcoding and related fields charged that the 2013 paper that indicted an entire industry and launched a new phase in Newmaster's career was itself a fraud. In a forty-three-page allegation letter, sent to UG in June 2021, the researchers—from UG, the University of Toronto, the University of British Columbia, and Stanford University—cited major problems in that study and two others by Newmaster. "The data which underpin [the papers] are missing, fraudulent, or plagiarized," they flatly stated. The group also charged that Newmaster "recurrently failed to disclose competing financial interests" in his papers. He had launched his first testing companies just before the influential paper was published.

The accusers included coauthors of two papers that were later retracted. They said Newmaster misled them. The critics included evolutionary biologist Paul Hebert, sometimes called the "father of DNA barcoding," who directs UG's Centre for Biodiversity Genomics.

"The 2013 herbal supplement paper reflects a pattern of deception and academic misconduct. The university has chosen to stand back for reasons that I don't understand," Hebert told me. "I am disturbed to sit in a building where someone has been running a fabrication mill."

Newmaster did not respond to my interview requests or written questions. But in a defense sent to UG he denied all charges. "I have never committed data fabrication, falsification, plagiarism, or inadequate acknowledgment in the publications as claimed," he wrote. "I have never engaged in any unethical activity or academic misconduct." Newmaster also denied making money from his network of businesses.

My 2022 investigation for *Science* found problems in Newmaster's work beyond the three papers. They included apparent fabrication, data manipulation, and plagiarism in lectures, teaching, biographies, and scholarly writing. A review of thousands of pages of his publications, conference speeches, and training and promotional videos, along with interviews with two dozen current and former colleagues or independent scientists and sixteen regulatory or research agencies, revealed a charismatic and eloquent scientist who often exaggerated, fabulized his accomplishments, and presented other researchers' data and teaching materials as his own.

In one particularly odd boast during an October 2020 radio interview, Newmaster said he was working on tests of SARS-CoV-2, the Covid-19 virus, partly at the request of the US Centers for Disease Control and Prevention (CDC). That was in the summer and fall of 2019, he said, months before the pandemic erupted. "In the scientific community we were already sequencing samples—blood samples, saliva samples—and looking at this virus," he told an incredulous host. The CDC said it could not locate information about working with Newmaster.

Among his various entrepreneurial ventures, Newmaster has served as science advisor to Purity-IQ, which tests and certifies the authenticity of comestibles, including cannabis. In a 2020 promotional video by the company, he warned about the risks of data manipulation. "We could have all the testing in the world," he said. "And if that data could be counterfeited or could be changed in any way it doesn't really matter how good the test is." One month later, in a training video for the Association of Food and Drug Officials in which Newmaster promoted Purity-IQ testing, he displayed graphics from other sources without credit and described them as his own work, an analysis of his talk and PowerPoint slides showed.

"Here's the little experiment that we ran," Newmaster said in the video, calling it "a real-life scenario" to guide industry quality control. The image he showed, purportedly representing a fifty-point technical analysis of cannabis strains, is identical to one assembled by other researchers for something unrelated to marijuana or scientific testing of any kind. It depicts US arrest data—one point for each of the fifty states.

A UG panel charged with investigating allegations of misconduct by Newmaster included no experts in DNA barcoding and looked strictly at the three challenged papers. It ignored my findings. Newmaster "displayed a pattern of poor judgment and failed to apply the standards reasonably expected in research activity in his discipline," the panel chairman wrote. Yet despite "many shortcomings" it found "insufficient evidence" to support a charge of misconduct. Newmaster was exonerated.

Given the panel's dubious conclusions and qualifications, the Canadian government required UG to do it over. In June 2024, the new examination of Newmaster's work found "with high probability" that the scientist engaged in "data fabrication and falsification," failed to acknowledge sources of data, and mismanaged conflicts of interest for all three papers it reviewed. It called for the landmark nutritional supplement paper to be retracted. (The journal did so a few weeks later.) The new review failed to address evidence of fraud in his other work.

Those conclusions were leaked to me, but only Newmaster and UG administrators know whether he has been or ever will be penalized for transgressions that make a mockery of academic integrity. The saga serves as an archetype of what often happens when an institution with the most to lose from a determined, dispassionate, far-reaching investigation—prestige, funding, and public respect—holds the authority to assess the conduct of its own scientists.

HISTORICAL RAMPARTS

Newmaster might seem extreme. But consider that dozens of cases involving apparent misconduct in Alzheimer's research—many exposed for the first time in these pages—traveled under the radar for decades. The same is true in other scientific realms. Part of the reason traces back to cultural imperatives born in the years following World War II.

After the war's massive Manhattan Project created the atomic bomb, like other wartime advances a military-managed venture, President Franklin Roosevelt's science advisor Vannevar Bush called for an end to government taking the lead role in scientific research. In 1945, he delivered an influential report that proposed a framework for future success based on substantial autonomy. Universities must have "internal control of policy, personnel, and the method and scope of research," Bush wrote in *Science: The Endless Frontier*. To succeed, they had to be self-directed and managed, he insisted, earning accolades from the academy.

Bush's advice was largely adopted. Still, in following decades governments layered on regulations for lab and patient safety, environmental pollution, and ethical practices, along with a close watch on how grant funds were spent. Regulatory mission creep deeply concerned many in the scientific community. "Freedom of inquiry is being stifled," as ethicist Sissela Bok described that reaction, "because of nameless fears always directed to what is new and bold." A landmark study by the premier US scientific organization, the National Academy of Sciences, warned: "Real dangers are involved . . . when the nonscientist attempts to impose his own value system on what should be largely scientific decisions."

Individuals can think big only if protected by the shared understanding that science depends on experimental trial and error, failure leading to success. It thrives on creativity that can threaten conventional wisdom. To break new ground, scientists must feel sure that institutional authorities—funders, regulators, and universities—have their backs.

Yet science, like any human activity, must endure mistakes and weaknesses. *Retraction Watch* has amassed a database of more than fifty thousand retractions of scholarly papers. Retractions, some the result of fraud, show scientific self-regulation in action.

But when universities use their substantial autonomy to defend, ignore, or hide corrupt practices that skew experimental outcomes or overall research directions, public trust—the active ingredient of democratic consent—can break down. How universities handle cases of egregious misconduct offers a barometer of academic vitality and reliability. Fairly or not, such cases play an outsized role in whether the public vests its faith in experts and their institutions. When universities conceal such problems, they feed the kind of mistrust that became reprehensible attacks on public health officials during the Covid-19 pandemic.

Arrogance and defensiveness have drained credibility from the maxim, "Trust us, we are the experts." Scientists have applied that idea to a multitude of political and values-based conflicts and challenges for which they often hold no special expertise, or despite obvious conflicts of interest—such as examining misconduct inside their own institutions.

STUDENTS TAKE CHARGE

When federal authorities become aware of credible claims of research fraud, they send the cases back to the universities where alleged misconduct took place. Yet in case after case, universities fall short, particularly when problems involve prestige and power. A 2009 study published in the journal *PLOS ONE* found that one in every fifty scientists admits to having fabricated or falsified experimental data. Perverse incentives account for that alarming figure.

"Universities can make a lot of money from sham science. They lose money from catching fraudsters. Uncovering fraud also brings negative publicity and a host of other headaches," criminal justice scholar and whistleblower Justin Pickett wrote in 2020. "Even in biomedical cases, where the public health consequences of fake research are most severe, universities dismiss almost 90 percent of fraud accusations without an investigation, or even an auditable record."

"Imagine a world in which police and prosecutors basically didn't exist, and most crime was caught only if there was a private vigilante around. Crime would be higher. But that's the world that researchers live in: No official agency *proactively* investigates important published papers to check for signs of fraud," added Stuart Buck, who directs the non-profit Good Science Project. So anonymous sleuths on PubPeer or gutsy whistleblowers do the most heavy lifting.

To the shame of major universities, idealistic students often become the most-determined whistleblowers. At great reputational risk—sometimes sacrificing their careers—they police the misdeeds of powerful professors and administrators.

Stanford University freshman and journalist Theo Baker's takedown of university president and Alzheimer's expert Marc Tessier-Lavigne was one such high-profile case. Suspicions about his work had been percolating for years before Baker's exposé, which was largely based on findings by Schrag and Elisabeth Bik. It forced administrators to act, leading to the resignation of one of the most powerful players in American education. It was also a gutsy move for Baker. If he had been wrong, his career might have been over before it got off the ground.

The Tessier-Lavigne example followed a litany of others in which students risked even more, and some paid dearly for doing the right thing.

In 2006, Chantal Ly, a PhD student in genetics at the University of Wisconsin–Madison, found strong evidence that her mentor, Elizabeth Goodwin, had invented data in grant applications and scholarly papers. Eventually, five other students sided with Ly and the group reported Goodwin to administrators. It altered their careers, tied to Goodwin, forever.

"Three of the students, who had invested a combined sixteen years in obtaining their PhDs, have quit school. Two others are starting over . . . extending the amount of time it will take them to get their doctorates by years," according to a report in *Science*. "The five graduate students who spoke with *Science* also described discouraging encounters with other faculty members, whom they say sided with Goodwin before all the facts became available." Ly, set back by years, abandoned her goal of earning a doctorate after Goodwin initially claimed innocence. Four years later, the professor pled guilty to a criminal charge in the case.

In 2008, Duke University medical student and researcher Bradford

Perez thought he had won the lottery when he landed a job helping develop revolutionary cancer chemotherapy treatments that were individualized to the genetic profile of each patient's tumor. FDA Commissioner Rob Califf, then vice chancellor of clinical research at Duke, called it "the holy grail of cancer." More than one hundred desperate patients signed up for the experimental therapy. Major journals published the findings about what looked like a fundamental breakthrough.

But Perez concluded that the technique developed by his professor, Anil Potti, was based on doctored data. He removed his own name as a coauthor from the Potti articles and reported his concerns in detail to Potti's senior collaborator Joseph Nevins and Duke administrators. Perez was urged, in effect, to shut up and not report anything to the funders that gave millions of dollars for the work. The student's career was set back by a year while he started fresh in a new research posting he felt he could trust.

Some eighteen months after complaints from Perez, the episode exploded. A report on *60 Minutes* described how outside researchers, and finally Nevins, found the kinds of problems Perez first saw in Potti's data. Perez appeared nowhere in that coverage. Duke officials denied having heard from any internal whistleblower. Potti resigned in the wake of retractions and lawsuits by dead patients' families. Despite the scale of apparent fraud, he went on to treat cancer patients at Unity Medical Center in Grafton, North Dakota, whose website bragged about his teaching awards and time on Duke's faculty.

"The system believes that scientists are honest, and I think usually they are. But it's never true in a large operation that everybody's morally and ethically the same," Schrag said. "Principal investigators want to get published. Your boss wants you to get published. Journals want to publish big, high-profile papers. Funding institutions want big results. So, when problems arise, who do they ask to investigate? They go back to the university that has everything to lose. The whole system is designed not to catch this stuff."

That's why students have had to step into the breach time after time.

In 2010, they nailed a Harvard expert on cognition and morality, who admitted "significant mistakes." Top Harvard economists were undone in 2013 when a University of Massachusetts grad student, for a class assignment, tried to replicate their analysis of economic growth during times of high public debt. The numbers didn't add up.

In 2018, Pickett, the criminology scholar, now at the State University of New York at Albany, outed his former mentor at Florida State University for cooking the books on five studies that Picket coauthored as a student. The university initially declined to conduct a thorough investigation. But after Pickett published a detailed review of the problems, all five papers—and one more—were retracted. The professor was finally fired in 2023.

The Newmaster inquiry was triggered in 2020 by Ken Thompson, who in 2012 was one of the first two students to enroll when Newmaster helped launch UG's undergraduate biodiversity major. "We're getting one-on-one time with this famous, super-successful, important professor," Thompson recalls thinking with excitement. Newmaster asked Thompson to work on a paper comparing the cost of traditional taxonomic typing and DNA barcoding for identifying forest plants. Newmaster provided summary data; Thompson had to analyze them and draft the paper. The resulting 2014 paper in *Biodiversity and Conservation* was his first.

Years later, working on his PhD at the University of British Columbia, Thompson grew queasy. He realized that the perfect species identification claimed in the paper was virtually impossible for some of the plants. Newmaster had never shown him the raw data or uploaded data to an online repository. The professor didn't reply to Thompson's requests for clarification, adding to his doubts. In early 2020, Thompson asked UG to investigate. "I wasn't 100 percent confident that it was fraudulent," he told me. "I was 100 percent confident that it was worth asking the question."

Thompson—who later detected other cases of Newmaster's ostensible fabrication or plagiarism—said UG administrators slow-walked his request, recast it as an informal query, and in early 2021 rejected his claims as insufficiently supported. "They thought that I was just one person, and

I didn't have a lot of power—that they could squash me," he said. Thompson then asked the editor of *Biodiversity and Conservation* to conduct an independent review. The editor deferred to UG. (Eventually, the paper was retracted.)

In May 2021, Thompson self-published his concerns and posted a related commentary on a biodiversity blog, *Eco-Evo Evo-Eco.* "Doing this alone behind the scenes has been incredibly isolating," he wrote. "I . . . hope that by sharing an evidence-based critique of our paper some people will choose to support me." Indeed, DNA barcoding titan Hebert soon added a note of support, and the yearslong investigation ensued.

SHARING THE BLAME

In fairness to the universities, misconduct investigations can be a hard slog.

So said Susan Garfinkel, the former ORI executive who manages research compliance at the Ohio State University. Universities often face legal threats from lawyered-up faculty members accused of wrongdoing, who receive further support from faculty unions. Students and junior researchers might have been coerced into misconduct in service of their mentors, and understandably feel terrified to talk openly because their careers could be crippled by a finding of fraud. Internal investigators at universities sometimes lack logistical or staffing support—or face hostility from higher-ups. (The Hoau-Yan Wang–CUNY case would prove an object lesson in those challenges.)

Francesca Gino, a well-known Harvard Business School social scientist, has studied influences on honesty. In a paper with a colleague she found, for example, that signing a pledge to be truthful at the top, rather than the bottom, of an insurance form can profoundly affect the honesty of replies. Data Colada, a team of social-behavioral scientists who moonlight as numbers sleuths, dived deeply into Gino's work. They found "evidence of fraud," such as fabrication, in several cases, including the insurance paper. Harvard's integrity office independently verified the findings and Gino was suspended. Several of her papers were retracted. Gino sued Data Colada, Harvard, and its business school dean for defamation, demanding "not less than $25 million" in damages.

Although the case against Data Colada was ultimately thrown out by a federal judge, the group's members had to mount a GoFundMe appeal to pay legal bills—a reason why so many sleuths publish their findings on PubPeer under pseudonyms. "It's maddening to find ourselves in a situation where scientists who find evidence of serious malpractice and data manipulation have to share their findings in secret lest their own livelihoods be ruined," noted an analysis in *Vox*.

Conflicts of interest, lawsuits, embarrassment, and financial risk aversion combine to make universities inherently unreliable, often feeble investigators of their own people. So eventual crackdowns on corruption—for example, in the Duke and Florida State cases—often occur, as in the manner of a quip often attributed to Winston Churchill about American efforts to combat the Nazis during World War II: "After all the other possibilities have been exhausted."

Buck and others have argued convincingly that a better approach could be an independent review process that includes subject matter experts, stakeholders, and forensic analysts.

When Schrag placed his findings into the hands of the federal authorities, the journals, and the universities, he didn't know whether their strengths would overcome their foibles. But he never anticipated that his actions would soon provoke a research-integrity crisis that cut to the core of his personal history and would destroy a relationship at the core of his identity as a scientist.

Chapter 17

Shock and Duty

Grand Forks, Nashville

2006 and 2022

"If the rules apply to others, they have to apply to [all of] us."
—MATTHEW SCHRAG

Five weeks after my *Science* article in July 2022 exposed a major scandal in Alzheimer's research and named Matthew Schrag as the whistleblower, he faced a shock unlike anything he'd experienced as a scientist or a person.

Schrag received automated emails from PubPeer linked to complaints that two of his own articles contained dubious images. The papers described the first research Schrag had ever participated in, more than fifteen years earlier, as a callow undergraduate at the University of North Dakota (UND). They were his earliest attempts to unravel the mysteries of Alzheimer's disease.

Meme-stock trolls who supported Cassava Sciences tweeted that Schrag was a hypocrite who denigrated others' work while closeting his own skeletons. That seemed unsurprising. After all, he had flagged apparently doctored images in Cassava-linked Alzheimer's papers and research underpinning a key aspect of the dominant amyloid hypothesis of the disease.

Schrag had earlier told me he "expected every project that I ever participated in to be carefully scrutinized, and that my work would stand up to that scrutiny." He assumed that if the PubPeer posts revealed actual flaws, there would be innocent explanations.

The now-suspect articles had been points of pride for a young student working as a lab assistant. Allegations of doctored images included studies on amyloid proteins in rabbit brains. Schrag had been learning about science and building his résumé to apply to medical school. He owed the training and the publications to the nurturing mentorship of neuropharmacologist Othman Ghribi, the senior author and principal investigator.

Ghribi designed the tests and directed Schrag's activities. Ghribi prepared the scientific images and packaged them for publication. Ghribi handled the back-and-forth of peer review and editing. Schrag felt sure that his former mentor, whom he trusted deeply, would dispatch the PubPeer concerns with simple clarifications.

Schrag told me that he owed Ghribi an enormous debt of gratitude. The scientist had played an outsized role in launching Schrag's career, instilling a sense of wonder in the world of biomedical research, and reinforcing the primacy of reliable experimentation. In no small part, Ghribi's influence explained the "Everything Is Figureoutable" sign that occupies precious real estate on the small, utilitarian desk in Schrag's Vanderbilt University office. Years later, he dedicated his PhD dissertation "To my dear friend Dr. Othman Ghribi who introduced me to research. I am grateful for his patient training and encouragement to pursue science as a career."

In 2011, when Schrag finished his PhD at Loma Linda University, Ghribi raised the ceremonial hood over his head in the age-old ritual marking the ultimate academic rite of passage. A photo taken that day shows the two men at a post-ceremony reception. Schrag, in full academic regalia, grasps the tassel on his cap with pride as he leans forward, gaze locked on the older man. Ghribi gestures intently—as if conveying one last fine point of biology to his newly launched protégé.

A few years later, as a professor at Vanderbilt—several notches higher than UND in the academic pecking order—Schrag prepared a talk filled with "to-do's" for aspiring grad students. Tip #3 shows Schrag, arm around

Ghribi earlier on that graduation day, with his PhD advisor, Wolff Kirsch, on Ghribi's other side. The caption reads: "Pick the right mentor."

Schrag credited Ghribi as key to shaping his professional choices. He recalled what his high school teacher told him, when he felt deflated that despite high test scores and visions of the Ivy League, he ended up at UND as an undergrad. That teacher admonished him to "Stop feeling sorry for yourself and go do something."

Ghribi opened the doors to doing something, and to Schrag's career. Ghribi's own literal "it takes a village" inspirational story fed the wellspring of his appeal. The ethnic Berber spent teenage years tending sheep in his native Tunisia. His family—with the help of village friends—somehow scraped together enough money to send him to France for his education. In 1994, Ghribi earned his PhD in neuropharmacology at René Descartes University in Paris.

"There was a certain humanity about him," a vestige of the humble shepherd boy, Schrag said.

In 2019 UND honored Ghribi, after his nomination by the faculty, with an award for research, teaching, and service to the university and the profession. It was one more sign of success in the ultracompetitive world of science. The award reflected great skill and equal dedication to truth. Or so it seemed.

Schrag figured—hoped—that like some other concerns posted to PubPeer, the criticisms would prove false or trivial. Still, he dropped everything to take a hard look at the papers. His stomach churned when Schrag realized that the anonymous critics seemed to have a point. The western blots looked false.

At that moment, he had to confront a sobering question: Had a beloved mentor faked data?

CONFRONTATION AND REMORSE

The next day, he called Ghribi, naturally fearing an excruciating conversation.

Within minutes, the older man broke down in tears, Schrag said. He admitted to "problems" in many papers. He explained that there had been a misconduct inquiry in 2006 or 2007—news to Schrag—about an improperly duplicated image in the rabbit paper. Ghribi gave the journal a false excuse, Schrag said his mentor admitted. The editors bought the story, and the paper survived with just a correction.

During their discussion, Ghribi defended his underlying findings as correct but admitted to exaggerating data. In his shame, Ghribi had hidden it all, Schrag said he was told. In a way, Schrag said he thought Ghribi's "certain humanity" was preserved, even heightened, in that wretched moment. Deep sadness hung like a pall over their words as Schrag could see Ghribi's reputation, based on a lifetime of struggle and accomplishment against all odds, leaking away.

"I'm nauseated talking about it," Schrag told me two days later. Abject betrayal by one of the most important people in his life—a man he loved—left him deflated, emotionally adrift.

Yet Ghribi was not prepared to correct the scientific record. So Schrag knew he had to do it himself. First, he immediately approached the journals of the two dubious papers he had coauthored to say he could no longer stand behind them. He requested retractions.

Despite the initial Twitter attacks, Schrag knew he wouldn't be held responsible for the fraudulent papers, given they were prepared when he was still an undergrad just learning how a lab operates. Unlike postdoctoral fellows or staff scientists—scholars with years of training—he had had no idea how to engineer false images or even how that might support a scientific point.

But he felt a moral and professional obligation to correct the record. And he knew that institutional authorities, such as the journals in question, don't always fix even the most obvious stumbles, even if a coauthor begs them to do so.

Schrag didn't rest until he completed a deep dive into Ghribi's body of work, including all their joint papers. It's rare, he had observed, that a scientist who manipulates images stops at one or a few. He enlisted help from Elisabeth Bik and the pseudonymous sleuth Cheshire, who had originally detected and posted to PubPeer some of Ghribi's issues.

I then had my first contact with Cheshire by phone, to check up on Schrag's views and get his ideas about how the problems likely unfolded. He responded with sober thoughtfulness, a quality that would later prove crucial to my own bigger examination of Alzheimer's research.

Schrag, Bik, and Cheshire soon uncovered a litany of questionable research spanning much of Ghribi's career, both before and after he had worked with Schrag. As the only person on every paper, and normally as the responsible first or last author, Ghribi formed the throughline—another validation that Schrag's integrity was intact.

In their assessment of the work from 2001 through 2019, when Ghribi stopped doing lab science, the three found suspect images in thirty-four papers, adding one more coauthored with Schrag. The ostensible problems included duplicated western blots used in experiments representing different circumstances, and brain micrographs that seemed to have artificial features—such as amyloid plaques—that supported Ghribi's hypotheses. In case after case, seemingly doctored images haunted Ghribi's work.

They sent their joint sixty-seven-page dossier, including more than one hundred suspicious images, to the National Institutes of Health (NIH), which had underwritten some $3.8 million of Ghribi's work. Agency officials declined to comment, but in an email to Schrag said they would look into the concerns, and alerted UND officials.

The possible misconduct included six papers in the *Journal of Neurochemistry* and four in the *Journal of Alzheimer's Disease (JAD)*. George Perry, chief editor of *JAD*, whose editorial board included Ghribi, said he contacted Ghribi for more information. Soon after, Ghribi dropped off the board. The journal would assess the claims, Perry told me. In March 2024, it retracted one of the papers.

Schrag contacted a UND official to see whether original images for the papers he coauthored could be found. It was due diligence. If innocent explanations for some of the problems existed, they would emerge from uncropped, high-resolution images used to prepare papers for publication. The official said he could not identify any relevant documents. But

UND found that Schrag's larger set of concerns, along with PubPeer comments on publications by Ghribi, warranted a full inquiry, according to a notification sent to Ghribi.

"We are taking all reasonable steps to secure records related to the research in question," John Mihelich, a UND vice president, told me in an email. "We are in communication with the appropriate federal research offices and sponsors."

In 2019, Ghribi had moved to a campus of the University of Texas (UT) Rio Grande Valley, located in remote Harlingen near the Mexican border. That complicated the process of unearthing any records he might have left behind in North Dakota.

In a text message Schrag provided to me, Ghribi told him, "I am sorry to say I couldn't find a trace of our work. I asked [a relative] to check on an external drive I had in my stuff in [North Dakota] but no data in it. As I said, I take full responsibility of any problem with the data."

Ghribi later acknowledged that out of remorse, he had discarded his scholarly awards and purged his computers and files of raw experimental data, Schrag said. If so, absolute proof of image manipulation might prove impossible. If Ghribi was trying to thwart a misconduct probe, Schrag said, he also seemed to be backing away from his entire career.

The *Journal of Neurochemistry*, where Schrag and Ghribi's original rabbit paper appeared, retracted it a few months after Schrag's request. The editors of a paper he and Ghribi shared in *Experimental Neurology* told Schrag that they were waiting to see what the UND investigation turned up before acting. (The third joint paper, which appeared in 2008 in the journal *Hippocampus*, was retracted in June 2024, after UND concluded that Ghribi had fabricated data. Two other Ghribi papers were retracted after he failed to provide original images for comparison.)

I had to get the story into *Science* quickly—it was leaking into the public domain and another reporter would write it soon enough if I didn't. The key question: What would Ghribi say about himself and about Schrag? I sent the dossier to Ghribi and said I'd like to talk.

AGONIZING EXONERATION

He agreed to an in-person interview, and I planned a trip to Texas. Beforehand, Ghribi emailed me to clear up one key matter: "My primary reason for speaking with you is to exonerate Matthew of any wrongdoing with the manuscripts he coauthored in my lab," he wrote, reinforcing the message he sent to Schrag. But Ghribi backed out of telling his whole story a few days before our appointment, citing the pending UND investigation.

My article appeared in early November 2022. I took no pleasure in the piece, headlined, "'I'm nauseated': Alzheimer's whistleblower finds possible misconduct by his mentor in their papers"—which almost certainly crushed Ghribi's hard-won reputation forever.

Soon after, Ghribi emailed me with complaints, and contradicted some of his earlier statements. "Your article is biased, reporting only the claims made by Dr. Matthew Schrag. It could have been ethical to wait on the outcome of the investigation by the University of North Dakota for you to provide both sides of the story. The statements attributed to me in the articles were not all true," he wrote. Ghribi blamed other coauthors for some of the problems—including Schrag in two cases. He provided no evidence.

In 2024, I tried twice more to speak with Ghribi—to get his story firsthand. The last attempt was in June after the UND investigation had been completed. The full results were not announced publicly, but the university sent Schrag and Ghribi a letter stating that they had determined that one of their joint papers was tainted due to misconduct—a doctored image—by Ghribi and should be retracted. He rejected my request for an interview.

Schrag called the episode the most agonizing of his professional career. It offered a poignant reminder that humility can be essential to scientific credibility. And it posed for Schrag a painful warning about hidden problems in Alzheimer's research. He said he had rededicated himself to teaching students his own bitter lesson.

"You have to have a near-religious commitment to research integrity," he said. "If the rules apply to others, they have to apply to [all of] us."

Schrag kept his eyes on the gatekeepers of misconduct investigations. He hoped they would restore his faith that the scientific community could police its own in Ghribi's case, that of Sylvain Lesné at the University of Minnesota, and Cassava Sciences' consultant Hoau-Yan Wang. If each faced meaningful consequences after an avalanche of well-documented concerns, it might instill hope that the scientific enterprise could be trusted to self-correct.

A big test case for that noble aspiration—the final report from a City University of New York probe of work by Wang—seemed to be buried, forgotten in the CUNY bureaucracy. Then something unexpected changed the equation. Someone inside one of the many institutional probes into the scientist and his work would reveal the university's report. Cassava and Wang would once again face a searing public spotlight.

Chapter 18

Slow-Motion Meltdown

New York City, Austin

2022–2023

"It's all about the money,
and always has been."

—ADAM FEUERSTEIN, JOURNALIST WITH *STAT*

By the late summer of 2023, investors, scientists, and regulators following the controversies swirling around Cassava Sciences had long been waiting impatiently for the City University of New York (CUNY) to deliver its investigation of Professor Hoau-Yan Wang, the key researcher behind Austin, Texas–based Cassava's experimental Alzheimer's drug simufilam. Papers by Wang and colleagues that had been questioned by Matthew Schrag and others underpinned simufilam's jump from the lab into clinical studies for thousands of patients.

In August, a confidential source leaked that CUNY report—to me. It was marked "draft," but the sender and recipients were clear, adding substantial credibility. From the context, it seemed final. But CUNY would not confirm its provenance, so I waited. Then, in October, my source provided the final version and emails that validated its authenticity. It was identical to the draft. The investigation was completed in May 2023, according to the emails. The four-member investigative panel had been led by CUNY neuroscientist Orie Shafer, I learned from metadata embedded in the file. In an interview, he confirmed the report's authenticity. (SAVAges later targeted Shafer in the social media, including a blatantly antisemitic rant.)

The university's investigative committee found numerous signs that images were improperly manipulated, such as in a 2012 paper in the *Journal of Neuroscience* suggesting that simufilam can blunt the pathological effects of amyloid-beta. The report concluded that Lindsay Burns, Cassava's senior vice president for neuroscience and a coauthor on several of the papers, bears primary or partial responsibility for some possible misconduct or scientific errors.

The committee could not definitively prove its suspicions, however, because Wang did not produce the original raw data. Instead, investigators found "long-standing and egregious misconduct in data management and record keeping by Dr. Wang."

Their fifty-page report said he failed to turn over to the panel "even a single datum or notebook in response to any allegation." It cited "Wang's inability or unwillingness to provide primary research materials to this investigation" as a "deep source of frustration."

Wang's attorney said neither she nor her client would comment until they had spoken with CUNY, and that university representatives had not responded to their inquiries. But the report said Wang offered several defenses, including a claim that much of his original data had been "thrown away in response to a request from CCNY [City College of New York] to clean the lab during the Covid-19 pandemic." CCNY, part of CUNY, said it made no such request.

The CUNY investigation into Wang began in the fall of 2021, after Schrag provided a dossier of concerns to the National Institutes of Health, which had provided millions of dollars to Wang. Following normal procedures, NIH sent it to the Office of Research Integrity (ORI), which asked CUNY to examine Wang-authored papers published from 2003 through 2021, a conference poster, and a grant proposal. Many included apparently improper alterations of western blots that could skew the interpretation and validity of experimental findings. The committee said it "found evidence highly suggestive of deliberate scientific misconduct" in four-teen cases.

To check for image doctoring, investigators sought high-resolution, un-cropped originals to compare against published versions. Wang provided none, the report said, adding: "It appears likely that no primary data and no research notebooks pertaining to the thirty-one allegations exist." The panel also found that Wang "starkly siloed" work in his lab, preparing nearly all such images himself. That highly unusual practice for a lab's principal in-vestigator was reminiscent of Sylvain Lesné at the University of Minnesota.

Among his defenses, Wang told the panel that "at least one hard drive" containing key data was destroyed by CCNY officials when they seques-tered his materials for review. (He separately told the Food and Drug Administration that the US Department of Justice had seized two stor-age drives.) Wang also accused the committee of bias, "failing to follow the CUNY guidelines for this investigation, and of lacking a basic un-derstanding of western blot analysis." The committee noted in its report, however, that three of its four members routinely conduct similar experi-ments and two often prepare and publish western blots.

The CUNY report suggested that scientists beyond Wang and Burns might also be faulted. Harvard University neurologist and Cassava ad-visor Steven Arnold, senior author of the influential 2012 study in the *Journal of Clinical Investigation*, "may bear a measure of responsibility" for failing to ensure the integrity of data in that paper and others coauthored by the CUNY scientist. Arnold declined to comment, saying he needed time to review the report.

The panel recommended that journals retract the Wang papers if he couldn't provide the original data. Multiple journals had already done so, after Schrag notified them of his findings. The CUNY report noted that *PLOS ONE*, which retracted five of Wang's papers, "discovered evidence of research misconduct in his response to the concerns raised." Others, including the *Journal of Neuroscience*, posted corrections or expressions of concern on Wang papers, with some editors saying they would wait for CUNY's investigation before taking further steps.

The panel had been stonewalled for six months by university officials after requesting files confiscated from Wang's computers, according to the report. Investigators received the files only after appealing directly to Vincent Boudreau, president of CCNY.

The university forwarded the report to ORI, emails indicated. But by the fall of 2023, neither organization had taken any public step regarding Wang during the roughly five months since the review was completed. Boudreau advisor Dee Dee Mozeleski said the president could not comment on the matter ahead of the story I was preparing for *Science*, but that "action on the report is imminent."

CUNY biochemist Kevin Gardner, who helped prepare a preliminary assessment of Wang's work but was not involved in the final review, called what the panel found "embarrassing beyond words." Wang's record of research is "abhorrent," he said. That the work supported clinical trials, Gardner added, "makes it doubly sickening."

In a written statement, Cassava declined to comment about the CUNY report because the school had not confirmed it as authentic. It said CUNY did not interview any Cassava employees, "and refused all requests for information and offers of assistance from Cassava." The company said it "looks forward to continuing the development of simufilam."

The scientific basis for the drug, including the critical "misfolding" of the protein filamin A, came from Wang's lab. But in its statement, Cassava said six basic research studies by organizations that "have no connection to CUNY" also support simufilam. The company noted one paper, which it funded, showed simufilam "may promote brain health." Researchers at the Cochin Institute in Paris conducted some of that work, but notwithstanding Cassava's statement, much of it took place in Wang's lab. Burns and Wang were the chief authors.

Two more papers cited by the company, both coauthored by Burns, suggest simufilam might be effective to treat pituitary tumors or seizures. The other papers examined issues surrounding filamin A, amyloid-beta, and tau, but did not directly test simufilam's ability to reverse or prevent brain pathologies.

In October 2023, I made the CUNY investigation public in *Science*, and the magazine posted the report. Schrag called it "detailed, thorough, and credible. But a two-year delay is somewhat astonishing," he added. "The phase 3 simufilam clinical trials should never have started. And they should certainly be shut down on the basis of this report." Phase 3 trials are the last major experimental hurdle before possible FDA approval.

My story was picked up in the *New York Times,* the *Wall Street Journal,* and elsewhere, and Cassava was soon named the "most shorted" health care company and the third-most shorted among all companies by the industry analysis firm S&P Global Market Intelligence. About 38 percent of its shares were controlled by short sellers betting that the price would decline.

STAT's Adam Feuerstein, a pharma-industry journalist with a reputation for applauding companies that deliver on their promises and castigating those whose practices he regards as dishonest, penned a caustic critique calling for the FDA to halt Cassava's clinical trials.

"It's all about the money, and always has been. The scientific illegitimacy of simufilam revealed in the CUNY investigation underscores a point I made about Cassava three years ago," Feuerstein wrote. "This entire project has nothing whatsoever to do with helping people suffering from Alzheimer's. It has everything to do with [CEO Remi] Barbier's desire to enrich himself, and the executives who work for him, at the expense of investors, and worse, people suffering from Alzheimer's."

But two weeks after my article appeared—following Cassava's attacks on the report and how it was produced—CUNY reversed Mozeleski's assertion of imminent action on the Wang report. "Because questions regarding the confidentiality and integrity of this investigation have been raised, CUNY will stay the underlying inquiry," the statement noted, "until such time as the University completes a comprehensive investigation of the process." The Wang report went on ice for up to a year longer, when the CUNY Board of Trustees—despite confirming its authenticity—budgeted $1,250,000 for a mole hunt to find my source.

As he was scrutinized, Wang continued to publish with Burns. One paper in June 2023 said that simufilam restores insulin sensitivity in certain white blood cells of Alzheimer's patients. Soon after, image sleuths—including a short seller of Cassava stock—posted critiques to PubPeer that revealed apparent examples of image manipulation in that paper. They closely resembled the style of anomalies identified in earlier, retracted papers by Wang.

FDA BOMBSHELL

Then in March 2024 another devastating development engulfed Wang and Cassava.

It involved an event in September 2022. FDA officials had arrived at an imposing, glass-dominated, CUNY research facility to review records and practices by Wang, who two years earlier had analyzed patients' blood and cerebrospinal fluid for a key simufilam trial. CUNY received advance warning but rebuffed the inspectors. Guards escorted them off the premises. When officials relented two days later, the FDA found an array of problems with Wang's work. Inspectors noted that he didn't routinely calibrate equipment or complete verification tests to ensure that his findings were "accurate, sensitive, and [conducted] with appropriate precision." They reported that Wang used improper statistical tests to determine concentrations of samples. On a ten-point scale, with ten being the worst score, the findings amounted to an eight, said Jerry Chapman, a senior quality expert at Redica Systems who reviewed the document. (Redica has cataloged nearly one million such reports, and guides clients on FDA compliance.)

"Essentially, the FDA said, 'You can't trust any of this.' But the company used the results" nevertheless, as evidence of the drug's efficacy, said University of Southern California neuroscientist Lon Schneider, who also reviewed the report. Indeed, Cassava publicly described the findings as positive, and they helped pave the way for phase 3 clinical trials.

The FDA report, disclosed under the Freedom of Information Act, raised new questions about the credibility of claims by Wang and Cassava about simufilam. (The report was obtained by a short seller and provided to me by his colleague; Cassava had sued both earlier for defamation.)

The FDA and CUNY declined to comment about the report. So did Wang, through his attorney. Cassava said in a statement that the CUNY lab was not required to comply with the FDA's Good Laboratory Practices (GLPs) for its "exploratory research." (The analysis of trial samples is considered clinical, not exploratory, under the FDA's definition, however. GLPs don't apply to clinical work.) The company also said the work from Wang's lab had been "validated" by subsequent academic work elsewhere.

The FDA report suggested that Wang's work on clinical trial samples was as suspect as his basic-science experiments. And that work was crucial to hopes for simufilam.

In May 2020, Cassava had announced disappointing results for its phase 2 study. Simufilam failed to reduce tau and amyloid-beta markers of the disease. Cassava stock lost three-quarters of its value overnight. In a press release months later, the company rejected those results, suggesting a contractor had analyzed patient samples improperly. It offered better news from a twenty-eight-day study of sixty-four Alzheimer's patients, including some given a placebo. This time, simufilam sharply reduced tau, amyloid-beta, and other biomarkers. Although Cassava didn't say so at the time, those were the suspect results generated by Wang. Its share value immediately more than doubled, and some biotech analysts became more optimistic about simufilam.

It's not clear why the FDA waited two years to investigate how Wang handled those samples—or why they only looked at that study, given that Wang tested samples for other Cassava studies. In any case, inspectors found concerns that went beyond poor lab practices. A key problem involved how Wang handled "outlier" data. For each patient sample, he ran three tests for biomarkers, then discarded readings that diverged sharply from the others. That practice is accepted, but criteria for doing so should be set in advance, the FDA inspectors noted. Wang told them that he didn't use clearly defined criteria. Instead, he "based it on his judgment."

Wang agreed he erred, according to the FDA report, and rechecked the rest of the data, finding no more anomalies. "However, our independent review of the same spreadsheets identified several additional examples affected by similar errors," the inspectors wrote, noting fifteen such cases. Wang "agreed with our findings," they added.

The CUNY scientist later told the officials that he corrected all mistakes and emailed updates to a person whose identity was redacted in the report—presumably Burns. Cassava declined to comment on why it had not updated published data with the new figures, saying that they "resulted in no material change to the data."

Even the corrected figures remain suspect, according to the report, due to Wang's failure to calibrate his equipment and other lapses. Echoing the CUNY report on problems in Wang's basic-science studies, FDA inspectors said the scientist had not retained original western blot films necessary to audit the accuracy of some results. Wang said he discarded them as "cumbersome to maintain," the report noted. Nor did he keep records on the storage, tracking, or testing of fluid samples. He didn't lock his lab or password-protect its computers.

Rather than publishing the data in a journal, Burns and Wang posted it without editing or peer review to a preprint server. In an unusual move, the preprint site posted a link to my story above the Cassava paper with a comment: "In light of concerns about the credibility of claims by Wang and Cassava about their Alzheimer's drug simufilam, it's important for readers to be aware of allegations of data manipulation and the ongoing US criminal probe and SEC scrutiny. While the FDA has allowed ongoing trials to continue, these regulatory and investigative challenges cannot be overlooked. We encourage a balanced view on this preprint considering the potential benefits of the drug alongside the current investigations into Cassava Sciences' research practices."

Critics said the findings reinforced their long-standing concerns. "This report extends a pattern of data that lacks rigor and reliability, and further undermines my confidence in any clinical trial results from this program," Schrag said. "The simufilam clinical trials should be shut down."

CORPORATE UPHEAVAL

Even before my stories reminded the world of the doubts about simufilam, Cassava faced a head-spinning array of legal troubles.

Barbier, Burns, and other Cassava executives faced a shareholder class-action lawsuit winding its way through federal court. (Similar class actions had been consolidated into that single case.) It accused them of a "fraudulent scheme" that deployed exaggerated claims about simufilam to sell shares at an inflated price. Some investors lost money when the stock plunged after news of Wang's problematic work came to light. Cassava said the claims were "without merit," and that it would "defend against these lawsuits vigorously."

Two other class-action shareholder suits were filed in early 2024. Those claimed that shareholders lost money when Cassava's stock fell sharply after *Science* published the CUNY investigative report on Wang. The company was also fighting those suits. Cassava settled a separate suit alleging that Barbier and others had set up a bonus plan to enrich themselves to the detriment of shareholders. The company denied the claims.

Then in March 2024, a federal judge tossed Cassava's defamation lawsuit against the short sellers, for lack of any convincing legal argument. It was a major blow. Cassava had burned enormous shareholder resources to make the case its primary legal defense of its science and credibility. The company almost immediately refiled a similar suit against some of the short sellers.

Meanwhile, the company continued efforts to promote its drug. Shortly after I reported on the CUNY investigation findings, Cassava offered optimistic portrayals of data from a simufilam trial at an international Alzheimer's conference.

It described results for 155 participants in its phase 2 clinical trial meant to establish baseline safety and efficacy information to inform the larger, more important phase 3 trials in process. Based on cognitive tests taken at the experiment's outset, trial volunteers were divided into "mild" and "moderate" disease groups. All then took simufilam for a year. Half of each group continued on the drug and half received a placebo during the following six months. Cassava said simufilam slowed cognitive decline sharply in each group that took the drug for the full eighteen months compared to the placebo groups.

Those assertions seemed farfetched. Placebo and simufilam patients in the mild group showed the normal variations of the imprecise psychological exams used. And some had no cognitive impairment prior to taking the drug, according to pretrial tests. They could be classified as the "worried well," rather than people with Alzheimer's. Treatment would be irrelevant to their mental acuity.

Those in the moderate group who took simufilam for eighteen months showed, on average, a tiny improvement in cognitive results at month thirteen. Again, this would not be uncommon among any small group of Alzheimer's patients taking those tests. Performance depends a lot on whether a patient is having a good day or a bad day. After that, the two groups showed parallel declines in cognitive testing.

Nicolas Villain, a neuroscientist at the Sorbonne and an expert in Alzheimer's trials, called the Cassava data "very sloppy work" that didn't reach statistical significance in any outcome measure. In essence, it was meaningless as an evaluation of simufilam, he said.

Admitting as much, the company included this presentation disclaimer: "Results . . . do not constitute, and should not be interpreted as, clinical evidence of therapeutic safety or benefit."

STAT's Feuerstein described the study with characteristic bluntness: "The conclusion, of course, is obvious: Simufilam is inactive. It's an inert compound no more effective than a placebo." He added: "With this new visibility into the simufilam data, the [FDA] has more cause to halt Cassava's two ongoing phase 3 studies and require the company to conduct a futility analysis of simufilam." Such an analysis could shutter those trials, but the FDA has not made that demand.

In a sign of the desperation people feel when faced with the slow, inexorable decline of Alzheimer's disease, none of that litany of challenges facing Cassava—lawsuits, federal investigations, CUNY's findings, the

FDA's dismal lab assessment, or dubious outcomes in the phase 2 study—impeded the company from enrolling about 1,900 Alzheimer's patients into phase 3 trials. Preliminary results were expected in late 2024, and the final results are due in late 2025 or 2026

But Cassava faced a monumental setback in June 2024. The DOJ announced that Wang had been indicted for "a scheme to fabricate and falsify scientific data in grant applications made to the NIH on behalf of himself and the biopharmaceutical company," which was Cassava, the company conceded.

"Wang's alleged scientific data falsification in the NIH grant applications related to how the proposed drug and diagnostic test were intended to work and the improvement of certain indicators associated with Alzheimer's disease after treatment with the proposed drug," the DOJ noted. "Wang is charged with one count of major fraud against the United States, two counts of wire fraud, and one count of false statements." Wang and his attorney could not be reached for comment. If convicted, the scientist faces a possible ten years in prison for major fraud, twenty years for each count of wire fraud, and five years for false statements.

Cassava distanced itself from Wang in a public statement calling him a former advisor who "had no involvement in the Company's Phase 3 clinical trials of simufilam."

The following Monday, the company filed an astonishing statement with the Securities and Exchange Commission (SEC). It admitted that two unnamed senior employees were being investigated by the SEC and DOJ.

The short SEC filing revealed mind-bending admissions. Lab tests by Wang that were the subject of the FDA inspection—central to the experiment that supported moving to the current phase 3 trials—were indeed unreliable. Even more remarkable, Cassava admitted that the cognitive testing results for that trial had been cherry-picked. Subjects who received simufilam and performed poorly were excised from the analysis—rendering it virtually worthless.

The next month, Cassava faced another dramatic rupture: The top players in the simufilam saga—the husband-wife team known for dogged and aggressive attacks on critics—were out. Barbier resigned as chief executive and board chair, picking up a $1.2 million golden parachute out the door. Burns pocketed half a million dollars, and Cassava retained the right to hire her for up to one year as an hourly consultant, with no guaranteed contract. Cassava did not reveal if Barbier and Burns were the two unnamed employees targeted by the feds.

New management lost no time trying to clean up the legal quagmire Barbier, Burns, and Wang left in their wake.

Cassava immediately dropped the lingering short-seller defamation lawsuit. To no one's surprise, three of the defendants in that case quickly sued Cassava for legal harassment under New York's anti-SLAPP law.

Then in September 2024, Cassava agreed to pay $40 million to settle SEC charges that it had misled investors about clinical results for simufilam. Subject to court approval, Barbier and Burns separately agreed to pay $175,000 and $85,000, respectively, and would be barred from serving as company officers or directors for years. Wang agreed to pay $50,000 to settle charges in a related administrative proceeding.

Barbier, Burns, and Wang did not admit or deny guilt, according to SEC's statement, and none could be reached for comment. "Cassava is pleased to put this matter behind us," and would focus on its ongoing simufilam trials, said CEO Richard Barry in a written statement.

The SEC said Cassava and Barbier knew that Wang's lab was not qualified to conduct the biomarker testing that suggested simufilam was effective for Alzheimer's, among other problems. The agency also charged that Wang had been "unblinded" for patient fluid samples that he tested. That means he would have known which samples came from patients given the drug rather than a placebo, introducing bias into his data. The complaint cited Burns as well. It said she "negligently failed to fully disclose" that she had improperly removed data from 40% of the volunteers in a phase 2 simufilam clinical trial after learning which ones received simufilam or the placebo.

Cassava allegedly withheld its knowledge of all of those matters, and its shares rose sharply after Barbier and Burns announced the favorable results—including cognitive improvements. The company then raised more than $260 million from investors. In fact, the complete data showed that the drug failed to improve memory in Alzheimer's patients, the SEC said.

Schrag considered this the final insult to integrity. "Experimenting on many hundreds of people with memory problems in this context is highly unethical," he said. "These [phase 3] trials should be stopped."

The FDA, the key entity with the power to do so, declined to comment.

With its meme stock fluctuating wildly, the company continued to put an optimistic, Barbie-like spin on its future: It would redouble its efforts to prove simufilam to be the long-predicted Alzheimer's miracle. A Cassava spokesperson said that a hybrid study—combining an open-label design in which all patients knew they were getting simufilam, with an interlude comparing the drug against a placebo—had shown favorable cognitive results. "There are good reasons to believe our [first phase 3] trial could be successful," the spokesperson said.

AS STRANGE AS FICTION

Lindsay Burns has never agreed to speak with me. Her only public comments have been occasional talks at scientific conferences or quips on social media to charge up simufilam boosters.

I kept thinking about Burns's ceaseless drive that began on her family's cattle ranch in Big Timber, Montana—an upbringing that helped her become one of the world's top rowers, a Harvard and Cambridge scholar, and a wealthy biotech scientist, notwithstanding Cassava's endless drama. Until her ouster, she had lived out a prototypically combative American success story true to her iconoclastic origins. But in recent years, her outwardly romantic family saga began to take on the kind of dramatic friction that popularized the prime-time soap opera *Yellowstone*. The show depicts love-hate sibling relationships in a fictional Montana cattle-ranching family during the waning years of its dominant patriarch.

After Burns's father, Horatio Burns, died in 2018, a bitter dispute broke out over his estate. Lindsay and her brother, Cameron Burns, locked horns in court about dividing their father's assets. In his own waning years, Horatio had suffered a stroke. Cameron and his wife, Alison, helped the old man manage his ranch and personal affairs. Before he died, Horatio cut Lindsay and a third sibling out of his will, leaving his assets to Cameron and Alison. A classic legal squabble, common among families of means, followed. It seemed another emblem of Lindsay's exalted status that the Burns family feud would reach its final adjudication not at Big Timber's Sweet Grass County Courthouse, but in the august chambers of the Montana Supreme Court.

The case of Horatio Burns also echoed the battles over what is true or false in depictions of people with Alzheimer's at the heart of Lindsay's work with Cassava. She claimed that her father suffered from dementia and paranoia before he died and had been improperly manipulated by Cameron and Alison. Cameron (who did not reply to a request for an interview) and Alison insisted—and a jury agreed—that Horatio was of sound mind. The prevailing party stood to gain a fortune. As Lindsay's nature seemingly dictated, she fought to the end. But this time, when the Supreme Court ruled in December 2023, she lost the fight. I wondered if it represented a harbinger of Cassava's eventual fate.

As the Burns court case reached its denouement, something shocking happened in another Alzheimer's research scandal that, for me, would forever be linked to Cassava. Karen Ashe adopted an extraordinary new effort to transform how the Alzheimer's world perceives her role in the $A\beta^*56$ image-doctoring scandal, to exonerate her legacy and restore her career luster. And I was integral to her plans.

Chapter 19

Survival Mode

Caen, France; Minneapolis

2023–2024

"It's not my soul. It's your soul."

—KAREN ASHE, UNIVERSITY OF MINNESOTA NEUROSCIENTIST

"Clothe yourselves in compassion, kindness, humility, gentleness
and patience . . . forgive one another . . . and above all,
bind these virtues with love."

—COLOSSIANS 3:12–14

After my 2022 article about apparent scientific misconduct in research by University of Minnesota (UMN) scientist Sylvain Lesné, he went to ground. Lesné's once-active, playful social-media presence—environmental advocacy, gourmet meals, picturesque sunsets, plaudits for colleagues and students—had gone dark.

I tried to learn what led to the debacle that prompted doubts about the amyloid hypothesis and chaotic backpedaling by eminent researchers who seemed desperate to plausibly excuse their embrace of tainted work for more than fifteen years. I wanted Lesné to answer a simple question: Why? What led him to apparently produce false and misleading data? I hoped he would take stock and shed light on his actions, to offer some closure for the research record and perhaps a bit of redemption for himself. He never replied to my entreaties.

To explore possible answers, I traveled to Normandy, where Lesné grew up and trained as a researcher. But just before that trip, a new wrinkle emerged in his scholarly origin story. At my request and to satisfy his own concerns, Matthew Schrag had been chipping away at work by Lesné's three French mentors apart from their now-notorious trainee. The idea was to see if one or more of those senior scientists had also conducted suspect studies.

Schrag found thirteen such problem papers, spanning more than two decades. He produced a thirty-two-page dossier showing clear signs of doctored or improperly reused images in studies about protections for brain cells, the blood-brain barrier—tiny blood vessels that shield the brain from toxic substances—and tau and amyloid-beta in Alzheimer's.

One of the scholars, neuroscientist Denis Vivien, now leads a large team at a research unit in Caen, where Lesné earned his doctorate. Prior to my exposé in 2022, Vivien, one of Lesné's PhD advisors, confided his doubts—then horror—about his student, who seemed to have created images "too beautiful to believe" for a paper about amyloid proteins. Vivien said he had to withdraw the paper when he saw the problem, and he stopped collaborating with Lesné.

After my story appeared, the French media pursued Vivien aggressively. He wanted to leave the Lesné matter behind and rebuffed my attempts to meet or talk by phone. But after Schrag's dossier about Vivien and his colleagues reached me, things shifted. I sent him a copy a few days ahead of my trip in July 2023. To his credit, Vivien replied in detail before I arrived. He downplayed problems for which he was responsible, admitting that he erred and skipped steps for expediency. Vivien described those actions as trivial, with no impact on experimental findings, perhaps warranting something akin to a scientific parking ticket.

He reluctantly agreed to meet me for lunch at a Caen hotel near the university. I faced pangs of regret. Vivien had, after all, shown rectitude by pulling back the paper with Lesné years earlier. He showed uncommon openness reflecting on his own missteps, even if he downplayed their significance. Lesné's other PhD advisor, Alain Buisson, had left Caen for a post in Grenoble a few years earlier. The third mentor, Fabian Docagne, had taken a job in Paris. They played larger roles than Vivien in the most recent dubious studies, including those that suggested serious manipulations. Neither responded to requests to meet or talk by phone.

I asked Jean-Charles Lambert, a leading neuroscientist at the University of Lille, to review the dossier. He said certain problems during older studies, acknowledged by Vivien, involved reusing a "positive control"—an experiment that shows known results from a treatment. Scientists compare the control result against tests that introduce variables with unknown effects. Reusing images from past controls as if new was improper then as now—but unfortunately common to save time and money, Lambert said. Other problems, such as the duplication of microscopic images within the same paper, might have been simple errors.

"What is very problematic is the use of the same result with different labeling—(suggesting) different cell types, different proteins measured. Playing with the background to contrast the results and make them more striking is also problematic," Lambert added. "These various points are undoubtedly scientific fraud, calling into question the validity of the results presented and therefore the conclusions of the articles concerned."

Another noted French neuroscientist spoke anonymously to avoid jeopardizing long-standing relationships with other Caen scientists. His views echoed Lambert. "Overall, I would say that this is misconduct, but at a different level than Lesné's," the scientist said. "Lesné clearly invented data and experiment results that were never performed or observed"—more severe than his mentors' lapses. "Lesné's misconduct led to his main publications in top-class scientific journals and made his career," the French scientist said.

Then he added a thought that had never been far from my mind during my time in France: "You could propose a nice 'psychological interpretation' for your story: When you are mentored, like Lesné, by scientists that cut corners, then it's like the 'boiling frog experiment': You've seen it once, why couldn't you do it a little bit more?"

It's a seductive hypothesis: A young scientist emerges from an environment with an apparently lenient posture on scientific integrity, then recreates it in more extreme form on the next rung of his career ladder—with far-reaching consequences. (The notion seemed to gain credence when I later learned that another Caen graduate—younger than Lesné—was for years a key assistant for a prominent Alzheimer's scientist later ensnared in a major research misconduct scandal.) And as I considered UMN history, I could hardly blame Lesné alone for an environment that sometimes seemed to lose contact with its ethical tether.

HISTORY OF LAPSES

Carl Elliott, the UMN physician and bioethicist who wrote the book about whistleblowers, *The Occasional Human Sacrifice*, spent years pressing the university to conduct a probe of how some of its professors and administrators handled the suicide of Dan Markingson, who died at age twenty-seven in 2004. Markingson, who experienced mental-health struggles, had been a subject in a clinical experiment involving an antipsychotic drug. He used a box cutter to slash his own throat. Elliott was convinced that UMN hadn't conducted an adequate review of the tragedy—which the university disputes—and spent years organizing his colleagues and the local community to force a better probe, without much success. He became a persistent, at times unyielding antagonist, as he acknowledged in his book.

A reference in that book to the Markingson affair grabbed me. It involved a conversation with another bioethicist, Leigh Turner—Elliott's ally at UMN. Turner, who has since moved to the University of California Irvine, has been a longtime, trusted expert source of mine. Elliott wrote that Turner "had watched the university's response with a growing sense of anger and disbelief. Leigh told me he felt like someone who had taken a job as a waiter only to discover that the restaurant was actually a front for a drug operation, like [the fried-chicken eatery] Los Pollos Hermanos in *Breaking Bad*," the television series.

The extreme comparison made me wonder about the history of UMN bioethics. Was there something in the university culture that led to bad outcomes? Did it accommodate someone like Lesné, creating a kind of cover for what he would become?

Elliott said he wasn't sure, then added: "It felt like that to me."

He recounted a series of UMN scandals during the 1980s and 1990s. One involved a psychiatrist who headed another antidepressant study and allegedly submitted false reports. He asked his assistant, who had no medical background, to provide therapy for trial volunteers. The Food and Drug Administration (FDA) debarred the psychiatrist from participating in clinical studies after he was convicted of lying to the agency about the matter. He ended up serving time in federal prison. In a separate case, the FDA disqualified another UMN psychiatrist for failing to obtain informed consent in a study to treat patients addicted to opioids.

A bigger problem involved pioneering UMN transplant surgeon John Najarian, widely seen as among the university's most illustrious scientists. His 1980s drug to prevent a transplant patient's immune system from rejecting a donated kidney, liver, or pancreas outperformed anything else available. UMN sold it to eager transplant centers nationwide, developing a profit center. The FDA said Najarian hadn't correctly communicated risk information to the agency. He blamed drug companies behind competing products for the accusations against him. "The FDA and the drug houses were in bed together," Najarian said in an oral history.

UMN forced Najarian out. The administration, which previously had vigorously supported his work, publicly denounced Najarian in what many viewed as scapegoating amid the glare of national media attention and legal prosecution. Najarian was ultimately acquitted. The judge in the case castigated the FDA, saying the scientist "literally saved thousands of lives."

The UMN Medical School lost scores of faculty members and respect in the biomedical research community in the wake of the scandal. It took many years to recover.

My first contact with the school came in 2020, during my investigation for *Science* of how the FDA fails to enforce rules to protect patients in human experiments. The agency had criticized—but not penalized—UMN professors working at an affiliated hospital over studies of the powerful sedative and anesthetic ketamine to treat agitated patients who came to the hospital for emergency treatment. In 2018, the consumer advocacy group Public Citizen and more than sixty clinicians and medical ethicists alleged that the hospital, operated by Hennepin Healthcare, had violated informed consent requirements in trials comparing ketamine to other drugs. The critics said doctors did not obtain consent from trial participants, although ketamine was much more likely to cause serious breathing problems and movement disorders. Many patients developed such symptoms. FDA inspectors confirmed the lapses. They also said doctors failed to properly report serious "adverse events"—possible side effects.

I found similar problems in FDA records on UMN ketamine studies from 2014 and 2016. Doctors failed to properly report thirteen patient deaths to Hennepin's institutional review board, which oversees trials. The FDA requires such reporting to help ensure that an experiment does not pose undue safety hazards.

In a response to the agency, Professor Brian Driver acknowledged his reporting error in three of the deaths but did not address the other ten. Driver conceded to me that he failed to report the thirteen deaths initially flagged by the agency, and ten others in the trial that the FDA did not document. He attributed all twenty-three to acute illnesses or injuries, including stroke and heart attack, unrelated to the study drugs. Hennepin officials refused to say why—after years of FDA inspections citing serious problems in ketamine trials—its review board and emergency department continued to greenlight trials without special precautions to protect patients.

Elliott compared such official silence to church leaders who decline to comment on priestly misdeeds. "The medical school seems to be saying, 'We are engaged in something morally important—making the world better,'" he said. "That can justify trying to hide problems from the outside world, because if [outsiders] find out what really happens, they might try to slow things down, or it might hurt the institution. Even if we do need to make things better, do it quietly, without letting the commoners actually understand."

DEFEND AND DEFY

Those words resonated as I thought about Karen Ashe, Lesné's mentor, who had spent decades at that medical school. "The University's review into concerns raised about her work has concluded," Jake Ricker, who directs UMN public relations, told me via email in July 2023. "If there is no disciplinary action, we can only disclose the existence and status (open or closed) of the complaints." Ashe was off the hook as far as UMN was concerned. But this is a scientist who had once been on a Nobel Prize trajectory. What now?

A Twin Cities Public Television program that aired in 2023, funded partly by UMN, featured Ashe seated at an exquisite grand piano, exuding calm grace. She masterfully played Chopin's Fantaisie-Impromptu, Opus 66—a fiendishly difficult piece that requires each hand to use different rhythms amid changing tempos.

Then Ashe made a sales pitch about her start-up company, Myriel. She sees it as her vehicle to cure Alzheimer's, someday, with a drug to inhibit caspase-2—a compound that affects the death of brain cells and might inhibit memory. Just as each of her hands worked independently to render the challenging Opus 66, Ashe described her excitement about recent findings in an oddly downbeat tone. And as she explained how dementia pushes some memories out of reach, her once-glittering protein, $A\beta^*56$, seemed to have faded into oblivion.

I wondered if such talent—musical and scientific—fed overconfidence and complacency that might have made her overlook Lesné's apparently flagrant subterfuge under her own roof. Her response to my story proved revealing. She blamed Lesné publicly, despite having been his mentor, colleague, and boss. "It is devastating to discover that a coworker may have misled me and the scientific community through the doctoring of images," she told the hometown Star Tribune. Ashe publicly described my article, and the doubt it cast on her signature $A\beta^*56$ findings, as unfair, false, or misleading. In a podcast, Ashe also blamed the NIH—for failing to invest enough in $A\beta^*56$ and related issues to prove that she was right all along.

In an effort to regain control over the narrative about her scientific credibility—and legacy—Ashe quietly enlisted a new group of scientists, excluding her former protégé. The goal: Validate the once-monumental, now-disputed 2006 findings about a possible cause for Alzheimer's.

The group, comprising four fledgling UMN researchers—who had modest track records and depended on Ashe for employment or publications to advance their careers—seemed ill-suited to the task. Peng Liu occupied a spot akin to Lesné's when the fateful 2006 *Nature* article came out. Liu spent about a decade as a postdoctoral fellow in Ashe's lab and staff researcher at the institute she ran before becoming an assistant research professor with his own lab in 2017. Now in his forties, he still works closely with Ashe—her new protégé. In March 2023, eight months after my article appeared, they posted a self-published preprint—a paper made public without peer review or editing.

The 2006 *Nature* paper had two parts: isolating Aβ*56—the specific amyloid protein thought to cause Alzheimer's symptoms—from the brains of mice, then injecting it into rats to show that it caused memory loss.

With pretzel logic, the new preprint "confirmed" the star protein's existence and stability. Yet at the same time, it conceded the opposite: They couldn't find Aβ*56 at all. Rather, they identified an amyloid protein in the general vicinity of Aβ*56—calling it "~*56." That such proteins exist in the general range of *56—which refers to its relatively heavy molecular weight—was never in dispute. The point grew more tenuous in the paper's fine print. It revealed that even that vague finding occurred only in a fraction of many tested mice, and in almost no mice in the age group designated as central to the thesis of the *Nature* paper.

"As a lab head and the senior author, it's my responsibility to establish the truth of what we've published" in the 2006 *Nature* article, Ashe commented in the *Star Tribune*, which reported on the preprint a couple of months after it was published. The newspaper repeated, without independent comment, Ashe's claims of success.

Experts disagreed. "This preprint goes a very long way in disproving the *Nature* paper," neuroscientist Donna Wilcock, chief editor of the journal *Alzheimer's & Dementia*, told me. "I think it would behoove her to voluntarily retract that paper."

Schrag wrote to *Nature*, pointing out that the preprint disavowed the methods that the 2006 paper relied on and failed to replicate its findings. "Surely this necessitates retracting the 2006 study," he said. *Nature* took no public action.

I emailed Ashe to propose a meeting to discuss the preprint, to help me understand her work better and generally hear her out. "Should you ever choose to address the errors you printed, I will consider your request," she replied tersely. By then, despite professed confidence in Aβ*56, she and Lesné had let their joint patents on the protein lapse. That suggested they had abandoned hope for commercializing the work.

Meanwhile, Schrag had introduced me to Mu Yang, a neurobiologist at Columbia University's Institute for Genomic Medicine and Psychiatry. Yang directs the university's Mouse NeuroBehavior Core—a facility that cares for mice and oversees testing involving them for studies concerning Alzheimer's and other neurological conditions. She belongs to a rarefied club of specialists who deeply understand how rats and mice behave in such tests.

Yang looked at several Ashe papers that tested mice for signs of memory problems using the standard Morris water maze, named after its inventor, UK scientist Richard Morris. He developed the test in the early 1980s as a professor at the University of St. Andrews. The "maze" is actually a small, circular pool of water made opaque with nontoxic dye. Mice are trained to hop onto a small platform to rest from swimming. After learning that trick, the test begins: Scientists measure how fast a mouse hops out of the water onto the platform, now slightly submerged to make it invisible. Younger mice or rats, or those not treated to impair memory, normally find the platform faster. (In Ashe and Lesné's 2006 paper, they seemed to prove that after an injection of Aβ*56, rats forgot the platform's location.)

Yang has worked with more than eighty Columbia labs on tests using the maze and often supervises the procedure. She said some of Ashe's water-maze data looked improbable. For example, in one study very young and very old mice showed nearly the same test results—a finding that other experts also found doubtful. In two other papers about tau effects on altered mice, Ashe, Peng Liu, and their colleagues reused some results as if new—an improper practice for which they later published a clarification.

I emailed Ashe in October 2023 to see if she could shed any light on Yang's questions. "I'd like to express my gratitude for discussing these concerns with me," Ashe surprisingly replied. (Yang later said she found some of Ashe's later written responses credible, others implausible.) Ashe also reiterated her claims that I made "conceptual and factual errors in the depiction of Aβ*56."

Then she surprised me with this offer: "A detailed explanation of my perspective and addressing any queries you may have would be beneficial," she wrote. "I would like to extend an invitation for you to spend a few days in my lab . . . I've been reluctant to meet in the past, but now believe that it's in everyone's best interest."

In January 2024, I traveled to Minneapolis to take her up on the invitation.

SUBZERO

I arrived on Martin Luther King Day, greeted by a windchill factor of 20 degrees below zero. I hoped that would not prove a fitting metaphor for the interview.

I met Ashe on the next morning under frigid but sparkling-clear skies. Sunshine streamed auspiciously through the windows of the modern lab building. I entered the fifth-floor conference room and finally shook the hand of the scientist I had tried to understand for two years. Ashe, a small, slim woman in her late sixties with straight, jet-black hair accented with a few gray strands, dressed contrary to the science-nerd trope: turtleneck sweater under a brightly colored, loose-fitting blouse, trendy red glasses, dark skinny pants, fur-topped boots.

She somberly introduced me to her staff and Liu—a quick-to-smile, ruddy-faced man who proved faultlessly gracious. Then Ashe moved to the heart of the matter: complaints about me and my article—how it crushed her morale and stripped her of funding and prestige.

"It came as a terrible shock to us," she said, speaking for herself and her lab members. "I've lost funding. Two foundations have asked to return the money," noting that once grants are made, funders almost never claw them back. "Your piece was framed in a way that undermined my reputation." Ashe downsized her lab radically to three junior scientists, none PhDs, and an animal-care technician. She added: "It's the smallest it's ever been since I began my work here."

Ashe no longer directs the university's N. Bud Grossman Center for Memory Research and Care, with its ten faculty and a clinic—to concentrate on her research, she said. The change accounted for her tiny, cookie-cutter office. I supposed that she lost the post due to the scandal caused by my story, and its effects on her fundraising.

I asked about Lesné. Ashe replied behind welling, red-rimmed eyes. "I haven't spoken to him since June of 2022, when in this very room, he was here with his department head and the [UMN] Office of Research Integrity. They were asking questions," she said, about the dossier I provided. "We don't know for sure that he did manipulate those figures. He denied that he had done that—vehemently denied it. But he wasn't able to enlighten us on how it happened. So that's as much as I know. And I had no idea that he would ever do something like this, because he seemed fine—very bright, very hardworking."

She returned over and over to a refrain about my responsibility, in effect, to resurrect her career.

"It's not my soul. It's your soul," Ashe said as I walked into her office on day two of our meetings.

"Do you know that there are some ways of behaving that supersede the code of conduct of journalists?" she asked. "I'm accusing you of a lack of humility and a lack of patience." Ashe paraphrased a Bible verse, Colossians 3:12–14, which she had written in green marker on the whiteboard in her office. "Clothe yourselves in compassion, kindness, humility, gentleness, and patience . . . forgive one another . . . and above all, bind these virtues with love." In red she had underlined "humility" and "patience"— qualities I lack, she explained. Liu listened silently, looking as if he'd rather be anywhere else on the planet.

Misconduct, funding gaps, and technical challenges do not account for scant progress in curing Alzheimer's, she said. "The field has not moved forward as rapidly [as possible] because people have been sidetracked from following these rules of conduct" inscribed in the Bible.

Ashe objected to my article's framing and timing "at the height of the aducanumab controversy." That was the anti-amyloid drug Aduhelm, the first FDA-approved medicine for Alzheimer's in a generation. "Although

I do really regret that Sylvain did what he did in my lab . . . It's not true that Aβ* doesn't exist . . . and that we might have misled the field," as my article quoted experts as suggesting. She added that if I had shown the patience to put aside my reporting indefinitely, I could have written about her tainted *Nature* paper in a kinder light—as the prescient basis for lecanemab (Leqembi), the FDA-approved anti-amyloid drug. "You could actually have given me credit for the success of lecanemab. You could have said, despite the problems in the paper, it was still a really important discovery," Ashe said. "And my career would have been intact."

The moment's sheer awkwardness seized me. Leave aside that Ashe furthered her career from Lesné's magic hands—his ability to get experiments to work, or so it seemed, like no one else. Leave aside the idea that a study tainted by apparent misconduct should still be lauded. Leave aside that the deep divisions on whether Leqembi's meager benefits outweigh its substantial risks. Ashe seemed to believe that being an ethical journalist meant to stop being a journalist at all.

She nodded to the whiteboard again. "I try to live by it, and I fail. All people fail . . . we are all sinners," Ashe said, turning back to me. "You wrote something that hurt. Deeply hurt an innocent person. And in every field, in every religion, in every culture, this goes way beyond your journalist's code of conduct . . . This is what I want to convey to you." She paused a beat, then added: "It's for your own good. The reason you are here is because I've forgiven you."

She then compared me to Claudine Gay, who had recently resigned as president of Harvard after disastrously commenting at a congressional hearing that calls for genocide against Jews might or might not be deemed harassment, "depending on the context." Gay "completely ignored a universal value. You never, ever say it's okay to eliminate a whole group of people," Ashe continued, her voice rising with emotion. "It doesn't matter what your journalistic rules are. You don't hurt innocent people . . . And you hurt an innocent person—very, very severely.

". . . It was like losing a limb. I lost part of my reputation. It will never grow back. My limb will never grow back. I'm learning to live with it as best I can. I don't want to lose another limb," she added. "And it was you. You had choices to make in your writing. You have choices up ahead. You have the power to shut my lab down completely."

For a moment, my thoughts strayed to the framed poster I saw while visiting Harvard's Dennis Selkoe. It commemorated a centenary meeting in Tübingen, Germany, where Alois Alzheimer first described his famous case in 1906—honoring the discovery. The meeting took place eight months after the Lesné-Ashe paper in *Nature* appeared. Illustrious speakers and advisors—all famous names—appeared over and below a photo of Alzheimer. Ashe topped both lists. As she spoke to me now in her office with such conviction, I thought about how her life of continuous achievement and acclaim—superior student, wise doctor, researcher of global renown—might have inspired such certainty.

Ashe's humanity and struggle to be heard and believed—by me, and by extension the world—seemed deeply authentic. Her sincerity and commitment to finding a solution to an intractable medical mystery appeared absolute. Still, message and delivery clashed. She mixed pathos and condemnation, pleadings and demands, appeals to science and exaltations to faith. Ashe stared intently through piercing, unblinking dark eyes, with palpable anger, waiting for me to break the gaze.

"I honestly believe that we can help cure Alzheimer's," she said later. "If I didn't think so I wouldn't be doing it. And I would hate to see all this work not come to fruition. And even if it turns out we're wrong, I would still like to know why . . . You have the choice to portray me as an irresponsible [scientist]. That's your choice. If you do that, you will have made a choice that will hurt me again. And you could potentially hurt me so badly that I won't be able to continue my work . . . If you do that, well, I will accept that as, you know, God's judgment."

"YES, I AM RESPONSIBLE"

When the conversation shifted to substantive descriptions of her work, Ashe spoke passionately about developing her caspase-2 compound into a cure for Alzheimer's and other neurological conditions. Then Aβ*56 of the fated *Nature* paper took center stage. She emphasized her ongoing determination to prove the reality of Aβ*56 and its centrality to Alzheimer's. "Aβ* exists. I believe it's stable. I believe that it can be purified. I believe that it impairs memory when it's injected into animals," she said.

She also made a profound admission. "Had your article not come out, I would have retracted the paper" and the other suspect papers she shared with Lesné. "But if I were to retract it now, people would think that I don't believe a truth."

"Yes, I am responsible for what Sylvain did, because I was the head of the lab," Ashe finally conceded later. "The way I've been handling my responsibility is to replicate the results," she said, then added something extraordinary: "We have replicated all of the findings, thanks to Peng [Liu]. And that Aβ* exists and we think it's important. And we think it helps to fortify the amyloid-cascade hypothesis."

As Ashe and Liu laid out how they came to their conclusion, her reference to "Aβ*," rather than "Aβ*56" made sense. They had reworked their apparently contradictory preprint, that "confirmed" the existence and stability of Aβ*56, but admitted finding something unremarkable—a protein in the general range of Aβ*56.

They shared a draft of the revised paper, tentatively accepted for publication in the journal *iScience*. (It was published nearly unchanged in that journal in March 2024.) The revised paper holds steady to the preprint's conclusion, adding scores of pages of raw data. The results are the same. Again, they identified a protein in the general vicinity of Aβ*56—"~*56"—or call it "Aβ*." Again, it was found in only a fraction of many tested mice—and only about one in every nine in the six-to-nine-months age group at the heart of the 2006 findings, and none before seven months.

"People can spin whatever they want to spin," but the *iScience* paper will add pressure on *Nature* to retract, Schrag said after reviewing the new draft. The *iScience* peer reviewers did a good job, he added. "They basically went back to the literature and said, 'No, not everybody else is finding these results. No, it doesn't consistently correlate with memory.'"

He noted that the new draft adds an experiment that injects ~*56 into the brains of mice and shows memory deficits compared to mice that did not get injections. But some of the untreated mice also had memory problems, and the differences between groups were weak.

Ashe and Liu then described how Liu had reproduced Lesné's methods of refining and isolating Aβ*56—methods that Selkoe and others regard as biologically impossible. Ashe said she planned to send a "correction" to *Nature* for the 2006 paper. But instead of addressing the problem images, it would prove the basic truth of Lesné's methods.

Again, her statement seemed contradictory. She would have retracted the *Nature* paper if not for my investigation, yet they had cracked the Lesné code—proved that his methods work. And if so, why had Lesné apparently doctored the images in the original paper? Why does the *iScience* paper still call the protein ~*56 rather than the thing itself?

They are moving cautiously, Ashe replied, gathering more data to be absolutely sure.

Liu said he started with the published Lesné protocol. It involved measuring Aβ oligomer proteins—the form of amyloid protein that unlike sticky plaques can dissolve in cerebrospinal fluid that bathes the brain—separately in three places: brain cells, spaces outside the cells, and membranes that enclose the cell. That was the method Selkoe told me made no biological sense. But through trial and error, Liu said, he changed the types of chemicals added to the proteins, and the type of gel they would pass through in the western blot device. He filled gaps in Lesné's experimental cookbook and finally got the method to work after all.

But he needed someone else to replicate his approach. So he gave the needed experimental materials to Charles Glabe, the University of California Irvine scientist who had coauthored the 2006 *Nature* paper. Liu and Ashe hoped he would confirm the results. He could not. (Liu displayed Glabe's failed western blot findings on a video screen but would not provide them for closer examination.)

Then in the summer of 2023, Liu asked a high school lab intern to try her hand at finding Aβ* with the new protocol. To his delight, she did it.

The key that the intern picked up on, Liu said, was to very gently roll out air bubbles between the layers of the western blot gel package. Bubbles can distort blot interpretation. He called a common approach, pressing the roller fairly firmly to squeeze out the bubbles, a "bad practice." Rolling too hard squashes the proteins together, making it hard to detect ~*56 or Aβ*56 precisely, he said. He called gentle rolling—barely touching the roller to a pad over the package—a "good practice." Liu allowed that his more delicate method might be uniquely required to detect Aβ*56.

"The bottom line is that using such a protocol we do reliably reproduce Aβ*," he said. Notwithstanding the success of the intern, the process is so delicate that not everyone can repeat it, "even if I show them," Liu added. "You have to follow [the protocol] exactly. When I say exactly, it is exactly." He added that deviating from the prescribed timing "even one second more or one second less" throws off the results. So far, no one outside of the Liu-Ashe circle has succeeded.

"I find this 'virtuoso defense'—the case that somehow they're better at these techniques than everybody who's been doing them their whole career, including Glabe—hard to believe," Schrag said. "They have sort of made up their minds that Aβ*56 is there, and will stop at nothing to prove the point. But remember, if you believe them, take all their data with all of those caveats, give them the benefit of every single doubt, they still find it only half the time."

I asked a forensic image expert to look at Liu's prior work, and no examples of doctoring emerged. Still, it seemed like I had encountered another set of magic hands.

THE PRICE OF SURVIVAL

In June 2024, five months after my visit, Ashe finally made the move she had considered two years before—to retract the 2006 *Nature* paper. "Although I had no knowledge of any image manipulations in the published paper until it was brought to my attention two years ago," she wrote on PubPeer, "it is clear that several of the figures in Lesné et al. (2006) have been manipulated . . . for which I as the senior and corresponding author take ultimate responsibility."

Ashe said in another post that all of the authors except Lesné had agreed to retract. It became the second-most highly cited paper prior to retraction in scientific history.

"It's unfortunate that it has taken two years to make the decision to retract," Wilcock said. "The evidence of manipulation was overwhelming."

Although Ashe implied that *Nature*'s editors forced the retraction request, and despite her further PubPeer comments challenging some details of Schrag's findings that led to this moment, and her sustained, lonely defense of Aβ*56, Schrag took a charitable view. He called Ashe's decision to retract "an important step in the right direction" for a field plagued with research integrity issues. "It's taken a while, but she has taken a stand for integrity."

After two years, the investigation of Lesné—who was promoted to full professor just before my 2022 article appeared—continues. If he ever faces discipline, the particulars will be made public. By then it will probably seem a distant controversy, like the fading memories of an Alzheimer's patient. Meanwhile, he retains his federal research funds, his lab, his degree of deniability that anything is amiss, his American dream.

He even continues to publish, if rarely. One month after my story about his work appeared, Lesné and colleagues submitted a paper to *Acta Neuropathologica Communications*, showing a novel finding: The protein alpha-synuclein—studied for its role in Alzheimer's and Parkinson's—affects learning and memory differently in male and female mice. The journal accepted it in November 2022 and published it the following month. Schrag found evidence of improperly duplicated images within the paper. And another image seemed to have been improperly prepared. Those observations raised doubts about the experimental findings. I vetted Schrag's findings with image analysts, who concurred. Neither Lesné nor UMN replied to my query about the paper.

The other journals that published his dubious work are waiting for the final ruling by UMN before doing anything to set the scientific record straight. Meanwhile, Lesné and Ashe still cite those papers, as do other scholars who seem to have missed the controversy.

As if foreshadowing a conclusion, however, less than a month after my 2022 story appeared the Medical School erased one of Lesné's signature accomplishments—a plaque about the *Nature* paper on the school's Wall of Scholarship, reserved for the faculty's most influential work. The award vanished without a trace or comment. As of July 2024, despite the retraction, the Lesné lab website still pictured him standing with pride before the wall.

On my second day in Minneapolis, walking to Ashe's office I caught a fleeting glimpse of the "international man of mystery," as he once jokingly called himself. Through a wide stairwell, I spotted Lesné in the hall on the floor below. Trim and handsome as ever, albeit with grayer hair and beard, dressed in jeans, a sweater, and sneakers, coffee cup in hand, he looked the picture of a confident scientist and teacher. I had emailed him that I'd be in town; no reply. It was the interview I wanted most but would never get.

As I reflected on my uncomfortable meetings with Ashe, her efforts to validate Lesné's work, and his steady position at UMN, larger questions haunted me: How common and important are episodes of apparent misconduct and lapses of scientific integrity that seem to be overlooked, excused, or doggedly defended whatever the evidence? What do they mean for solving the Alzheimer's puzzle?

To answer, I had put in place an unprecedented plan to examine the reliability of work by scores of the field's scientists, including top innovators who wield vast influence. Big names in the United States, the United Kingdom, Europe, and Asia quickly rose to the surface. They included one of the field's most lauded, cited, and powerful leaders: University of Southern California neuroscientist Berislav Zlokovic.

Chapter 20

Brain Games

Los Angeles and Elsewhere

2022–2024

"It was not real science. He already knew
what he wanted to say . . . It made me sick."

—FORMER MEMBER, LAB OF UNIVERSITY OF
SOUTHERN CALIFORNIA NEUROSCIENTIST BERISLAV ZLOKOVIC

In 2022, the National Institutes of Health (NIH) placed a large bet on an experimental drug developed to limit brain damage after strokes. It committed up to $30 million to administer a compound called 3K3A-APC in a study of fourteen hundred people shortly after they experience an acute ischemic stroke, a perilous condition in which a clot blocks blood flow to part of the brain.

The gamble seemed warranted. Lab studies, mostly by longtime grantee and prominent University of Southern California (USC) neuroscientist Berislav Zlokovic, had generated promising data. A small safety trial in people, sponsored by ZZ Biotech, a company Zlokovic cofounded, also seemed encouraging. An analysis hinted that the treatment reduced the number of tiny, imperceptible brain hemorrhages after stroke patients received either surgery to remove the clot, the clot-busting drug tissue plasminogen activator (tPA), or both.

Scientists have long tried to diminish the brain cell death, bleeding, and inflammation that can follow a stroke, some of which results from disruption of the blood-brain barrier—a system of tiny blood vessels that delivers oxygen and nutrients but shields the brain from toxic substances. The only approved stroke drug in the United States and Europe, tPA reduces death and disability by clearing a stroke's blockage. But it can also cause risky brain bleeding. 3K3A-APC could mitigate such damage and prevent brain cells from dying, ZZ Biotech said.

Given that it could address an unmet medical need, the US Food and Drug Administration (FDA) gave the compound "fast track" status, and a chance for "accelerated approval and priority review." In November 2023, ZZ Biotech said it would start the new trial within a few months.

FITTING DATA TO A HYPOTHESIS

Concerns about Zlokovic and his drug came to light via a hunch. I knew that Sylvain Lesné and Hoau-Yan Wang could not be unique. I wanted to see if I could find an unmeasured, poorly understood pattern. In November 2022, I reached out to Boris Barbour and Brandon Stell, administrators of PubPeer, to try a methodical approach to find an answer.

They provided details for every posting on the site pertaining to Alzheimer's and directly adjacent science. I sifted through the flagged researchers to see who might warrant a close look. I used the PubPeer posts as a tip sheet to find examples of doctoring that I could flesh out to learn if research was sent astray.

Barbour and Stell delivered a spreadsheet containing posts on about 5,500 papers. I quickly identified some five hundred Alzheimer's scholars with five or more questioned papers and began to whittle down that list to a group whose work had meaningful influence. Matthew Schrag and I came up with sixty-five tempting targets. He agreed to examine twenty to fifty papers from each of them to see if a pattern of doctoring emerged.

To accomplish the massive task, Schrag recruited Kevin Patrick, aka "Cheshire," the skilled forensic image analyst who had organized the Prague meetings. (He uses the pseudonym on social media and a different name for his prolific contributions to PubPeer. He revealed his true name publicly via the article I would write about Zlokovic.) A nonscientist, Patrick leaves scientific implications of his work to others, comparing himself to a cancer-sniffing dog. "You wouldn't want the dog to treat the patient, but it might help save their life," he said. Schrag also reached out to Mu Yang, the Columbia neurobiologist and mouse-behavior expert. (They worked independently from their universities.) Schrag provided context—how image alterations can matter to an experiment.

Zlokovic quickly rose to the top tier of scientists who required a close look, not least because of the power he wields: He directs the Zilkha Neurogenetic Institute at USC, which collects more than $30 million in grants annually. Zlokovic enjoys global influence on lab and human studies on Alzheimer's and stroke. Hard-driving and prolific, he pioneered work on pericytes, cells that surround the brain's capillaries and help maintain the blood-brain barrier. His work showing that the barrier helps move amyloid-beta proteins out of the brain won him a share of the celebrated Potamkin Prize in 2009 from the American Academy of Neurology.

An eclectic scientist and entrepreneur, Zlokovic has rarely hit a false note—as a researcher, institute head, and even an amateur opera singer. Amid his steady climb into the academic stratosphere, the charismatic scholar always maintained his vocal gifts. "Science requires clear and perfect language, while music is a universal language," he told the Cure Alzheimer's Fund, a patron. Zlokovic proved that maxim a few years ago at a neuroscience conference, belting out a credible version of "O Sole Mio" to the evident delight of his youthful audience.

Over several months, Schrag and Patrick scrutinized Zlokovic's papers. Image after image looked wrong. Yang provided fresh eyes to backstop the findings. Their 113-page dossier folded in PubPeer posts on Zlokovic's research by Patrick, Elisabeth Bik, and others. (Neither *Science* nor I paid anyone to scrutinize the work of any scientist. Schrag said he, Patrick, and Bik might file a whistleblower lawsuit to receive a portion of NIH funds clawed back from USC if federal authorities deem Zlokovic's work fraudulent.)

Molecular biologist Mike Rossner—a former journal editor whose company, Image Data Integrity, consults on such matters—also evaluated the dossier. Bik reviewed images that she had not personally uncovered. Both saw strong evidence of errors or misconduct.

I soon realized that the path to apparent problems in Zlokovic's Alzheimer's studies passed through his work on stroke. The dossier included a look at the phase 2 trial of 3K3A-APC. There were no falsified images in the write-ups, but the experimental drug might have actually increased deaths in the first days after treatment: Six of sixty-six stroke patients who got it died within a week, compared to one of forty-four in the placebo group, although the death rate evened out after a month. And patients given 3K3A-APC trended toward greater disability and dependency after the trial. Zlokovic and colleagues reported it all obliquely—found by Schrag in the report's fine print.

Deepening Schrag's concerns, the dossier highlighted signs that many papers from Zlokovic's lab supporting the readiness of 3K3A-APC for human testing contained seemingly doctored data. Apparent changes to images might have skewed results in favor of the scientist's hypotheses about 3K3A-APC and the role of the blood-brain barrier in stroke and Alzheimer's.

Ground truth—four former members of Zlokovic's lab who agreed to speak with me anonymously—filled in the picture. They described a culture of intimidation, in which he regularly pushed them and others to adjust data. "There were clear examples of him instructing people to manipulate data to fit the hypothesis," one said.

I had to get the story out ahead of the impending phase 3 clinical trial. Lives were at stake.

UNFATHOMABLE

Given the dossier findings, its authors wanted clinical testing of 3K3A-APC halted at least until after an investigation by the correct authorities. Schrag submitted their work to the NIH with that request. Seven leading neurologists and neuroscientists who reviewed the dossier concurred.

"To have a fourfold increase in mortality in the first few days of giving the drug really gives me pause," said Wade Smith, a University of California San Francisco neurologist. Smith found the dossier so disturbing that he couldn't sleep the night after reading it. His reaction seemed profound, given that he serves as a regional leader for a consortium of clinical sites slated to conduct the larger phase 3 trial.

Because the drug has to be given soon after a stroke, Smith and others pointed out, hundreds of patients—or their family members by proxy—might have just hours or even minutes to decide whether to join the trial.

Given what Smith called possible "scientific fraud" in lab research supporting 3K3A-APC's supposed protective effects, he said the trial should not go forward until NIH and USC address the whistleblowers' allegations. "If we're wrong about the trial, and we really upset some people, well, then I'm sorry," Smith said. "But the opposite is unfathomable."

The dossier featured thirty-five basic research studies and data from two reports on the phase 2 trial. The publications had one common author: Zlokovic. In twenty-nine—including the main phase 2 report—he occupied the last author slot, denoting his senior role. The dossier authors and those who reviewed it noted that some duplicated images could be simple mistakes. Other anomalies might be innocent digital artifacts. For example, western blots sometimes look unnatural after digital changes during publication. Proof might require comparison of published versions against original, uncropped, high-resolution originals. Zlokovic did not respond to my request for those images.

Everyone who saw the dossier said it raised far-reaching questions about his lab practices, research results, and the pending clinical trial.

Much of the data "is clearly, undeniably, the result of misrepresentation," said a famous neuroscientist who studies some of the same topics. "That saddens me, because he's a very respected member of this community." The researcher requested anonymity, concerned about becoming embroiled in a controversy that he predicted would threaten Zlokovic's career.

Chris Schaffer, a Cornell University biomedical engineer, was taken aback by a pair of papers published five years apart that seem to use the same image to represent different results. In a 2004 paper in the prestigious journal *Neuron*, the image purportedly shows how natural APC, from which 3K3A-APC is derived, prevents brain cells from dying. But a 2009 paper in the *European Journal of Neuroscience* includes what appears to be the same image as evidence that the ZZ Biotech compound also protects the brain but without causing hazardous bleeding, a drawback of natural APC. It helped set the dose of 3K3A-APC initially tested in people.

The dossier suggests that cellular features had been removed from a raw image before its use in the 2004 paper, and that the original image was used in the later paper. The analysis left Schaffer shaken: "I immediately felt nauseous," he said. "The integrity of the scientific record is so fundamental to what we do that seeing this kind of data anomaly is distressing."

Schaffer, an expert in optical imaging for neuroscience, took the dossier's analysis of the two papers further. When he adjusted the image contrast, new details became obvious: In the 2004 paper, superimposed square boxes cover the nuclei of some brain cells. The boxes may mask fragmentation indicating that the supposedly protected cells were dying, he suggests. "It's hard to imagine those boxes emerging as a digital artifact," Schaffer said. "They're perfect squares."

The Cornell scientist said whoever apparently manipulated the image might have wanted to show "cleaner," more consistent data or, in a less charitable interpretation, tried to obscure signs that APC and 3K3A-APC didn't actually protect brain cells.

Another neuroscientist who reviewed the dossier anonymously for fear of courting a lawsuit was shocked to see seemingly doctored images in papers he had peer reviewed. "One of them is so clear in retrospect that I should have spotted it," he said, broadly agreeing with the dossier conclusions. Then he asked: "Why would one bother to go to these lengths to change images, when the guy has the resources to generate loads of great papers without doing this?"

"WE WERE ALL SILENT"

Two former lab members offered muted support for Zlokovic. Angeliki Nikolakopoulou, first author on three papers in the dossier, became principal scientist at Bionaut Labs in Los Angeles. Reached by phone, she said, "The only thing I can tell you after being a member of his lab for eight years is that there is no misconduct," then hung up.

Axel Montagne—also first author on three papers—coincidentally earned his PhD at the University of Caen, Lesné's alma mater. He left the Zlokovic lab to head his own at the University of Edinburgh. Except for a typo on a statistical calculation, none of the data he personally supplied had been flagged, Montagne said. "I am not aware of, nor did I witness any instances of misconduct in Professor Zlokovic," he added, nor "any behavior from him that I construed as exerting undue pressure." But Montagne saw image problems that might have been intentional and said that he would cooperate with official inquiries.

The four former lab members who allege Zlokovic pushed them and others to manipulate data paint a picture of a pressure-cooker environment in which their boss expected new data in line with his hypotheses almost every week. All worked with Zlokovic for years and published with him. All independently gave similar descriptions.

In lab meetings, the accusers said, researchers were discouraged from speaking up and contributing intellectually to the lab's work, tightly controlled by Zlokovic. "It's science. So normally you would express your opinions," one noted. Instead, that person said, newcomers soon learned that speaking up meant facing "humiliation"—a term three of the insiders used. Except to answer questions, one said, "we were all silent."

All four said Zlokovic routinely castigated junior scientists when they failed to obtain desired results. "If you are not in agreement with him, you will lose the lead authorship on a paper or on a project," one of the scientists said. "Of course, this is important for your career." Another said, "If the data does not look like the hypothesis, we were afraid to even bring it to the lab meeting." They described some staff scientists or long-tenured trainees as his enforcers or dependable cooperators.

Zlokovic hosted lavish parties that included celebrities and power players in science and philanthropy. He dangled invitations as rewards to lab members who reliably delivered what he wanted, said two former lab members.

One researcher described how a group of lab members approached Zilkha's human resources department about the "toxic environment." The complaint was rejected because they insisted on remaining anonymous for fear of retaliation.

Several former lab members detailed data that they said were falsified. That included experiments referenced in the dossier. Sometimes, they said, data points that would have invalidated desired results were removed and results planned in advance. "It was not real science. He already knew what he wanted to say . . . It made me sick."

Two insiders also said Zlokovic sometimes had his team improperly alter lab notebooks. Scientists use them to record details of experiments in process, providing ground truth for methods and results. They're often central to misconduct investigations. But two of the former lab members said that after an experiment was completed and published, Zlokovic sometimes admonished his scientists to make sure the notebooks were "clean." That was understood to mean pasting into them printouts of the published results and methodology or omitting contrary details that challenged the paper's conclusions. Zlokovic explained that those changes were needed in case of an "audit," the two scientists said.

Two former lab members had long wrestled with whether to speak out, fearing that blowback might damage their careers. "This is a moment in life when I must choose between what is right and what is easy," one said, sobbing. "The easy option would be not speaking with you. I decided that when I lay on my deathbed one day, I might regret not doing what is right."

A USC spokesperson said that the university "takes any allegations relating to research integrity seriously." Zlokovic declined interview requests. His attorney said in a statement that Zlokovic "is committed to fully cooperating" with the USC inquiry. Without offering specifics, the statement noted that part of the dossier is "based on information and premises Professor Zlokovic knows to be completely incorrect," or pertains to work not completed in his lab.

My story appeared in *Science* on November 13, 2023. Moving with rare speed, three days later NIH halted the trial, launched an investigation, and then clawed back $1.9 million in USC grant funds. Soon after, the editors of *Neuron* concluded that at least one image "appears to have been digitally manipulated" just as described in the dossier and by Cornell's Schaffer. High-profile papers on pericytes in *Nature Communications* and *Nature Medicine*, as well as the 2009 paper in the *European Journal of Neuroscience*, were retracted. In October 2024, Zlokovic went on indefinite leave from USC.

The Zlokovic case seemed extreme. But it fits a disturbing pattern: Authorities often ignore doubts about top Alzheimer's scientists and rainmakers for years.

IRRESISTIBLE TEMPTATIONS

In December 1991, Gerald Higgins, a respected researcher at the National Institute on Aging (NIA) and colleagues published what seemed like a landmark Alzheimer's paper in *Nature*. It described the development of a transgenic mouse whose brain seemed to produce telltale amyloid plaques and tau tangles. In short, they had produced one of the first direct animal models to test Alzheimer's therapies—a breakthrough.

A commentary by Dennis Selkoe praised the work. Soon after, he visited Higgins's lab near Washington, DC, to discuss possible collaborations. Selkoe left "dismayed," he said at the time. He had seen signs of what others were whispering about: Higgins might have produced no more than images of human brain tissue described as coming from a mouse. He denied wrongdoing, but the paper was retracted. NIA never publicly commented. (Decades later, driving in his hybrid sedan across Boston, Selkoe looked aghast when I asked about the episode, uttering only, "I was shocked.")

Yet a month after that humiliation, Higgins and UK biochemist John Hardy published what became the most influential paper in Alzheimer's history, this time in *Science*. They described the "amyloid cascade hypothesis," setting in motion decades of scientific dominance.

The episode seemed to prove a maxim that the benefits of data doctoring are great, the risks small. "Breakthroughs" can lead to riches, fame, and glory. Corner-cutting, or worse, can prove irresistible. Or so it seems, given that temptation has often triumphed, even among leaders in the field. Occasional bad behavior afflicts all of science—indeed, every human endeavor. In Alzheimer's such problems seem to occur with troubling regularity.

Dubious studies were piling up: Wang and Lindsay Burns of Cassava Sciences, Lesné and Karen Ashe, Schrag's teacher Othman Ghribi, former Stanford president Marc Tessier-Lavigne, and now Zlokovic.

Ashe and Tessier-Lavigne seemed to have engaged in misconduct "misdemeanors." They didn't falsify data personally or coerce underlings. But they turned a blind eye or provided what some considered inadequate oversight, then benefited from apparent corruption. Ashe bragged about seemingly fake findings and won awards and raised money from them. Tessier-Lavigne kept his skeletons in the closet, rising to one of the most important academic posts until the "cover-up," in typical fashion, eclipsed the "crime." (In a soft landing, he left Stanford shortly after his ouster to head Xaira Therapeutics, an artificial-intelligence drug-discovery start-up with $1 billion in funding.)

Ethically suspect actions go beyond image doctoring. In 2015, Alzheimer's authority Paul Aisen attempted to "hijack" the University of California San Diego (UCSD) research center he ran, and move it to USC, as the *Los Angeles Times* described it. According to court documents, Aisen allegedly arranged for a massive pay raise to move the program's grants and some faculty. He and others "agreed to become 'double agents'— ostensibly employed by UCSD . . . but in reality working to dismantle and destroy the [Alzheimer's] research program at UCSD and put the pieces of the program back together under the auspices of USC," UCSD alleged. The filings called Aisen and others "predatory."

Dean Carmen Puliafito then led USC's School of Medicine. "Is the golden rule part of USC's Code of Ethics, to treat others the way USC would want to be treated?" he was asked under oath. Puliafito answered simply: "No." (Soon after, he fell in his own scandal—among several that have plagued USC—when his drug problem and parties with addicts and criminals went public. Puliafito was bounced from his job, collecting a $1 million payout on the way out the door, according to the *Times*. The state later revoked his medical license.)

"USC is committed to, and wants to be known for, ethics, integrity and the pursuit of academic excellence, and it has already implemented sweeping changes to this end," the university said in its public *mea culpa* on the Aisen case, for which they paid UCSD a $50 million settlement. Yet Aisen's reputation didn't seem to suffer. He still headlines scientific conferences.

And Zlokovic evidently didn't get the memo.

OTHER BLOTS

The project that began with a glance through PubPeer data had grown rapidly. In my personal shorthand, I called it "Other Blots," after the title of my Lesné-Ashe article in 2022, "Blots on a Field"—a play on Lesné's western blot images. As I coordinated and monitored months of work by the image sleuths, I hoped the project could become an unprecedented review of misconduct across a major field of science.

After nearly a year, Schrag, Patrick, and Yang had examined forty-four scientists, using the software program Imagetwin and their own expert eyes. Bik contributed to the findings and vetted most of the suspected problems that she had not personally discovered. Rossner also reviewed a handful of high-profile cases. I showed the dossiers to noted neuroscientists. In many cases, they said that image doctoring seemed to clearly change experimental results in important ways. In other words, much of the work could not be trusted.

(All of those who created or checked the dossiers at my request agreed: Clear evidence suggests culpability, but final conclusions can require examination of nonpublic sources such as raw images and lab notebooks. That's why critics call even image-doctoring that seems obvious "probable," or "apparent" misconduct.)

Rather than looking for the isolated problems that often surface on PubPeer, Other Blots studied patterns—to create a map to help universities, funders, or regulators probe underlying data to illuminate bigger problems in a scientist's body of work. Robust responses from institutional authorities in the Zlokovic case lent that approach credibility.

The effort flagged respected, mid-level neuroscientists, including Domenico Praticò of Temple University, who has extensively studied amyloid and tau in Alzheimer's disease. (Years earlier, Yang had uncovered seemingly implausible data in his tests of mice in the Morris water maze. Richard Morris, inventor of the widely used test, concurred with her findings.) Other doubts about Praticò's work surfaced on PubPeer and elsewhere; four suspect studies were retracted. In January 2024 he filed suit against a trainee for "falsification of research data."

The *Philadelphia Inquirer* described some of the concerns and noted an ongoing Temple review. Praticò, through his attorney, "categorically denie[d] engaging in scientific misconduct." When I contacted him about thirty-one apparently doctored papers in the dossier, Praticò said the litigation limited his response. He blamed his trainee and a former colleague, adding, "I have been actively working since the allegations were first presented to me to understand and correct issues flagged in the noted papers." One of those papers was retracted in March 2024, two others in June 2024, and one more in August 2024. Regarding seven others that did not involve either of those scientists, Praticò blamed other collaborators or said he would examine the concerns.

Studies by P. Hemachandra Reddy at Texas Tech University involving amyloids, tau, and other topics central to Alzheimer's, showed extensive signs of image tampering and improper reuse of images in experiments going back twenty years. Reddy said only that he would address the matter within the university's confidential inquiry sparked by my messages.

Anuska Andjelkovic-Zochowska of the University of Michigan did not reply to requests for comment on the dossier I provided that questioned more than a dozen of her brain studies. A Michigan spokesperson said the dossier would be assessed, and an investigation launched if warranted.

In 2023 and 2024, *The Transmitter* wrote about problems in experiments by Gary Dunbar and Panchanan Maiti at Central Michigan University—also the subjects of an Other Blots dossier. Several of their papers have been retracted in the face of ostensible image doctoring.

Such problems extend well beyond US borders. Other Blots found thirty-eight apparently doctored papers by Myeong Ok Kim, a prominent Korean scientist who explores natural antioxidants, vitamins, caffeine, and chemicals derived from ginseng and turmeric as Alzheimer's treatments. Kim did not reply to requests for comment.

Twenty papers on a wide range of Alzheimer's topics—including amyloid plaques and insulin resistance in the brain—by highly regarded Thai researchers Siriporn and Nipon Chattipakorn, showed signs of tampering in dozens of western blots and microscopic images. Siriporn Chattipakorn blamed the problems on "unintentional procedural human error" in ten papers. She said that corrections have been made or submitted. In several cases, original data verified the questioned images, she added, but declined to provide original images for independent review. Chattipakorn did not address other examples showing signs of manipulation.

A trio of Chinese scientists—Bing-Qiao Zhao and Wenying Fan of Fudan University, and Yongliang Cao of Wuhan University—didn't reply to requests for comment about dubious images in five papers on blood flow issues in the brain related to Alzheimer's and stroke, published in prominent journals. One had been retracted in 2023. Jun Tan, who recently returned to his native China from the University of South Florida, did not respond to queries about apparent image doctoring in fifteen studies—many concerning amyloid-beta in animal testing.

Other Blots also identified consistent image anomalies in work from Daniel Alkon, formerly a high-level NIH neuroscientist, and his colleagues Jarin Hongpaisan and Miao-Kun Sun. Their studies underpin human trials to treat Alzheimer's with bryostatin, an anticancer agent. Alkon's company, Synaptogenix, sponsored the work, which suggested that the compound might halt or mitigate cognitive decline. The three scientists responded in detail—admitting to mistakes or to having deliberately doctored images. But they described the changed images as "illustrations" not meant to literally represent underlying data. Alkon called that approach standard at NIH and elsewhere. Yet in numerous cases, they corrected or said they would correct the images and would not use that approach in the future.

Stanford's Thomas Südhof said that 99.9 percent of scientists would agree that knowingly posting incorrect or doctored images—whatever the justification—violates basic scientific ethics and suggests misconduct. He added that such attitudes raise doubts about the credibility of a group's body of research.

Alkon argued that bryostatin shows great promise—as demonstrated in the questioned studies and in clinical trials. Investors see it differently. After disappointing results from a small clinical trial of the compound were announced in late 2022, Synaptogenix stock quickly lost three-quarters of its value. Even after a new study reanalyzed the trial data and found possible small benefits for a tiny subset of patients who had severe dementia—shares traded at about 3 percent of their former value.

BIG PLAYERS, BIG PROBLEMS

Other Blots looked closely at neuroscientists whose Alzheimer's contributions have gained global recognition. Südhof; George Perry, the *Journal of Alzheimer's Disease* editor; and Donna Wilcock of Indiana University and *Alzheimer's & Dementia*, reviewed many of the dossiers.

Steven Arnold, a longtime Cassava Sciences advisor and collaborator of CUNY's Wang, leads the Interdisciplinary Brain Center at Massachusetts General Hospital. His studies on post-mortem brain tissue with CUNY's Wang, Cassava's Burns, and others, support the idea that Alzheimer's might be caused by a diabetes of the brain. The fifty-four-page Arnold dossier covers thirteen papers—showing apparent doctoring of western blots and improper reuse of other images—including work without Wang and Burns. Arnold declined to comment. A Massachusetts General spokesperson said that officials would "undertake a robust and confidential process to assess and respond to any claims" in the dossier. In March 2024, the journal *PLOS ONE* issued an expression of concern about one of those papers.

A constellation of researchers headlined by UK scientist Peter St George-Hyslop, now at Columbia University and the University of Toronto (UT), and Frédéric Checler, an emeritus research director at the French National Institute of Health and Medical Research, made notable contributions to understanding amyloid precursor protein—the source of amyloid-beta—and genetic and molecular factors that drive early onset Alzheimer's. St George-Hyslop discovered presenilins, which play a role in the production of amyloid-beta.

The eighty-page dossier about their work showed apparent image doctoring in forty-four papers—casting doubt on widely accepted ideas. It expanded and updated concerns previously cited on PubPeer or elsewhere. (An image sleuth who uses the pseudonym Clare Francis first raised concerns about the two scientists.)

In response to the dossier, St George-Hyslop and Checler said that experts at UT and the University of Cambridge, St George-Hyslop's former employer, had already examined their work based on prior complaints. "The conclusions of these enquiries were the same. There was no evidence of misconduct. We were fully exonerated," they told me via email. The two universities confirmed that claim. The scientists would not provide the investigation reports.

Soon after, a UT spokesperson sent me the list of papers reviewed there. It included just three of the forty-four in the Other Blots dossier. One of the three had been retracted. Moreover, the spokesperson said that rather than modern benchmarks for ensuring image authenticity, it used less-rigorous "standards for data images that were in place at the time of the actual publication."

I informed Checler and St George-Hyslop of the UT disclosures, noting that the dossier included a range of possible doctoring and copied images or parts of images, sometimes across papers, including blots and micrographs. Some seemed to have been stretched vertically or horizontally to obscure reuse. I again asked if they would address those concerns, rather than referring to prior assessments whose relevance seems tangential.

St George-Hyslop and Checler did not respond.

Perry called the Checler–St George-Hyslop case "worrisome"—and worthy of careful review by institutional authorities. Südhof described Checler's role as very problematic, because he was the key investigator in half the papers and coauthor of thirty-four.

Frank LaFerla, a neuroscientist and dean of the University of California Irvine School of Biological Sciences, has contributed to widely shared views about how amyloid-beta plaques and tau tangles interact in Alzheimer's. His triple-transgenic—three mutations linked to Alzheimer's—"LaFerla mouse," developed in the early 2000s, became a widely used model for research. Over the last decade, NIA has awarded LaFerla more than $60 million for his Alzheimer's center—mostly for mouse-model development.

That investment, Perry said, was "predicated on bringing it to a place where the work is going to be executed with great care," adding that the dossier findings warrant institutional review.

LaFerla's former student Salvatore Oddo helped develop the famous mouse. He moved to the University of Messina via the University of Arizona—where some of his work came under fire, leading to two retractions. A dossier prepared for the Other Blots project included Oddo papers not connected with LaFerla. In a written statement, he accepted most findings, blaming "honest errors" that he said left experimental outcomes unaffected. (Such replies are common when images are challenged.)

LaFerla responded with forthright alacrity, describing himself as "embarrassed, confused, and perplexed." He informed his provost, triggering an internal review. LaFerla also quickly contacted a journal to correct a paper in which a manipulated image did not affect the experimental outcome, and said he would correct others and likely retract an influential paper from the *Journal of Neuroscience* describing how amyloid-beta, tau, and alpha-synuclein (which helps regulate synapses, the junctions that convey signals between nerve cells) combine to accelerate cognitive decline in mice.

The scientist seemed genuinely chastened. "The most important thing is that we get all of this right because many people's lives depend on it," LaFerla said.

AGUZZI'S ARGUMENT

Adriano Aguzzi, a native Italian at the University of Zürich (UZ), is one of the most revered neuroscientists of the twenty-first century. His groundbreaking work on prions—widely viewed as infectious proteins tied to rare, often-fatal brain disorders in animals and people—earned prizes and honors. Aguzzi has long penned influential commentaries, analyses, and neuroscience histories in *Science*. He founded and directs the Swiss National Reference Center for Prion Diseases and has introduced ideas on how prion-like processes might contribute to Alzheimer's.

"If I look at people who complain that they can't get grants because of the 'amyloid mafia,' often they aren't doing very good science," he said in 2023. By then PubPeer critics had been targeting his work for a decade.

In 2019, Aguzzi was caught in the searing spotlight of Leonid Schneider, the Ukrainian-German blogger and scientific critic who described PubPeer posts about Aguzzi's work with characteristic irreverence. The scientist engaged in an extended dialogue on Schneider's blog—acknowledging some errors but objecting to the mocking personal tone of the critique.

"The scorn, the ridiculing, and the meanness say more about Schneider than about myself. I think that no scientist is immune from making mistakes. In my research work, I try to be the severest reviewer of my own work," he wrote.

Schrag found problems in Aguzzi's work well beyond those previously cited, going back two decades. Rossner vetted Schrag's dossier, which was augmented by Bik, Patrick, and Yang. Südhof, Wilcock, and Perry concurred that some findings in that sixty-page document were relatively minor, but others posed serious questions.

I provided Aguzzi with the dossier in February 2024 and asked if I could see him in Zürich to talk it over. He immediately consented. Then he shared my inquiry with the university's vice president for research. She launched an investigation and vetoed my visit.

Still, in a lengthy email, Aguzzi replied with contrition. He primarily blamed trainees but said he would move aggressively to fix the record.

Aguzzi wrote that after 2019, he made some corrections and "voluntarily reduced the size of my lab by 50 percent, so that I could offer stricter supervision to my students and postdocs. It was an embarrassing experience, but it was a good thing—for my science and also for my own peace of mind."

Five papers noted in the Other Blots dossier appeared after 2019. Aguzzi addressed those and fresh concerns about earlier papers. For example, an important 2017 study in *PLOS Pathogens* described how brain-cell structures involved in transmitting nerve signals can be inhibited to protect against prions. He called the dossier's findings "worrisome," adding: "If the data was fake then this needs to come to light and the paper needs to be amended or retracted." (He later asked the journal to retract, according to emails to Schrag. "I am grateful for your work—even if I am finding myself, to some extent, in the crosshairs of your critique," Aguzzi told Schrag. "Maintenance of a correct, honest scientific record is fundamental to all science, and your work helps immensely towards this goal.")

A landmark 2011 paper showed that when mice inhaled aerosolized prions they quickly died. The results were partly corrected following Pub-Peer comments, but the dossier described new problems. Aguzzi conceded that data generated largely by a junior colleague "was of very poor quality" and might require a new correction. But he added that the study "triggered a rethinking of aerosol containment and I am convinced that it saved human lives." The journal retracted the paper in June 2024.

On two Lesné papers, Aguzzi received coauthor credit—a courtesy, he said, for providing transgenic mice to test oligomer forms of amyloid-beta in Alzheimer's. He was skeptical of Lesné's results and "briefly considered refusing to coauthor," Aguzzi said. "Probably I should have followed my instinct." Instead, he lent credibility and influence to the suspect work.

"Please consider that I have been publishing papers since 1982," and most have never been challenged, Aguzzi said.

Südhof, who has followed Aguzzi's work closely, said he saw "potentially severe instances of possible misconduct" in the dossier. But he felt that the problems left most of the scientist's major contributions unaffected.

"I don't run my lab like a military battalion, and I do not consider myself a policeman . . . If somebody is determined to cheat, they will always find a way to do it," Aguzzi said, calling the idea that a lab head can prevent all misconduct "an illusion heeded by people who don't know how labs function." (Most researchers agree that great science—a team sport with specialized contributions—demands trust. But heading a lab means taking responsibility for quality and ethics.)

A few months later, Aguzzi had a major medical emergency. Looking to his legacy in a moment of crisis, he wrote on X: "I have no wish to leave this valley of tears today, but if that happens, let it be known that I was an honest scientist. In 40 years of science, I have been wrong, sloppy, lazy, insufficiently vigilant/competent, and much more—but I was never dishonest."

COLLATERAL DAMAGE

Aguzzi added a sobering postscript in his message to me: "I witnessed . . . suicides of people who were caught cheating." In 1991, a UZ PhD student killed himself in his lab after data he provided for a groundbreaking paper were exposed as fabrication. Aguzzi said that when his own trainee delivered apparently invented data, "he seemed suicidal, and I really did not want to see [another] self-inflicted death of a scientist. The aggressivity with which the scientific record must be corrected . . . needs to be balanced against the risk of suicides."

That perspective, however heartfelt, might seem self-serving. Yet others concur. John Hardy—an originator of the amyloid hypothesis and one of the most lauded Alzheimer's researchers—has himself been accused of misconduct. And although he also has waded into such a controversy as a critic of an accused scientist, Hardy recently wrote of his fears about some of my work to a *Science* editor: "I am seriously concerned about the exposés run by *Science* on high-profile researchers who seem to have published fraudulent work," he said, adding that he knows three of the scientists in question. "I am concerned about the name-and-shame culture that has developed. I have met one of the 'victims' at a recent scientific meeting and he was a broken man. I say this because I fear that one of these exposed scientists will commit suicide. I hope *Science* is considering this possible outcome, especially since rarely do the allegations of individual fraud reach the threshold of 'beyond a reasonable doubt.'"

Each time I write about possible fraud by a scientist, I also worry: Might someone who has seemed to have falsified data be emotionally unstable? Hoau-Yan Wang's hospitalization for emotional exhaustion after concerns emerged about his apparent image doctoring comes to mind. Bik has shared misgivings about criticisms that escalate into personal attacks. Schrag often has said that he works hard to avoid "collateral damage" that can destroy junior scientists who might have been manipulated by powerful superiors.

Media coverage of misconduct hardly mentions "trainees who may be traumatized personally and harmed professionally by the clumsy, opaque, and slow way that institutions deal with these incidents," wrote Holden Thorp, editor of *Science*.

Charges of plagiarism—some minor—have recently become political brickbats. And some anonymous complaints about minor mistakes become excessively argumentative and aloof of context—verging on trolling or vigilantism.

Similarly, "weaponisation of forensic research" can have "a chilling effect on academic freedom and distracts from efforts to address more important systemic issues in research integrity," wrote Till Bruckner, an advocate for openness in clinical research. "Focusing research integrity efforts on targets selected by partisan actors or social media mobs is unlikely to improve science," he added, and deter systematic assessments of misconduct "across an entire field."

Südhof exemplifies the challenges of finding a balance. His own papers have been tagged on PubPeer, and he too was savaged by Schneider. A Nobelist offers a choice target, but far beyond the vast majority of scientists, Südhof has published voluminous raw data—to transparency advocates, the best show of integrity. Data sleuths, including Bik and Patrick, scoured his work, in some cases using AI tools, and said they found errors in dozens of papers. During a prolonged PubPeer debate and comments on his lab website, Südhof retracted one and corrected several others. But he argues, sometimes with prickly defensiveness, that most concerns were unfounded or insignificant.

Any body of work that spans hundreds of papers, like Südhof's, contains errors. The more data released, the easier to spot them. Schrag agreed that most problems had no clear impact on Südhof's experiments—with a couple of exceptions, including the one leading to the retraction. And he said he had "been impressed by Südhof's candor" and willingness to correct when needed. "Südhof is modeling a culture of integrity for his team," Schrag added. "We should destigmatize this process because this is how science is supposed to work."

Südhof decried what he sees as serious unintended effects of PubPeer. "Lab members have quit because they don't want to be in a profession where young scientists are prosecuted for minor errors," and others broke down in tears, he said. All are women and excellent scientists who made minor mistakes assembling illustrations in complex projects, Südhof added. "They are now being chased out of science by critics armed with artificial intelligence software who identify true but minor errors. People are deeply upset about the unfairness of all this."

I was reminded that a close friend of mine who spent much of his career studying how to improve health outcomes recoiled when my Zlokovic article appeared, despite agreeing with its premise. He worried about a related hazard of "overkill"—that such coverage promotes public cynicism. A rising focus on scientific error and ethical lapses without comparable treatment of solutions, he said, "creates a risk of people throwing up their hands and thinking 'the whole scientific enterprise is a cesspool of corruption.'"

A RECKONING

A vivid counter to arguments that scientific-integrity criticism is out of control involves Eliezer Masliah, director of the NIA Division of Neuroscience, principal federal funder for Alzheimer's research. Masliah's $2.6 billion annual budget and the influence it implies place him among the world's most powerful Alzheimer's scientists.

"NIA sets the agenda worldwide for age-related diseases," says Scott Ayton, director of a neuroscience center at the University of Melbourne, echoing US and European peers.

Masliah received medical training in his home country of Mexico. Before joining NIA in 2016, he headed experimental neuropathology at UCSD. His prolific output on Alzheimer's, Parkinson's, and other ailments led to some eight hundred papers and seventy book chapters. Masliah made discoveries involving alpha-synuclein, considered important in Alzheimer's and widely viewed as a cause of Parkinson's. He explored possible Alzheimer's treatments, including anti-inflammatory drugs, antidepressants, and compounds to decrease amyloid-beta production.

A Masliah dossier compiled largely by Yang with significant contributions by Schrag, Bik, and Patrick, weighed in at 300 pages, comprising 132 apparently doctored papers—by far the most for any scientist examined. It contained questionable western blots, micrographs, and images reused within and across papers going back to 1997.

"I started feeling like a curator or art historian—when you look at a piece of art without the label, you know the artist by the style," Yang said about examining Masliah's body of work. "Like a painting from Picasso's blue period, it's a signature style that I saw in many, many papers—the way they lay out the figures, even the color contrast." After finding hundreds of questionable images, the group had more than enough strong signs of misconduct and stopped looking, Yang says. But she suspects similar problems would emerge from a close examination of the hundreds of other Masliah papers.

As usual, the dossier's creators did not accuse Masliah or his colleagues of fraud or misconduct. Some problems might have been simple errors or visual artifacts that resemble improper changes. Distinguishing the two sometimes requires comparison to raw, high-resolution images and other data. But Masliah did not respond to my requests for those materials. The document's enormity stunned eleven leading neuroscientists I asked to review it. If substantially correct, the document would mean that a scientist near the pinnacle of power in the biggest funding agency engaged in wholesale misconduct or pervasive error for much of his career—a body blow to the field.

"A major issue in Alzheimer's disease has been synapse loss," and Masliah provided elements of the field's thinking about that key issue, Perry said. "Now I think that work was probably fabricated, in part."

The researchers who reviewed the dossier didn't personally verify every example of possible misconduct, but they agreed that most of the doubts identified cannot be explained as digital anomalies or careless errors.

"Breathtaking," said Ludwig Maximilians University Munich neuro-scientist Christian Haass, about the findings. "People will, of course, be shocked, as I was . . . I was falling from a chair, basically."

The dossier includes numerous studies relied on by pharma companies. Notably, Masliah's dubious work helped win a nod by the FDA for clinical trials of the Parkinson's drug prasinezumab, made by Prothena—a company backed by big money and big-name neuroscientists. (Selkoe is a board member. He did not reply to my message alerting him about the situation, and asking for comment.) It attacks alpha-synuclein. In a recent trial of 316 patients, prasinezumab showed no benefit compared to a placebo, and volunteers given the treatment suffered from far more relatively minor side effects from the infusions to deliver the drug. Another trial in progress involves 586 patients.

Masliah's Prothena connection began with his ties to the late Dale Schenk, an influential pioneer in vaccines and antibody treatments for Alzheimer's and Parkinson's. In 2001 Schenk won the coveted Potamkin neuroscience prize. He cofounded and served as chief executive of Pro-thena, spun off in 2012 from the former biopharma company Elan.

After Schenk's death from pancreatic cancer at age 59 in 2016, Masliah described an archetypal 2001 meeting: "Dale and I sat at a coffee shop . . . next to the Pacific Ocean and drew, on a napkin, the concept of how a potential synuclein vaccine might work," he wrote on Alzforum—the website frequented by Alzheimer's researchers. "People strongly doubted the potential use of a vaccine approach in Alzheimer's and even more so in Parkinson's. Dale was one of the few who listened and believed in the idea."

The two scientists worked together extensively. Four of their joint studies, published between 2005 and 2017, proved foundational for prasinezumab, according to Prothena. Schenk was senior author on two of those papers, Masliah on two. Those four and other Masliah papers cited as important to the drug used apparently doctored images. Masliah and Schenk shared inventor credit for several patents whose rights they assigned to Prothena. Those and other Prothena patents cite suspect work described in the dossier.

Apparently doctored images in studies underlying or related to prasinezumab occurred "to an astonishing level," said Tim Greenamyre, director of the University of Pittsburgh Institute for Neurodegenerative Diseases. "There can be no other conclusion."

The drug's lack of success in the recent trial by Prothena and its partner, Swiss pharmaceutical giant Roche, doesn't necessarily mean "that synuclein is a bad target or that targeting it with antibodies is never going to work," Greenamyre cautions. "There may be beneficial clinical effects in a subgroup of participants. But the discovery that key papers supporting this approach contained manipulated figures certainly muddies the waters," and begs an assessment of support from independent studies to determine if "the rationale for clinical development remains on firm ground—or if it is now a little shaky."

Roche joined forces with Prothena to develop prasinezumab in 2013, agreeing to pay the smaller company up to $620 million to meet a series of performance goals. So far, Roche has ponied up $135 million. Further payments depend in part on possible phase 3 trials—the last experiments before possible FDA approval. Masliah and Prothena did not reply to questions about how much, if anything, he earned in royalties from patents licensed to the company.

"The images are being used to substantiate the favored findings of the authors," says Northwestern University neuropathologist Rudy Castellani, regarding the papers cited by Prothena. "They need better-quality preclinical data, in my opinion, and an explanation for the digital duplications, before moving forward" on further clinical studies.

Neurologist Michael Okun, who directs the Fixel Institute for Neurological Diseases at the University of Florida, called it "deeply troubling" that the FDA greenlighted human trials of prasinezumab based largely on papers from Masliah's lab. (The FDA declined to comment.)

Some of Masliah's earliest work on alpha-synuclein is also being challenged, raising other questions about the foundations of Prothena's drug. Okun calls an apparently doctored image in a seminal 2000 Masliah paper in *Science* a sign of something amiss from the outset. It suggested that alpha-synuclein might cause the death of certain brain cells and the development of Lewy body lesions—key factors in Parkinson's. Other researchers have been unable to validate key aspects of that study, according to Okun and Ayton.

Science editor Thorp said that although the changes in one questioned image violated contemporary standards, "we don't have enough to say that the experiment was fraudulent." In that case and another, Masliah had not retained the original images that could confirm or refute his findings. (*Science*'s news department, where I work, is editorially independent of the journal.)

Neither Masliah nor the various drug companies, universities, or federal agencies that were provided the dossier rejected or challenged any of its examples of possible misconduct despite being given ample time to review it. Masliah and his boss, NIA Director Richard Hodes, via a spokesperson, declined to reply to detailed questions, provide an interview, or comment. National Institutes of Health Director Monica Bertagnolli also declined to comment. Masliah did not reply to a request for raw images and other data. Two days before my report on the Masliah affair was slated to go public, NIH contacted me to say that Masliah was no longer serving in his post—he had been ousted or resigned. They cited their own investigation of two papers without mention of the dossier.

"We do not interpret these claims as specifically relevant to the current prasinezumab clinical program," a Prothena spokesperson said in response to a lengthy sub-dossier on apparently doctored research relevant to the drug. Roche defended its clinical research on prasinezumab as well supported by other studies. In the interest of scientific integrity, a Roche spokesperson added, "We are working to further understand the details of this matter."

The influence of dubious work by Masliah in advancing drugs to market or clinical testing reflects "a deeply rooted problem" in neuroscience, Schrag said. "Too many people providing intellectual leadership in the field turn a blind eye when data look too good to be true, but were convenient for pet hypotheses" or commercial interests.

The Masliah dossier also raises questions about the vetting process at NIH. The agency acknowledged that Masliah's work was not checked for possible fraud before he was hired. "There is no evidence that such proactive screening would improve, or is necessary to improve, the research environment at NIH," the agency said.

Samuel Gandy, a prominent neurologist at the Mount Sinai Alzheimer's Disease Research Center who during an interview was visibly shaken over the enormity of the dossier, disagreed. "It has to be part of the process now," he said.

"For so important a job, you want somebody who is beyond reproach. You want somebody to be an exemplar of what you aspire to be," Greenamyre said of the agency's decision to hire Masliah. Echoing comments from Haass and others, he added: "[But] I worry about it giving science a further black eye, just as the public's confidence in science and scientists is sinking to new depths."

The Other Blots project was far from a comprehensive look at each researcher, let alone the multitude of other Alzheimer's experts. That would take an army of sleuths years. But it was the first major attempt to systematically assess the extent of image and data doctoring across a broad range of key scientists addressing any disease.

By 2024, it had sparked numerous corrections, retractions, institutional reviews, government investigations, and lawsuits. Strong evidence suggested that work by Arnold, Lesné, Zlokovic, Masliah, and many others had been doctored in ways that wasted funds and starved more-worthy studies. But did tainted work distort larger directions in research or drug development, or jeopardize patients? That question haunted me.

Chapter 21

Impact on Alzheimer's

Various Locations

2024

"As a field, we've had a lot of dead ends.
Maybe some of those were driven by bad science
and data manipulation."

—DONNA WILCOCK, EDITOR, *ALZHEIMER'S & DEMENTIA*

To find out if work by Eliezer Masliah, Steven Arnold, Adriano Aguzzi, Peter St George-Hyslop, and others had distorted Alzheimer's research in harmful, measurable ways, I needed more data. I turned to Dimensions Analytics, a premier system for cataloging scientific output and its reach from the UK company Digital Science. George Perry introduced me to Aaron Sorensen, an analyst for the company who years earlier had written an incisive analysis that ranked the premier influencers in the field.

Berislav Zlokovic offered a test case. His stature seemed clear. For example, in 2022 the *Journal of Molecular Neuroscience* described key "influencers" who had explored the role of the blood-brain barrier in people with early dementia. Zlokovic dominated. But I needed sharper data on his power and how his apparently doctored studies might have distorted Alzheimer's research.

I started by examining whether funding trends by the National Institutes of Health (NIH) tracked with Zlokovic's ascendancy. As his dozens of publications popularized the importance of the blood-brain barrier among Alzheimer's scientists, National Institutes of Health (NIH) support for those efforts jumped from $13 million in 2006 to $221 million in 2023.

According to Dimensions, he ranked first in the world in the number of published papers and citations to those papers by other scholars—important measures of influence—in several Alzheimer's subfields, including the blood-brain barrier and the impact of pericytes, cells that help move amyloids and other toxins out of the brain. His studies pertaining to the barrier, Alzheimer's, and cerebral amyloid angiopathy (CAA)—a closely related vascular condition—were also the most cited in the world. Those subfields could face a crisis of confidence if his dozens of papers unravel for sloppiness or misconduct.

The thirty-five suspect papers described in the Zlokovic dossier have been cited more than 8,400 times. On average, they have been twenty-seven times as influential as comparable work in the same fields published during the same years, according to Dimensions. They have been cited in forty-nine patents by thirty companies, universities, and foundations—a sign of broad interest in commercializing inventions based partly on Zlokovic papers that are now in doubt.

Chris Schaffer, a Cornell University biomedical engineer, said the dossier findings "unquestionably trigger the need for a robust investigation [of the questioned papers] that goes all the way back to raw data and includes interviews of the scientists who conducted this work." That would show which of Zlokovic's contributions rest on solid data from his own lab or others, Schaffer added. "Until that investigation has been conducted, the scientific community should use caution in building on these results."

Prior to helping create the Zlokovic dossier, Kevin Patrick and Elisabeth Bik had alerted journals that published some of the problem papers. Six corrections followed. By March 2024, four months after my Zlokovic article appeared in *Science*, nine papers noted in the dossier had been corrected, three retracted, and two labeled with expressions of concern by the publishers, pending findings by the USC investigation. The others remained in limbo.

Just how damaging a definitive invalidation of Zlokovic's work would be to other research on Alzheimer's, CAA, and other conditions remains "one of the million-dollar questions," said Andreas Charidimou, a Boston University expert in stroke, CAA, and Alzheimer's. "We need to clarify which of these findings are replicable and correct, and which are completely off."

That process might take years to play out, given the usual sluggish review process. But the Zlokovic model let me address looming "So what?" questions for Alzheimer's research raised by the Other Blots project in twenty-one dossiers comprising forty-six scientists. This chart shows the scope of the Other Blots project—and suggests the enormity of these issues for the field.

Scope of the Problem

Unique Suspect Papers	Nonduplicated Citations to Suspect Papers	Citations to Suspect Papers in Active Patents	Citations to Suspect Papers in Separate Active Patent "Families" *
571	77,655	487	379

Note: On average, each paper cites 1.4 Problem Papers.
*= Different aspects of the same intellectual property, or patents filed in multiple jurisdictions.

Matthew Schrag, Perry, and I selected keywords to pair with "Alzheimer's." Sorensen ran them through Dimensions. The next chart shows a sampling of a few influential scientists.

Influential Alzheimer's Scientists

Author	Subfield Terms (+ "Alzheimer's") in Title or Abstract	Total Papers	World Rank (Papers)	Citations to Papers	World Rank (Citations)
Adriano Aguzzi	Prion* (protein tied to neurological diseases)	229	7	15,046	46
Aguzzi	PrP mutation* (PrP = prion protein)	142	2	9,971	5
Steven Arnold	Brain insulin resistance (hypothesis for cause of Alzheimer's)	9	18	3,339	4
Peter St George-Hyslop	Presenilin (involved in amyloid production)	134	2	6,522	4
Hyslop	SORL1 (involved in amyloid production)	25	2	2,248	2
Hyslop	Sortilin (genetic association with Alzheimer's)	10	2	1,475	2
Frank LaFerla	Mouse models (to test Alzheimer's treatments)	199	2	26,036	2
LaFerla	"Triple transgenic mouse" OR 3xTG-AD	135	1	20,159	1
Eliezer Masliah	Nerve Degeneration	43	2	6,822	6
Masliah	Synaptophysin (regulates connections between brain cells)	57	1	10,447	1

Masliah	Synucleins (protein involved in nerve-impulse transmission)	88	2	12,108	4
Masliah	Amyloid (basis for dominant Alzheimer's hypothesis)	293	29	52,795	9
Masliah	Messenger RNA (mRNA; possible player in future treatments)	25	13	4,284	4
Masliah	Synapse (site for nerve-impulse transmission)	92	1	17,697	2
Masliah	Neuropathology	29	58	5,957	10
Masliah	Mouse models (to test Alzheimer's treatments)	139	6	20,767	3
Berislav Zlokovic	Blood-brain barrier (filter to block toxins)	91	1	28,623	1
Zlokovic	Cerebral amyloid angiopathy (vascular condition tied to Alzheimer's) + blood-brain barrier	7	4	1,675	1
Zlokovic	Pericyte (cells that help maintain the blood-brain barrier)	25	1	14,341	1

* = Alzheimer's anywhere in full article text.

Finally, here are some top names in the field who cited and therefore fostered the influence of tainted studies. They included such celebrated scientists as amyloid-hypothesis originator John Hardy; Dennis Selkoe, a key advocate of the hypothesis; Massachusetts General Hospital's Bradley Hyman; and the late University of Pennsylvania scholar John Trojanowski.

15 Top Alzheimer's Scientists Who Often Cited Suspect Papers

(H-Index is a widely used measure of scholarly influence. Scholars promoted to full professor in a biological science at top-tier US universities score 41 on average; 100 is regarded as truly exceptional.)

Scientist (H-Index)	Number of Papers Citing One or More Suspect Papers	Whose Suspect Papers Were Cited; Examples (Number of Times)
Henrik Zetterberg (178)	137	Aguzzi (6), Arnold (7), Ashe (24), Burns/Wang (7), LaFerla/Oddo (8), Lesné (26), Masliah (18), Zlokovic (31)
John Q Trojanowski (269)	134	Arnold (7), Burns/Wang (6), LaFerla/Oddo (22), Masliah (99), Zlokovic (8)
Kaj Blennow (184)	122	Arnold (6), Ashe (25), Burns/Wang (6), Lesné (26), Masliah (17), Zlokovic (24)
Virginia Man-Yee Lee (228)	117	Masliah (86), LaFerla/Oddo (20)
Bradley T Hyman (214)	105	Aguzzi (9), Ashe (20), LaFerla/Oddo (27), Lesné (24), Masliah (28), Zlokovic (14)
David M Holtzman (207)	104	Aguzzi (8), Ashe (15), LaFerla/Oddo (25), Lesné (16), Masliah (16), Zlokovic (29)
Mark P Mattson (246)	97	LaFerla/Oddo (52), Masliah (16)
Dennis William Dickson (227)	91	LaFerla/Oddo (13), Lesné (6), Masliah (61), Zlokovic (10)
David Alan Bennett (219)	88	Arnold (23), Ashe (13), Burns/Wang (23), LaFerla/Oddo (17), Lesné (14), Masliah (15), Zlokovic (11)
George Perry (173)	86	LaFerla/Oddo (15), Masliah (19)
Dennis J Selkoe (200)	83	Aguzzi (11), Ashe (22), Hyslop/Checler (16), LaFerla/Oddo (14), Lesné (22), Masliah (26)
Colin Louis Masters (183)	78	Ashe (15), LaFerla/Oddo (11), Lesné (17), Masliah (16)
Bart de Strooper (148)	74	Aguzzi (15), Ashe (9), Hyslop/Checler (23), LaFerla/Oddo (10), Lesné (10), Masliah (11), Zlokovic (8)
Rudolph Emile Tanzi (178)	63	Hyslop/Checler (13), LaFerla/Oddo (13), Lesné (9), Zlokovic (9)
John Anthony Hardy (195)	58	LaFerla/Oddo (8), Masliah (35), Zlokovic (10)

Note: Excludes self-citations by authors of suspect papers.

RABBIT HOLES

Schrag, Perry, Donna Wilcock, and Thomas Südhof assessed the Other Blots findings. As central author of the dossiers, Schrag knew the concerns intimately. Perry, an amyloid skeptic, offers a virtually unmatched breadth of knowledge of the field. Wilcock, an open-minded scholar who edits *Alzheimer's & Dementia*, is a rising star in the field. Südhof offered skepticism about everything—including the dossier findings and their importance. His Nobel Prize, trials by the fires of PubPeer and X, and willingness to share his raw data and correct his lab's errors, give him unusual standing to assess the meaning of Other Blots.

Each spent many hours reviewing thousands of pages of material. For context, I explained that the dossiers had sparked numerous university or federal investigations, and that Adriano Aguzzi, Domenico Praticò, Frank LaFerla, and others had conceded that some of the images flagged in their dossiers were false. I asked what the Other Blots project says about key scientists (beyond Zlokovic) whose work infuses the Alzheimer's research enterprise.

Arnold, of Harvard and Massachusetts General Hospital, hasn't been the only scientist to propose insulin resistance in the brain as a key to unlock the Alzheimer's black box, but his work has proved central to that hypothesis. Many of Arnold's ideas stemmed from dubious collaborations with Hoau-Yan Wang. Both scientists have ties to Cassava Sciences.

Arnold and Wang reinforced the idea of insulin resistance largely via studies of purportedly revivified frozen brain tissue that no other research group has replicated, dubbed "zombie science" by a skeptic. Arnold's status as head of an important research group at an elite institution attracted famous collaborators and added luster to the work. For example, NIH funding for related studies more than doubled within five years after Arnold, Wang, and others published their 2012 paper in the *Journal of Clinical Investigation*—which, despite dubious parts of twenty western blots, has been widely cited by other scholars. Over the ensuing ten-year span, the agency spent more than $500 million on that topic—four times as much as during the decade before. Yet insulin treatments for Alzheimer's have fallen flat.

"In Alzheimer's, obesity [a diabetes risk factor] is a hugely important question. In terms of impact, Arnold's work has been truly important," Südhof said, adding that the dossier raises questions about the foundation of the insulin-resistance hypothesis.

Wilcock concurred. "Arnold has shown the most direct evidence of insulin dysregulation," she said, using the term for problems that can occur when the brain doesn't respond to insulin normally. "This may be one [body of work] that has led us down a bad rabbit hole."

The eclectic range of suspect papers in the Peter St George-Hyslop–Frédéric Checler dossier examined neprilysin (thought to regulate degradation of amyloid-beta), presenilin (a protein tied to familial Alzheimer's), synuclein and secretase (proteins that affect brain-cell signaling), caspase (instrumental in inflammation and cell death), and prions (widely viewed as similar to amyloid-beta and tau).

Those forty-four seemingly doctored articles prompted many others to move in wrong directions, Wilcock said, resulting in "wasted time, wasted resources . . . grants going to the wrong places and funding the wrong kinds of science." Meanwhile, other ideas withered for lack of resources.

Papers conceded by Aguzzi as problematic have been cited some 4,500 times. Many top researchers relied on them to support their own ideas. For example, Nobelist Stanley Prusiner cited them twenty-one times, Alzheimer's heavyweight Bart de Strooper fifteen times, and Selkoe eleven times.

That pattern repeated for every notable scientist covered by the Other Blots project. Top neuroscientists took hundreds of challenged studies seriously and extended their impact dramatically, Perry said, speaking advisedly. That list included himself.

Südhof argued that important contributions by Aguzzi and St George-Hyslop remain solid, having been replicated by others. Yet questions shadow work by scientists who show a pattern of possible deception: Would an examination of their entire body of work generate fresh doubts? "When we find a couple of problems in somebody's CV, very often, if we look carefully, we see problems throughout their CV," Schrag said. "I don't think it's an immutable law. But understanding the source of the problems and why they occurred is critical." Even in egregious cases, comprehensive examinations rarely occur, because they require nonpublic images and other data accessible only to an employer or someone with subpoena power.

The scale of the Masliah dossier—132 papers that led to more than eighteen thousand citations, many by revered Alzheimer's scientists— sobered the experts. "Basically, everybody's citing his [dubious] work," Schrag said. Perry credited Masliah with "a huge amount of fundamental research on transgenic animals and pathological description—careful pathological description, and interfacing [pathology] with behavior." He added that "People are very dependent on all of these descriptions," calling the suspect papers "very problematic" for the field.

Südhof cautioned that ranking Masliah's influence based on citations might prove misleading, because he didn't originate many of the key ideas he was testing—one mark of a truly great scientist. To Schrag, influence can take other forms. He compared Masliah's work to an old music festival video. "Some uninhibited individual stands up on the side of the hill and starts dancing in a wild way. Everybody looks at him like he's weird. Then a second guy stands up and starts dancing with him. Little by little people jump in until the hillside is covered in people doing crazy dance moves," Schrag said. "It's something about the second and third voices that come in that normalizes a concept." The harm caused by Masliah's ostensibly doctored validation of such important ideas as the amyloid hypothesis and the use of mice to model human disease remains unclear.

Another number gave Perry, Schrag, Südhof, and Wilcock pause: Problem papers by Masliah supported approval for 238 active patents—by far the most for any scientist examined. Dozens of organizations hold the rights to the patents, including pharma giants AbbVie (32 patents), Leqembi partners Biogen (8) and Eisai (7), Selkoe's anti-amyloid company Prothena Biosciences (25), and leading universities. (The patent system seems alarmingly unable to police retracted or corrected papers supporting such filings, according to a 2023 article in the *Review of Economics and Statistics*.) What-

ever Masliah's research accomplishments and leadership in the funding bureaucracy, powerful organizations have used his problem papers to support
their ambitions to commercialize inventions aimed against dementia.

"STAGES OF GRIEF"

I asked the neuroscientists what they thought the Other Blots project says
about Alzheimer's research writ large.

"As a field, we've had a lot of dead ends" that have left patients waiting endlessly for treatments, said Wilcock. "Maybe some of those were
driven by bad science and data manipulation. Some people have put
their ego and fame ahead of performing rigorous science." She added,
"There's a knock-on effect on all of us. Zlokovic comes to my mind,
because his data is always very, very perfect. Now the expectation is
that everybody's data should be perfect. And if it's not, then you're not
doing good science." In the biological sciences, Wilcock said, perfect
data often should instead be seen as a red flag.

When I started talking to Schrag about these issues in December 2021,
he viewed misconduct in Alzheimer's research as rare. He said he's since
gone through "a stages-of-grief process," recognizing the impact it has on
his chosen profession. "It doesn't take that high a percentage of fraud in
this discipline to cause major problems, especially if it's strategically placed,"
he said. "Patients ask me why we're not making more progress. I keep telling them that it's a complicated disease. But misconduct is also part of the
problem."

To Südhof, "The biggest impact of apparently fraudulent or sloppy
science has been on commercial activities that lead to clinical trials that
are probably inappropriate and have wasted resources and endangered
patients. I'm particularly concerned about the Cassava [simufilam] trial."
He added that "Some labs and scientists who have had a significant presence in the field serially publish papers with major problems." Others
have had far more potentially harmful impact with fewer problem papers
that have "suggested conceptual paradigms that are innovative or differ-

ent from dominant ideas," Südhof said. "Among those, I would count, for example, St George-Hyslop and Aguzzi."

The neuroscientists also saw exposure of such problems as a path to course corrections.

"Many fundamentals of Alzheimer's research are built on very weak foundations," Perry said, and Other Blots "found a reason for it, a new way to detect it." He expressed optimism that the project could foster innovation in how to police scientific integrity without the need to repeat suspect experiments at astronomical cost.

Journals have begun to adopt artificial-intelligence software such as Imagetwin and Proofig that rapidly detect some forms of image doctoring. And mandates to publish full datasets should help reduce the number of fraudulent or simply erroneous experiments that can often be much harder to detect than faked images.

Incentive systems also must change, according to Schrag. "We need to push back on 'publish or perish,' and focus on basic, good-science principles. It's a balancing act. There's no point in doing this if you're not productive," he said. "But let's make sure we measure it the right ways—not promoting people solely based on the number of papers they produce, without regard to the quality of the underlying work."

The primary lesson, Schrag added, is to "very intentionally teach research ethics and integrity when we're training students so that it becomes ingrained in our identity as scientists."

After three years of work trying to clean up the scientific record, he holds out hope that such cultural pressure, combined with the evidence provided by image sleuths, "will help break people out of the idea that 'yeah, this is shocking, but it's rare,' and, 'it gets too much attention and damages the reputation of science.'" At the end of some days he spends unearthing such problems, Schrag feels deflated, he conceded. "Yet I still believe that the vast, vast majority of scientists attempt to do good work."

I next took a look at some of that work—at innovators whose ideas might shape the future of Alzheimer's research and the lives of patients.

Chapter 22

Innovation and Hope

Boston; Washington, DC; Oxford; New York; Nashville

2024

"Very few diseases of aging have a single cause.
It's just not logical."

—MATTHEW SCHRAG

Andreas Charidimou, a soft-spoken physician and neuroscientist at Boston University, responded sadly when asked to project the future of Alzheimer's research and treatment.

The Greek native sports a fulsome black beard that covers the knot of his tie. It seems to capture a rebellious spirit against neuroscience orthodoxy that sometimes emanates from Harvard and University College London, where he trained. Charidimou studies cerebral amyloid angiopathy, or CAA—a condition in which amyloid plaques replace muscle supporting blood vessels to the brain. Most Alzheimer's patients live with CAA, which also can cause fatal brain bleeding. Many also have Lewy bodies—brain lesions that contribute to dementia associated with Parkinson's disease. Such combinations, Charidimou said, leave him troubled when top scientists describe the "amyloid cascade" cause of Alzheimer's as settled science.

He offered a brutal near-term outlook on better treatments for Alzheimer's. "I see a lot of resistance to change from the leaders of the field" who headline big conferences and start biopharma companies, Charidimou said. "Multiple labs and investigators have invested their careers, their funding—their whole narrative—on the amyloid hypothesis. It's hard for them to even think about being wrong."

Expectation bias—deeming all results as somehow consistent with prevailing ideas—makes thousands of scientists complicit in what amounts to a kind of self-deception, he said. Healthy skepticism that polices science and pushes it forward often seems missing. "We need to be more inclusive . . . to come up with different narratives of what dementia is and Alzheimer's disease is. But this requires fundamental change at many levels," said Charidimou. "I'm not optimistic that change will come very soon."

It didn't seem surprising that most of the 571 suspect papers examined by Other Blots concerned aspects of the amyloid hypothesis. To Thomas Südhof, it "reflects that most misconduct is in papers that confirm something that somebody else believes. That's how scientists who are not honest get their papers published"—playing to journals' deference to conventional wisdom.

Matthew Schrag extended the idea. "You have a group of people who have achieved such intellectual dominance over the field that it may have contributed to an environment where people felt like they had to bring their findings into general alignment with this dominant hypothesis to reach some level of acceptance," at times even doctoring data to align more neatly, he said.

INNOVATION AND OPTIMISM

Yet in recent years, the notion that a mysterious disease concerning the most complex structure in the body will require many solutions has gained currency and influence. Even if amyloids play a role, other ideas have begun to force themselves into the discussion—giving innovators a sense that the frozen supremacy of the amyloid hypothesis is beginning to thaw. One of those involves testing the seemingly miraculous weight-loss drug Wegovy to treat early Alzheimer's. It might reduce cognitive symptoms by targeting inflammation in the brain. Those trials could provide some answers by early 2026. (A similar drug, liraglutide, also shows intriguing possible benefits.)

Madhav Thambisetty, until recently a senior scientist at the National Institute on Aging in Washington, DC, conducts research with a normal, methodical approach. But as a thinker, he's a radical who traces his inspiration to a courageous exploration half a millennium ago. Thambisetty grew up in Calicut (also called Kozhikode), on the southwest coast of India. In 1498, Portuguese explorer Vasco da Gama landed there to complete his historic journey that tied together Asia and Europe via the Cape of Good Hope.

Like da Gama, Thambisetty, an amyloid-hypothesis skeptic, won respect via a long and hard journey. He trained as a medical doctor in India, where his mentors—even his scientist parents—"took a very dim view of physicians doing science . . . India didn't have a culture of physician scientists." Thambisetty defied the odds, gaining a scholarship to study for a PhD at the University of Oxford.

Decades later, his accomplishments earned him a place on the Food and Drug Administration (FDA) advisory committee for aducanumab. In 2022 the panel rejected Biogen's anti-amyloid drug aducanumab as a travesty. The FDA vetoed their recommendation. But Aduhelm, as it was later branded, never gained acceptance and Biogen discontinued it a couple of years later.

More than one thousand Alzheimer's papers appear every month, with little to offer patients, Thambisetty said, noting a wisecrack often attributed to Mark Twain: "Researchers have already cast much darkness on the subject, and if they continue their investigations, we shall soon know nothing at all about it."

Thambisetty's work focuses on a big idea: First, look for abnormalities in brain tissues from people who died in their thirties or forties, with or without risk factors for Alzheimer's. Then he compares the findings to tissues from deceased Alzheimer's patients and people who didn't have the disease. Where the samples overlap, drug targets might emerge. But rather than develop new drugs via lab and animal testing, followed by multiphase clinical trials with people—which can cost billions of dollars and take decades—he looks for compounds that have already been approved as reasonably safe and effective for other conditions.

Some of those "target some of the same pathways that we've identified in Alzheimer's disease," he said. Using computer algorithms that address the clinical, molecular, and biological factors that lead to dementia, he then maps treatments to targets. For example, anti-inflammatory rheumatoid arthritis drugs—including hydroxychloroquine, which gained a dreadful reputation when then-President Donald Trump falsely promoted it as a cure for Covid-19—show promise.

The profit challenge of standard drug development presents the big challenge. Many of the drugs under consideration are off-patent and sold cheaply as generics—affordable for patients, but far less interesting to drugmakers, which most commonly underwrite costs of testing and development. New financial models might be needed to realize Thambisetty's dream.

Another radical, Ruth Itzhaki of the University of Oxford, stirred curiosity in the 1990s with evidence associating Alzheimer's with the herpesvirus—spread by oral or genital contact and causing incurable, often painful, but nonfatal infections. She faced a long slog to gain traction in the research community. Somehow boosters of the amyloid hypothesis rendered the infection hypothesis virtually invisible, Itzhaki said with evident exasperation. "They don't understand concepts like virus latency and reactivation," in which viruses hide out undetected in various organs for years, including the brain, then cause symptoms divergent from the original infection.

But her ideas might finally be catching on. Nearly five thousand papers have been written about infections and the risk of Alzheimer's since Itzhaki began her work. Annual National Institutes of Health funding to explore that line of research jumped from a mere few million dollars a year when Itzhaki began her work to nearly $250 million annually in 2023. Eighty scientists met in 2024 to discuss promising developments in the viral hypothesis. For example, the vaccine for shingles—an ailment that causes a painful rash from latent effects of the virus that causes chicken pox—shows signs of reducing risks of dementia. Although still a fraction of Alzheimer's literature and funding, the infection hypothesis has slowly gained credibility. Two clinical trials have targeted the treatment of herpes among Alzheimer's patients. Results should come in 2025 or 2026. They fuel Itzhaki's optimism that effective treatments outside the amyloid mold might emerge.

SOLUTIONS IN PLAIN SIGHT

Forestalling Alzheimer's offers a bridge from today's difficult reality to effective treatments or a cure someday. Miguel Arce Rentería is one in a cadre of dementia experts who ask fundamental questions about how a better system of treatment can forestall the worst of Alzheimer's, enriching lives with prevention.

The sacrifice of care on the altar of cure particularly afflicts Latino Americans, who are up to 1.5 times as likely to develop Alzheimer's as whites, and far less likely to be participants in research to find solutions to Alzheimer's conundrums. Arce, a bilingual Mexican American neuropsychologist at Columbia University, said he has often been the only Spanish speaker available to assess cognitive decline in concerned patients coming into a clinic. The problems are often even worse for African Americans, who suffer from Alzheimer's at up to twice the rate for whites, and disproportionately lack adequate access to specialized care.

Of course, it's a general problem for the working poor. When conditions that can exacerbate Alzheimer's go untreated, years of better life can be lost. That problem of access represents a great challenge, but also a great opportunity, Arce said. No one can stop growing older or change their genetic predispositions. But risk factors like diabetes, high blood pressure, high cholesterol, obesity, depression, hearing loss, sedentary lifestyles, poor diets—can be targeted to sometimes forestall or moderate the worst aspects of Alzheimer's.

"There are studies looking at 'cognitive reserve,' meaning that despite evidence of increasing pathology in the brain you can still function for a longer period of time," Arce said. "We know that a poor quality of education during childhood is associated with an increased risk of dementia. Higher education can be protective."

In short, Alzheimer's can afflict anyone, but it's also a disease of inequality. Although the vast majority of research and funding looks for the magic bullet of an elusive cure, the mood is shifting. In the last generation, annual funding for prevention-linked studies has exploded into the hundreds of millions of dollars.

At long last, Arce said, "There's somewhat of a balance," which brings a measure of hope.

SCHRAG'S PRACTICE

In 2024, Matthew Schrag's lab produced a three-dimensional animation of blood vessels in brain tissues from deceased patients. First up, normal tissue, what he called an "elegant lacy network of capillaries," perfectly formed and branching like a grove of illuminated young trees, rotating with grace in the image. Then comes CAA. The trees become gnarly, misshapen tubes. Bulbous growths, like redwood burls, begin to populate the once-pristine microscopic woodland. Then the last shift, severe CAA: In the devastated forest the brittle bulbs burst, spewing precious blood—destroying tissue and claiming a life.

Sometimes a disease can have a single, clear origin, as in genetic mutations that cause some cases of CAA or the excruciating and deadly sickle cell disease. But "very few diseases of aging have just one cause. It's just not logical," Schrag says. It would show up earlier in life and be more clearly present in everyone who suffers from the disorder.

"It's time for the field to move on," he said. "And I think that's happening. There is an entrenched echo chamber that involves a lot of big names, but I don't think it's anywhere near the majority of scientists in this space. I'm hearing from a lot of people, some publicly, but many privately, who are anxious to see us move past the amyloid hypothesis, even if amyloid-beta is part of the story of Alzheimer's."

A part. Not all of it.

"We see a lot of inflammation in the brain with neurodegenerative disorders," he said. "Looking at why—that's an area where I expect we'll get some traction," beginning with the blood vessels. "They do a lot more than simple plumbing," Schrag said. "When you think about something, the part of your brain that activates suddenly needs a lot more blood supply, and those blood vessels dilate, and more blood goes to that part of your brain." It's clearly visible on a brain scan. "We have cholesterol medications, blood pressure medications, and things that can destress the blood vessels. Hopefully we'll have more targets coming," he added.

Schrag also studies lysosomes—cellular structures integral to digesting waste products that can cause inflammation.

"Almost all neurodegenerative diseases accumulate too much of one protein or another in the brain. In Alzheimer's, it's plaques and tangles. In Parkinson's, it's alpha-synuclein," Schrag said. "Lysosomes are a way that neurons clear their waste products, get rid of those abnormal proteins. It suggests this unifying concept that neurodegenerative diseases are essentially age-related, lysosomal-storage diseases. If we could get lysosomes working better, there's some hope that you might have a therapeutic that could work across neurodegenerative diseases."

I asked Schrag how long we will have to wait for effective Alzheimer's treatments, or a cure. He wouldn't take the bait. "Sometimes these things are pretty stochastic," he said, using a ten-dollar word for random and unpredictable.

But Schrag takes heart from progress in Parkinson's, and major gains in stroke—until recently an untreatable event that many people never fully recovered from.

"It's easy to get disappointed, to think that there's no hope. But there is a lot of growth in this discipline. Despite high-profile problems, there are a lot of troops on the ground determined to make headway. Every time I sit through a student's dissertation defense or qualifying exams, it builds back whatever optimism I've lost from doing this research-integrity work. There are a lot of really talented people being drawn to this field."

To keep his lab research grounded in real life, Schrag treats about two hundred Alzheimer's patients a year. That often means helping them and their families accept new realities while preserving dignity and quality of life.

It doesn't always work well, Schrag said. "One patient was an insurance salesman, and I talked with his family about their financial situation. Everything was fine, they said. He was still good at taking care of the books. Not two weeks later, they're calling me to send a letter to prevent a foreclosure."

But respect and self-worth can also survive against steep odds. "I have a patient who ran a chain of furniture stores, an extremely successful businessman. Instead of retiring him one day, his family gradually transitioned who handled the major financial decisions. He continued to come to their main shop when he was wheelchair bound and horribly demented," Schrag said. "That was a big part of his identity, being a salesman, talking to people. They found a way to evolve his role so that it continued to be a positive thing in his life. They did it by intervening together before there were problems.

"People don't want to give up autonomy. Coming to grips with relinquishing a little bit of autonomy can help you keep more of it," Schrag added.

"I've told people they have cancer and had an easier go of it than telling somebody they can't drive," he said. The solution is adding perspective. "I say, 'sooner or later, we're all going to have to quit driving. It goes much better if you make that decision for yourself. Don't make a family member do it. Don't make a cop do it. Don't make a doctor do it.'" He proposes solutions—ride services, visits with friends—to stave off the fear of isolation. Schrag added, "The worst thing for anybody aging with a neurological disease is to get stuck at home."

It's a matter of helping people maintain something that Alzheimer's gradually steals—agency in one's own life. That means anticipating the hardest moments, like moving into assisted living. "Many times, families won't make the decisions for a patient that the patient would have wanted. There can be a lot of guilt associated with putting a parent in an assisted living facility, but a primary goal for a lot of elderly people is not to be a burden. So, you start early with these conversations. You want to make sure that the right person drives the decisions."

Matt Price and his mom, Toni, were facing that issue. After the disappointing, yearslong trial with the Cassava Sciences drug simufilam, they worried what would come next for their beloved father and husband as Stephen struggled to hold on to his agency, to play a role in deciding his own future.

Epilogue

Tabernacle Township, New Jersey; Nashville

2024

"Memory is still forbidden, but this book is stubborn."

—AUGUSTO GÓNGORA, AUTHOR OF
CHILE: LA MEMORIA PROHIBIDA
(CHILE: THE FORBIDDEN MEMORY)

In his youth, Augusto Góngora, a Chilean TV journalist, reported on the military coup and terror that afflicted that nation in the 1970s and 1980s. His striking visage informed millions in their darkest hours. Decades later, Augusto faced a personal, growing darkness, living with advanced Alzheimer's. Yet his life remained full of joy. His spouse, Chile's former culture minister Paulina Urrutia, and their daughter helped him stay tethered to a misty, fading world.

The Eternal Memory, a feature documentary Academy Award finalist in 2024, tells their story. In a compelling scene, Augusto expresses shock that he's known Paulina more than twenty years. "No way!" he says. With tender patience, she helps him shower, dries his hair and ears, shaves him with an electric razor. "I love you very much," he says softly.

She answers, "Me too."

Later, with bold openness, Paulina asks, "Would you like to die?"

"No. I don't want to die . . . I'm going to fight until the end."

"Do you like life that much?"

"Yes. I like it very much."

A slim man with short white hair and penetrating eyes, Augusto laughs easily. He asks Paulina to dance to a romantic song in the studio of his physical therapist. At times, he can even joke about his condition. Augusto's essence remains. But he recognizes Paulina less and less. She cries about losing him, and he reassures her in his way. It's a love story. The simplest things—touch, garden scents, walks—connect them. And always love.

Paulina reads him the inscription he wrote for her decades before, in his book *Chile: La Memoria Prohibida* ("Chile: The Forbidden Memory"), written during the nightmare of the military regime. "There is pain here. The horrors are denounced. But there is also a lot of nobility. Memory is still forbidden, but this book is stubborn. Those who have memory, have courage, and are the sowers, like you."

STEPHEN'S LIFE

Matt Price recommended that film to me in the fall of 2023, shortly after Augusto died. Then in early 2024, I reconnected via videoconference with him, his mother, Toni, and his father, Stephen—who lives with Alzheimer's and takes Cassava's simufilam in a clinical trial. Stephen reminds me of Augusto: thin, still-handsome face; trim, combed white hair; eyes soulful even during moments of confusion.

I hadn't spoken with Stephen in more than a year. He still wore a plaid shirt and jeans, suggesting his years as a construction contractor, but had obviously declined. Matt said his dad can usually put on a T-shirt unassisted, but it might take twenty minutes to get the correct arm in each sleeve. He struggles with which foot goes in which boot. The boots feature a twist-dial lace tightener, which Stephen can sometimes operate.

Below the dial on one boot, Matt placed a wireless tracker so he and his mom can locate Stephen when he moves out of view of their video cameras while "working" on their large, rural property. The temperature that day, in the thirties, suited him. "I like to have a little bit of chill, to keep you from falling asleep," Stephen said. Sleepiness is a symptom.

"I'm feeling good. I was out working this morning. Doing, you know, I don't know what, to get things shaped up. I was cleaning up the shop. So when Matthew goes out there to work he can get something done," he added. Stephen enjoys moving tools around in his storage building. "I try and keep everything shape, shape ship, sorted out. But just keep, I-I-I try to keep busy."

"Things are going nice for me," he later added with a chuckle, charmingly upbeat. Increasing problems with speaking and understanding have him reaching for simple answers that might make a good impression, Matt told me later. "He'll often try to find, 'What does this person want to hear?'"

"I feel lucky that I have all this support in my family because some days are not good," Stephen added. Today was a good day. "I'm lucky that it works for me," he said when I asked about simufilam. "And I haven't had any issues." Stephen meant that he can take the pills easily, not that they help.

When I asked about his experience with the doctors for the clinical trial, he didn't understand until Matt reminded him. "I didn't have any issues," he repeated, like a mantra. "Everything's straightforward, if you just do the meds and follow them. What you should be doing at that time. Everything works out fine. I didn't have any real issues."

I asked Stephen if he feels optimistic about his future. "Yes, I don't know. Pretty good," he said.

During visits Matt takes pressure off Toni, who at seventy-five is cognitively normal but has medical and physical limitations. Helping Stephen bathe, dress, eat, and much more, is becoming too much for her, even with part-time, paid help. In the prior few months, Stephen's symptoms had worsened sharply. "It's been jarring to see his loss of insight," Matt said. "I think he often feels bad because he perceives my mom's stress. He's still quite perceptive emotionally.

"I've been reluctantly working on some applications for nursing homes," Matt added. Stephen's role in that decision or its timing remained to be seen. But as each day passes, his agency diminishes.

When I checked in with Matt in June 2024, things had grown substantially worse. Stephen increasingly was having trouble with eating and toileting, and rarely spoke in sentences longer than a few words. He had gone wandering. Once, terrifyingly, he took his truck off the property, and needed help from the police to get home. Another time he left on foot and was returned by a Good Samaritan neighbor. It was becoming hard to judge how much self-awareness he had left. Toni had recently suffered a minor heart attack, which Matt attributed to the stress of being the primary caregiver for a person experiencing advanced Alzheimer's.

Matt spent years finding and helping his dad try treatments, including unconventional ones discovered during his travels as a global-health epidemiologist. Simufilam became a last resort when Stephen's symptoms grew too severe for other trials. But as Matt learned more about the drug and Cassava, he concluded that it would never help his dad. He struggled with whether to pull Stephen out of the trial. "I often feel ethically compromised by enabling continued participation," Matt said. "He wants a source of optimism. It's hard to be the person to take that away."

Matt said he feels particularly disturbed that by enrolling in Cassava's trials, patients foreclose their ability to try drugs based on firmer scientific footing. "It's especially upsetting to think that this happens mostly to people who either don't realize [simufilam's problems], or don't have the ability to make their own decisions," he said.

The simufilam experience angers him, Matt said, particularly since the fraud indictment of Hoau-Yan Wang, one of the drug's two key developers, for allegedly fabricating data. "There's a kind of poisoning of the well. It's hard to describe until you've walked through that door. There's a dire need for medical research and the trust upon which that always depends. To undermine that hope for people in desperate circumstances seems so unnecessary. It makes people start to distrust the clinical research enterprise." Recent polling supports his concern. Faith in doctors and medical scientists has fallen sharply in recent years.

"I wanted to believe that trying to learn more, spending more time digesting research, would make a difference. I've seen that it mostly does not, or has not in his case. That's been quite humbling," Matt said, reflecting on how his dad's condition also affected himself. "Trying to teach my father to shave changed my outlook on life and what's important. Time is the most precious resource."

SCHRAG'S NEW REALITY

Matthew Schrag decided long ago that for a person with Alzheimer's, time doesn't count down a life like sand through an hourglass. The now is primary. The lesson began during his teens while helping his father, then a nurse in a senior-care home. "There were these two teeny-tiny grandmas, Ella and Willa." Lifelong friends, Schrag said. "Willa had serious memory problems, but she could get around okay, and Ella was cognitively sharp, but couldn't walk. The two of them sort of completed each other. We used to round them up to play pinochle or dominos. Willa was pleasantly confused, and it frustrated Ella to see her best friend drifting away. Yet, Willa was still a very happy person."

The memory reminds him, Schrag said, that even without a cure or a good treatment, many Alzheimer's patients live life as the protagonist in their own stories. It's an idea of genuine hope he holds out for his patients.

The hope he holds out for himself, as a doctor and scientist, seems more complicated. Since 2021, when he began to examine possible scientific misconduct in his chosen field, Schrag's life has transformed. He's gone from an early career research scientist into a leading authority on research integrity and a go-to source for journalists—and still managed to win a prestigious National Institutes of Health R01 grant, with substantial funding.

Schrag hasn't been doxed or sued. But he has become a target for internet trolls who support Cassava Sciences. And brutally long hours take him away from his spouse and two young kids.

"One of the bigger costs has been losing my relationship with Othman," Schrag said with evident sorrow. He was referring to Othman Ghribi, his first scientific mentor, whom he had to expose for apparent misconduct. He doesn't dwell much on regrets, or life's disappointments, but that one still stings, Schrag said. "As I get older, I realize that you don't have that many real friends, good friends who hang with you a long time. Othman was one of those."

Throughout his sometimes painful journey, Schrag reminded himself over and over why he was doing it. "It's hard to ignore the scale of the problem, particularly when it involves patients," like the simufilam trial, he said. "It's hard to ignore what's happening to patients who have put a lot of trust in those who run clinical experiments," Schrag added, echoing Matt Price. "It's changed the way I think.

". . . Occasionally I've found myself in the thrill of making these misconduct discoveries," he said, riffing on his contributions after some prodding. "But pretty quickly that gives way to a bit of discouragement. We've not had significant breakthroughs in Alzheimer's treatment."

Image doctoring didn't cause that desolate reality. "But it's certainly a contributor. It's created a major distraction," Schrag said. "I go to clinic, and I talk to these beautiful, wonderful people who are confronting this disease. The cost of misconduct is very hard to measure. But it's a real, tangible cost. We need to build generational change, cultural change in this field, that makes it much harder for this to happen going forward.

"Why does misconduct happen? What are the motivations? I find it very interesting—the human elements," Schrag said. "But much more important: Can we move the field forward, individually and collectively, if we take some time to carefully clean it up?"

A Note on Reporting

This book is based on a review of thousands of scientific papers, and hundreds of interviews with scientists, doctors, forensic image analysts, financial experts and other specialists, as well as patients and family members. Quotes from interviews are verbatim, except where indicated in the source notes that they have been slightly condensed for clarity. No quotations were invented or reconstructed from anyone's memory.

I originated, designed, and coordinated the process for creating and assessing the dossiers described in chapters 20 and 21. Experts in the relevant science and forensic image analysts built and reviewed the documents. I did not analyze images or their scientific significance. After this book's publication, the dossier authors plan to post to PubPeer most of the thousands of images that contain evidence of errors or misconduct.

Except in a few cases where I relied on court documents or news articles, I contacted every scientist named as connected to apparently doctored work. I reached out two or more times in every case, provided each scientist with their dossier, and allowed ample time for either an interview or reply to written questions after review and reflection. Often, I made several attempts to speak with implicated scientists, whose perspectives

I consider vitally important. Some wrote replies, and a few agreed to discuss the issues; most, regrettably, did not.

Sometimes innocent digital artifacts that resemble signs of doctoring occur during the publishing process. That's why I always requested original, uncropped, high-resolution images for the examples described in a dossier. Comparing those to published versions can validate or disprove concerns. Scientists provided the originals in only a handful of cases. I also asked for unpublished, full experimental datasets, to ensure that I had not overlooked factors that might exonerate a challenged scientific paper. No scientist provided those materials.

I expected the subjects of the dossiers to dispute some findings. I knew some might describe intentional changes as "cosmetic"—to make an image look more balanced or pleasing without affecting experimental findings. Although such changes would be improper, some scientists distinguish them from outright misconduct, such as alterations that artificially fit results to an experimental hypothesis. I leave it to readers to decide if a history of such cosmetic changes or errors suggests bigger doubts about a scientist's reliability.

None of the dossiers reviewed the full corpus of any researcher's work, which can comprise hundreds of papers. Nor can they be the final word on possible misconduct. But a pattern of suspect work suggests a logical reason for institutional authorities to look more deeply.

Acknowledgments

This book could not have been written without Matthew Schrag—whose integrity, wisdom, and determination never faltered during three years of conversations. He schooled me on neuroscience and Alzheimer's with patience and wit. Matt became much more than just a source, and I'll forever be grateful that he trusted me to tell so much of his story—despite the personal risks he ran to do so.

I was fortunate to receive support and friendship from journalists at *Science*, particularly my editors Tim Appenzeller, John Travis, Martin Enserink, and Kelly Servick; and my colleagues Meredith Wadman, Jon Cohen, Meagan Weiland, Cathleen O'Grady, and Jessica Slater. Thanks also to Editor-in-Chief Holden Thorp, Executive Publisher Sudip Parikh, and the AAAS board of directors, for their deep commitment to telling hard truths about the scientific world.

My editor at One Signal, Nicholas Ciani, saw the potential of this story from the start. His sound judgment, advocacy, thoughtfulness, and deft editing vastly improved the manuscript. Nick's colleagues Abby Mohr and Hannah Frankel made the publication process far smoother and easier.

I'm deeply grateful to Doron Weber and the Sloan Foundation, whose grant helped me increase my ambitions. Doron's confidence also cemented my belief that this book could influence public understanding of Alzheimer's in meaningful ways. I was privileged to become a small part of the foundation's Public Understanding of Science, Technology & Economics program, which has contributed mightily to comprehension of society's fast-moving complexity.

My investigative articles for *Science* that were integral to *Doctored* were honored by the National Academies of Science and Eric and Wendy Schmidt, and twice by the National Institute of Health Care Management—until recently led by the inspiring Nancy Chockley. The illustrious journalists who judged those awards built my confidence that exposing and correcting misconduct in research has to be a priority for the worlds of science and medicine.

I relied often on the astute advice of my dear friend, the brilliant writer and editor Marianne Szegedy-Maszak. Marianne introduced me to my incomparable agent, Jill Grinberg. Jill's confidence and guidance touched the book from start to finish—finding One Signal, offering insightful suggestions for the manuscript, and introducing me to the savvy Mary Pender-Coplan of William Morris Endeavor for negotiations with TV and film producers. Jill's extraordinary skill and encouragement buoyed my spirits throughout the challenges inherent to a major investigative project. Thanks also to her colleague Denise Page; among her many behind-the-scenes contributions was the main title for the book.

I received important help from expert fact-checker Eamon Whalen, and am indebted to Wesley Lowery, Lynne Perry, and Margot Susca of the Investigative Reporting Workshop at American University—founded by my close friend Chuck Lewis. Talented IRW journalists Madeleine Sherer, Sophia Steele, Chaya Tong, and Maya Cederlund provided essential background reporting.

I was privileged to receive data and insights from the creators of two unique and invaluable resources in service of scientific integrity. My friend Ivan Oransky of *Retraction Watch* delivered key elements of the group's database. Boris Barbour and Brandon Stell of PubPeer did likewise for comments on Alzheimer's research posted to their site. That streamlined my efforts to understand the extent of possible misconduct in the field. Many thanks also to Jia You, who helped me organize the voluminous datasets.

Matt, Toni, and Stephen Price generously shared their experience living with Stephen's Alzheimer's, showing extraordinarily gracious candor. I can't thank them enough for their courage. I'm indebted to Yvonne Vasquez and other family members of patients who died after treatments with aducanumab or lecanemab, who understood that the details of their loved ones' tragedies were critical to bringing the dangers of those drugs to public attention.

The pioneering reporting of the late Sharon Begley, my friend and colleague, provided key insights about Alzheimer's research that helped guide my efforts.

Tom Südhof, Donna Wilcock, and George Perry were among the brilliant scientists who spent many hours helping me understand some of the complexity of the world of Alzheimer's research and candidly sharing their views. George connected me with Aaron Sorensen, until recently with Digital Science, who proved instrumental to my efforts to assess the influence of key figures in the book whose work was tainted by image doctoring. Andreas Charidimou and Nicolas Villain—thoughtful, independent-minded neuroscientists—also helped me understand ideas central to the book's thesis. Alexander Trevelyan provided a number of key documents from his own important research into Cassava Sciences.

In addition to Schrag, three other accomplished forensic image analysts—Mu Yang, Kevin Patrick, and Elisabeth Bik—spent months assessing the work of dozens of scientists to help me tell a bigger, more meaningful story about image doctoring in neuroscience research. Mike Rossner provided expert oversight on some of that work, as did Nick Brown for some thorny questions on statistics. Many other eminent scientists interrupted their frenetic lives to provide essential insights and guidance.

Only a few of the researchers whose work this book challenges agreed to be interviewed. I'm grateful that Karen Ashe welcomed me to her lab for a two-day visit, and that she shared her views of how I portrayed her work in *Science* with forthright openness. Denis Vivien showed honesty and insight that revealed his honor as a scientist and a person. Dennis Selkoe cogently described his important contributions to the field, and responded to tough questions, with extraordinary courtesy.

The unnamed, heroic source for the CUNY report on Hoau-Yan Wang, and other anonymous sources, gave me key documents, tips, and insights into the work of many scientists whose research I scrutinized— often taking serious personal risks to do so.

I'll forever appreciate the support and thoughtful perspectives of my close friends Jim Bellows, Linda Rudolph, Jeff Pector, Shelley Coppock, Marjie Lundstrom, and Usha McFarling, who reinforced my ambition to provoke change in the field of Alzheimer's research and beyond.

My beloved wife, Surry Bunnell, has been my steadfast counsel, trusted advisor, and most-insightful sounding board—particularly during our long walks during which I obsessed over neuroscience minutiae. Our son, Nathan Piller, and daughter-in-law, Sandra Harpster, provided unflagging encouragement while juggling challenging careers and young parenthood with humor, grace, and love. Finally, my tiny granddaughter, Maya, always reminded me not to take myself too seriously, and pushed me to live in each moment.

Notes

PROLOGUE

My investigative story for *Science* magazine in July 2022: "Blots on a Field? A Neuroscience Image Sleuth Finds Signs of Fabrication in Scores of Alzheimer's Articles, Threatening a Reigning Theory of the Disease," *Science*, July 21, 2022.

what many described as one of the most dramatic developments: Eisai Co. Ltd. press release, September 28, 2022.

Alzheimer's afflicts nearly seven million Americans: "2023 Alzheimer's Facts and Figures," Alzheimer's Association, 20.

Up to 360,000 adults in the prime of life: Mayo Clinic, "Young-Onset Alzheimer's: When Symptoms Begin Before Age 65," August 29, 2022, https://www.mayoclinic.org/diseases-conditions/alzheimers-disease/in-depth/alzheimers/art-20048356.

figures in the United Kingdom, Europe . . . totals will more than double by 2050: "Prevalence of Dementia in Europe," Alzheimer's Europe, 2019, Alzheimer's Disease International, https://www.alzheimer-europe.org/dementia/prevalence-dementia-europe?language_content_entity=en —viewed August 12, 2024.

$350 billion in care . . . nearly matching the amount paid for dementia care: "Alzheimer's Disease Facts and Figures Report: Executive Summary," Alzheimer's Association, 2024.

so modest a benefit that doctors and patients might not perceive any effect: For example: Madhav R. Thambisetty, MD, PhD, senior scientist, National Institute on Aging; "Targeting Pathology in Neurodegenerative Disease," presentation at the 2023 American Academy of Neurology Annual Meeting, 13.

CHAPTER 1

"I have to handle things differently" and later quotes and personal information about the Price family: Interviews with Stephen, Toni, and Matt Price, 2022 and 2023.

APOE4—**a risk factor:** "Study Reveals How APOE4 Gene May Increase Risk for Dementia," National Institute on Aging, March 16, 2021, https://www.nia.nih.gov/news/study-reveals-how-apoe4-gene-may-increase-risk-dementia#:~:text=APOE4%20is%20the%20strongest%20risk,lipid%20imbalances%20in%20brain%20cells.

common Alzheimer's symptom: "Depression," Alzheimer's Association, https://www.alz.org/help-support/caregiving/stages-behaviors/depression#:~:text=Depression%20is%20very%20common%20among,difference%20in%20quality%20of%20life.

Stephen had enrolled in a "phase 2" trial (and subsequent trial references): Simufilam: ClinicalTrials.gov record NCT04388254; supplemented by a recording of the trial testing visit from December 2022. Psilocybin: ClinicalTrials.gov record NCT04123314; Vaccine: ClinicalTrials.gov record NCT04507126.

Treatments for late-stage cancers, for example: "FDA's Drug Review Process," Food and Drug Administration (accessed March 7, 2024), https://www.fda.gov/drugs/information-consumers-and-patients-drugs/fdas-drug-review-process-continued.

Inclusion criteria for simufilam: National Library of Medicine, ClinicalTrials.gov records: NCT04388254 (phase 2), NCT05026177 and NCT04994483 (phase 3).

widely considered imprecise and easily susceptible to coaching: "The Mini-Mental State Examination: pitfalls and limitations," *Practical Neurology* (2017) 17:79–80.

so do other conditions that cause dementia: LA van de Pol, A Hensel, WM van der Flier, et al., "Hippocampal Atrophy on MRI in Frontotemporal Lobar Degeneration and Alzheimer's Disease," *Journal of Neurology, Neurosurgery & Psychiatry,* Published Online First: November 23, 2005, doi: 10.1136/jnnp.2005.075341: 77(4): 439–442.

debunked the idea that it is an accurate test: "FDA Position Statement 'Early Alzheimer's Disease: Developing Drugs for Treatment, Guidance for Industry,'" *Alzheimer's & Dementia, Translational Research & Clinical Interventions,* 5 (2019): 13–19.

consent forms Stephen signed: "Informed Consent Form and Authorization to Disclose Health Information. Cassava Sciences, Inc. / A 12-Month, Open-Label Safety Study of Simufilam Followed by a 6-Month Randomized Withdrawal and 6 Additional Months Open-Label in Mild-to-Moderate Alzheimer's Disease Patients," March 9 and July 8, 2021.

tested by Cassava's close collaborator: Freedom of Information law: "FOIL—Cassava-Related—Robbins Geller—Exhibit 1 2022-06-27 Responsive Documents FINAL_Redacted.pdf," 87–92; CSF testing is indicated as having occurred at CUNY, 202–203 (via Adrian Heilbut).

violated a New York State lab licensing and inspection requirement: https://www.wadsworth.org/regulatory/clep/clinical-labs.

no lab at CUNY was on the certified list: https://www.wadsworth.org/regulatory/clep/approved-labs.

abruptly changed the trial protocol: ClinicalTrials.gov, history of changes in Cassava's trial protocol, https://clinicaltrials.gov/ct2/history/NCT04388254?A=1&B=5&C=Side-by-Side#StudyPageTop.

Theranos's testing evidently violated the same state rules: John Carreyrou, *Bad Blood: Secrets and Lies in a Silicon Valley Startup* (New York: Alfred A. Knopf, 2018), 195.

the idea that the drug was promising, partly due to its impact on TLR4: Cassava Sciences, "We focus on Alzheimer's Disease," April 2022: 9, 11.

CHAPTER 2

"It's zombie science": "Jordan Thomas's Army of Whistle-Blowers," *The New Yorker*, January 24, 2022.

Born in 1965: https://worldrowing.com/athlete/1614.

He migrated out west and by 1884 (and his ranching history): Ancestry.com, "1946 Horatio Hutchinson Burns 1860–1946"; https://www.ancestry.com/genealogy/records/horatio-hutchinson-burns-24-21pk26w; Michael Cassity, *Stock-Raising, Ranching, and Homesteading in the Powder River Basin: Historic Context Study* (Broken Arrow, OK: 2007), 164.

Robert Horatio Burns, became a cow puncher (and other early life and civic engagement details): *Big Timber (MT) Pioneer*, June 28–July 4, 2002, 7.

Robert Redford shot . . . in and around Big Timber: https://www.imdb.com/search/title/?locations=Big%20Timber,%20Montana,%20USA&ref_=ttloc_loc_2; http://movie-locations.com/movies/r/River-Runs-Through-It.php; https://www.imdb.com/search/title/?locations=Big%20Timber,%20Montana,%20USA&ref_=ttloc_loc_2.

according to a declassified Federal Bureau of Investigation report: Record 124-10330-10067, file 62-107261-503, July 31, 1964.

"None Dare Call It Treason": John Stormer obituary, *The Washington Post*, July 16, 2018, "A 1964 Lesson in Fake News That Still Applies," *The New York Times*, January 10, 2017.

voted solidly for Goldwater: https://uselectionatlas.org/RESULTS/datagraph.php?year=1964&fips=30&f=0&off=0&elect=0.

Horatio "Rasch" Winspear Burns: *Big Timber (MT) Pioneer*, August 23, 2018.

Sheridan, Wyoming . . . population: http://eadiv.state.wy.us/demog_data/cntycity_hist.htm.

to shoot a polar bear: *Big Timber (MT) Pioneer*, March 20, 1969, 4.

sack races: *Big Timber (MT) Pioneer*, May 11, 1972, 1.

joyful, rural Americana: *Big Timber (MT) Pioneer*, August 9, 1973, 5.

Christmas bazaar: *Big Timber (MT) Pioneer*, November 26, 1975, 3.

10,560 trees: *Big Timber (MT) Pioneer*, June 27, 1974, 1.

cutting hay on a giant mower: *USA Today*, March 15, 1995, 10C.

followed in his footsteps to Milton: *Milton Magazine* (Fall 2018): 88.

whose alumni include: *Forbes.com* (April 29, 2010); *BostonMagazine.com* (March 26, 2013).

glide path to Harvard: Biographical Sketch, NIH application, Grant 12925953, August 28, 2019.

Weighing no more than 130 pounds: *Big Timber (MT) Pioneer*, September 23, 1987, 1.

cracked a rib: Harvard Varsity Club profile, undated, https://www.harvardvarsityclub.org/article.html?aid=532.

rattlesnake earrings . . . edged out competitors: *Big Timber (MT) Pioneer*, September 23, 1987, 1; *World Rowing*, https://worldrowing.com/event/1987-world-rowing-championships-bagsvaerd-copenhagen-denmark.

Tasmania, Vienna: *The Boston Globe*, October 17, 1996, C1.

PhD . . . University of Cambridge . . . fellow at . . . McLean: Biographical Sketch, NIH application, Grant 12925953, August 28, 2019.

Her work involved the successful transplantation: *Experimental Neurology* 140, no. 1 (July 1996): 1–13.

Burns extended her rowing career . . . glittering capstone: *The Boston Globe*, October 17, 1996, C1.

"Lindsay Burns Day": *Big Timber (MT) Pioneer*, August 23, 1996, 13.

bouncing around . . . joined the tiny pharma company: Biographical Sketch, NIH application, Grant 12925953, August 28, 2019; as of December 3, 2021, the company had 25 employees, according to interview with Barbier, https://www.youtube.com/watch?v=0SIqNWbPCFE (at 31:10).

Its big idea: Pain Therapeutics press release, June 26, 2018; and "FDA Advisory Committee Briefing Document: Remoxy™ ER" (June 26, 2018): 9.

narcissistic mash-up: "Failure Has Paid Cassava's CEO Well. His Latest—a Risky Alzheimer's Drug," *STAT*, October 2, 2020.

may save lives: Pain Therapeutics press release, February 5, 2019.

Barbier, a finance guy: Cassava Sciences bio, https://www.cassavasciences.com/board-directors-management/remi-barbier.

They wed in June 2005: Remi Barbier, Securities and Exchange Commission Form 4, February 15, 2007.

luxury home in Austin: Nuwber public records search, https://nuwber.com/person/563a9d7a98f8a849c1813d4e; https://www.zillow.com/homes/3800-Cassava-Dr-Austin,-TX-78746_rb/120900038_zpid/.

trained under . . . Trevor Robbins: Biographical Sketch, NIH application, Grant 12925953, August 28, 2019.

forty-three of Robbins's students: Neurotree, Trevor Robbins, https://neurotree.org/beta/tree.php?pid=839.

half of the brain trust: Biographical Sketch, NIH application, Grant 12925953, August 28, 2019.

earned his PhD degree: Biographical Sketch, NIH application, Grant 13154950, June 29, 2020.

became part of Drexel University: https://drexel.edu/medicine/about/history/timeline/.

grueling daily commute: *The Philadelphia Inquirer*, September 11, 2005, B3; September 18, 2006, B1.

research collaborator and scientific advisor: Cassava Science, "Public Statement Regarding Recent Allegations Against Cassava Sciences, Inc.," September 3, 2021, 6; "Cassava Sciences Inc., Plaintiff, v. David Bredt, et al," Case 1:22-cv-09409 Document 1 Filed 11/02/22, 99.

one of their earliest joint scholarly papers: *PLOS ONE* 3, no. 2 (February 2008): E1554.

fourteen patents: US Patents, 8,580,808 B2; 8,614,324 B2; 8,653,068 B2; 9,340,558 B2; 9,354,223 B2; 9,500,640 B2; 8,492,349 B2; 8,580,809 B2; 8,722,851 B2; 10,017,736 B2; 9354223 B2; 10017736 B2; 10760052 B2; 20150148318 A1.

Barbier and his company settled the case: KB Partners I, LP, et al v. Pain Therapeutics, Inc., et al, Case No. A-11-CV-1034-SS, United States District Court, Western District of Texas, Austin Division, Notice of Proposed Settlement of Class Action, Document 251-1 (filed August 31, 2016): 4.

"horrible travesty": "Investors Club," https://www.youtube.com/watch?v=0SIq NWbPCFE.

"math errors . . . shambolic regulations": Pain Therapeutics press release, February 5, 2019.

was worth just $19 million: Yahoo Finance.

"She has a lot more explaining to do": Lindsay Burns, LinkedIn, 2016.

PTI-125 purportedly offers a grab bag of "mechanisms of action": *Neurobiology of Aging* 55 (July 2017): 99–114.

His grandmother and both of his parents-in-law were living with Alzheimer's: The United States vs. Hoau-Yan Wang, Case 8:24-cr-00211-TDC, Document 49-1, 10/28/24, 3.

abandoned its moribund opioid business: Being Patient, Barbier interview, March 1, 2021, https://www.facebook.com/beingpatientalzheimers/videos/2849545 868635704/ (at 1:30).

changed its name to . . . Cassava Sciences: Cassava Sciences press release, March 27, 2019.

Cassava root . . . as . . . remedy: https://www.stylecraze.com/articles /benefits-of-cassava-on-your-skin-hair-and-health/; https://www.getatoz.com/con tent/10-health-benefits-of-cassava/2216; https://www.webmd.com/vitamins/ai/ingre dientmono-1473/cassava#:~:text=Reviews%20(0)-,Overview,evidence%20to%20sup port%20these%20uses; https://www.ncbi.nlm.nih.gov/pmc/articles/PMC9315608/; https://www.fic.nih.gov/News/GlobalHealthMatters/january-february-2014/Pages /brain-disorders-cassava.aspx.; https://msutoday.msu.edu/news/2021/reducing-cas sava-cyanide-improves-cognitive-development; https://www.medicalnewstoday.com /articles/323756#safe-preparation.

chemical structure of the hallucinogen LSD: Cassava Sciences, "Corporate Overview" (May 2019): 9.

LSD diagram apparently came from Wikipedia: https://upload.wikimedia.org /wikipedia/commons/7/7b/Lysergide_stereoisomers_structural_formulae_v.2.png 1/.

"what's in a name" . . . transposed two vowels to rename his drug: Cassava Sciences press releases, August 24 and November 27, 2020.

revivified long-dead brain tissue . . . lent support to the overall idea: *Neurobiology of Aging* 55 (July 2017): 99–114; *The Journal of Clinical Investigation* 122, no. 4 (April 2012); "Statement of Concern Regarding the Accuracy and Integrity of Clinical and Preclinical Data Supporting the Ongoing Clinical Evaluation of Compound PTI-125, Also Known as Simufilam," Citizen petition to Food and Drug Administration (August 18, 2021): 2,15.

has been cited 1,600 times: Google search, January 26, 2023.

"It's hard for me to imagine how you could get any life": "Jordan Thomas's Army of Whistle-Blowers," *The New Yorker*, January 24, 2022.

the late John Trojanowski: *The New York Times*, March 4, 2022, B11.

one of the most prolific and influential Alzheimer's scholars: *Journal of Alzheimer's Disease* 16 (2009): 51–465.

tracing back to earlier work by Wang himself: For example, *The Journal of Clinical Investigation* 122, no. 4 (April 2012); *Nature Medicine* 12 (2006): 824–828; *Annals of Neurology* 88 (2020): 513–525; *Molecular Psychiatry* 20 (2015): 1091–1100; *PLOS ONE*, DOI:10.1371, August 5, 2016.

members of Cassava's paid advisory board: https://web.archive.org/web /20210305232445/; https://www.cassavasciences.com/scientific-advisory-board.

$20 million in grants: NIH grants: R01 AG067972, R44 AG060878, R44 AG065152, R44 AG056166, R44 AG050301, R01 MH116463, R21 AG065890, R44 AG057329.

tens of millions more: NIH grants: R21 AG051958, RF1 AG059621, R01 MH075916, P50 MH096891, R44 DA042639, R01 AG054434, NS084965.

would ultimately underwrite clinical trials: Cassava Sciences press release, November 10, 2021.

"Today's top-line results disappoint": Cassava Sciences press release, May 15, 2020.

blamed the earlier disappointing results . . . "It's hard for anyone to fess up": "Failure Has Paid Handsomely for Cassava Sciences' CEO," *STAT*, October 2, 2020.

patients taking simufilam showed memory improvements . . . "represent an important advance": Cassava Sciences press release, September 14, 2020.

improved even more: Cassava Sciences press release, February 2, 2021.

it had raised $200 million: Cassava Sciences press release, February 12, 2021.

"With solid science": Cassava Sciences press release, March 23, 2021.

unveiled more impressive data: Cassava Sciences press release, July 29, 2021.

"Uninterpretable" . . . "Overblown": "Alzheimer's Scientists Critique Cassava Sciences' Study Results—Overblown, Inappropriate, Uninterpretable," *STAT*, July 30, 2021.

"It's an evil necessity": "Being Patient Alzheimer's," March 1, 2021, https://www .facebook.com/beingpatientalzheimers/videos/2849545868635704/ (at 13:20–13:25).

Barbier and Burns family was suddenly worth $147 million: Remi Barbier, Securities and Exchange Commission Form 4, July 21, 2021.

"These clinical data": Cassava Sciences press release, July 29, 2021.

submitted a lengthy "citizen petition": https://www.regulations.gov/docket /FDA-2021-P-0930.

looked like it had been doctored: FDA Citizens Petition: https://www.regula tions.gov/docket/FDA-2021-P-0930; "FDA-2021-P-0930-0161_attachment_1.pdf," 1.

appeared to be "fraudulent": FDA Citizens Petition: https://www.regulations .gov/docket/FDA-2021-P-0930; "FDA-2021-p-0930-0004_content-cassava.pdf," 6.

The public announcements hit Wang hard: The United States vs. Hoau-Yan Wang, Case 8:24-cr-00211-TDC, Document 49-1, 10/28/24, 9.

"Hit job by a law firm": Lindsay Burns, LinkedIn, September 3, 2021, https:// www.linkedin.com/in/lindsay-burns-61b67229/recent-activity/.

"I remembered a meme from the '90s TV show *The X Files*": Interview with Matt Price, January 11, 2023.

CHAPTER 3

Quotes and personal information about Matthew Schrag and family: Interviews with Schrag, 2022–2023; some quotes condensed slightly for clarity.

A few sentences appeared in similar form in articles by me in *Science.*

"Gateway to the Lake Roosevelt Recreation Area": Official website of the City of Davenport, https://www.davenportwa.us.

Harvard, first in the biological sciences . . . UND ranks 186th: *US News and World Report* rankings: https://www.usnews.com/best-graduate-schools/top-science-schools/biological-sciences-rankings?_sort=rank-asc.

Harvard's vast, ultramodern labs garnered about $350 . . . compared to UND's $9 million: National Institutes of Health, 2006 data.

Othman Ghribi . . . PhD in neuropharmacology: Othman Ghribi CV, 2016.

studied that topic in rabbits for his first-ever scientific paper: "Deposition of Iron and B-Amyloid Plaques Is Associated with Cortical Cellular Damage in Rabbits Fed with Long-Term Cholesterol-Enriched Diets," *Journal of Neurochemistry* 99 (2006): 438–449.

Marcus Munafo at the University of Bristol has worked for years to mitigate the replication problem: *The Naked Scientists* (podcast), November 15, 2022, https://www.thenakedscientists.com/articles/interviews/are-reproducibility-rates-concern.

"We want to be discovering new things" . . . researchers have attempted to replicate: "Is There a Reproducibility Crisis?" *Nature* 533 (May 26, 2016): 452.

CHAPTER 4

Biographical information on Sylvain Lesné included: IdRef, http://www.idref.fr/069067929/id; Copains d'avant, https://copainsdavant.linternaute.com/p/sylvain-lesne-20198575; Lesné Lab, https://lesnelab.org/people/.

Comments from Denis Vivien: Emails and interviews with Vivien, 2022 and 2023.

Comments from Jean-Charles Lambert: Interview with Lambert, 2023.

"We are never safe": Email from Denis Vivien, June 15, 2022.

looked much as it did on that fated day in 1944: https://earthobservatory.nasa.gov/images/145143/forecasting-d-day.

"As I grew up on Normandy beaches . . .": Sylvain Lesné Twitter post, June 6, 2019.

scarcely more than two thousand residents when Lesné grew up: Insee, RP2009, RP2014, and RP2020, main holdings, geography as of 01/01/2023.

a handsome, gabled behemoth built in 1883: https://www.annuaire-mairie.fr/ville-luc-sur-mer.html.

destroyed military vehicles and equipment began to litter Sword Beach: "We Landed in Luc-Sur-Me on D-Day, Tuesday 6 June 1944," *BBC*, October 15, 2014.

The town owns the casino: "Casinos: A Financial Windfall but a Budgetary Trap for Normandy Municipalities," *France 3*, June 22, 2020.

Bertrand, who worked for the French national railways: "Jean-François Pillet dévoile sa liste un nouvel élan pour Beauvoir," *Ouest-France*, March 10, 2014.

alumni include pioneering chemists and mathematicians: "75 Notable Alumni of University of Caen Normandy," Edurank.org.

British troops moved inland to capture Caen: Caen Memorial Museum displays; Tiane R. Gardner, "Bombing Caen: A Thesis Presented to the Faculty of the U.S. Army Command and General Staff College," 2020; Ministry of the Armed Forces of France, "French Civilian Victims of the Battle of Normandy," https://www.cheminsdememoire.gouv.fr/en/french-civilian-victims-battle-normandy.

nation's thirty-eighth best university: "Best Global Universities in France," *US News and Global Report*, 2023.

compare his hair to George Clooney's: "Stalking Alzheimer's," *Minneapolis Star Tribune*, February 12, 2012, 1.

cited by other scholars more than a thousand times: Google Scholar, Lesné profile.

Docagne recently said his work: "Portrait de Fabian Docagne—Faire de la recherche à l'Inserm permet d'exercer des métiers très différents," Inserm Podcast, March 15, 2022.

without ever speaking with anyone from Caen: Interview with Ashe, January 17, 2024.

CHAPTER 5

"I was astonished": "Alzheimer's Damage May Be Reversible," *Townsville* (Australia) *Bulletin-Sun*, July 16, 2005.

high-achieving Chinese immigrants . . . Joyce Hsiao, was a biochemist . . . "CC" Hsiao, was a highly regarded aerospace engineer: "Dr. Karen Ashe: Stalking Alzheimer's," *Minneapolis Star Tribune*, February 13, 2012; "C. C. Hsiao Obituary," *St. Paul Pioneer Press*, August 10, 2009; "Hsiao Left Corporate World for Classroom," *Minneapolis Star Tribune*, September 19, 2009, 6B.

"close off the rest of the world" . . . "school project on how the brain works" . . . excelled at science and math . . . entered Harvard University: "Dr. Karen Ashe: Stalking Alzheimer's," *Minneapolis Star Tribune*, February 13, 2012.

inducted Ashe into its pantheon: "Past DAA Recipients," https://www.spa.edu/alumni/connect/daa/past-daa-recipients (accessed August 3, 2023).

first Asian American to attend . . . steely high school portrait: SPA (Spring 2011), 21.

with Ashe's essential contributions—won him the Nobel: The Nobel Foundation, Stanley B. Prusiner Biographical, 1997.

created transgenic mice that churn out human amyloid proteins: "Correlative Memory Deficits, Aβ Elevation, and Amyloid Plaques in Transgenic Mice," *Science* 274, no. 5284 (October 4, 1996): 99–102.

"the mouse equivalent of finding your car in the parking lot": "Dr. Karen Ashe: Stalking Alzheimer's," *Minneapolis Star Tribune*, February 13, 2012.

plaque in the UMN Medical School Wall of Scholarship: University of Minnesota Medical School, https://med.umn.edu/research/wall-scholarship (accessed August 3, 2023).

impress US Senator Amy Klobuchar: Amy Klobuchar Twitter post, April 6, 2018.

talk up Lesné as a "brilliant" experimentalist: Interview with Dennis Selkoe, 2022.

groundbreaking paper suggested that amyloid oligomers can disrupt cognition: "Natural Oligomers of the Amyloid-β Protein Specifically Disrupt Cognitive Function," *Nature Neuroscience* 8, no. 1 (January 2005): 79–84.

transgenic mice she engineered to generate human tau proteins: "Tau Suppression in a Neurodegenerative Mouse Model Improves Memory Function," *Science* 309 (July 15, 2005): 476–481.

the $250,000 MetLife Foundation Award: "Memory, Mice and Molecules—2005," MetLife Foundation Awards for Medical Research in Alzheimer's Disease (2016): 13.

"My dream is for the [UMN] to take the lead": "Medical Miracles Brewing at the U of M," *Triumph of the Spirit* (blog), March 30, 2009, https://bolstablog.word press.com/2009/03/30/medical-miracles/ (accessed August 3, 2023).

she founded a new Alzheimer's center: N. Bud Grossman Center for Memory Research and Care, https://www.memory.umn.edu/about/center-profile/ (accessed Aug 3, 2023).

CHAPTER 6

Ancient history: "Evolution in the Conceptualization of Dementia and Alzheimer's Disease: Greco-Roman Period to the 1960s," *Neurobiology of Aging* 19, no. 3 (May–June 1998): 173–189; "History of Alzheimer's Disease," *Dementia and Neurocognitive Disorders* 15, no. 4 (2016): 115–121; "The Ancient History of Dementia," *Neurological Sciences* 39, no. 11 (July 17, 2018): 2011–2016.

began to change markedly after the industrial revolution . . . nearly twenty-three million Americans: US Census Bureau, Population Division, "2020 Census: 1 in 6 People in the United States Were 65 and Over," May 25, 2023.

born in 1864, was a cigar chain-smoking: "Profile: Alois Alzheimer, Neuroscientist (1864–1915)," *Alzheimer Disease and Associated Disorders* 13, no. 3 (1999): 132–137.

joined the boisterous fraternity: "Alois Alzheimer—Who Was the Person Behind the Disease?," *Dementia Science*, October 17, 2020.

earned a saber scar . . . German aggression in World War I: "A Brief Biography of Alois Alzheimer," *Neurosciences and History* 1, no. 3 (2013): 125–136.

German Racial Hygiene Society . . . "Moral decadence, social deviancy, tuberculosis": "Alois Alzheimer: His Life and Times," *Brain Pathology* 17 (2007): 57–62.

Emil Kraepelin, gained fame . . . a theorist for crackpot eugenics theories: "On Human Self-Domestication, Psychiatry, and Eugenics," *Philosophy, Ethics, and Humanities in Medicine* 2, no. 21 (2007).

Ernst Rüdin, cofounded the Racial Hygiene Society: "Alois Alzheimer: His Life and Times," *Brain Pathology* 17, no. 1 (2007): 57–62; "Science and Inhumanity: The Kaiser-Wilhelm/Max Planck Society," *If Not Now* 2 (Winter 2000).

Nitsche, was executed for war crimes . . . was a junior doctor . . . psychiatric conference in Tübingen . . . Alzheimer died in 1915: "Alois Alzheimer: His Life and Times," *Brain Pathology* 17 (2007): 57–62; "Alois Alzheimer—Who Was the Person Behind the Disease?," *Dementia Science*, October 17, 2020.

created the National Institute on Aging: https://www.nia.nih.gov/about /history#:~:text=October%207%2C%201974,Institute%20on%20Aging%20is%20es tablished.

the cholinergic hypothesis: "The Cholinergic Hypothesis of Age and Alzheimer's Disease–Related Cognitive Deficits: Recent Challenges and Their Implications for Novel Drug Development," *Journal of Pharmacology and Experimental Therapeutics* 306, no. 3 (September 2003): 821–827.

Glenner isolated the main component of plaques: "Alzheimer's Disease and Down's Syndrome: Sharing of a Unique Cerebrovascular Amyloid Fibril Protein," *Biochemical and Biophysical Research Communications* 122, no. 3 (August 16, 1984): 1131–1135.

In a bitter irony, he died in 1995 of systemic senile amyloidosis: "Dr. George G. Glenner, 67, Dies; Researched Alzheimer's Disease," *The New York Times*, July 14, 1995.

new discovery about what was affecting brain cells in Alzheimer's: "Immunostaining of Neurofibrillary Tangles in Alzheimer's Senile Dementia with a Neurofilament Antiserum," *Journal of Neuroscience* 2, no. 1 (January 1982): 113–119.

created her transgenic, University of Minnesota (UMN) mice: *Alzforum*, March 29, 2013, "Research Models: Tg2576," https://www.alzforum.org/research -models/tg2576.

landmark analysis by life-science data specialist Aaron Sorensen: "Alzheimer's Disease Research: Scientific Productivity and Impact of the Top 100 Investigators in the Field," *Journal of Alzheimer's Disease* 16, no. 3 (2009): 451–465.

medical research beat back other relentless assassins: "Deaths, Percent of Death, and Death Rates for the 15 Leading Causes of Death," Center for Disease Control and Prevention/National Center for Health Statistics System, 1999 and 2015; "The State of US Health, 1990–2016," *JAMA* 319, no. 14 (April 10, 2018): 1444–1472.

Year after year, drug candidates that seemed promising in mice: "Amyloid-modifying Therapies for Alzheimer's Disease: Therapeutic Progress and its Implications," *Age* 32 (April 20, 2010): 365–384.

at least forty-three drugs—many designed to attack amyloid deposits—had failed: "Researching Alzheimer's Medicines: Setbacks and Stepping Stones," PhRMA, Fall 2018.

delivered a breathtaking experiment: "A Specific Amyloid-β Protein Assembly in the Brain Impairs Memory," *Nature* 440 (March 16, 2006): 352–357.

called Aβ*56 "a star suspect": "A Needle from the Haystack," *Nature* 440 (March 16, 2006): 284–285.

"Aβ Star Is Born?": "Aβ Star Is Born? Memory Loss in APP Mice Blamed on Oligomer, " *Alzforum*, March 21, 2006.

"clearly a key finding in the field" . . . "It changes the focus": "U Study Finds Possible Agent in Alzheimer's; Lead researcher Says the Protein May Offer Clues to Treating the Brain-Destroying Disease Early," *Star Tribune*, March 16, 2006, 1A.

landmark overview of the field: "Aβ Oligomers—a Decade of Discovery," *Journal of Neurochemistry* 1, no. 5 (January 4, 2007): 1172–1184.

won the $100,000 Potamkin Prize: American Academy of Neurology press release, March 23, 2006.

donated $5 million to a new research center: "Dr. Karen Ashe: Stalking Alzheimer's," *Minneapolis Star Tribune*, February 13, 2012.

CHAPTER 7

Quotes and personal information about Matthew Schrag and family: Interviews with Schrag, 2022–2023 (some quotes condensed slightly for clarity).

research on soluble oligomer amyloids: "Why Do Trials for Alzheimer's Disease Drugs Keep Failing? A Discontinued Drug Perspective for 2010–2015," *Expert Opinion on Investigational Drugs* 26, no. 6 (June 2017): 735–739; "History and Progress of Hypotheses and Clinical Trials for Alzheimer's Disease," *Signal Transduction and Targeted Therapy* 4, no. 29 (2019).

Oligomers are shapeshifters: "Amyloid Beta: Structure, Biology and Structure-based Therapeutic Development," *Acta Pharmacologica Sinica* 38 (2017): 1205–1235.

scarier sounding and more accurate: "Paris: Renamed ARIA, Vasogenic Edema Common to Anti-Amyloid Therapy," *Alzforum*, July 29, 2011.

Impressive results . . . 167 times: *Alzforum*, "Aduhelm," https://www.alzforum.org/therapeutics/aduhelm.

amyloid levels had plummeted: "Biogen Antibody Buoyed by Phase 1 Data and Hungry Investors," *Alzforum*, March 25, 2015.

But in March 2019 . . . Seven months later . . . 27 percent to 30 percent more slowly: *Alzforum*, "Aduhelm," https://www.alzforum.org/therapeutics/aduhelm.

four-tenths of a point: Food and Drug Administration. Webcast recording of the November 6, 2020 meeting, Peripheral and Central Nervous System Drugs Advisory Committee, at 04:03:47 to 04:04:14, https://collaboration.fda.gov/p2uew93ez7dw/.

clear benefits can be seen only after a full point difference: "Disease Severity and Minimal Clinically Important Differences in Clinical Outcome Assessments for Alzheimer's Disease Clinical Trials," *Alzheimer's & Dementia: Translational Research & Clinical Interventions* 5 (2019): 354–363; "Establishing Clinically Meaningful Change on Outcome Assessments Frequently Used in Trials of Mild Cognitive Impairment Due to Alzheimer's Disease," *Journal of Prevention of Alzheimer's Disease*, December 8, 2022, http://dx.doi.org/10.14283/jpad.2022.102; "Lecanemab for Alzheimer's Disease: Tempering Hype and Hope," *The Lancet* 400, no. 10367 (December 3, 2022): 1899.

painful brain swelling or bleeding afflicted: "Amyloid-Related Imaging Abnormalities in 2 Phase 3 Studies Evaluating Aducanumab in Patients with Early Alzheimer Disease," *JAMA Neurology* 79, no. 1 (2022): 13–21.

they delivered a stinging rebuke . . . ten voted no: *Alzforum*, "Aduhelm," https://www.alzforum.org/therapeutics/aduhelm.

"Texas sharpshooter fallacy . . . video on the TV are out of sync": Food and Drug Administration. Webcast recording of the November 6, 2020 meeting, Peripheral and Central Nervous System Drugs Advisory Committee, at 01:00:27 to 01:01:02 and 03:35:22 to 03:36:30, https://collaboration.fda.gov/p2uew93ez7dw/.

required only the removal of amyloid as a biological marker: *Alzforum*, "Aduhelm," https://www.alzforum.org/therapeutics/aduhelm.

"the totality of the evidence": "FDA Approves Alzheimer's Drug Despite Fierce Debate Over Whether It Works," *The New York Times*, June 8, 2021, A1.

"This historic moment": Biogen press release, June 7, 2021.

company's top revenue-producing product: Biogen press release, February 3. 2022.

quadruple Medicare spending: US Department of Health and Human Services, Centers for Medicare & Medicaid Services, "Medicare Part D Drug Spending by Drug, 2022."

"Appropriate Use Recommendations": "Aducanumab: Appropriate Use Recommendations Update," *Journal of Prevention of Alzheimer's Disease* 2, no. 9 (2022): 221–230.

scientists have denied . . . Biogen cited writings: "The Loudest Physician Proponents of Aduhelm Have All Taken Money from Biogen," *STAT*, November 1, 2021; Biogen, letter to Centers for Medicare & Medicaid Services, February 10, 2022, 30.

found people who offered heartrending tales: Patient comments: https://www.cms.gov/medicare-coverage-database/view/ncacal-public-comments.aspx?ncaId=305&fromTracking=Y&; Laura Thornhill, director, regulatory affairs, Alzheimer's Association, comment to Centers for Medicare & Medicaid Services, February 10, 2022.

Eisai and Biogen had poured as much as $1.7 million: "Pharmaceutical Industry Contributions," Alzheimer's Association, fiscal years 2021 and 2022.

"This was a disgraceful decision" . . . "dumping duffel bags of money": *Science—In the Pipeline*, "The Aducanumab Approval," June 8, 2021 and "Had Enough, Eh? Come Back and Take What's Coming to You!" June 16, 2022.

"not supposed to be the backup": Aaron Kesselheim, Twitter post, June 7, 2021.

scornful resignation letter: Letter to Acting Commissioner Janet Woodcock, June 10, 2021.

castigated the agency: "The FDA Has Reached a New Low," *The New York Times*, June 15, 2021.

an eerie side effect: "Anti-Amyloid Drugs and the Mystery of Treatment-Associated Brain Shrinkage," *STAT*, November 8, 2022.

"I do not think this excess volume loss": Email from Nick Fox, March 13, 2023.

"Brain volume changes consistent with atrophy": Email from Scott Ayton, February 13, 2023.

a vivid example of the revolving door: "Is FDA's Revolving Door Open Too Wide?," *Science* 361, no. 6397 (July 6, 2018): 21.

"serves as a model": "Alzheimer's Drug Approval Could Affect Other Diseases," *Nature* 595, no. 7866 (July 8, 2021): 162.

Relax already-weak FDA rules: "FDA Advisory Committees Under Scrutiny," *Pharmtech.com*, June 22, 2021.

"emotional undertone or overtones": "Inside 'Project Onyx,'" *STAT*, June 29, 2021.

recounted a harrowing series of events: FDA Adverse Event Reporting System (FAERS), Case ID: 19787426, received by FDA November 19, 2021.

"**died following a prolonged and refractory epileptic seizure**": Bureau du coroner of Quebec, October 10, 2023, "Coroner's investigation report." (Name withheld by agreement with the family.)

European Medicines Agency rejected . . . UK . . . Japan . . . United Arab Emirates: "Refusal of the Marketing Authorisation for Aduhelm," EMA statement, December 21, 2021; "What is Aducanumab and What Could This Dementia Drug Mean for People with Alzheimer's Disease," Alzheimer's Society UK, December 22, 2021; "Japanese Health Ministry Panel Rejects Biogen's Aducanumab," *FDA News*, December 23, 2021; "Biogen Receives Approval of Aducanumab in the UAE for the Treatment of Alzheimer's Disease," Biogen statement, undated.

made a paltry $300,000: "Biogen's Aduhelm Sales Fall Dramatically Below Wall Street's Expectations," *STAT*, October 20, 2021.

scathing investigative report: U.S. House of Representatives, "The High Price of Aduhelm's Approval: An Investigation into FDA's Atypical Review Process and Biogen's Aggressive Launch Plans," at 5, 15 (December 2022).

"**high-touch engagement strategy**": "How the FDA Got Too Cozy with an Alzheimer's Drugmaker," *The Washington Post*, January 11, 2023.

In January 2024, the company discontinued all efforts: Biogen press release, January 31, 2024.

terminated an ongoing clinical trial: "Years after a Polarizing Approval, Biogen Walks Away from Aduhelm," *STAT*, January 31, 2024.

an ethical lapse that insults the trial volunteers' sacrifices: Madhav Thambisetty, X post, January 31, 2024.

"**Now that the bar has been lowered**": "The FDA Has Reached a New Low," *The New York Times*, June 15, 2021.

"**If the amyloid thing continues**": Interview with George Perry, October 7, 2022.

"**I don't like it**": "'I Don't Like It:' Biogen's latest Alzheimer's Ad Rouses Fresh Aduhelm Concerns—and Some Defense," *Fierce Pharma*, July 27, 2021.

"**hoping for a recalibration**": "The Controversial Approval of an Alzheimer's Drug Reignites the Battle over the Underlying Cause of the Disease," *The Washington Post*, July 16, 2021.

CHAPTER 8

"**Cheat professionally**": Interview with Alena Kozunda, May 5, 2022.

Quotes and personal information about Matthew Schrag and family: Interviews conducted with Schrag, 2022–2023; some quotes condensed slightly for clarity.

fifteen years of existence: *The Wall Street Journal*, Cassava Science profile, accessed March 24, 2021, https://www.wsj.com/market-data/quotes/SAVA.

"**can dramatically suppress**": Pain Therapeutics press release, July 18, 2012.

They were getting better. They remembered more.: Cassava Sciences press release, February 2, 2021.

"**Is [simufilam] a drug that you would stay on for the rest of your life**": "An Inside Look at Cassava's Experimental Alzheimer's Drug," *Being Patient* (webcast), March 1, 2021, https://www.facebook.com/beingpatientalzheimers/videos/2849545868635704.

proprietary test . . . said could find misfolded filamin A: Hoau-Yan Wang, et al, "SavaDx, a Novel Plasma Biomarker to Detect Alzheimer's Disease, Confirms Mechanism of Action of Simufilam," https://www.cassavasciences.com/static-files /0854aec6-59b3-4e2b-ac20-c32b7c307b08.

Alzheimer's might be caused by a kind of diabetes of the brain: "Alzheimer's disease: the new promise," *The Journal of Clinical Investigation* 122, no. 4 (April 2012): 1191.

Burns announced early results: Cassava Sciences press release, February 11, 2020.

Institutional investors . . . literally weren't buying it: https://www.nasdaq.com /market-activity/stocks/sava/institutional-holdings (accessed March 22, 2024).

the norm for publicly traded companies . . . biotech funds . . . have stayed away: Nasdaq, "Cassava Sciences, Inc. Common Stock (SAVA) Institutional Holdings," https://www.nasdaq.com/market-activity/stocks/sava/institutional-holdings.

"opened up a market frenzy": "Biogen's Aduhelm Win Opened Up Market Frenzy for Alzheimer's-Focused Companies," *Fierce Biotech*, July 15, 2021.

suddenly worth $5.4 billion: Yahoo Finance.

huge bonuses were tied to the rising share prices: "Failure Has Paid Handsomely for Cassava Sciences' CEO," *STAT*, October 2, 2020; Cassava Sciences Inc., Securities and Exchange Commission Form 10-Q, Document date: September 30, 2020.

Years later, the FDA . . . would reveal: Food and Drug Administration, Establishment Inspection Report, The City College of New York (CCNY)/CUNY, #3006508031, September 14–16, 2022.

Investors filed suit against Barbier: "Cassava Investor Sues Over Pay Plan Adopted Before Stock Spike," *Bloomberg Law*, August 25, 2022.

settle the suit out of court: Cassava Sciences Inc., Securities and Exchange Commission Form 10-Q filed February 28, 2024, for December 31, 2023, 78.

investors who called themselves "SAVAges": "Jordan Thomas's Army of Whistle-Blowers," *The New Yorker*, January 24, 2022.

YouTube investment promoter Joe Springer: "The Alzheimer's Casino: Big Money and Bad Science," *Slow Newscast*, November 14, 2022.

making it one of the most shorted stocks: *MarketWatch*, https://www.market watch.com/tools/screener/short-interest (accessed March 22, 2024).

offered by the likes of Dr. Oz or Gwyneth Paltrow: "What's Wrong with Dr. Oz?," *Missouri Medicine* 112, no. 5 (September–October 2015): 332–333; E J Dickson, "We Fact-Checked Four of the Most Outrageous Claims in Gwyneth Paltrow's Netflix Show," *Rolling Stone*, January 29, 2020.

John Smith, a neuroscientist and friend: Interviews with Smith, 2022.

Cassava said it had spent more than $100 million: Cassava Sciences, Inc., Plaintiff, v. David Bredt; Geoffrey Pitt, et al, defendants, Civil Action No. 22-cv-9409, Complaint, November 2. 2022, 1.

Stephen Price was signing revised consent forms: Cassava Sciences, "Informed Consent Form and Authorization to Disclose Health Information," dated July 29, 2021, signed August 20, 2021.

With the help of his son, Matt, a global health epidemiologist: Interviews with Stephen and Matt Price, 2022 and 2023.

That paper in the *Journal of Neuroscience* helped spark: "Reducing Amyloid-Related Alzheimer's Disease Pathogenesis by a Small Molecule Targeting Filamin A," *The Journal of Neuroscience* 32, no. 29 (July 18, 2012): 9773–9784.

Peculiarities immediately seemed apparent: Schrag dossier on Cassava Sciences, Wang, Burns, 2022, unpublished; description of some of the image issues: https://pubpeer.com/publications/F91E0D22B887598445BB1F908393EE#28; publishers position: "Expression of Concern: Wang et al., 'Reducing Amyloid-Related Alzheimer's Disease Pathogenesis by a Small Molecule Targeting Filamin A,'" *The Journal of Neuroscience* 42, no. 3 (January 19, 2022): 9773–9784.

"cheat professionally": Interview with Alena Kozunda, May 5, 2022.

"Cassava Sciences apparently didn't get the Theranos memo": Jordan A. Thomas, August 18, 2021, letter to Bill Dunn, director, Office of Neuroscience, FDA Center for Drug Evaluation and Research.

plummeted nearly 60 percent from its peak value: Yahoo Finance.

CHAPTER 9

Quotes from Matthew Schrag: Interviews with Schrag, 2022–2023; some quotes condensed slightly for clarity.

"It is not conceivable that features in the images": "Biotech's Data Supporting Alzheimer's Trials under Scrutiny," *Retraction Watch*, August 27, 2021.

Schrag described many of those anonymously: PubPeer, https://pubpeer.com/search?q=Hoau-Yan+Wang.

"Let me be very clear": Cassava Science press release, September 3, 2021.

unveiled what Wang and Burns described as the protein filamin A's central role: "Reducing Amyloid-Related Alzheimer's Disease Pathogenesis by a Small Molecule Targeting Filamin A," *The Journal of Neuroscience* 32, no. 29 (July 18, 2012): 9773–9784.

Technical descriptions from lab-equipment companies supported his comments: For example, https://stoeltingco.com/Neuroscience/McIllwain-Tissue-Chopper~9991.

survived after having been frozen at -112 . . . "Neurons in the human brain do not survive": Jordan A. Thomas, "Statement of Concern Regarding the Accuracy and Integrity of Clinical and Preclinical Data Supporting the Ongoing Clinical Evaluation of Compound PTI-125, Also Known as Simufilam," August 18, 2021.

and a related Wang-Arnold study: "Alzheimer's Disease: The New Promise," *The Journal of Clinical Investigation* 122, no. 4 (April 2012): 1191.

scientists mocked Cassava and simufilam: "Cassava Sciences: A Shambolic Charade," November 3, 2021, Cassavafraud.com.

"fact" vs. "fiction" rebuttal: Cassava Science statement, August 25, 2021.

the analytics firm flatly refuted Barbier's claim: Quanterix press release, August 27, 2021.

already initiated a review . . . "the allegations are false" . . . changed its initial in-

quiry into a formal misconduct investigation: City University of New York, "Exhibit 1 Response to Robbins Geller FOIL Request," 143, 640, 921–922 (via Adrian Heilbut).

issued a correction involving one of the nine challenged images: "Erratum: Wang et al., 'Reducing Amyloid-Related Alzheimer's Disease Pathogenesis by a Small Molecule Targeting Filamin A,'" *The Journal of Neuroscience* 41, no. 50 (December 15, 2021): 10405.

A flurry of rejoinders: https://pubpeer.com/publications/F91E0D22B887 598445BB1F908393EE.

editors issued an "expression of concern": "Expression of Concern: Wang et al., 'Reducing Amyloid-Related Alzheimer's Disease Pathogenesis by a Small Molecule Targeting Filamin A,'" *The Journal of Neuroscience* 42, no. 3 (January 19, 2022).

Cassava shareholders filed a class action lawsuit: Pierre Brazeau, et al, vs. Cassava Sciences, et al, Civil Action 1:21-cv-00751, filed August 27, 2021, United States District Court, Western District of Texas, Austin Division, 3, 20.

US Securities and Exchange Commission (SEC) had launched an investigation: "SEC Investigating Cassava Sciences, Developer of Experimental Alzheimer's Drug," *The Wall Street Journal*, November 17, 2021.

Federal Bureau of Investigation began inquiries: Email correspondence, December 13, 2021, between FBI Special Agent Jeffrey Weeks and software engineer Alexander Trevelyan (via Trevelyan).

weighed in with skeptical reports about Cassava and simufilam: "Jordan Thomas's Army of Whistle-Blowers," *The New Yorker*, January 24, 2022; "Scientists Question Data Behind an Experimental Alzheimer's Drug," *The New York Times*, April 18, 2022.

The rejection was signed by Patrizia Cavazzoni: US Food and Drug Administration, February 10, 2022, Re: Docket Nos. FDA-2021-P-0930 and FDA-2021-P-0967.

Cassava Sciences acknowledged anxiety in a filing: Cassava Sciences, Securities and Exchange Commission Form 10-K, for the period ending December 31, 2021, 40.

The company would later acknowledge . . . "a toxic environment": Cassava Sciences, Inc., Plaintiff, v. David Bredt, et al, Defendants, Complaint, US District Court Southern District of New York, Civil Action No. 22-cv-9409, Document 1, Filed November 2, 2022, 166–167.

apparently a criminal probe by the US Department of Justice: "Exclusive: Cassava Sciences Faces US Criminal Probe Tied to Alzheimer's Drug, Sources Say," *Reuters*, July 27, 2022.

CHAPTER 10

Quotes from Matthew Schrag: Interviews with Schrag, 2022–2023; some quotes condensed slightly for clarity.

both members of Cassava's paid advisory board: "Corporate Overview," Cassava Sciences, May 2019.

provided a respected patina: Arnold and Cummings later declined to be interviewed or to answer written questions.

an important player on six doubtful papers: For example, "Demonstrated Brain Insulin Resistance in Alzheimer's Disease Patients Is Associated with IGF-1 Resistance, IRS-1 Dysregulation, and Cognitive Decline," *The Journal of Clinical Investigation* 122, no. 4 (April 2012): 11316–1338; "Altered Neuregulin 1–erbB4 Signaling Contributes to NMDA Receptor Hypofunction in Schizophrenia," *Nature Medicine* 12, no. 7 (July 2006): 824–828.

One of them . . . has been cited 1,600 times . . . accompanied by an editorial: "Demonstrated Brain Insulin Resistance in Alzheimer's Disease Patients Is Associated with IGF-1 Resistance, IRS-1 Dysregulation, and Cognitive Decline," *The Journal of Clinical Investigation* 122, no. 4 (April 2012): 11316–1338; "Alzheimer's Disease: The New Promise," *The Journal of Clinical Investigation* 122, no. 4 (April 2012): 1191.

largely funded out of the highly competitive federal grants: NIH funded these relevant grants to Lindsay Burns and/or Hoau-Yan Wang, listed by grant number, total funding $19.8 million, NIH Reporter, R44 AG065152, R01 AG067972, R44 AG050301, R44 AG056166, R44 AG060878, R01 MH116463, R21 AG065890, R44 AG057329.

The first article on the results list: "NMDA Receptor Activation Inhibits α-Secretase and Promotes Neuronal Amyloid-β Production," *The Journal of Neuroscience* 25, no. 41 (October 12, 2005): 9367–9377.

"ton of questionable stuff [had appeared] in *Brain* and *PNAS* and *Nature*": "Brain Amyloid-β Oligomers in Ageing and Alzheimer's Disease," *Brain* 136 (2013): 1383–1398; "Selective Lowering of Synapsins Induced by Oligomeric α-Synuclein Exacerbates Memory Deficits," *PNAS*, published online (May 22, 2017): E4648–E4657; "A Specific Amyloid-β Protein Assembly in the Brain Impairs Memory," *Nature* 440, no. 16 (March 2006): 352–357.

Selkoe, a chief progenitor of the amyloid hypothesis: National Library of Medicine database PubMed.

CHAPTER 11

Quotes from Matthew Schrag: Interviews with Schrag, 2022–2023; some quotes condensed slightly for clarity.

Nancy Olivieri, a hematologist at the University of Toronto: Carl Elliott, *The Occasional Human Sacrifice* (New York: W. W. Norton, 2024), 58; "The Canadian Corporate-Academic Complex," *Academe*, October 29, 2010.

John Pesando, who leaked the story of a scandal: Carl Elliott, *The Occasional Human Sacrifice* (New York: W.W. Norton, 2024), 132; "Uninformed Consent—What Patients at 'The Hutch' Weren't Told about the Experiments in Which They Died," *The Seattle Times*, March 11, 2001.

"Some people manage to blow the whistle without being fired": Carl Elliott, *The Occasional Human Sacrifice* (New York: W.W. Norton, 2024), 58.

one suspect Hoau-Yan Wang paper had been retracted: *Molecular Neurodegeneration*, February 4, 2022, retraction notice: https://molecularneurodegeneration.biomedcentral.com/articles/10.1186/s13024-021-00438-3. Paper was changed, augmented, and republished June 15, 2022, with Wang's work and name excised:

https://molecularneurodegeneration.biomedcentral.com/articles/10.1186/s13024
-022-00549-5.

heads an Alzheimer's institute at Rush University and leads the Religious Orders Study: https://www.rushu.rush.edu/faculty/david-bennett-md; https://www.rushu.rush.edu/research/departmental-research/religious-orders-study.

By contract, he becomes a coauthor: "Rush Alzheimer's Disease Center Resource Sharing Policies" (August 25, 2017), 2.

"dossier is a fraction of the anomalies easily visible on review": Note within the Sylvain Lesné dossier, unpublished.

That standard process: https://ori.hhs.gov/about-ori.

a nurse at the university's medical center was tried: "In Nurse's Trial, Investigator Says Hospital Bears 'Heavy' Responsibility for Patient Death," Kaiser Health News, March 24, 2022, https://kffhealthnews.org/news/article/radonda-vaught-fatal-drug-error-vanderbilt-hospital-responsibility/; "Ex-Nurse Convicted in Fatal Medication Error Gets Probation," *The New York Times*, May 15, 2022.

Bik had been profiled often in leading media, including *Science*: "How a Sharp-Eyed Scientist Became Biology's Image Detective," *The New Yorker*, June 23, 2021; "Microbiologist Elisabeth Bik Queried Covid Research—That's When the Abuse and Trolling Began," *The Guardian*, August 2, 2021; "Scientists Rally Around Misconduct Consultant Facing Legal Threat After Challenging Covid-19 Drug Researcher," *Science*, May 27, 2021.

CHAPTER 12

Comments and personal information from Dennis Selkoe: Except as noted, interviews with Selkoe, 2022 and 2023.

Comments from Matthew Schrag: Interviews with Schrag, 2022 and 2023; some quotes condensed slightly for clarity.

chastised me . . . I had just broken a story: "Second Death Linked to Potential Antibody Treatment for Alzheimer's Disease," *Science*, November 27, 2022.

UC-San Diego pathologist George Glenner: "Neuritic Plaques and Cerebrovascular Amyloid in Alzheimer Disease Are Antigenically Related," *Proceedings of the National Academies of Science* 82 (December 1985): 8729–8732.

1992 paper by neuroscientists John Hardy and Gerald Higgins: Unpublished manuscript provided by the author, 2023.

boasts more than three hundred researchers in twenty-five labs: Interview with Dennis Selkoe, 2023.

"It became gradually an infallible belief system": "Why There's No Cure for Alzheimer's: The Invention of a Disease and the Pursuit of one Molecule," *APM Reports*, October 15, 2019, https://www.apmreports.org/episode/2019/10/15/senility-alzheimers-amyloid-plaques.

Oligomer funding from NIH skyrocketed . . . out of a total Alzheimer's budget of about $3 billion: NIH Reporter.

Since 2002, the majority of clinical trials: "Why There's No Cure for Alzheimer's: The Invention of a Disease and the Pursuit of one Molecule," *APM Reports*,

October 15, 2019, https://www.apmreports.org/episode/2019/10/15/senility-alzhei
mers-amyloid-plaques.

2022 review of Alzheimer's clinical trials: "Alzheimer's Disease Drug Development Pipeline: 2022," *Alzheimer's & Dementia*, May 4, 2022.

I examined records in ClinicalTrials.gov: Records from https://fdaaa.trials
tracker.net/ for trials with completion dates January 1, 2017 or later; details of trials from https://clinicaltrials.gov/ and https://www.alzforum.org/; pharma company
rankings from https://www.icapsulepack.com.

"To be blunt, [amyloid] lowering" . . . "The hope was that": "Lowering of
Amyloid-Beta by β-Secretase Inhibitors—Some Informative Failures," *The New
England Journal of Medicine* 380 (April 11, 2019): 1476–1478; "Amyloid Gains
Converts in Debate Over Alzheimer's Treatments," *The Wall Street Journal*, Febru-
ary 27, 2023.

**compiled a chart describing all fifty-one anti-amyloid trials conducted since
2002:** Private communication from Alberto Espay, March 14, 2024, updated from
"Soluble Amyloid-Beta Consumption in Alzheimer's Disease," *Journal of Alzheimer's
Disease* 82 (2021): 1403–1415.

Less than a month later, a new source came forward: "Scientists Tie Third
Clinical Trial Death to Experimental Alzheimer's Drug," *Science*, December 21, 2022.

"We may have reached the limit of what amyloid lowering can do": "Amyloid
Gains Converts in Debate Over Alzheimer's Treatments," *The Wall Street Journal*,
February 27, 2023.

Data will be kept secret: "Lecanemab in Early Alzheimer's Disease," *The New
England Journal of Medicine* 388 (January 5, 2023): 9–21; "data sharing plan" posted
November 29, 2022.

The *New York Times* reported in 2024: "What Drugmakers Did Not Tell Volunteers in Alzheimer's Trials," October 23, 2024.

Thambisetty and others have pointed to another key doubt: Interview with
Thambisetty, 2023.

**long-understood approach of using a placebo meant to closely resemble the
treatment:** "Blinding, Unblinding, and the Placebo Effect: An Analysis of Patients'
Guesses of Treatment Assignment in a Double-Blind Clinical Trial," *Clinical Pharmacology and Therapeutics* 41, no. 3 (March 1987): 259–265.

Seven required immediate intervention, emergency care: Eisai, Inc., Briefing
Document, June 9, 2023, Peripheral and Central Nervous System (PCNS) Drugs Advisory Committee Meeting, BLA 761269 S-001, Appendix 2.

provisionally approved lecanemab even before seeing the major trial results:
"FDA Grants Accelerated Approval for Alzheimer's Disease Treatment," FDA News
Release, January 6, 2023.

In July 2023, it delivered full approval: "FDA Converts Novel Alzheimer's Disease Treatment to Traditional Approval," FDA News Release, July 6, 2023.

European Medicines Agency recommending in 2024 against approval: "Meeting highlights from the Committee for Medicinal Products for Human Use (CHMP)
22-25 July 2024," July 26, 2024, https://www.ema.europa.eu/en/news/meeting-high
lights-committee-medicinal-products-human-use-chmp-22-25-july-2024.

UK authorities approved the drug: "Debate rages over Alzheimer's drug lecanemab as UK limits approval," *Nature*, August 22, 2024.

added a "black box warning" to the approved lecanemab product label: Eisai Inc. and Biogen, Prescribing Information, "LEQEMBI® (lecanemab-irmb) Injection, for Intravenous Use Initial U.S. Approval: 2023," 1.

detailed case report by Schrag and colleagues: "Fatal Iatrogenic Cerebral β-Amyloid-Related Arteritis in a Woman Treated with Lecanemab for Alzheimer's Disease" (published as a preprint prior to FDA black box decision), *Nature Communications* 14 (December 2023).

By early 2024, only two thousand patients had been treated with lecanemab: "Biogen Alzheimer's Drug Launch Off to Slow Start," *The Boston Globe*, February 13, 2024.

but decided to hold an advisory committee meeting: "FDA Delays Action on Closely Watched Alzheimer's Drug," *The New York Times*, March 8, 2024.

gave donanemab a green light: "FDA Panel Backs New Alzheimer's Drug, Despite Risks and Uncertainties," *Science*, June 11, 2024.

FDA approved it under the brand name Kisunla: "FDA Approves Treatment for Adults with Alzheimer's Disease," FDA, July 2, 2024, https://www.fda.gov/drugs/news-events-human-drugs/fda-approves-treatment-adults-alzheimers-disease.

meta-analysis examined results from many studies: "Clinically Important Benefits and Harms of Monoclonal Antibodies Targeting Amyloid for the Treatment of Alzheimer Disease: A Systematic Review and Meta-Analysis," *Annals of Family Medicine* 22, no. 1 (January/February 2024): 50–58.

"So much of the amyloid world is built on an almost biblical end-of-times story": This and other comments, interview with Lon Schneider, 2023, except where noted.

"Optimism is good but not if it hurts others": "No Easy Answers on Clinical Meaningfulness of Alzheimer's Treatments," *Alzforum*, February 16, 2023.

Eisai and Biogen expect to earn more than $10 billion a year: Eisai press conference presentation, March 7, 2024, 30.

run the bill to as high as $90,000: "When It Comes to Lecanemab (and Donanemab), How Might We Think about 'Reasonable and Necessary'?" *Journal of Prevention of Alzheimer's Disease* 3, no. 10 (June 13, 2023): 342–343.

would owe $6,600 in copays: "The Real Costs of the New Alzheimer's Drug, Most of Which Will Fall to Taxpayers," *Kaiser Health News*, August 2, 2023.

substantial portion of the $50,290 median annual household income: "Income in the United States: 2021," US Department of Commerce, Census Bureau, September 2023, 2.

almost certainly spike drug premiums for all Medicare recipients: "Lecanemab Prescriptions Could Increase Medicare Annual Spending by Up to $5 Billion," *Neurology Today*, May 12, 2023.

"Having actual therapies that even have a small beneficial effect is positive": This and other comments, interview with Thomas Südhof, 2023.

Cassava Sciences CEO Remi Barbier agrees: "An Inside Look at Cassava's Experimental Alzheimer's Drug," *Being Patient* (webcast), March 1, 2021, https://www.facebook.com/beingpatientalzheimers/videos/2849545868635704.

targeting amyloid deposits in patients as young as eighteen: Washington University School of Medicine press release, December 20, 2021.

"'Not treating early enough' is why [companies] are targeting young adults": Albert Espay Twitter post, December 1, 2022.

But consider "prediabetes": "The War on 'Prediabetes' Could Be a Boon for Pharma—but Is It Good Medicine?" (slightly adapted from this article), *Science*, March 7, 2019.

National Institute for Health and Care Excellence recently endorsed: "Wegovy Made Available in the UK for Weight Loss in People with Prediabetes and Type 2 Diabetes," Diabetes UK, January 5, 2024.

the term "preclinical Alzheimer's" has come into play: "Global Estimates on the Number of Persons across the Alzheimer's Disease Continuum," *Alzheimer's & Dementia* 19, no. 2 (June 2, 2022): 658–670.

Once upon a time a pathologist saw plaques & tangles: Lon Schneider Twitter post, December 7, 2022.

***Los Angeles Times* exposé detailed plans by the FDA:** "Inside the Plan to Diagnose Alzheimer's in People with No Memory Problems—And Who Stands to Benefit," *Los Angeles Times*, February 14, 2024.

sixty-year-old who tests positive for amyloid and tau biomarkers: "Lifetime Risks of Alzheimer's Disease Dementia Using Biomarkers for Preclinical Disease," *Alzheimer's & Dementia* 14, no. 8 (August 2018): 981–988.

Mordant critics suggested that Alzheimer's treatments in the womb: Albert Espay Twitter post, March 9, 2023.

George Perry retains the relaxed informality: Perry comments and personal history from interviews, 2022.

written often that they play a role: "The Amyloid Cascade and Alzheimer's Disease Therapeutics: Theory Versus Observation," *Laboratory Investigation* 99, no. 7 (July 2019): 958–970.

he's collected $250 million in research funds: Dimensions database, Digital Science & Research Solutions, Inc., 2023; funds to Selkoe as principal investigator or coinvestigator; excludes some private funding or corporate grants.

something comparably effective has been around since 2004: "Donepezil for Dementia Due to Alzheimer's Disease," *The Cochrane Collaboration*, Issue 6, Art. No. CD001190, 2018.

Perry has written more than 1,100 scholarly articles: Dimensions database, Digital Science & Research Solutions, Inc., 2024.

article about the "amyloid cabal" by the late Sharon Begley: "The Maddening Saga of How an Alzheimer's 'Cabal' Thwarted Progress Toward a Cure for Decades" (Tesi, Itzhaki quotes), *STAT*, June 25, 2019.

neurobiologist Rachael Neve of Massachusetts General Hospital: Comments from interview via email, 2022, except as noted.

"My program officer at NIH recommended": Good Science Project, July 6, 2022, https://goodscienceproject.org/articles/essay-rachael-neve/.

late Harvard scientist Robert Moir faced headwinds: "How an Outsider in Alzheimer's Research Bucked the Prevailing Theory—and Clawed for Validation,"

STAT, October 29, 2018; "Unorthodox Alzheimer's Researcher Robert Moir Dies at Age 58," *STAT*, December 20, 2019.

one of the top advances of the year: "2016's Top 5 Advances in Neurology," *MedPage Today*, December 21, 2016.

Malú Tansey . . . was shot down: "The Maddening Saga of How an Alzheimer's 'Cabal' Thwarted Progress Toward a Cure for Decades," *STAT*, June 25, 2019.

"we wouldn't be here": Interview with Tansey, 2022.

describes both tau and microgliosis as direct results of the cascade: "A Calcium-Sensitive Antibody Isolates Soluble Amyloid-β Aggregates and Fibrils from Alzheimer's Disease Brain," *Brain* 145 (July 27, 2022): 2528–2540.

sits on the board of Prothena: https://www.prothena.com/management/dennis-j-selkoe/.

Cummings disclosed . . . Salloway has taken: "Lecanemab Appropriate Use Recommendations," *Journal of Prevention of Alzheimer's Disease*, March 27, 2023; OpenPaymentsData.CMS.gov and NIH Reporter, searched June 26, 2023.

CHAPTER 13

A few paragraphs adapted from "Blots on a Field?" my article published in *Science*, July 22, 2022.

"What is more shocking: reading that the discovery": "Sylvain Lesné, Who Found Aβ*56, Accused of Image Manipulation," *Alzforum*, July 22, 2022.

Comments from Dennis Selkoe: Except as noted, from interviews, 2022 and 2023.

Comments from Matthew Schrag: Interviews with Schrag, 2022 and 2023; some quotes condensed slightly for clarity.

tried and failed to find the protein: According to Donna Wilcock, University of Indiana; Dennis Selkoe, Harvard University; and "Sylvain Lesné, Who Found Aβ*56, Accused of Image Manipulation," *Alzforum*, July 22, 2022.

2006 paper he coauthored with Lesné . . . includes a graphic later reprinted as if original: "Orally Available Compound Prevents Deficits in Memory Caused by the Alzheimer Amyloid-β Oligomers," *Annals of Neurology* 60 (2006): 668–676; "Oligomers of the Amyloid-B Protein Disrupt Working Memory: Confirmation with Two Behavioral Procedures," *Behavioural Brain Research* 193 (2008): 230–234; "Soluble Aβ Oligomer Production and Toxicity," *Journal of Neurochemistry* 120 (Supplement 1): 125–139.

with a carefully lawyered brush-off: Email from David Bennett, June 24, 2022.

Barbier replied via email that Schrag's "allegations are false": Email from Remi Barbier, June 20, 2022.

Cassava later conceded investigations: Cassava Sciences Inc. Securities Litigation, Case 1:21-cv-00751-DAE, Document 108 Filed 07/03/23, 2 (DOJ and SEC).

Ashe agreed to talk, then demurred (and subsequent quotes): Emails from Karen Ashe, June 2022.

"It's very difficult to say 'no' to a potentially very big publication": Interview with Jean-Charles Lambert, July 28, 2023.

"Ashe obviously failed in that very serious duty": Interview with John Forsay-eth, April 9, 2022.

she tried to get ahead of my story with a defense on PubPeer: https://pubpeer .com/publications/8FF7E6996524B73ACB4A9EF5C0AACF, posted June 2022.

One for a 2012 paper in the *Journal of Neuroscience*: "Erratum: Larson, et al., Soluble α-Synuclein Is a Novel Modulator of Alzheimer's Disease Pathophysiology," *The Journal of Neuroscience* 42, no. 24 (June 15, 2022): 4953–4955.

Schrag and Bik showed in detailed posts to PubPeer: https://pubpeer.com /publications/8FF7E6996524B73ACB4A9EF5C0AACF.

appeared in a 2013 paper in the influential journal *Brain*: "Correction to: Brain Amyloid-β Oligomers in Ageing and Alzheimer's Disease," *Brain* 145, no. 8 (August 2022): e72–e76.

it had corrected two of the Lesné papers: Megan E. Larson et al., "Soluble α-Synuclein Is a Novel Modulator of Alzheimer's Disease Pathophysiology," *The Journal of Neuroscience*, May 26, 2022; Stephanie W. Fowler et al., "Genetic Modula-tion of Soluble Aβ Rescues Cognitive and Synaptic Impairment in a Mouse Model of Alzheimer's Disease," *The Journal of Neuroscience*, June 4, 2014.

posted expressions of concern for studies from 2016 and 2017: "The Amyloid β Oligomer Aβ*56 Induces Specific Alterations in Neuronal Signaling That Lead to Tau Phosphorylation and Aggregation," *Science Signaling*, June 21, 2022; "Gain-of-Function Mutations in Protein Kinase Cα (PKCα) May Promote Synaptic Defects in Alzheimer's Disease," *Science Signaling*, May 10, 2016.

***Nature* posted a notice:** *Nature*, Editor's note for "A Specific Amyloid-β Protein Assembly in the Brain Impairs Memory," July 14, 2022.

one of the most discussed articles in recent scientific history: https://www .nature.com/articles/nature04533/metrics (accessed April 27, 2024).

Alzheimer's research community reacted with alarm: "Sylvain Lesné, Who Found Aβ*56, Accused of Image Manipulation," *Alzforum*, July 22, 2022.

citing the *Nature* paper in fourteen of his own articles . . . cited nearly seven thousand times: All citation data: Digital Science & Research Solutions Inc., Dimen-sions, June 28, 2023.

Ashe told *NBC News*: NBC News, "Allegations of Fabricated Research Under-mine key Alzheimer's Theory," July 25, 2022, https://www.nbcnews.com/science /science-news/alzheimers-theory-undermined-accusations-fabricated-research -rcna39843 (accessed July 18, 2023).

defended the amyloid hypothesis and the role of oligomers: *Science*, Letter, 377, no. 6609 (August 26, 2022): 934–935.

CHAPTER 14

A few paragraphs adapted from my articles in *Science*, as noted.

"It is a wonder that the ORI accomplishes much at all": "Rooting Out Scien-tific Misconduct," *Science*, 383, no. 6679 (January 12, 2024): 131.

Quotes from Matthew Schrag: Interviews with Schrag, 2022 and 2023, some quotes condensed slightly for clarity.

As the largest biomedical research funder in the world, NIH provided about $37 billion: https://www.nih.gov/about-nih/what-we-do/impact-nih-research/serv ing-society/direct-economic-contributions#:~:text=With (accessed November 21, 2023).

About 10 percent went to Alzheimer's: NIH Reporter, accessed November 23, 2023.

City University of New York (CUNY) ... took in $55 million ... (UMN) ... gained $433 million: NIH Awards by Location and Organization, 2022, https://report.nih .gov/award/index.cfm?ot=&fy=2022&state=&ic=&fm=&orgid=&distr=&rfa=&om =n&pid=.

that agency paid for most of the work on the two scientists' star protein: Based on grants cited in papers flagged as containing suspect images.

When NIH receives a concern about misconduct: NIH, "NIH Process for Handling Research Misconduct Allegations," https://grants.nih.gov/policy/research_in tegrity/process.htm (accessed November 16, 2023).

As of the end of 2023, it had just thirty-seven employees: Department of Health and Human Services, "Fiscal Year 2022 Justification of Estimates for Appropriations Committees," 89.

It's far from a new problem: "Top U.S. Scientific Misconduct Official Quits in Frustration with Bureaucracy," *Science*, March 12, 2014.

ORI normally hands off investigations: Office of Research Integrity, "Frequently Asked Questions," https://ori.hhs.gov/frequently-asked-questions (accessed November 21, 2023).

ORI recently floated proposals to tighten deadlines: Department of Health and Human Services, "Public Health Service Policies on Research Misconduct, Notice of Proposed Rulemaking," October 5, 2023.

moves strongly opposed by many universities: "New Proposals for Scientific Misconduct Investigations Worry Some Research Universities," *STAT*, December 8, 2023.

the agency caved to that pressure: Department of Health and Human Services, "HHS Finalizes Rule on Research Misconduct to Foster Research Integrity," September 12, 2024.

"further evidence of academic institutions capturing ORI": "Final U.S. misconduct rule drops controversial changes," *Science*, September 13, 2024.

Susan Garfinkel, who formerly directed ORI's investigative oversight: Interview with Garfinkel, December 1, 2023.

360 have been disciplined since the agency's inception ... Of the eighty-seven cases: "Life After Research Misconduct: Punishments and the Pursuit of Second Chances," *Journal of Empirical Research on Human Research Ethics*, December 14, 2016; Office of Research Integrity, "Case Summaries," https://ori.hhs.gov/content /case_summary (accessed November 2023); additional case summaries accessed via internet archive.

more than two-thirds of PubPeer comments report possible misconduct: "Classification and Analysis of PubPeer Comments: How a Web Journal Club Is Used," *Journal of the Association for Information Science and Technology* 73 (2022): 655–670.

In late 2023, ORI proposed another option: "Federal Agency's Plan to Disclose University Misconduct Findings Splits Academics," *Science*, December 8, 2023.

several thousand concerns about doctored Alzheimer's research: PubPeer, November 2023.

The academy successfully quashed the proposal: Health Care Compliance Association, "Penn Calls for Withdrawal of ORI's Misconduct Proposed Reg; Many Commenters Also Critical," February 26, 2024, https://www.jdsupra.com/legalnews /penn-calls-for-withdrawal-of-ori-s-3003981/.

"Give the scientific integrity official enough of a budget": "Comments on Draft NIH Scientific Integrity Policy," Good Science Project, *Good Science Newsletter*, October 31, 2023.

my 2020 investigation of the FDA's track record overseeing patient safety . . . called that failure to inform "a travesty": "Official Inaction: A Science Investigation Shows that FDA Oversight of Clinical Trials Is Lax, Slow Moving, and Secretive— and That Enforcement Is Declining," *Science*, October 1, 2020.

Califf had millions of dollars in investments: Robert Califf, "Executive Branch Personnel Public Financial Disclosure Report," October 13, 2021.

Scott Gottlieb, joined the board of directors of Pfizer: https://www.pfizer.com /people/leadership/board_of_directors/scott_gottlieb-md (accessed November 23, 2023).

eleven of sixteen FDA medical examiners: "FDA's Revolving Door: Companies Often Hire Agency Staffers Who Managed Their Successful Drug Reviews," *Science*, July 5, 2018.

Biogen, Aduhelm's maker, donated heavily to patient advocacy groups: Alzheimer's Association, "Pharmaceutical Industry Contributions: FY21 (and) FY22."

Billy Dunn, the FDA's top regulator for Aduhelm and other Alzheimer's drugs: "Inside 'Project Onyx,'" *STAT*, June 29, 2021.

"Regulatory capture has now infiltrated the Food and Drug Administration": Public Citizen, "Outrage of the Month: FDA's Inappropriate Close Collaboration with Biogen on Alzheimer's Disease Drug," *Health Letter*, January 2021.

"It says right there in the agency's charter": "The Underside of the Aducanumab Approval," *Science*, In the Pipeline, July 2, 2021.

join the board of Prothena . . . received options to buy thirty thousand shares: US Securities and Exchange Commission, Prothena Biosciences Form 4, May 19, 2023.

CHAPTER 15

"It was one of those roles": Email from Jason Karlawish, September 30, 2023.

Comments by Thomas Südhof: Interview with Südhof, 2023.

JPAD had published a paper by Cassava's Lindsay Burns: "PTI-125 Reduces Biomarkers of Alzheimer's Disease in Patients," *The Journal of Prevention of Alzheimer's Disease* 7, no. 4 (February 7, 2020).

a French neuroscientist and then coeditor-in-chief, handled the query: Emails provided by Matthew Schrag, dated September 30, 2021 through October 9, 2021.

Vellas and Wang coauthored a similar 2017 article: "RETRACTED ARTICLE: Increased Aβ42-α7-Like Nicotinic Acetylcholine Receptor Complex Level in Lymphocytes Is Associated with Apolipoprotein E4-Driven Alzheimer's Disease Pathogenesis," *Alzheimer's Research & Therapy* 9, no. 54 (July 27, 2017).

coeditor-in-chief Paul Aisen of the University of Southern California took over: Emails provided by Matthew Schrag, dated August 18, 2022.

Vellas also stepped down as coeditor-in-chief: *The Journal of Prevention of Alzheimer's Disease* Editorial Board, January 17, 2022, via internet archive, https://web.archive.org/web/20220117011950/https://www.jpreventionalzheimer.com/editorial-board.html.

Aisen later told Schrag that they had run the images by experts: Emails provided by Matthew Schrag, dated August 18, 2022.

Selkoe sharply criticized my 2022 "Blots on a Field?" article: "News Story Miscasts Alzheimer's Science," *Science* 377, no. 6609 (August 25, 2022): 934–935.

Cummings augments his income—by nearly $1 million (and payments to others as noted): OpenPaymentsData.CMS.gov, accessed September 5, 2023.

Vellas has received consulting fees from Eisai and others: For example, "Designing the Next-Generation Clinical Care Pathway for Alzheimer's Disease," *Nature Aging* 2, no. 8 (August 2022): 692–703.

Biogen and Eisai employees have actually served on that board: *The Journal of Prevention of Alzheimer's Disease*, Editorial Board, https://www.jpreventionalzheimer.com/editorial-board.html (accessed September 5, 2023).

received favorable coverage in *JPAD* in papers written by Cummings: "Two Randomized Phase 3 Studies of Aducanumab in Early Alzheimer's Disease," *The Journal of Prevention of Alzheimer's Disease* 2, no. 9 (March 18, 2022): 197–210; "Aducanumab: Appropriate Use Recommendations" 4, no. 8 (July 20, 2021).

***Nature* journals . . . average 213 days from submission to acceptance:** "Journal Metrics," *Nature*, https://www.nature.com/nature-portfolio/about/journal-metrics (accessed Aug 25, 2023).

***Science* journals move at a comparable pace:** "Journal Metrics," *Science*, https://www.science.org/content/page/journal-metrics (accessed September 5, 2023).

"peer reviewed" guidelines for Aduhelm took eight days: "Aducanumab: Appropriate Use Recommendations," *The Journal of Prevention of Alzheimer's Disease* 4. no. 8 (July 20, 2021).

Cassava biomarker study took seven days: "PTI-125 Reduces Biomarkers of Alzheimer's Disease in Patients," *The Journal of Prevention of Alzheimer's Disease* 7, no. 4 (February 7, 2020).

2016 study of the anti-amyloid drug tramiprosate: "Clinical Benefits of Tramiprosate in Alzheimer's Disease Are Associated with Higher Number of APOE4 Alleles: The 'APOE4 Gene-Dose Effect,'" *The Journal of Prevention of Alzheimer's Disease* 3, no. 4 (October 26, 2016): 219–228.

Alzheon, paid all three of those scientists: "Clinical Effects of Tramiprosate in APOE4/4 Homozygous Patients with Mild Alzheimer's Disease Suggest Disease Modification Potential," *The Journal of Prevention of Alzheimer's Disease* 4, no. 3 (June 22, 2017): 149–156.

"This casts a shadow on the whole publishing and peer review process": Interview with Donna Wilcock, March 15, 2023.

prominently notes a ScD degree in his biographical materials: Jeffrey Cummings, University of Nevada biography, https://www.unlv.edu/news/expert/dr-jeffrey-l-cummings (accessed August 25, 2023); Jeffrey L. Cummings, MD, ScD, December 14, 2016, "Curriculum Vitae"; University of Wyoming Laramie, "2011 Honorary Degree Recipient," https://www.uwyo.edu/honorarydegree/past_honorary_degree_recipients/2011-honorary-degree-recipients/Jeffrey-L.-Cummings--M.D..html (accessed August 25, 2023).

2018 JPAD article suggested that pimavanserin: "Pimavanserin in Alzheimer's Disease Psychosis: Efficacy in Patients with More Pronounced Psychotic Symptoms," *The Journal of Prevention of Alzheimer's Disease* 6, no. 1 (August 16, 2018).

a second paper extolling the benefits of the drug: "Pimavanserin: Potential Treatment for Dementia-Related Psychosis," *The Journal of Prevention of Alzheimer's Disease* 5, no. 4 (August 16, 2018).

They sent a joint reply that they review quality: Email from *JPAD* editors, October 15, 2023.

he disclosed receiving "fees and/or stock options" from the company: "Clinical Effects of Tramiprosate in APOE4/4 Homozygous Patients with Mild Alzheimer's Disease Suggest Disease Modification Potential," *The Journal of Prevention of Alzheimer's Disease* 4, no. 3 (June 22, 2017):149–156.

"My experiences were precisely none": Email from Jason Karlawish, September 30, 2023.

a study by Elisabeth Bik of 960 papers: "Analysis and Correction of Inappropriate Image Duplication: The Molecular and Cellular Biology Experience," *Molecular and Cellular Biology* 38, no. 20, October 2018.

in June 2020 a major scandal hit Covid-19 pandemic research: "Two Elite Medical Journals Retract Coronavirus Papers over Data Integrity Questions," *Science*, June 4, 2020.

For a January 2021 article: "Many Scientists Citing Two Scandalous Covid-19 Papers Ignore Their Retractions," *Science*, January 15, 2021.

more than 100 academic articles—many in leading journals: Digital Science & Research Solutions, Inc., Dimensions, accessed March 24, 2024.

The most influential Cassava-related paper: "Demonstrated Brain Insulin Resistance in Alzheimer's Disease Patients Is Associated with IGF-1 Resistance, IRS-1 Dysregulation, and Cognitive Decline," *The Journal of Clinical Investigation* 122, no. 4 (April 2012):1316–1338.

As of March 2024, other papers had cited it: Google tabulation.

Ahima had coauthored three suspect papers with Wang and Harvard's Steven Arnold: "Brain Insulin Signaling and Cerebrovascular Disease in Human Postmortem brain," *Acta Neuropathologica Communications* 9, no. 71 (April 15, 2021); "Insulin and Adipokine Signaling and Their Cross-Regulation in Postmortem Human Brain," *Neurobiology of Aging* 84 (August 20, 2019): 119–130; "Brain Insulin Signaling, Alzheimer Disease Pathology, and Cognitive Function," *Annals of Neurology* 88, no. 3 (July 27, 2020): 513–525.

and shared $7 million in grants: NIH Reporter, Projects 1RF1AG059621-01,

5R01NS084965-05, 5R01NS084965-04, 5R01NS084965-03, 5R01NS084965-02, 1R01NS084965-01A1.

Ahima recused himself: Email from *JCI* editor Sarah Jackson to Alexander Trevelyan, November 21, 2021.

"was a major part of the foundation": Interview with Matthew Schrag, 2023.

McNally used her editorial soapbox to threaten short sellers: "Conflicting Interests: When Whistleblowers Profit from Allegations of Scientific Misconduct," *The Journal of Clinical Investigation* 132, no. 21 (November 1, 2022).

language Cassava Sciences had deployed: Cassava Sciences, "Public Statement Regarding Recent Allegations Against Cassava Sciences, Inc.," September 3, 2021.

editorial unsealed "a Pandora's box": "Losing Interest: When Scientific Journals Fail to Take Whistleblowers Seriously," Substack, Primary Endpoints, November 6, 2022, https://ajtrev.substack.com/p/losing-interest-when-scientific-journals.

a takeoff on the name of his first cat: "Smut Clyde, Scout of Mushrooms and Bogus Science," *Le Monde*, July 18, 2023.

where he outed his true identity: "What Makes an Undercover Science Sleuth Tick?," *Nature* 608 (August 18, 2023): 463.

his comedic YouTube "Science Police" videos: https://www.youtube.com/@Sholto_David.

problematic studies by scientists at Dana-Farber Cancer Institute: "Dana-Farber Cancer Institute Researchers Accused of Manipulating Data," *The Harvard Crimson*, January 12, 2024.

monthly contributions from fans of just over $200: "Science Sleuths Are Using Technology to Find Fakery and Plagiarism in Published Research," *Associated Press*, January 28, 2024.

"I'm just stretching my meagre savings": "'A Lot of It Is Sloppiness': The Biologist Who Finds Flaws in Scientific Papers," *The Guardian*, January 29, 2024.

Features in *Le Monde, The New Yorker*: "Elisabeth Bik, A Lynx Eye Against Falsified Images," *Le Monde*, July 25, 2023; "How a Sharp-Eyed Scientist Became Biology's Image Detective," *The New Yorker*, June 23, 2021; "Scientists Rally Around Misconduct Consultant Facing Legal Threat After Challenging Covid-19 Drug Researcher," *Science*, May 27, 2021; "Seeing Double," *Nature* 581 (May 14, 2020):132–136.

Patreon donations total about $2,300 per month: Patreon page for Elisabeth Bik, https://www.patreon.com/elisabethbik (accessed April 4, 2024).

Bik counts more than one thousand papers retracted: https://scienceintegritydigest.com/about/.

Japanese scientist who hung himself: "Stem-Cell Pioneer Blamed Media 'Bashing' in Suicide Note," *Nature*, August 13, 2014.

journals have been slow to react, some prominent ones are changing: "How Journals Are Fighting Back Against a Wave of Questionable Images," *Nature*, February 12, 2024.

Thorp wrote in early 2024: "Genuine Images in 2024," *Science* 383, no. 6678 (January 5, 2024): 7.

CHAPTER 16

"reflects a pattern of deception and academic misconduct": Interview with Paul Hebert, January 5, 2022.

In 2013, a team led by University of Guelph (UG) botanist Steven Newmaster: Newmaster and Ken Thompson sections adapted from my articles. "Failing the Test," *Science* 375, no. 6580 (February 4, 2022): 485–489; "Controversial Botanist Cleared," *Science* 376, no. 6598 (June 10, 2022): 1145; "Star Botanist Likely Made Up Data About Nutritional Supplements, New Probe Finds," *Science* 384, no. 6701 (June 24, 2024): 1163.

After the war's massive Manhattan Project: Vannevar Bush Section adapted from my book, *The Fail-Safe Society* (New York: Basic Books/Harper Collins, 1991).

has amassed a database of more than fifty thousand retractions: https://retractionwatch.com/ (accessed August 14, 2024).

A 2009 study published in the journal *PLOS ONE*: "How Many Scientists Fabricate and Falsify research? A Systematic Review and Meta-Analysis of Survey Data," *PLOS ONE* 4, no. 5, May 2009.

"Universities can make a lot of money from sham science": "How Universities Cover Up Scientific Fraud," *Areo*, February 2, 2020.

"Imagine a world in which police and prosecutors basically didn't exist": "Why We Need More Quality Control in Science Funding," Good Science Project, October 3, 2022, https://goodscience.substack.com/p/why-we-need-more-quality-control.

Chantal Ly, a PhD student in genetics: "Truth and Consequences," *Science* 313, no. 5791 (September 1, 2006): 1222–1226.

student and researcher Bradford Perez (and subsequent Perez references): "Duke Officials Silenced Med Student Who Reported Trouble in Anil Potti's Lab," *The Cancer Letter* 41, no. 1 (January 9, 2015).

called it "the holy grail of cancer" . . . Potti resigned: "Deception at Duke," *CBS 60 Minutes*, February 12, 2012.

went on to treat cancer patients at Unity Medical Center: https://www.cancercenternd.com/about-ccnd (accessed August 23, 2023).

"The system believes that scientists are honest": Interview with Matthew Schrag, 2022.

In 2010, they nailed a Harvard expert on cognition and morality: "Harvard Finds Scientist Guilty of Misconduct," *The New York Times*, August 21, 2010; "FAS Dean Smith Confirms Scientific Misconduct by Marc Hauser," *Harvard Magazine*, August 20, 2010.

Top Harvard economists were undone: "Reinhart, Rogoff . . . and Herndon: The Student Who Caught Out the Profs," *BBC News*, April 20, 2013.

after Pickett published a detailed review: "Why I Asked the Editors of Criminology to Retract Johnson, Stewart, Pickett, and Gertz," *SocArXiv Papers*, 2011.

all five papers—and one more—were retracted: "Florida University Fires Criminology Professor Blemished by Retractions," *Retraction Watch*, July 20, 2023.

professor was finally fired in 2023: Letter from James J. Clark, provost, Florida

State University, July 13, 2023, https://retractionwatch.com/wp-content/uploads /2023/07/Final-Termination-Letter-7.13.23.pdf.

a team of social-behavioral scientists: "Fasificada" (parts 1–4), *Data Colada*, June 17, 20, 23, 30, 2023, https://datacolada.org/.

Harvard's integrity office independently verified the findings: United States District Court, District of Massachusetts (Boston), Civil Case 1:23-cv-11775-MJJ, "Gino v. President and Fellows of Harvard College et al," Exhibit 4, June 13, 2023.

demanding "not less than $25 million" in damages: "Professor Accused of Faking Data in Studies on Dishonesty Sues Harvard," *The Washington Post*, August 3, 2023.

Although the case against Data Colada: United States District Court, District of Massachusetts (Boston), Civil Case 1:23-cv-11775-MJJ, "Gino v. President and Fellows of Harvard College et al," Memorandum of Decision, September 11, 2024.

"It's maddening to find ourselves in a situation": "A Disgraced Harvard Professor Sued Them for Millions. Their Recourse: GoFundMe," *Vox*, August 23, 2023.

CHAPTER 17

Portions of this chapter adapted from my article "'I'm nauseated': Alzheimer's Whistleblower Finds Possible Misconduct by His Mentor in Their Papers," *Science*, November 10, 2022.

Comments from Matthew Schrag: Interviews with Schrag, 2022 and 2023.

his own articles contained dubious images: https://pubpeer.com/publications /B460F45981DF6CE6E8FEC316FE3795#11; https://pubpeer.com/publications/5DE B389769963DDCA2B44742190D83#7.

Ghribi's own literal "it takes a village" inspirational story: Interview with Matthew Schrag, 2022.

Ghribi earned his PhD in neuropharmacology: Othman Ghribi, "Curriculum Vitae."

UND honored Ghribi: https://und.edu/academics/ttada/awards.html#2019.

the three found suspect images in thirty-four papers: Most of the papers, https://pubpeer.com/search?q=authors%3A%22Othman+Ghribi%22.

had underwritten some $3.8 million of Ghribi's work: NIH Reporter.

In March 2024, it retracted one of the papers: "Retraction to: Potential Mechanisms Linking Cholesterol to Alzheimer's Disease-like Pathology in Rabbit Brain, Hippocampal Organotypic Slices, and Skeletal Muscle," *Journal of Alzheimer's Disease* 98, no. 1 (March 5, 2024): 341.

Journal of Neurochemistry, **where the original rabbit paper appeared:** "Retraction: Deposition of Iron and β-Amyloid Plaques Is Associated with Cortical Cellular Damage in Rabbits Fed with Long-Term Cholesterol-Enriched Diets," *Journal of Neurochemistry* 165, no. 1 (March 7, 2023): 106.

paper he and Ghribi shared in *Experimental Neurology:* "High Cholesterol Content in Neurons Increases BACE, Beta-Amyloid, and Phosphorylated Tau Levels in Rabbit Hippocampus," *Experimental Neurology* 200, no. 2 (August 2006): 460–7.

retracted in June 2024, after UND concluded: "Hippocampus of Ames Dwarf Mice Is Resistant to β-Amyloid-Induced Tau Hyperphosphorylation and Changes in Apoptosis-Regulatory Protein Levels," *Hippocampus* 18 (2008): 239–244 (first pub-

lished online November 13, 2007); retracted August 1, 2024, https://onlinelibrary
.wiley.com/doi/10.1002/hipo.23626.

"My primary reason for speaking with you is to exonerate Matthew": Email
from Othman Ghribi, October 5, 2022.

My article appeared in early November: "'I'm Nauseated': Alzheimer's Whistleblower Finds Possible Misconduct by His Mentor in Their Papers," *Science* 378,
no. 6621 (November 18, 2022): 694–695 (published online November 10, 2022).

"Your article is biased": Email from Othman Ghribi, December 16, 2022.

CHAPTER 18

Portions of this chapter adapted from my articles in *Science*: "Codeveloper
of Cassava's Potential Alzheimer's Drug Cited for 'Egregious Misconduct,'" October
12, 2023; "'Damning' FDA Inspection Report Undermines Positive Trial Results of
Possible Alzheimer's Drug," March 11, 2024; "Company misled investors on possible
Alzheimer's drug, SEC charges," September 30, 2024.

such as in a 2012 paper in the *Journal of Neuroscience*: "Reducing Amyloid-
Related Alzheimer's Disease Pathogenesis by a Small Molecule Targeting Filamin A,"
The Journal of Neuroscience 18, no. 32(29) (July 18, 2012): 9773–9784.

"It's all about the money, and always has been": "It's Time for the FDA to Halt
Cassava Sciences' Alzheimer's Clinical Trials," *STAT*, October 17, 2023.

**The report concluded that Lindsay Burns (and subsequent report refer-
ences):** City University of New York, "Final Investigation Report of Associate Professor Hoau-Yan Wang, Ph.D.," https://www.science.org/do/10.1126/science.adl3444
/full/cuny_wang_final_report-1698701360173.pdf.

Wang's attorney said neither she nor her client would comment: Email from
Jennifer Beidel Scramlin, October 10, 2023.

said it made no such request: "Scientists Investigating Alzheimer's Drug Faulted
in Leaked Report," *The New York Times*, October 14, 2023.

He separately told the Food and Drug Administration: Food and Drug Administration, Establishment Inspection Report, The City College of New York
(CCNY)/CUNY, #3006508031, September 14–16, 2022, p. 7.

Arnold declined to comment, saying he needed time: Email from Steven Arnold, October 10, 2023.

Boudreau advisor Dee Dee Mozeleski said the president could not comment:
Email from Mozeleski, October 10, 2023.

called what the panel found "embarrassing beyond words": Interview with
Kevin Gardner, August 22, 2023.

In a written statement, Cassava declined to comment: "Statement of Cassava
Sciences, Inc. in Response to an Inquiry from *Science*," Cassava Sciences, October 11,
2023, https://www.science.org/do/10.1126/science.adl3444/full/cassava_statement_to
_science_101123-1698701360173.pdf.

SAVAges later targeted Shafer in the social media: For example, on X, Hard-
coreX (@scudmissle), October 24, 2023, https://twitter.com/scudmissles/status/171
6785482858721612.

Schrag called it "detailed, thorough, and credible": Interview with Matthew Schrag, October 9, 2023.

Cassava was soon named the "most shorted" health care company: "Short Sellers Boost Bets Against Healthcare Stocks," S&P Global Market Intelligence, November 15, 2023, https://www.spglobal.com/marketintelligence/en/news-insights/latest-news-headlines/short-sellers-boost-bets-against-healthcare-stocks-78457247.

One paper in June 2023: "Simufilam Suppresses Overactive mTOR and Restores Its Sensitivity to Insulin in Alzheimer's Disease Patient Lymphocytes," *Frontiers in Aging* 4 (June 29, 2023).

penned a caustic critique: "It's Time for the FDA to Halt Cassava Sciences' Alzheimer's clinical trials," *STAT*, October 17, 2023.

CUNY reversed Mozeleski's assertion of imminent action: "Statement from The City University of New York," CUNY, October 27, 2023, https://www1.cuny.edu/mu/forum/2023/10/27/statement-from-the-city-university-of-new-york/#.

CUNY Board of Trustees—despite confirming its authenticity: "Summary of Actions Taken at the December 18, 2023 Special Board Meeting," Board of Trustees, The City University of New York, December 18, 2023.

FDA found an array of problems with Wang's work (and all subsequent report references): Food and Drug Administration, Establishment Inspection Report, The City College of New York (CCNY)/CUNY, #3006508031, September 14–16, 2022.

On a ten-point scale, with ten being the worst score: Interview with Jerry Chapman, March 1, 2024.

"Essentially, the FDA said, 'You can't trust any of this'": Interview with Lon Schneider, March 1, 2024.

The report was obtained by a short seller and provided to me by his colleague: Obtained by Jesse Brodkin, provided by Adrian Heilbut.

Cassava said in a statement that the CUNY lab: https://www.science.org/do/10.1126/science.z7wo4zp/full/statement_cassavasciences_to_science030824-1710187507643.pdf.

The analysis of trial samples is considered clinical, not exploratory: "Nonclinical Laboratories Inspected under Good Laboratory Practices," Food and Drug Administration, 2024, https://www.fda.gov/inspections-compliance-enforcement-and-criminal-investigations/inspection-references/nonclinical-laboratories-inspected-under-good-laboratory-practices; https://www.fda.gov/inspections-compliance-enforcement-and-criminal-investigations/fda-bioresearch-monitoring-information/definitions.

In May 2020, Cassava had announced disappointing results: Cassava Sciences press release, May 15, 2020.

months later, the company rejected those results: Cassava Sciences press release, September 14, 2020.

the preprint site posted a link: "Effects of Simufilam on Cerebrospinal Fluid Biomarkers in Alzheimer's Disease: A Randomized Clinical Trial—Editorial Note," Research Square, March 20, 2024.

"This report extends a pattern of data that lacks rigor and reliability": Interview with Matthew Schrag, March 1, 2024.

Cassava executives faced a shareholder class-action lawsuit: Cassava Sciences, Securities and Exchange Commission Form 10-K for December 31, 2023.

It accused them of a "fraudulent scheme": United States District Court, Western District of Texas, Austin Division, Case 1:21-cv-00751-DAE Document 1 Filed 08/27/21, for example: 6.

Cassava said the claims were "without merit": Cassava Sciences, Securities and Exchange Commission Form 10-K for December 31, 2023.

Two other class-action shareholder suits were filed in early 2024: United States District Court, Northern District of Illinois, February 2, 2024, Case: 1:24-cv-00977; United States District Court, Northern District of Illinois, March 18, 2024, Case: 1:24-cv-02223.

a federal judge tossed Cassava's defamation lawsuit against the short sellers: United States District Court, Southern District of New York, Case 1:22-cv-09409-GHW-OTW, Document 119, Filed 03/28/24.

Cassava offered optimistic portrayals of data: "Results of a Phase 2 Randomized Withdrawal Study of Simufilam in Mild-to-moderate Alzheimer's Disease," Cassava Sciences, October 26, 2023.

some had no cognitive impairment: "Results of a Phase 2 Randomized Withdrawal Study of Simufilam in Mild-to-Moderate Alzheimer's Disease," at slide 12 (shows scores of 26 to 30 in Mini-Mental State Examination; 30 denotes no cognitive decline and above 25 normal performance), Cassava Sciences, October 26, 2023.

called the Cassava data "very sloppy work": Email from Nicolas Villain, November 29, 2023.

"The conclusion, of course, is obvious": "Cassava Pulled Back the Curtain on Its Alzheimer's Study—and Revealed Insurmountable Problems," *STAT*, October 30, 2023.

final results are due sometime in 2026: ClinicalTrials.gov, "NCT05575076," "Open-label Extension for Phase 3 Clinical Trials of Simufilam."

DOJ announced that Wang had been indicted: The United States vs. Hoau-Yan Wang, Case 8:24-cr-00211-TDC, 06/27/24.

distanced itself from Wang in a public statement: "Cassava Sciences Issues Statement on Former Science Advisor," Cassava Sciences, June 28, 2024.

the company filed an astonishing statement: Cassava Sciences, Securities and Exchange Commission Form 8K, filed July 1, 2024.

quips on social media: LinkedIn, linkedin.com/in/lindsay-burns-61b67229/recent-activity/.

The top players in the simufilam saga . . . were out: Cassava Sciences, Securities and Exchange Commission Form 8K, filed July 15, 2024.

dropped the lingering short-seller defamation lawsuit: Cassava Sciences vs David Bredt, et al, Case 1:22-cv-09409-GHW-OTW, 08/02/24.

defendants in that case quickly sued: Adrian Heilbut, Jesse Brodkin, Enea Milioris vs Cassava Sciences, Case 1:24-cv-05948, 08/06/24.

Then in September 2024, Cassava agreed to pay $40 million: "SEC Charges Cassava Sciences,Two Former Executives for Misleading Claims About Alzheimer's Clinical Trial," Securities and Exchange Commission, release 2024-151, September 26, 2024.

The SEC said Cassava and Barbier knew: Securities and Exchange Commission vs Cassava Sciences, et al, Case 24:cv-1150, document 1, September 26, 2024, 2–4.

"Experimenting on many hundreds of people": "Company misled investors on possible Alzheimer's drug, SEC charges," *Science*, September 30, 2024.

After Burns's father, Horatio Burns, died in 2018, a bitter dispute broke out: Supreme Court of Montana, "In Re: The Estate of: Horatio W. Burns, Deceased," DA 22-0456, Decided: December 27, 2023.

CHAPTER 19

A few paragraphs adapted from my article, "Official Inaction," *Science*, October 1, 2020.

Comments from Karen Ashe (unless otherwise noted) and Peng Liu: Interviews with Ashe and Liu, January 16 and 17, 2024.

"Clothe yourselves in compassion": *The Bible*, Colossians 3:12–14, paraphrase by Karen Ashe.

Vivien replied in detail: Email from Vivien, July 7, 2023.

Comments from Jean-Charles Lambert: Email from Lambert, August 26, 2023.

Comments from Carl Elliott: Interview with Elliott, October 18, 2023.

A reference in that book to the Markingson affair (and subsequent references): Carl Elliott, *The Occasional Human Sacrifice: Medical Experimentation and the Price of Saying No* (New York: W. W. Norton, 2024).

One involved a psychiatrist who headed another antidepressant study: *Federal Register* 62, no. 63 (April 2, 1997): 15713; "Top Psychiatrist Is Guilty in Fraud," *The New York Times*, August 8, 1993, 31.

disqualified another UMN psychiatrist for failing to obtain informed consent: "DHHS-FDA Regulatory Hearing on the Proposal to Disqualify James A. Halikas, M.D. from Receiving Investigational New Drugs-Commissioner's Decision," Food and Drug Administration, January 17, 2001.

problem involved pioneering UMN transplant surgeon John Najarian: "The Crime of Saving Lives: The FDA, John Najarian, and Minnesota ALG," *Archives of Surgery* 130 (October 1995): 1035–1039.

"in bed together": "John Najarian, Pioneering Transplant Surgeon, Dies at 92," *The New York Times*, September 19, 2020.

UMN Medical School lost scores of faculty members: "U of M Med School Still Recovering 10 years After ALG Scandal," Minnesota Public Radio, February 28, 2006.

how the FDA fails to enforce rules to protect patients: Official Inaction: A *Science* Investigation Shows That FDA Oversight of Clinical Trials is Lax, Slow Moving, and Secretive—and that Enforcement is Declining. *Science*, October 1, 2020.

A Twin Cities Public Television program: "Playing New Notes in Dementia Research," Twin Cities Public Television, May 12, 2023, https://www.pbs.org/video/playing-new-notes-dementia-research-ubghsk/.

"a coworker may have misled me": "University of Minnesota Scientist Responds to Fraud Allegations in Alzheimer's Research," *Minneapolis Star Tribune*, July 22, 2022.

posted a self-published preprint: "Aβ*56 Is a Stable Oligomer That Correlates with Age-Related Memory Loss in Tg2576 Mice," bioRxiv, March 21, 2023.

Ashe commented in the *Star Tribune*: "University of Minnesota Researcher Seeks to Put Tarnished Alzheimer's Discoveries Back on Track," *Minneapolis Star Tribune*, May 13, 2023.

Ashe publicly described my article: "Alzheimer's Target Still Viable but Untested," *Science* 377, no. 6609 (August 26, 2022): 935.

In a podcast, Ashe also blamed the NIH: "An Alzheimer's Uproar," *Vox Unexplainable*, September 14, 2022, at 27:20.

Ashe quietly enlisted a new group of scientists: "Aβ*56 Is a Stable Oligomer That Correlates with Age-Related Memory Loss in Tg2576 Mice," bioRxiv, March 21, 2023, https://www.biorxiv.org/content/10.1101/2023.03.20.533414v1.full (accessed July 18, 2023).

"As a lab head and the senior author, it's my responsibility": "University of Minnesota Researcher Seeks to Put Tarnished Alzheimer's Discoveries Back on Track," *Minneapolis Star Tribune*, May 13, 2023.

"it would behoove her to voluntarily retract": Interview with Donna Wilcock, May 16, 2023.

"Surely this necessitates retracting the 2006 study": Matthew Schrag email to *Nature*, May 15, 2023, reprinted in PubPeer, June 2023, https://pubpeer.com/publications/8FF7E6996524B73ACB4A9EF5C0AACF.

developed the test in the early 1980s: "Developments of a Water-Maze Procedure for Studying Spatial Learning in the Rat," *Journal of Neuroscience Methods*, May 1984, 47–60.

"Should you ever choose to address the errors you printed": Email from Karen Ashe, May 16, 2023.

had let their joint patents on the protein lapse: US Patents US20090258824A1, US20080044356A1.

some of Ashe's water-maze data looked improbable: Mu Yang, confidential analysis provided by the author.

published nearly unchanged in that journal: "Aβ*56 Is a Stable Oligomer That Impairs Memory Function in Mice," *iScience* 27, March 15, 2024.

Ashe finally made the move she had considered two years before: PubPeer, https://pubpeer.com/publications/8FF7E6996524B73ACB4A9EF5C0AACF.

the second-most highly cited paper prior to retraction in scientific history: "Top 10 most highly cited retracted papers," *Retraction Watch*, December 2020.

"It's unfortunate that it has taken two years" . . . "step in the right direction": "Authors Move to Retract Discredited Alzheimer's Study," *Science* 384, no. 6700 (June 7, 2024): 1055.

Lesné and colleagues submitted a paper: "SNCA Genetic Lowering Reveals Differential Cognitive Function of Alpha-Synuclein Dependent on Sex," *Acta Neuropathologica Communications* 10, no. 180 (December 14, 2022).

erased one of Lesné's signature accomplishments: Medical School Wall of Scholarship, https://med.umn.edu/research/wall-scholarship (accessed August 16, 2022, October 26, 2023, and in archival form May 2022).

pictured him standing with pride before the wall: https://lesnelab.org/goals/ (accessed January 26, 2024).

CHAPTER 20

Descriptions of work by Berislav Zlokovic and quotes from his lab members were drawn or adapted from my articles in *Science*: November 12, 2023, "Brain Games?" and December 1, 2023, "NIH Puts Hold on $30 Million Trial of Potential Stroke Drug." Some descriptions of work by Eliezer Masliah and quotes from scientists were drawn or adapted from my article in *Science*, September 27, 2024, "Picture Imperfect."

committed up to $30 million: ZZ Biotech press release, May 24, 2022.

a study of fourteen hundred people: "Efficacy and Safety Evaluation of 3K3A-APC in Ischemic Stroke (RHAPSODY-2)," ClinicalTrials.gov, NCT05484154.

a company Zlokovic cofounded: University of Rochester press release, October 2, 2009.

US Food and Drug Administration (FDA) gave the compound "fast track" status: ZZ Biotech press release, June 12, 2020.

He directs the Zilkha Neurogenetic Institute: https://keck.usc.edu/faculty-search/berislav-v-zlokovic/ (accessed March 3, 2024).

won him a share of the celebrated Potamkin Prize: American Academy of Neurology press release, April 14, 2009, "Three Researchers Awarded AAN Potamkin Prize for Alzheimer's Research."

"Science requires clear and perfect language": "Featured Researcher: Berislav V. Zokovic, MD, PhD," Cure Alzheimer's Fund, July 21, 2015, https://curealz.org/news-and-events/featured-researcher-berislav-v-zlokovic-m-d-ph-d/.

credible version of "O Sole Mio": https://twitter.com/jonykipnis/status/1085423489824288768?s=42.

experimental drug might have actually increased deaths: *Annals of Neurology* 85, no. 1 (2018): 131.

trended toward greater disability and dependency: Unpublished analysis by Matthew Schrag, confirmed by several neuroscientists.

Comments from Wade Smith: Interviews with Smith, September and October 2023.

Comments from Chris Schaffer: Interviews with Schaffer, September and October 2023.

"I am not aware of, nor did I witness any instances of misconduct": Letter from Axel Montagne, February 2, 2024.

halted the trial, launched an investigation, and then clawed back $1.9 million in USC grant funds: Letter from Director Clinton Wright, NIH Division of Clinical Research, to USC, November 16, 2023.

at least one image "appears to have been digitally manipulated": "Activated Protein C Prevents Neuronal Apoptosis via Protease Activated Receptors 1 and 3," Editorial Expression of Concern, *Neuron* 111, no. 24 (December 20, 2023): 4116.

papers on pericytes in *Nature Communications* **and** *Nature Medicine* **were retracted:** "Retraction Note: Pericyte Loss Influences Alzheimer-Like Neurodegeneration in Mice," *Nature Communications*, April 3, 2024; "Retraction Note: Pericyte Degeneration Causes White Matter Dysfunction in the Mouse Central Nervous System," *Nature Medicine*, April 5, 2024; "Retraction: Neuroprotective Activities of Activated Protein C Mutant with Reduced Anticoagulant Activity," *European Journal of Neuroscience*, October 29, 2024.

In October 2024, Zlokovic went on indefinite leave: "Transition update at Zilkha and Physiology & Neuroscience," email from Carolyn C. Meltzer, MD, dean, Keck School of Medicine of USC, October 22, 2024.

published what seemed like a landmark Alzheimer's paper: "Amyloid Plaques, Neurofibrillary Tangles and Neuronal Loss in Brains of Transgenic Mice Overexpressing a C-Terminal Fragment of Human Amyloid Precursor Protein," *Nature* 354 (December 12, 1991): 476.

Selkoe left "dismayed": "Alzheimer's Research Suffers Major Setback," *The Washington Post*, March 10, 1992.

He denied wrongdoing, but the paper was retracted: *Nature* 356 (March 19, 1992): 265.

Selkoe looked aghast: Interview with Dennis Selkoe, March 7, 2023.

published what became the most influential paper in Alzheimer's history: "Alzheimer's Disease: The Amyloid Cascade Hypothesis," *Science* 256 (April 10, 1992): 184.

In a soft landing, he left Stanford: "Chutes & Ladders—Ex-Stanford President Will Lead New Billion-Dollar Biotech," *Fierce Biotech*, April 26, 2024.

"hijack" the University of California San Diego (UCSD) research center: "Project Money Going to USC; In Battle's Latest Twist, School Siphons Funds for Alzheimer's Study from UC San Diego," *Los Angeles Times*, August 30, 2015, B1.

Aisen allegedly arranged for a massive pay raise to move the program's grants . . . "'double agents'" . . . "predatory" . . . "golden rule": California Superior Court, County of San Diego, Case 37-2015-22082-CU-BT-CTL, First Amended Complaint, January 3, 2019, 11,17–18.

collecting a $1 million payout: "Doctor at USC Got Big Payout: Medical School Dean in Drug Abuse Scandal Received $1 Million in Severance and Bonus," *Los Angeles Times*, May 20, 2019, B1.

the state later revoked his medical license: Medical Board of California, Licensing details for: G 88200.

said in its public *mea culpa* on the Aisen case: California Superior Court, County of San Diego, Case 37-2015-22082-CU-BT-CTL, Settlement Agreement, July 3, 2019, 1, and "Exhibit A: USC Public Statement."

Morris, inventor of the widely used test, concurred: Letter from Richard Morris to Mu Yang, February 11, 2020.

filed suit against a trainee: Court of Common Pleas, Philadelphia County, Pennsylvania, Case ID: 240101083, Complaint.

described some of the concerns: "Critics Claim to Find Flaws in Dozens of Alzheimer's Studies by Temple Scientist: Domenico Praticò Denies Any Research Misconduct, but in a Lawsuit, He Accused a Former Grad Student of Copying Images," *The Philadelphia Inquirer*, January 18, 2024.

blamed his trainee and a former colleague: Emails from Domenico Praticò, February 26 and March 25, 2024.

One of those papers was retracted in March 2024, two others in June 2024, and one in August 2024: "Retraction: 5-Lipoxygenase Gene Transfer Worsens Memory, Amyloid, and Tau Brain Pathologies in a Mouse Model of Alzheimer [sic] Disease," *Annals of Neurology*, March 28, 2024; "Retracted: Pharmacologic Inhibition of 5-Lipoxygenase Improves Memory, Rescues Synaptic Dysfunction, and Ameliorates Tau Pathology in a Transgenic Model of Tauopathy," *Biological Psychiatry*, June 24, 2024; "Retracted 5-Lipoxygenase Activating Protein Reduction Ameliorates Cognitive Deficit, Synaptic Dysfunction, and Neuropathology in a Mouse Model of Alzheimer's Disease," *Biological Psychiatry*, June 24, 2024; "Retraction Note to: Learning Impairments, Memory Deficits, and Neuropathology in Aged Tau Transgenic Mice Are Dependent on Leukotrienes Biosynthesis: Role of the cdk5 Kinase Pathway," *Molecular Neurobiology*, August 2, 2024.

he would address the matter within the university's confidential inquiry: Email from P. Hemachandra Reddy, February 23, 2024.

A Michigan spokesperson said the dossier would be assessed: Email from Colleen Mastony, February 21, 2024.

wrote about problems in experiments by Gary Dunbar: "After Retractions, Alzheimer's Scientist Is Left Cleaning Up a Prolific Collaborator's Mess," *The Transmitter*, January 9, 2024; "U.S. Government Requested Inquiry into Alzheimer's Scientist over Misconduct Allegations," February 7, 2024.

blamed the problems on "unintentional procedural human error": Emails from Siriporn Chattipakorn, March 2 and 11, 2024.

Comments from Alkon and colleagues: Emails from Daniel Alkon, Jarin Hongpaisan, Miao-Kun Sun, February and March 2024.

Comments from Thomas Südhof: Interviews and emails with Südhof, March and April 2024.

"undertake a robust and confidential process": Email from Massachusetts General spokesperson Michael Morrison, February 9, 2024.

PLOS ONE **issued an expression of concern:** *PLOS ONE*, March 20, 2024, "Expression of Concern: Synaptic Dysbindin-1 Reductions in Schizophrenia Occur in an Isoform-Specific Manner Indicating Their Subsynaptic Location," https://doi.org /10.1371/journal.pone.0301152.

Comments by George Perry: Interview with Perry, March 8, 2024.

Comments from Donna Wilcock: Interview with Wilcock, March 15, 2024.

Comments from Checler and St George-Hyslop, and Universities of Cambridge and Toronto: Emails from Peter St George-Hyslop, Frédéric Checler, and representatives from the universities, March 2024.

he accepted most findings, blaming "honest errors": Email from Salvatore Oddo, March 15, 2024.

Comments from Frank LaFerla: Interview with LaFerla, March 15, 2024.

"people who complain that they can't get grants": Good Science Project, January 17, 2023, https://goodscienceproject.org/articles/interview-adriano-aguzzi/.

PubPeer critics had been targeting his work for a decade: https://pubpeer.com /search?q=adriano+aguzzi.

Aguzzi was caught in the searing spotlight of Leonid Schneider: "Aguzzi and the Lowlifes," *For Better Science*, December 12, 2019.

Aguzzi replied with contrition: Email from Aguzzi, February 6, 2024.

2017 study in *PLOS Pathogens***:** "Inhibition of Group-I Metabotropic Glutamate

Receptors Protects Against Prion Toxicity," *PLOS Pathogens* 13, no. 11 (November 27, 2017).

A landmark 2011 paper showed: "Aerosols Transmit Prions to Immunocompetent and Immunodeficient Mice," *PLOS Pathogens* 7, no. 1 (January 2011).

"I have no wish to leave this valley of tears today": Aguzzi post on X, April 25, 2024.

a UZ PhD student killed himself: "Tragedy revealed in Zürich," *Nature* 255 (February 13, 1992).

accused of misconduct: "Famed Alzheimer's Researcher John Hardy a Knight . . . but Not in Shining Armor," *Real Clear Investigations*, February 8, 2022.

waded into such a controversy as a critic: "Top geneticist 'should resign' over his team's laboratory fraud," *The Guardian*, February 1, 2020.

Hardy recently wrote of his fears: Email to Stella Hurtley, October 1, 2024.

"trainees who may be traumatized personally": "Misconduct's Forgotten Victims," *Science*, March 14, 2024.

Charges of plagiarism—some minor: "Plagiarism Charges Downed Harvard's President. A Conservative Attack Helped to Fan the Outrage," Associated Press, January 3, 2024.

"weaponisation of forensic research": "The Weaponisation of Forensic Research Auditing Will Not Resolve Systemic Research Misconduct," *London School of Economics and Political Science Blog,* January 4, 2024, https://blogs.lse.ac.uk/impactofsocialsciences/2024/01/04/the-weaponisation-of-forensic-research-auditing-will-not-resolve-systemic-research-misconduct/.

Südhof . . . has published voluminous raw data . . . most concerns were unfounded: "Integrity Initiatives in the Südhof Laboratory," https://med.stanford.edu/sudhoflab/science-resources/integrity---pubpeer.html.

found errors in dozens of papers: PubPeer, https://pubpeer.com/search?q=thomas+sudhof.

During a prolonged PubPeer debate and comments on his lab website, Südhof retracted one: "Retraction for Lin et al., Neurexin-2 Restricts Synapse Numbers and Restrains the Presynaptic Release Probability by an Alternative Splicing-Dependent Mechanism," *Proceedings of the National Academy of Sciences* 21, no. 11 (March 5, 2024).

The more data released, the easier to spot them: Matthew Schrag email to a journalist with *Science*, March 29, 2024.

prolific output on Alzheimer's, Parkinson's, and other ailments: NIH biography of Eliezer Masliah, https://www.nia.nih.gov/about/staff/masliah-eliezer.

"Dale and I sat at a coffee shop": Alzforum, October 3, 2016, "Dale Schenk, 59, Pioneer of Alzheimer's Immunotherapy," https://www.alzforum.org/news/community-news/dale-schenk-59-pioneer-alzheimers-immunotherapy.

Four of their joint studies: Prothena, "Publications," https://www.prothena.com/pipeline/publications/#prasinezumab (second, third, and fifth publications listed), and *Movement Disorders* 32, no. 2, 2017, "First-in-Human Assessment of PRX002, an Anti–a-Synuclein Monoclonal Antibody, in Healthy Volunteers" (references 16 and 35).

up to $620 million to meet a series of performance goals: Prothena, "Corporate Overview," May 2024, 45, https://s201.q4cdn.com/351053094/files/doc_finan cials/2024/Prothena-Corporate-Overview-Final-May-2024.pdf.

a seminal 2000 Masliah paper in *Science*: "Dopaminergic Loss and Inclusion Body Formation in a-Synuclein Mice: Implications for Neurodegenerative Disorders," *Science* 287 (February 18, 2000): 1265–1266.

CHAPTER 21

Comments by Donna Wilcock, George Perry, Matthew Schrag, and Thomas Südhof: Interviews, March 2024.

Some information on Berislav Zlokovic is adapted from my article in *Science*, **"Brain Games?"** November 13, 2023.

jumped from $13 million in 2006 to $221 million: NIH Reporter.

"unquestionably trigger the need for a robust investigation": Interview with Chris Schaffer, October 13, 2023.

"one of the million-dollar questions": Interview with Andreas Charidimou, September 22, 2023.

promoted to full professor: Email from Jake Ricker, November 9, 2023.

full professor in a biological science at top-tier US universities score 41 on average: "H-Index Distributions in Biology," The Bioinformatics CRO, January 15, 2021, https://www.bioinformaticscro.com/blog/h-index-distributions-in-biology/.

an open-minded scholar who edits *Alzheimer's & Dementia*: https://alz-jour nals.onlinelibrary.wiley.com/hub/journal/15525279/homepage/editorial-board.

[sources for Arnold and Wang and their links to Cassava detailed in prior chapters]

Insulin treatments for Alzheimer's have fallen flat: "Safety, Efficacy, and Feasibility of Intranasal Insulin for the Treatment of Mild Cognitive Impairment and Alzheimer Disease Dementia: A Randomized Clinical Trial," *JAMA Neurology* 77, no. 9 (September 2020).

Over the ensuing ten-year span, the agency spent more than $500 million: NIH Reporter.

The patent system seems alarmingly unable to police: "Is the Patent System Sensitive to Incorrect Information?," *The Review of Economics and Statistics* (July 24, 2023): 1–38.

mandates to publish full datasets: "2023 NIH Data Management and Sharing Policy," National Institutes of Health, January 25, 2023, https://oir.nih.gov/source book/intramural-program-oversight/intramural-data-sharing/2023-nih-data-man agement-sharing-policy.

CHAPTER 22

Portions of this chapter are adapted from my article in the *New York Times*, **July 7, 2024, "All the Alzheimer's Research We Didn't Do."**

Comments from Andreas Charidimou: Interview with Charidimou, September 22, 2023.

To Südhof, it "reflects that most misconduct": Interview with Thomas Südhof, March 11, 2024.

Comments from Matthew Schrag: Interviews with Schrag, February 7, 2024, March 12, 2024.

Comments from Madhav Thambisetty: Interview with Thambisetty, February 8, 2024.

One of those involves testing the seemingly miraculous weight-loss drug Wegovy: ClinicalTrials.gov, "A Research Study Investigating Semaglutide in People with Early Alzheimer's Disease (EVOKE)" and "A Research Study Investigating Semaglutide in People with Early Alzheimer's Disease (EVOKE Plus).

A similar drug, liraglutide, also shows intriguing possible benefits: "Expert Reaction to Conference Abstract on Phase 2b Trial of Liraglutide in Alzheimer's Disease," Science Media Centre, July 30, 2024, https://www.sciencemediacentre .org/expert-reaction-to-conference-abstract-on-phase-2b-trial-of-liraglutide-in-alz heimers-disease/.

In 1498, Portuguese explorer Vasco da Gama landed: Britannica Online Encyclopedia, https://www.britannica.com/print/article/224711.

Comments from Ruth Itzhaki: Interview with Itzhaki, February 5, 2024.

funding to explore that line of research jumped: NIH Reporter.

Eighty scientists met in 2024 to discuss promising developments: "Hunt for Infectious Causes of Alzheimer's Gains Momentum," Science 385, no. 6708 (August 2, 2024): 479–480.

vaccine for shingles . . . shows signs of reducing risks of dementia: "The Recombinant Shingles Vaccine Is Associated with Lower Risk of Dementia," Nature Medicine, July 25, 2024.

Results should come in 2025 or 2026: ClinicalTrials.gov, Anti-viral Therapy in Alzheimer's Disease, NCT03282916; and Valacyclovir for Mild Cognitive Impairment (VALMCI), NCT04710030.

Comments from Miguel Arce Rentería: Interview with Arce, January 30, 2024 (condensed slightly for clarity).

Latino Americans, who are up to 1.5 times as likely to develop Alzheimer's . . . African Americans, who suffer: "Quantification of race/ethnicity representation in Alzheimer's disease neuroimaging research in the USA: a systematic review," Nature Communications Medicine, 2023.

EPILOGUE

Comments from the Price family: Interviews, February 2024 (some Matt Price quotes condensed slightly for clarity).

Faith in doctors and medical scientists has fallen sharply in recent years: Gallup, December 2023, "Honesty/Ethics in Professions, https://news.gallup.com /poll/1654/honesty-ethics-professions.aspx; Pew Research Center, November, 2023, "Americans' Trust in Scientists, Positive Views of Science Continue to Decline."

Comments from Matthew Schrag: Interviews with Schrag, February 2024 (some quotes condensed slightly for clarity).

Index

Massachusetts General Hospital, 136,
237, 238, 253, 255
Massachusetts Institute of Technology
(MIT), 6, 46, 47
Masters, Colin Louis, 254
Mattson, Mark, 254
Mayo Clinic, 60, 124
McIlwain Chopper, 86
McNally, Elizabeth, 167–68
measles, 56
Medical College of Pennsylvania, 18
Medicare, x, 67, 71, 129, 130
Medicines and Healthcare Products
Regulatory Agency, 71
MetLife Foundation, 50
mice, *see* mouse and rat experiments
Michael J. Fox Foundation, 136
microbes, 136
microglia, 134, 137
micrographs, 37, 82, 88, 100, 189, 239,
245
Mihelich, John, 190
Milton Academy, 14–16
Mini-Mental State Examination
(MMSE), 6–7
Minneapolis Star Tribune, 212, 213
Minutemen, 13
Moir, Robert, 136
Molecular and Cellular Biology, 165
monoclonal antibodies, 63
Montagne, Axel, 230
Morris, Richard, 214, 235
mouse and rat experiments, 57, 59, 63,
64, 74, 101, 134, 213, 222, 232
by LaFerla, 239–40
prion, 241
water maze, 48–50, 59, 104, 214,
235
Mozeleski, Dee Dee, 196, 197
Müller-Schiffmann, Andreas, 139, 148
multiple sclerosis, 42, 62, 122
Munafo, Marcus, 38
Myriel, 212

N
Najarian, John, 210
National Academy of Sciences, 178

National Health Service, 127
National Institute for Health and Care
Excellence (UK), 132
National Institute of Health and
Medical Research (Inserm), 42,
238
National Institute on Aging (NIA), 55,
69, 122, 126, 232, 239, 244–45,
248, 262
National Institutes of Health (NIH),
23, 32, 61, 82, 90–92, 93, 102, 116,
122–23, 136, 151–53, 236, 237,
255–56, 263
Ashe and, 212
Ghribi and, 189
ORI and, 151–53, 194
Schrag and, 79, 87–88, 94, 96–97, 99,
111–12, 142, 151–52, 194, 273
simufilam and, 24, 79
study sections and, 151–52
3K3A-APC and, 224, 226–28, 232
Wang's grant application to, 203
Zlokovic and, 249–50
National Library of Medicine, 76
National Reference Center for Prion
Diseases, 240
Nature, 134, 162, 170, 171, 232
Lesné-Ashe paper in, 59, 61, 101–4,
122, 140–43, 145–50, 153, 166,
213, 217–23
Nature Communications, 232
Nature Medicine, 136, 232
Nature Neuroscience, 42–44
Nazi Germany, 39–41, 54, 184
NBC News, 149
neprilysin, 256
neurodegenerative disorders, 266
Neuron, 134, 229, 232
Neurotree, 18
Neve, Rachael, 136
Nevins, Joseph, 181
Newcastle University, 170
*New England Journal of Medicine
(NEJM)*, 165
Newmaster, Steven, 174–77, 182–83
New Yorker, 90, 171
New York Times, 90, 175, 197

Puliafito, Carmen, 234
Purity-IQ, 176
Pythagoras, 51

Q
Quanterix Corp., 89

R
Raoult, Didier, 172
rat experiments, *see* mouse and rat
    experiments
Reddy, P. Hemachandra, 235
Redford, Robert, 13
Redica Systems, 156, 198
Redman, Barbara, 151, 153
Religious Orders Study, 110
Remoxy, 17–20
René Descartes University, 187
Retraction Watch, 151, 153, 166, 178
Review of Economics and Statistics, 258
Ricker, Jake, 212
Risk Evaluation and Mitigation Strategy
    (REMS), 127
River Runs Through It, A, 13
Robbins, Trevor, 18, 23
Robinson, Kim Stanley, 118
Roche, 132, 137, 157, 246, 247
Romney, Ann and Mitt, 122
Roosevelt, Franklin, 178
Rossner, Mike, 227, 234, 240–41
Rouelle, Guillaume-François, 41
Rüdin, Ernst, 54
Rush University, 23, 110–11, 143
Russian Revolution, 121

S
Sahakian, Barbara, 23
St George-Hyslop, Peter, 238–39, 249,
    252, 256, 259
St. John's University, 18
St. John's wort, 174
St. Paul Academy, 47
St. Paul Pioneer Press, 50
Salk Institute, 93
Salloway, Stephen, 66, 67, 137, 162
S&P Global Market Intelligence, 197
San Francisco–Oakland Bay Bridge, 115

SavaDx, 75
SAVAges, 77–78, 83, 88, 109, 172, 194,
    109, 172, 194
Schaffer, Chris, 229, 232, 250
Schenk, Dale, 246
Schneider, Julie, 23
Schneider, Leonid, 171, 172, 240, 243
Schneider, Lon, 25, 128–29, 132, 134,
    138, 198
scholarly journals, *see* journals
Schrag, Matthew, 27–28, 29–38, 39, 74,
    79, 93–105, 106–17, 123, 128, 135,
    159, 167, 181, 197, 214, 219–20,
    222, 240–41, 243–44, 247–48, 251,
    255–57, 259, 260, 265–67, 273–74
    Aduhelm and, 72–73, 83, 162
    cerebral amyloid angiopathy and,
        36–37, 265
    Christian faith of, 31, 34
    FDA and, 155
    Ghribi and, 32–34, 186–92, 233,
        273–74
    JPAD and, 160–64
    Kirsch and, 34, 35, 187
    misconduct investigated by, 28,
        37, 38, 73, 78, 80–83, 84–92, 94,
        96–105, 107–17, 139–50, 152, 153,
        160–61, 166–68, 171, 173, 174,
        180, 184, 185, 193, 194, 207, 222,
        225–27, 234, 273–74
    NIH and, 79, 87–88, 94, 96–97, 99,
        111–12, 142, 151–52, 194, 273
    PubPeer and, 185–88, 190
Schrag, Nanette, 30, 31, 33, 34
Schrag, Paul, 29–32
Schrag, Sarah, 31, 36, 39, 73, 95, 112
science, 37, 138, 167, 178, 179, 242, 259
    fraud in, *see* fraud
    replication in, 37–38, 141
    self-correction in, 37, 142
    trust in, 142
    values and, 178, 179
Science, ix, 48–50, 57, 62, 68, 69, 93–94,
    98, 106, 111, 113–14, 116, 118,
    125, 134, 153, 154, 157, 158, 162,
    166, 171, 173, 180, 190–91, 210,
    226, 233, 240, 243, 247

Thomas, Jordan, 78, 79, 83
Thompson, Ken, 182–83
Thorp, Holden, 98, 173, 243
3K3A-APC, 224–29, 232
TLR4 nerve-cell receptors, 10
Touchon, Jacques, 163
Toulouse University Hospital, 110
tPA (tissue plasminogen activator),
    224–25
tramiprosate, 163, 164
Transmitter, 236
transplant patients, 210
Travis, John, 98, 109
Trevelyan, Alexander, 168
Trojanowski, John, 23, 253, 254
Trump, Donald, 45, 142, 165, 263
Turner, Leigh, 209
Twain, Mark, 262
Twin Cities Public Television, 212
Twitter (X), 45, 77, 88, 132, 169, 172,
    188, 242, 255

U

United Arab Emirates, 71
Unity Medical Center, 181
universities, 174–84, 257
University College Dublin, 49, 60
University College London, 26, 69, 101,
    260
University of Arizona, 239
University of British Columbia, 175,
    182
University of Caen, 41, 44, 45, 207–9,
    230
University of California Irvine, 99, 209,
    220, 239
University of California San Diego
    (UCSD), 119, 233–34, 245
University of California San Francisco,
    23, 145, 158, 228
University of Cambridge, 16, 18, 204,
    238
University of Chicago, 148
University of Cincinnati, 124, 131
University of Edinburgh, 230
University of Florida, 136, 247
University of Grenoble, 42

University of Guelph (UG), 174–77, 182
University of Kentucky, 115, 141
University of Lille, 43, 145, 208
University of Manchester, 136
University of Massachusetts, 182
University of Melbourne, 69, 244
University of Messina, 239
University of Michigan, 236
University of Minnesota (UMN),
    44–45, 46, 48–50, 57, 61, 100, 102,
    104, 108, 112, 144, 149, 152–54,
    174, 192, 205, 206, 209–13, 216,
    222–23
  scandals at, 210–11
  Wall of Scholarship at, 49, 50, 61, 223
University of Munich, 54
University of Nevada, 23–24, 67, 96,
    161
University of North Carolina Chapel
    Hill, 156
University of North Dakota (UND),
    32–33, 185–87, 189–91
University of Oxford, 262, 263
University of Pennsylvania, 23, 127,
    160, 164, 253
University of Pittsburgh, 246
University of St. Andrews, 214
University of Southern California
    (USC), 25, 67, 128, 138, 161, 198,
    223, 224, 226, 231–34, 251
University of South Florida, 236
University of Texas Rio Grande Valley,
    190
University of Texas San Antonio, 72,
    115, 133, 189, 237
University of Toronto (UT), 108, 175,
    238–39
University of Virginia, 121
University of Wisconsin–Madison, 180
University of Wyoming Laramie, 163
University of Zürich (UZ), 101, 240–42
Urrutia, Paulina, 269–70

V

vaccines, 57, 58, 128, 246, 264
Vanderbilt University, 28, 29, 36,
    112–13, 186

About the Author

Charles Piller is an investigative journalist for *Science* magazine and his work has appeared in the *Los Angeles Times*, the *New York Times*, the *Sacramento Bee*, and more. Piller has been honored with many national journalism awards, and is the author of *Gene Wars* and *The Fail-Safe Society*. He has reported on public health, biological warfare, infectious disease outbreaks, and other topics from the United States, Africa, Asia, Europe, and Central America. Follow him on X @CPiller.